BATTLE OF BRITAIN
Volume I
The Gathering Storm

*Dedicated to the aircrew of Fighter Command,
Bomber Command and Coastal Command killed,
posted missing or wounded in Britain's defence,
2–9 July 1940*

BATTLE OF BRITAIN
Volume I
The Gathering Storm
Prelude to the Spitfire Summer of 1940

Dilip Sarkar MBE, FRHistS

BATTLE OF BRITAIN: VOLUME I
THE GATHERING STORM
Prelude to the Spitfire Summer of 1940

First published in Great Britain in 2023
and reprinted in 2026 in this edition by
Air World
An imprint of
Pen & Sword Books Ltd
Yorkshire – Philadelphia

Copyright © Dilip Sarkar, 2023, 2026

ISBN: 978 1 39905 637 3

The right of Dilip Sarkar to be identified as Author of this work has been asserted by him in accordance with the Copyright, Designs and Patents Act 1988. A CIP catalogue record for this book is available from the British Library All rights reserved.

All rights reserved. No part of this book may be reproduced, transmitted, downloaded, decompiled or reverse engineered in any form or by any means, electronic or mechanical including photocopying, recording or by any information storage and retrieval system, without permission from the Publisher in writing. NO AI TRAINING: Without in any way limiting the Author's and Publisher's exclusive rights under copyright, any use of this publication to "train" generative artificial intelligence (AI) technologies to generate text is expressly prohibited. The Author and Publisher reserve all rights to license uses of this work for generative AI training and development of machine learning language models.

Typeset by SJmagic DESIGN SERVICES, India.
Printed and bound in the UK by CPI Group (UK) Ltd.

The Publisher's authorised representative in the EU for product safety is Authorised Rep Compliance Ltd., Ground Floor, 71 Lower Baggot Street, Dublin D02 P593, Ireland.
www.arccompliance.com

For a complete list of Pen & Sword titles please contact:

PEN & SWORD BOOKS LTD
George House, Units 12 & 13, Beevor Street, Off Pontefract Road,
Barnsley, South Yorkshire, S71 1HN, England
E-mail: enquiries@pen-and-sword.co.uk
Website: www.pen-and-sword.co.uk
or
PEN AND SWORD BOOKS,
1950 Lawrence Road, Havertown, PA 19083, USA
E-mail: uspen-and-sword@casematepublishers.com
Website: www.penandswordbooks.com

Contents

Author's Note and Glossary..vi
Acknowledgements..x
Foreword by Prince Michael of Kent, GCVO, CD, KStJ...xi
Introduction..xii

Chapter 1   Locusts, 'Bomber Barons', 'Strawberries and Cream
            and Fruitcake for Tea'...1
Chapter 2   'Real Killer Fighters'..12
Chapter 3   Dowding, Park, Fighter Command and 'The System'....................37
Chapter 4   'We Lacked Experience but were Certainly Keen'.......................55
Chapter 5   Göring, Hitler and 'Mein Kampf'..76
Chapter 6   'The Personnel of the Luftwaffe ... Took the Oath of
            Allegiance to the Führer'..82
Chapter 7   Messerschmitts, Spain and Mölders...86
Chapter 8   'Barking Creek' and 'A Queer War'..94
Chapter 9   Operation Weserübung: The German Invasion of Norway..........112
Chapter 10 Fall Gelb: Blitzkrieg in the West..126
Chapter 11 Dunkirk: Operation Dynamo...150
Chapter 12 'We Never Considered Being Beaten. It Was Just Not
            Possible in Our Eyes'..173
Chapter 13 'The Beaver'..196
Chapter 14 'Unleash a Storm of Wrath and Steel Upon the British!'............203
Chapter 15 'Events are Much Livelier'..212
Chapter 16 'I Have Therefore, Somewhat Arbitrarily Chosen
            the Events of 10 July as the Opening of the Battle'....................270

Appendix   RAF Fighter Command Operational Aircraft and Aircrew
            Casualties, 2–9 July 1940...275
Bibliography...278
Other Books by Dilip Sarkar...287
Index...289

Author's Note and Glossary

The aviation-minded reader will notice that I have referred to German Messerschmitt fighters by the abbreviation 'Me' (not 'Bf', which is more technically correct), or simply by their numeric designation, such as '109' or '110'. This not only reads better but is authentic: during the Battle of Britain, Keith Lawrence, a New Zealander, flew Spitfires and once said to me 'To us they were just 'Me's', '109s' or '110s', simple, never 'Bf'.'

In another attempt to preserve accuracy, I have also used the original German, wherever possible, regarding terms associated with the *Luftwaffe*. These include the following:

Adlerangriff	'Attack of the Eagles'.
Adlertag	'Eagle Day'.
Eichenlaub	The Oak Leaves, essentially being a bar to the Ritterkreuz.
Erprobungsgruppe	Experimental group, in the case of Erprobungsgruppe 210 a skilled precision bombing unit.
Experte	A fighter 'ace'. Ace status, on both sides, was achieved by destroying five enemy aircraft.
Freie hunt	A fighter sweep.
Gefechstand	Operations headquarters.
Geschwader	The whole group, usually of three gruppen.
Geschwaderkommodore	The group leader.
Gruppe	A wing, usually of three squadrons.
Gruppenkeil	A wedge formation of bombers, usually made up of vics of three.
Gruppenkommandeur	The wing commander.
Jagdbomber ('Jabo')	Fighter-bomber.
Jagdflieger	Fighter pilot.
Jagdgeschwader	Fighter group, abbreviated JG.
Jagdwaffe	The fighter force.
Jäger	Hunter, in this context a fighter pilot or aircraft.
Kampfflieger	Bomber aircrew.

AUTHOR'S NOTE AND GLOSSARY

Kampfgeschwader	Bomber group, abbreviated KG.
Kanal	English Channel.
Katchmarek	Wingman.
Lehrgeschwader	Literally a training group, but actually a precision bombing unit, abbreviated LG.
Luftflotte	Air Fleet.
Oberkannone	Literally the 'Top Gun', or leading fighter ace.
Oberkommando der Wehrmacht (OKW)	The German armed forces high command.
Ritterkreuz	The Knight's Cross of the Iron Cross.
Rotte	A pair of fighters, comprising leader and wingman, into which the Schwarm broke once battle was joined.
Rottenführer	Leader of a fighting pair.
Schwarm	A section of four fighters.
Schwarmführer	Section leader.
Schwimmweste	Life-jacket.
Seelöwe	*Sealion*, the codenamed provided Hitler's proposed seaborne invasion of the UK.
Stab	Staff.
Stabschwarm	Staff flight.
Staffel	A squadron.
Staffelkapitän	The squadron leader.
Störflug	Harassing attacks, usually by lone Ju 88s.
Stuka	The Ju 87 dive-bomber.
Sturkampfgeschwader	Dive-bomber group, abbreviated StG.
Vermisst	Missing.
Zerstörer	Literally 'destroyer', the term used for the Me 110.
Zerstörergeschwader	Destroyer group, abbreviated ZG.

Each geschwader generally comprised three gruppen, each of three staffeln. Each gruppe is designated by Roman numerals, i.e. III/JG 26 refers to the third gruppe of Fighter Group (abbreviated 'JG') 26. Staffeln are identified by numbers, so 7/JG 26 is the 7th staffel and belongs to III/JG 26.

Rank comparisons may also be useful:

Gefreiter	Private 1st Class.
Unteroffizier	Corporal, no aircrew equivalent in Fighter Command.
Feldwebel	Sergeant.
Oberfeldwebel	Flight Sergeant.
Leutnant	Pilot Officer.

Oberleutnant	Flight Lieutenant.
Hauptmann	Squadron Leader.
Major	Wing Commander.
Oberst	Group Captain.

RAF and British Abbreviations:

AAF	Auxiliary Air Force.
AASF	Advance Air Striking Force.
A&AEE	Aeroplane & Armament Experimental Establishment.
AFC	Air Force Cross.
AFDU	Air Fighting Development Unit.
AI	Airborne Interception radar.
AOC	Air Officer Commanding.
AOC-in-C	Air Officer Commanding-in-Chief.
ATA	Air Transport Auxiliary.
ATS	Armament Training School.
BEF	British Expeditionary Force.
CAS	Chief of the Air Staff.
DCAS	Deputy CAS.
CFS	Central Flying School.
CGS	Central Gunnery School.
CO	Commanding Officer.
DES	Direct Entry Scheme.
DFC	Distinguished Flying Cross.
DFM	Distinguished Flying Medal.
DSO	Distinguished Service Order.
E/A	Enemy Aircraft.
FAA	Fleet Air Arm.
EFTS	Elementary Flying Training School.
FIU	Fighter Interception Unit.
FTS	Flying Training School.
ITW	Initial Training.
LAC	Leading Aircraftman.
MRAF	Marshal of the Royal Air Force.
MSFU	Merchant Ship Fighter Unit.
NCO	Non-Commissioned Officer.
ORB	Operations Record Book.
OTC	Officer Training Corps.
OTU	Operational Training Unit.
PDC	Personnel Distribution Centre.
RAFVR	Royal Air Force Volunteer Reserve.

AUTHOR'S NOTE AND GLOSSARY

RFS	Reserve Flying School.
RN	Royal Navy.
R/T	Radio Telephone.
RNAS	Royal Navy Air Service.
SASO	Senior Air Staff Officer.
SEAC	South East Asia Command.
SOO	Senior Operations Officer.
SSC	Short Service Commission.
UAS	University Air Squadron.
U/S	Unserviceable.
W/T	Wireless Telephone.

Acknowledgements

This series of books has arisen from over forty years of research and study of the subject, throughout which time I led a privileged relationship with survivors, and the relatives of casualties – too many to thank individually, but all have my appreciation.

As ever, my old friend Andy Long was ever-helpful, and I would also acknowledge kind assistance from Andy Straw, who runs a Facebook page dedicated to HMS *Foylebank*, Eddie Palmer, Sandy Weatherburn, and Chloe Taylor of Portland Museum, who all helped unravel the violent events of, and provide some colour to, 4 July 1940. Linda Duffield of the Kenley Revival Project was also ever-helpful, and Frances Hills, daughter of Squadron Leader E.G. Alford GM.

In relation to this particularly special project, I must thank Charles Hewitt, Martin Mace and Matthew Potts of Pen & Sword, and the production and marketing teams, who are always a pleasure to work with and collectively do a first-class job.

Finally, it has been an absolute privilege to produce this work for the Battle of Britain Memorial Trust and National Memorial to The Few, and I must thank our Chairman, Richard Hunting CBE, Honorary Secretary, Group Captain Patrick Tootal OBE DL RAF, Trustee Wing Commander Andrew Simpson RAFVR(T), Major (Ret'd) Jules Gomez, Site Manager, National Memorial to The Few, and both Malcolm Triggs and Becca Collier-Cook for their help in promoting 'Battle of Britain: The People's Project'.

Foreword

Prince Michael of Kent, GCVO, CD, KStJ

Patron, The Battle of Britain Memorial Trust CIO

The Battle of Britain Memorial Trust, in addition to maintaining the National Memorial to the Few, is dedicated to preserving the memory of the men and women who took part in the Battle of Britain, commemorating their achievements and sacrifices. It sets out to educate the public about the unique nature of the Battle of Britain and ensure that future generations are aware of the importance of this event and its place in history. Dilip Sarkar MBE, in association with the Trust, has produced a detailed and broad ranging history of the Battle of Britain in eight volumes, drawing upon his personal archive and other rare sources, in this partnership project.

This volume covers the essential background: from the birth of air power to the end of the lull following the Dunkirk evacuation.

In subsequent volumes each phase of the Battle of Britain will be dealt with as a separate volume with a final volume presenting a study of how the Battle of Britain has been commemorated over the years and its place in popular culture together with a guide to memorials, museums and other sites of interest.

Much has been written about the Battle, but the eight volumes will present a unique review of the conflict using the personal recollections of many of those who took part in or witnessed this significant part of World War Two.

The author has produced an invaluable work which contributes greatly to our understanding of the Battle, which also helps sustain the Trust's invaluable work.

Kensington Palace May 2023
London

Introduction

The time will come when thou shalt lift thine eyes
To watch a long-drawn battle in the skies;
While aged peasants, too amazed for words,
Stare at the flying fleets of wondrous birds.
England, so long the mistress of the sea,
Where wind and waves confess her sovereignty;
Her ancient triumphs yet on high shall bear
And reign, the sovereign of the conquered air.

The English poet Thomas Gray wrote *Luna Habitabillas*, in which that verse appears, in 1737 – 166 years before the Wright brothers made the world's first powered flight and 177 years before the first German bomb fell on England. Gray's verse was, therefore, a far-sighted prophecy indeed.

Nearly 2,000 years before Gray's vivid imagination turned skywards, in 55 BC, the Roman Emperor Julius Caesar invaded Britain. Finding Dover heavily defended, the Romans continued along the Kentish coast, ultimately landing, it is believed, at Pegwell Bay. After Roman times, England was variously invaded from the sea by Angles, Saxons and Vikings. Famously, in 1066, William of Normandy, assisted by King Harold Hardrada of Norway, who staged a diversionary landing on the east coast, landed, unopposed, at Pevensey in East Sussex, subsequently defeating the Anglo-Saxon King Harold near Hastings and taking the crown. Significantly, none of these seaborne invasions were challenged at sea. In time, it was recognised that the 'Sceptered Isle' was best defended by a strong navy and any invasion threat met off the English coast.

In 1588, Philip II's Spanish fleet was the largest ever seen in Europe, and together with the Duke of Parma the Spanish Monarch resolved to invade Britain with a force of 30,000 men. As the great armada approached England's South Coast, beacons were lit, warning of the approaching threat. The English Royal Navy (RN), founded by Henry VIII in 1546, responded, successfully attacking the Spaniards off Calais and Gravelines before a storm scattered Philip's ships, rendering his proposed invasion impossible. Later, after the Restoration in 1660, Charles II significantly strengthened the RN, competing with both the Dutch and French for maritime supremacy – vital to imperial expansion and trade.

INTRODUCTION

In 1804, during the 'Age of Fighting Sail', what had become the United Kingdom of Great Britain (in 1707) was again threatened with a seaborne invasion – this time by the French Emperor Napoleon. The RN blockaded the French and Spanish fleets, however, and in 1805 Admiral Nelson destroyed the combined French-Spanish Fleet off Cape Trafalgar, neutralising the threat. From then until the Second World War, Britannia ruled the waves, its navy the undisputed supreme power at sea.

From the second aeroplanes were harnessed for military purposes, though, Britain was again imperilled. By June 1940, Germany was the undefeated master of Europe, and looked to mount a seaborne invasion of southern England. To facilitate this, certain conditions were pre-requisite, including the destruction of the RAF. The resulting, unprecedented, aerial conflict was fought out by the opposing air forces over sixteen bloody weeks, between 10 July – 31 October 1940. This epic aerial duel became known as the Battle of Britain – which is a huge story of human experiences, of great courage and determination, ranging from the airmen in the skies to civilians on the ground 'taking it', not to mention those who worked in aircraft factories and at other high priority targets. If Britain's overall part in the Allied Total Victory is the high point of modern British national pride, then Britain's victory in the Battle of Britain has to be the most pivotal moment of all.

The traditional and heavily myth-laden narrative is that this victory belonged exclusively to 'The Few', nearly 3,000 young aircrew of Air Chief Marshal Sir Hugh Dowding's Fighter Command, whom Churchill apparently immortalised in his speech of 20 August 1940. But was he only talking about Fighter Command? That actually appears doubtful, because concurrently with the defensive battle being fought by Dowding's men, aircrews of Bomber Command were both taking the war to Germany by night, and by day attacking the enemy's invasion preparations and airfields. Moreover, RAF Coastal Command also contributed through minelaying and attacking German shipping, and photographic reconnaissance also played its part in the air. So the Battle of Britain is actually a much more holistic and inclusive story than has largely been understood until comparatively recent times – and the individual stories of those involved are frequently as inspirational as they are deeply moving and fascinating.

My lifelong desire to document and share these stories, in fact, led to the creation of 'Battle of Britain: The People's Project', a partnership between the all-important Battle of Britain Memorial Trust and National Memorial to The Few, and my publisher, Pen & Sword. Aimed squarely at public engagement and harvesting previously unshared personal material from family archives, the Project focuses on those who lived through and experienced the 'Finest Hour', in whatever way – because only that collective experience enables us, nearly a century later, to better understand what happened, and why.

Some may question whether this story still resonates, has any relevance to today. The answer is yes, because this is history – our history – and all history is important. As Herman Kell, a German bomber pilot in the Battle of Britain said, without history 'we humans would be without a past, without parameters for our judgement and guidance; without hope and just a black hole as the future'. And that, more than anything, is why the Battle of Britain story – and all history – is important.

This, the first of eight volumes covering the big Battle of Britain story, covers the essential background, providing context to the day-by-day events occurring between 10 July and 31 October 1940. It has been a challenging book to write, given the myriad of concurrent stories and threads, on both sides of the Channel, defying a traditionally chronological approach. Volumes two to seven inclusive cover each phase of the Battle of Britain, day-by-day, and are far more than dispassionate lists of combat losses and claims – although that said, reverting to primary source material, especially actual RAF pilots' combat reports, has frequently untangled hitherto incorrectly documented events and proves the crucial importance of an evidence-based approach.

All of these seven books, then, are not only about events, but equally about people and their experiences, seeking to set the air battles within a far wider context of human experience. The final book of the whole eight-volume series explores how the Battle of Britain has been remembered and commemorated over the years, its place in popular and cultural history, and a guide to the various museums, memorials and certain sites of interest.

My brief has been not to produce an academic text, but something setting these aerial events into a wider context, appealing to military aviation experts and the 'general reader' alike. Collectively, the seven works represent the Battle of Britain Memorial Trust's official history of the epic aerial conflict – at the conclusion of which, regardless of historical debate, Britain emerged unbowed, unconquered – and, where it counted, 'sovereign of the conquered air'.

Dilip Sarkar MBE, FRHistS, 2022

Chapter 1

Locusts, 'Bomber Barons', 'Strawberries and Cream and Fruitcake for Tea'

Considering that the Wright brothers had only made their mark on history in 1903, with their first successful powered flight at Kittyhawk, manned flight remained a new concept when the First World War broke out in 1914. This, of course, was the world's first global war of the industrial age, and the American Civil War (1861–1865) had already hinted at the scale of casualties involved with modern warfare. During that conflict, however, aircraft had not existed, whereas aviation was at the military's disposal in 1914. Today, the strategic and tactical benefits of what became known as 'air power' are many and obvious, but back then there was no precedent; it was a matter of starting from scratch.

During the First World War, belligerent countries aligned themselves with one or other of the two sides: the 'Triple Entente', or 'Allies', namely Britain, France and Russia, or the 'Central Powers', headed-up by Germany and Austria-Hungary. Ultimately, fifty-seven nations fought in the war, but only eight of these had a dedicated air arm, among them Britain and Germany. Initially, the most obvious use of aircraft for military purposes was reconnaissance, because they could fly higher and were more versatile than tethered observation balloons. Such 'gas bags' were operated by the Royal Engineers (RE), the aviation side of which was expanded in 1911 to battalion strength with headquarters and a balloon company at Farnborough, Hampshire, and another equipped with aircraft at Larkhill, Wiltshire. The following year, on 13 April 1912, the Royal Flying Corps (RFC) was formed to provide aviation for both the army and RN.

In 1913, however, the Admiralty insisted upon its own air arm, and so in 1914, the Royal Naval Air Service (RNAS) was created, leaving the RFC alone providing aircraft for the army. From the early 1900s, though, an early advocate and supporter of air power, Captain Bertram Dickson, argued that Britain required a dedicated and independent air force, arguing that 'The fight for supremacy of the air in future wars will be of the first and greatest importance'; he was both far-sighted and correct.

On 25 August 1914, Lieutenant Harvey-Kelly and two other pilots of 2 Squadron RFC forced down a German Rumpler reconnaissance aircraft in what was the first recorded clash between British and German airmen. The victory was achieved by the RFC pilots making diving passes at the Rumpler – the remarkable thing being that all aircraft involved were unarmed. Things soon changed, it rapidly became clear that aircraft could also be used for what was later known as 'close air support', attacking ground targets, and bombing. Defence was required against such machines, however, and to deal with enemy reconnaissance aircraft, and so the fighter was born. At first, the aircrew involved were armed purely with revolvers and rifles, then fixed machine-guns, either forward-firing above the propeller arc, operated by the pilot, or synchronised to shoot through the spinning airscrew, while in two-seaters a rear gunner was also armed with a machine-gun. This, then, was the start of military aviation and fighter warfare.

War always accelerates technology, and First World War military aviation was no exception. Airframes were refined, engines continually developed and improved, all these advances increasing all-important range, operational ceiling and speed. Significantly, these first military aircraft were all biplanes, which is to say they have two wings, stacked one atop the other. The advantage is a light but strong wing design, low wing loading and a smaller span. The two wings and necessary bracing wires created much drag, however, reducing performance, and therefore aircraft designers began looking at fixed wing monoplanes with just a single mainplane. Such a wing was more efficient, producing less drag, and was easier to build; the disadvantage was greater weight, owing to the mainplane's larger surface area, and reduced manoeuvrability. In 1915, the German Fokker Eindecker monoplane fighter appeared, which temporarily dominated the skies during what became known as the 'Fokker Scourge'.

Nonetheless, the period 1914 to the late 1920s saw comparatively few monoplanes produced, because the engines available were too slow to produce sufficient thrust for the larger, heavier, monoplane. Ultimately, as mightier engines and more advanced construction materials became available, the monoplane's advantages and performance substantially outweighed the biplane's attributes and so became standard. During the First World War, though, the biplane, and even triple-deckers, held sway, and it was around these comparatively primitive machines that combat tactics were devised.

A new word – 'ace' – also entered common language. Coined by the French, it described a fighter pilot who had achieved three victories. An American journalist picked this up and decreed that five aerial victories were required for ace status, while the Imperial German Air Service decided upon ten, preferring to call their aces *Kanone*. The ever-understated British authorities were less enthusiastic and initially refused to use the term, failing to see what Germany grasped immediately: that the fighter pilot was a glamorous aerial knight and a star to the ground-borne general public: true heroes in a time for heroes – and a great weapon in the propaganda war. Nonetheless, by the Armistice, there were over a thousand British aces, many of whom, like Captain Albert Ball VC, DSO, MC and Major Lanoe George Hawker VC, DSO, had become household names, their exploits enthusiastically followed by schoolboys and adults alike. In short, the fighter pilot had become a star.

On 19 August 1915, Lieutenant-Colonel Hugh Trenchard took command of the RFC in France. It would prove a most significant appointment. Trenchard argued that the RFC should be an autonomous service, not tied to the army, and on 1 April 1918, this came to pass when the Royal Air Force (RAF) was created. 'Boom' Trenchard became the first Chief of the Air Staff (CAS) and remembered as 'Father of the Royal Air Force'. It was when the guns fell silent, at long last, on 11 November 1918, the Allies victorious, that Trenchard's real battle began to preserve and move forward his so-called 'junior service', as the vast armies and air components which had fought on and over the First World War's battlefields were rapidly dismantled and much reduced.

In November 1919, Trenchard submitted a White Paper outlining his plan for the peace-time air force. The junior service was to remain independent, and include a substantial proportion of commissioned short-term pilots, a cadet training college for permanent officers, an auxiliary facility, and, among other things, a school for aero-engineering apprentices. In 1922, the Lloyd George government became conscious of the fact that while the French Air Force included a striking force of 600 machines, the RAF Home Defence capacity comprised just three squadrons. Consequently, it was decided to increase the RAF's establishment to 500 aircraft at a cost of £1.1m annually.

The RAF, however, was actually still fighting a battle for survival in the corridors of Whitehall and Westminster, owing to hostility from the more senior services resentful of having lost their air arms, and given the determination of many to disarm completely. In 1923, the Salisbury Committee, appointed to review and decide upon the air force's fate, decreed a new and enlarged expansion programme for the RAF. Although this involved increasing establishment to fifty-two Home Defence squadrons, to be complete by 1928, given that war with France was unimaginable, and with no other enemy threatening Britain's island shores at that time, this ambitious and early expansion plan soon lost momentum. Indeed, peace, not war, was very much in the air following the Western powers signing the Locarno Treaty in 1925, binding each other to preserve peace and unite against any would-be aggressor. Nevertheless, the RAF remained in existence and an independent service.

Upon formation, the RAF was modelled upon the British Army's organisation and rank structure. Army officers were trained at the Royal Military Academy at Sandhurst, which was, according to James, 'for gentlemen who could afford to pay the fees'. Those 'gentlemen' had exclusively been educated privately at so-called 'public' schools, as were RAF officers between the wars. Indeed, Branson and Heinemann describe a society 'still stratified into layers divided by rigid class barriers'. Air force officers were trained at the fee-paying RAF College Cranwell, meaning the commissions – legal authority granted by the sovereign to bear arms and issue orders to subordinates – were effectively bought.

Cost, in fact, dominated entry to all of the professions, preserving them, like commissions, exclusively for the upper classes. Coming from a family of means able to fund a private education prompted Mowat to ask 'Did the public schoolboy enjoy advantages beyond his desserts in public and professional life?' According to Branson and Heinemann, in 1937, 35.7 per cent of the population earned under £2 10s per week; 37.8 per cent earned between that figure and £4; 21.3 per cent earned between £4 and £10, but only 5.2 per cent earned over £10. The lowest wage-earners represented 4,318,000 families, while the top earnings concerned just 635,000. Moreover, by one estimate in 1935, less than half of working-class children of 'higher ability' were receiving a secondary, state-funded, education, which was the minimum standard for any kind of advancement, even if not socially – leading Pugh to conclude that 'interwar Britain was still a very undereducated society'.

From 1905 onwards, all public schools had Officer Training Corps (OTC), delivering a specific military syllabus and examination. Those who passed were awarded Certificate 'A', armed with which, together with a good school report and an application counter-signed by any colonel, they were entitled to a commission as of right. Trenchard modelled the new RAF's system on this long-established tradition, preserving commissions for the upper classes. Indeed, before the Second World War, 'the RAF had no definition of leadership', such 'skills were absorbed rather than taught', and the services reflected the social attitudes of the time – which were rather more inclined to assume leadership on the basis of social class.

In Trenchard's new service, this also extended to flying: all pilots were to be officers, commissioned into the General Duties (flying) branch. The ability to fly is, of course, over and above the traditional officer function of leading men in battle. Aircrew are, in fact, a breed apart, as Wells explained: 'From the earliest days of aviation, airmen have been regarded as members of an élite group ... it took a special type of man to brave the obvious perils.' The training of Trenchard's officers was undertaken at the RAF College Cranwell, although Flight Cadets, according to Air Vice-Marshal H.A.V. Hogan, which he was himself between 1929–30, were not at Cranwell 'because we wanted to be leaders of men, but simply because we wanted to fly!'

Nonetheless, enthusiasm for aviation and a burning ambition to fly was not enough: the fees payable to attend Cranwell were substantial, the amount involved preserving the pilot's cockpit for the British socio-economic pyramid's top 5.2 per cent. Means, however, may have opened the door to a commission – but it could not automatically assume the ability to fly: the failure rate in flying training was 50 per cent, so a privileged social and educational background was no guarantee towards receiving the coveted flying brevet.

Cranwell alone, though, was too small to produce the quantity of pilots required by the RAF. In 1921, contrary to his original elitist vision for officer pilots, Trenchard, to both achieve the number of pilots he needed and create a trained reserve, permitted a small number of non-commissioned officers (NCO) as pilots. The concept was that these men would fly for five years before resuming their original trades, while eligible for recall to flying duties in the event of an emergency. The initiative was both popular and economic, but numbers remained small: in 1925, only 13.9 per cent of pilots were NCOs, rising to 17.1 per cent in 1935.

The first half of the 1930s had seen Britain and other nations 'hell-bent', according to Sir Maurice Dean, 'for collective security and prepared to accept incalculable risks in that cause'. In 1932, Britain abandoned what had been a miniscule RAF expansion programme. The following year, Adolf Hitler – leader of the Nazis – became Chancellor of Germany, changing everything. The Führer immediately set about contravening and reversing what were seen as injustices arising from the Versailles Peace Treaty of 1919, namely restrictions on the German military and territorial concessions. Already Weimar Germany had begun secretly rebuilding its prohibited *Luftwaffe*, far away from prying Western eyes, deep in Soviet Russia. The Great Depression caused by the Wall Street stock-market crash of 1929, had not helped, the resulting financial chaos affecting the next decade. The British government, therefore, had serious socio-economic issues to address at home, which it tried its best to do – while Germany fervently rearmed.

Between the wars, especially before the various rearmament programmes, the RAF was comparatively small, more like an elite flying club, in which everyone knew each other. With no one, as yet, to fight (fortunately, considering it remained biplane equipped until 1938), squadrons competed in various competitions, such as aerobatics and gunnery, and participated in annual air displays like the Hendon Air Pageant. A young Welshman, Fred Roberts, remembered those days:

> Another airman, Jimmy Belton, and myself joined 19 Squadron as rooky armourers direct from our six-month course at Manby. Full of enthusiasm and expecting to see aircraft everywhere, we arrived at Duxford to find everything quiet and partly closed for the weekend. Of course, this was still the 'strawberries and cream and fruit-cake for tea' period enjoyed by the pre-war air force.

Of fundamental significance is that between the wars, even though far-sighted novelists like H.G. Wells had written of great future battles fought by huge aerial armadas, those actually deciding aerial strategy failed to give any credence to such ideas. As A.J.P. Taylor wrote:

> Those who determined air strategy after the war had to proceed by dogma alone, a dogma that was little more than guesswork. The dogma was simple: 'The bomber will always get through'. General Giulio Douhet said this in Italy; Billy Mitchell said it in the United States. Both were detached theorists. It was more important that Lord Trenchard said it in England, for Trenchard was CAS for ten years, from 1919–1929.

And Trenchard was a confirmed 'Bomber Baron' – which was not great news for Britain's fighter force, such as it was.

Many influential people in both the services and in civilian life, in fact, believed in the so-called 'knock-out blow' – which could only be delivered by bombers. Indeed, such was the bomber's perceived power, Trenchard considered it unnecessary,

> for an air force, in order to defeat the enemy nation, to defeat its armed forces first. Air power can dispense with that immediate step, can pass over the enemy navies and armies, and penetrate air defences and attack direct the centre of production, transportation and communication from which the enemy war effort is maintained. It is on the destruction of enemy industries and, above all, in the lowering of morale of enemy nationals caused by bombing that the ultimate victory lies.

In 1932, Stanley Baldwin, then Prime Minister, emphasised the all-pervasive fear of bombing:

> I think it is as well for the man in the street to realise that there is no power on earth that can save him from being bombed. Whatever people may tell him, the bomber will always get through. The only defence is offence, which means that you have to kill more women and children more quickly than the enemy if you want to save yourselves.

What precious little spending there was on British air power between the wars, certainly until 1935, was overwhelmingly focused on the bomber force. This is unsurprising considering Trenchard's view in 1921 that the aeroplane was 'a shockingly bad weapon for defence' and that the use of fighters was 'only necessary to keep up the morale of your own people'. Trenchard's doctrine revolved almost entirely, therefore, around offensive operations. Defence was side-lined with the absolute bare minimum of resources.

In 1934, Britain revisited rearmament, but given the restricted spending involved, Dean charged that 'even now Britain was not taking its problems seriously'. It was not just a reluctance to rearm that had contributed to this sorry scenario, however. According to Calder, the 1930s were 'the best of times, the worst of times'. In 1929 the world had been plunged into an economic crisis when the Wall Street stock market infamously crashed. The resulting fiscal chaos directly affected the next decade. Indeed, the British novelist and broadcaster J.B. Priestley famously made his celebrated *English Journey* in 1934, finding 'three Englands': the old and traditional, green and pleasant land; that of Victorian industrialisation, and finally a new, American inspired, revived, England of 'motor coaches, wireless, hiking, factory girls looking like actresses', and belonging 'far more to the age itself than to this particular island'.

Prosperity was largely confined to the 'New Britain' of the area south of a line between the rivers Severn and Humber. North of that line was the demoralised and declining 'Nineteenth-century Britain'. The countryside too was hard-hit by the depression. In 1932, unemployment stood at 2,750,000. The British government between the wars, therefore, had serious social issues at home to deal with. Against this calamitous backdrop Nazi Germany busied itself with rearmament, while Churchill later wrote that so far as British military spending was concerned the years 1931–35 were those of 'the locust'.

Locusts or not, in November 1934, Stanley Baldwin told the House of Commons that Britain would 'in no conditions ... accept any position of inferiority with regard to what Air Force may be raised in Germany in the future'. According to Dean, though, 'the plan of air rearmament adopted was quite inadequate to fulfil the pledge, and was indeed little more than a façade'. The simple truth was that neither the government or British people were yet ready to pay the price required for aerial parity with Nazi Germany. Moreover, the price would now be paid for Trenchard's offensive doctrine.

In the mid-1930s the Air Staff still believed in a strict numerical ratio of fighters to bombers. This was, however, meaningless, because, again as Dean wrote, 'the requirements of defence' should be 'determined by the area to be defended and the nature of the probable attack'. The size of the bomber force, of course, was dictated by quite different factors. In sum, the complete lack of substantial rearmament and deficiencies in doctrinal thinking were caused by three things: financial constraints, the indifference of or opposition by politicians, and Trenchard's offensive thinking.

Trenchard's next initiative, however, was revolutionary: Short Service Commissions (SSC). In the senior services, officers usually served for the duration of their working lives (hence the term 'Permanent Commission'). This, however, led to a 'dead man's shoes' scenario, which Trenchard wished to avoid, given that flying is obviously a young man's activity. The SSC scheme, therefore, provided for officers to serve a fixed contract of four years active service, followed by six on the reserve list. Such officers were only eligible for promotion as far as flight lieutenant, but could transfer to a permanent commission upon successfully passing the required examination. The SSC scheme also reached out to young men of the Commonwealth, keen to fly and hungry for adventure. Among them was an Australian, James Baird Coward, who remembered that:

> Shortly after my twenty-first birthday in 1936, I applied for a SSC in the RAF. My father had gone broke in the depression, so I had to leave school aged fifteen.
>
> I went up to the Air Ministry and after a short wait was shown into a room where there were three group captains sitting at a table.

The one in the middle asked me what games I played. 'Rugby and cricket, Sir.'

'Go down the corridor and see the doctor'. I was astonished. I was in!

Pilot Officer Coward completed his service flying training and was then posted to 19 Squadron at Duxford, near Cambridge:

> It was very pleasant at Duxford because it was a small Mess, brand new, lovely rooms with fitted wardrobes and washbasins. It was absolute luxury. One was woken up in the morning with a cup of tea, they ran you a bath and while you were having it your uniform would be pressed, buttons and shoes polished. Then you went down to breakfast. There was a great hotplate along the side with a choice of eggs, bacon, kippers, herrings or kedgeree, or anything.
>
> It was a beautifully run Mess with excellent food. There were no senior people, and no air traffic control. The Mess was full of young chaps. We dined in four nights a week, in full mess kit. In the mornings, all we had to do was parade and march the airmen down to the flights, and then fly a lovely fighter all day or as often as we could.
>
> We had squash and tennis courts, played games on Wednesday and Saturday afternoons, and on Sunday there was a church parade. We had the Gloster Gauntlet aircraft, which was easy and very pleasant to fly.

Another SSC officer entering the service in 1936 was John Wray, who described the training involved:

> In those days, officers and NCO pilots on limited service engagements spent three months at Elementary Flying Training School, completing fifty hours dual and solo flying, and engaging in associated ground subjects. Flying training at EFTS was mainly on the De Havilland Tiger Moth biplane, although where I was, at Hamble, we also had Avro Cadets, which were similar.
>
> After EFTS, we then proceeded to the RAF Depot at Uxbridge for general introduction into the service, including issue of, or in the case of officers, the purchase of uniform. This lasted about a month. Then onwards to Service Flying Training School for one year and ten months' conversion to service aircraft types, and instruction into their use as military weapons.
>
> Ground subjects were also studied and the whole training experience was now in a service environment, with we officers learning how to be such, and the NCOs learning how to be NCOs.

Together with Direct Entrants from the University Air Squadrons (UAS), SSC officers were not trained at Cranwell, which remained exclusively for professional career officers, but at Service Flying Training Schools (SFTS). Interestingly, the minimum entry requirement for a SSC was the School Certificate, obtainable not just at public but also grammar schools. Nonetheless, it was still assumed that 'all applicants would come from the social class that filled the public schools'. Furthermore, the Direct Entry Scheme (DES) provided a small number of permanent commissions offered to university graduates via competition for limited places.

Another sound initiative was the creation of the Auxiliary Air Force (AAF) in 1924, based upon the territorial concept; by 1930 such squadrons comprised 5 per cent of the air force's strength. There was no question, though, that auxiliary officers would be anything but public schoolboys. If Cranwellians were drawn from Britain's socio-economic élite, then auxiliaries were the élite of the élite.

James Edgar 'Johnnie' Johnson, a police inspector's son from Melton Mowbray, had a grammar-school education and a degree in civil engineering. An exceptional sportsman, this intrepid young man began private flying lessons in 1938, and applied to join the AAF:

> I went along for this interview and the senior officer there, knowing that I came from Leicestershire, said 'With whom do you hunt, Johnson?'
>
> I said 'Hunt, Sir?'
>
> He said 'Yes, Johnson, hunt; with whom do you hunt?'
>
> I said 'Well, I don't hunt, Sir, I shoot.'
>
> He said 'Oh, well thank you then, Johnson, that will be all!'
>
> Clearly the fact that I could shoot game on the wing impressed him not one bit. Had I been socially acceptable, however, by hunting with Lord so-and-so, things would have been different, but back then, that is what the auxiliaries were like, and do not forget that many members were of independent means, which I certainly wasn't!

William James Green was born in Easton, Bristol, on 23 April 1917, and attended St Gabriel's Church of England School before first working as an errand boy, then a travelling salesman; like Johnnie Johnson, 'Bill' did not come from the top 5.2 per cent of Britain's socio-economic pyramid – but he did become a pilot in the pre-war AAF. For that reason alone, his story is remarkable:

> By October 1936, I was working for a company that encouraged its employees to join the territorial army, or navy or air force reserve. Therefore I joined 501 'County of Gloucester' Squadron of the AAF, at Filton, as an Aircraftsman 2nd Class, Fitter under Training.

This, of course, was part-time. Every Thursday evening and at weekends I attended lectures, and fourteen months later took a practical, written and oral examination, in which I obtained over 80 per cent. Anyone getting 80 per cent or more skipped AC1 and went straight to LAC rank, and posted to a crew of two, looking after engines, which I did.

There were essentially two groundcrew trades: the fitter, who looked after the engine, and the rigger, who looked after everything else. We used to cycle out to the airfield every weekend, sometimes staying overnight. We had a skeleton staff of experienced regular airmen and NCOs, to train us 'weekenders'. Just after Munich, in 1938, my friend, Farr, who had enjoyed a better education than me, at a grammar school, told me that he was moving to the other side of the airfield to become a pilot, in the RAF VR. In all honesty I was green with envy, because I felt that I was every bit as good as he was, so I wrote to the CO and applied to do likewise. I was, in due course, ushered before a regular squadron leader who said 'Wouldn't you rather remain with the squadron and fly?'

To which I said 'Well, yes, but that's only for commissioned officers.' The AAF flyers at that time, of course, were the 'blue bloods', whereas I had not been to public school or university, and was not from a wealthy family. So, that is why I thought my only chance to fly was with the VR, which was not a social elite. The squadron leader, however, said 'I can tell you in confidence, that I am getting an establishment for six NCO pilots, so, if you like, you can stay on and train to be one of those.' So I did.

Something an observer today, looking back on all this, could not fail to note is that between the wars the RAF was exclusively white and male. Air Ministry regulations, under the Air Force (Constitution) Act, 1917, which provided the legal mechanism required to create the new service, explicitly excluded recruits 'not of pure European descent' from serving, similar racial restrictions also being observed by the British Army and RN. In August 1923, the Air Ministry's 'Recruiting Regulations for the Royal Air Force' confirmed that the nationality and ethnic origin of recruits must be restricted to those of 'pure European descent and the sons of natural born or naturalised British subjects'.

This was, of course, the age of Imperialism and colonial expansion by white nations, and the white man had steel and industry, providing the necessary means to dominate non-industrial nations – and those concerned people of colour. The policy was relaxed in October 1939, to appease the Empire and encourage the participation of people of colour in the war against the Axis, but, even so, numbers actually serving in the RAF (as opposed to, say, the Royal Indian Air Force) would remain comparatively low throughout the war. Also worthy of note is that the Recruiting Regulations refer only to 'sons'.

Between 1918 and 1920, women had served in the Woman's Royal Air Force in non-combatant roles – but were not permitted to serve again until 1939, when war with Germany appeared imminent and the Women's Auxiliary Air Force was created. In today's much more multi-cultural, diverse and equal society, such racial and sexist discrimination would clearly be completely unacceptable, but that was then, when times were very different and society was strictly hierarchical, and very much white and male dominated. This cannot be changed and simply has to be seen within the context of those very different times.

Information received in Britain during 1935 confirmed that although Germany was unlikely to be ready for war until 1939, Hitler's preparations towards that end were so substantial that the threat could no longer be ignored. So it was that, albeit tentatively, Britain at last began to rearm in earnest. On 25 February 1936, Expansion Scheme 'F' was approved: 124 squadrons (1,736 aircraft of all types) by April 1937. Unfortunately, while Scheme 'F' increased the bomber force to 1,000 aircraft, the number of fighters was only maintained. The most significant and forward-thinking feature of 1936's Expansion Scheme 'F' was recognising that a trained reserve was essential – leading to creation of the RAF Volunteer Reserve (RAFVR). This intended to,

> have wide appeal based upon the Citizen Volunteer principle with a common mode of entry and promotion and commissioning on merit ... So far as aircrew training was concerned, the system was based upon local town centres for spare time ground training and upon aerodrome centres associated with the town centres for flying training at the weekend, also for a fortnight's annual camp.

All such volunteer aircrew were automatically made sergeants – much to the chagrin of regular NCOs who had taken years to attain that exulted rank. The RAFVR, however, was a huge step forward to seeing fighter pilots and leaders eventually selected not on the basis of social class, but on ability – a prime example being Johnnie Johnson, rejected by the AAF on the grounds of social class and who subsequently joined the RAFVR – and became both the RAF's official top-scoring fighter pilot of the Second World War and an air-vice marshal.

Things were changing – just in time.

Chapter 2

'Real Killer Fighters'

Financial constraints and, of course, disarmament, severely restricted the resources made available to the RAF for research and development in the 1920s. Similar restrictions applied to the British aircraft industry generally. Paradoxically, though, it was an exciting time for aviation. There were many and various flights of endurance. In April 1919, for example, Major Keith Park and Captain Stewart completed a non-stop circuit of the British Isles in a Handley-Page 0/400. The route of 1,880 miles was flown at an average speed of 66 mph in twenty-eight hours and thirty minutes flying time.

In 1939, Alex Henshaw, piloting a single-engine Percival Mew Gull, flew non-stop from England to Cape Town. Most exciting of all, however, was the Schneider Trophy air race. Seven tenths of the world's surface is covered by water, and the Frenchman Jacques Schneider, son of an armament manufacturer, could not understand why, this being so, marine lagged so far behind land-based aviation. He saw the seaplane as being possessed of massive potential with water providing cheap airports.

As an incentive for aircraft designers to invest in seaplanes, Schneider presented his famous trophy for an international air race. The winner would be the nation whose seaplane flew the fastest over a measured water-course. Whichever country won the trophy three consecutive times would keep it. This was a time of emerging nationalism on a global basis, and so what undoubtedly remains the most emotive air race to date developed into a competition of immense national pride. More importantly, the races led directly to the Supermarine Spitfire and Hawker Hurricane monoplane fighters.

Between 1919 and 1931, the Schneider races were spectacular competitions being held at low-level over water, giving spectators on the ground an excellent view of events. Schneider's trophy – a silver nymph kissing the sea – became coveted. Both aircraft manufacturers and governments spent large sums of money designing, developing and racing their entrants. The first race, in 1913, was won by a Frenchman, whose top speed was 45.75 mph. Importantly, the winning design was not, as might be assumed, a biplane: it was a monoplane.

Although Britain's first win came the following year, Sopwith's victorious design was a biplane. This achieved, however, a new seaplane speed record of 86.78 mph. Given that the speed involved was almost double that of the previous winner, the biplane's supremacy appeared both assured and justified. The biplane dominated the war of 1914–18, the conflict interrupting the Schneider races until 1919. That year saw an entry submitted by the Supermarine Aviation Works, whose factory was situated on the Itchen estuary at Southampton.

With no time to produce a new machine, Supermarine's Chief Designer, Reginald Joseph Mitchell, and the company's owner, Hubert Scott-Paine, modified the Supermarine Baby, a biplane seaplane produced during the First World War. The resulting machine – the Sea Lion – competed over Bournemouth Bay but sank when the pilot was forced to land due to poor visibility. The Sea Lion was more flying boat than seaplane, as were subsequent developments of that design which competed in later races. Significantly, however, when the Sea Lion competed in the 1922 race held at Naples, Britain's was the only entry not government funded. Nonetheless, that year Mitchell's team won with a top speed of 145.7 mph – just 2.5 mph faster than the Italians in second place. In 1923, however, the Sea Lion was beaten – by 20 mph – by the American government-sponsored Curtiss CR-3 seaplane. Inspired, Mitchell went back to Southampton – and designed a monoplane.

The Curtiss, Mitchell had noted with interest, boasted a number of new features, including a liquid-cooled engine, wing surface radiators and a metal airscrew. Mitchell's new monoplane – the S.4 – was even more advanced than the American machine. Instead of employing the usual external bracing struts and wires, Mitchell's monoplane's wing was cantilevered. This represented both an important juncture in both Mitchell's personal career and aircraft design generally. Interestingly, the Air Ministry funded the design and construction of both the S.4 and the Gloster Aircraft Company's entry. The S.4 looked stunning. The single wing was made in one piece, covered not in doped fabric but in plywood. The fuselage was similarly covered and was of a monocoque construction which included both fin and tailplane. The nose – housing the Napier Lion engine – was covered in aluminium and the two-bladed propeller was also metal.

On 13 September 1925, the S.4 set a new air speed record over Southampton Water: 226.75 mph. However, the aircraft failed to meet expectations when it crashed during the Schneider race a month later. Fortunately the pilot survived, but the reason for the crash remained unclear; aileron flutter was thought most likely. 'Aviation experts,' wrote Gordon Mitchell, 'believed that Mitchell's ambitious use of the cantilever wing had exceeded the bounds of aerodynamic and structural knowledge available at the time.' Nonetheless, Mitchell still believed that the monoplane represented the best chance of preventing America winning once more and therefore keeping the Schneider Trophy.

Mitchell had no time to produce an entrant in the 1926 race, which was won by the Italians, meaning that the contest remained ongoing. In a bright red Macchi M.39, Major de Barnardi set a new air speed record of 258.87 mph. Mitchell set-to and designed the S.5, which had a metal covered fuselage much smaller in cross-section than the S.4. In fact everything about the S.5 was intended to reduce drag, including flush rivets and a highly polished surface.

Most importantly, this 1927 entry was Air Ministry funded and flown by an RAF pilot of the High Speed Flight – which had been formed specifically for the race. Two S.5s competed – winning first and second place, the victor setting yet another speed record at 281.66 mph. Quite rightly, Mitchell and his triumphant team returned from Venice to a heroes' welcome in Southampton.

In March 1928, Flight Lieutenant S.M. Kinkead was killed in a finely tuned S.5 while making his attempt on the world air speed record over the Solent. Mitchell was devastated. That month also saw de Barnardi push the boundaries further still in a Macchi M52R and increase the record to 318.57 mph. Speeds were now being reached which were unimaginable back in 1913. Towards the end of the year, Flight Lieutenant D'Arcy Greig hit 319.57 mph in an S.5 – but the margin over de Barnardi was insufficient to be accepted as a new record. By now the contest was being held every two years, giving Mitchell more time to develop his existing – excellent – racing seaplane into the S.6.

One thing the gifted designer was uncertain about, though, was the Napier engine. This led to him enquiring about the Derby based firm Rolls-Royce. Sir Henry Royce's Chief Designer and engineers assured Supermarine that they could deliver a new engine of 1,900 hp – 500 hp more powerful than the Italian engine. Mitchell then designed the S.6 around the potent new Rolls-Royce engine. This new machine featured further revolutionary improvements: the wings and fuselage were completely constructed of duralumin, and the heavy copper radiator internals replaced with much lighter alloy.

The 1929 race, described as 'The World's Greatest Aerial Spectacle' took place at Calshot on the Solent. Flight Lieutenant H.R.D. Waghorn won, flying an S.6, at an average speed of 328.63 mph. Mitchell was ecstatic: Britain had now won the Schneider trophy twice. Shortly afterwards, Squadron Leader A.H. Orlebar reached speeds of 336.3 and 357.7 mph, setting new world records in the process. The S.6 was now confirmed as both the fastest and most technologically advanced aircraft in the world.

That same year, however, also saw the Wall Street Crash. As the effect of this severe economic depression resounded throughout the world, people had more important things on their minds than fancy air races. In spite of pressure upon the Treasury exerted by many influential individuals and organisations sympathetic to Mitchell's plight, in January 1931 Prime Minister Ramsay MacDonald announced his Labour government's understandable decision: there would be no money made available from the public purse to finance Britain's Schneider Trophy that year.

This decision was immediately attacked by the press, which accused the government of being anti-British. MacDonald remained unmoved. Italy, however, which had also won twice, was competing and at this time looked set for a third and final victory in the S.6's enforced absence. Then an astonishing and inspirational thing happened: Lady Houston – a tremendous patriot and nationalist – paid the £100,000 necessary for Mitchell to compete. With the race but seven months away there was no longer time for Mitchell to produce his proposed S.7. Instead he improved the S.6 – now powered with a 2,350 hp 'R' engine. So was born the S.6B. Gordon Mitchell, son of 'R.J.', colourfully described what this meant to many people:

> People who were sick and tired of the hopeless struggle to find work and the humiliation of the dole queues, longed for some excitement to relieve the monotony of everyday life. The sight of Mitchell's seaplanes thundering across the sky at breath-taking speeds raised a cheer from lips which had forgotten to smile. England might be in a depression, but in the world of aviation she still had something of which to be proud.

On 12 September 1931, Flight Lieutenant J.N. Boothman flashed over the cheering crowds at 340.08 mph – with the throttle not even fully open – winning the Schneider Trophy outright for Britain. That afternoon, Flight Lieutenant G.H. Stainforth took up another S.6B in which he set a new world record: 379.05 mph. The depressed nation was delighted, British aviation supreme, and Mitchell deservedly made a Commander of the Most Excellent Order of the British Empire (CBE).

Although Schneider's original concept was that the first nation to win three consecutive times would keep the trophy – and thus bring an end to the famous air race – after Britain's win many people wanted the competition to continue with a new prize. According to historian Vincent Orange, Britain's 1931 win was, in fact, 'a hollow one because no rival machine got to the starting line', although conceding that Britain did win the trophy five times. Air Marshal Sir Hugh Dowding, Air Member for Supply and Research, however, disagreed with continuing the race:

> I was strongly opposed to this', he wrote, 'because the float-planes we had developed were perfectly useless for any military purpose. There was absolutely no value in them as a combat machine, and what value they did have was limited to flying from sheltered waters in light wind conditions. What I wanted to do was invite private tenders from two firms to cash in on the experience that had been gained in aircraft construction and engine progress so that we could order two of the fastest machines which it was possible to build with no restriction except landing speed, and that had to be on grass airfields.

The far-sighted Dowding's proposal was agreed by the Air Ministry.

When Dowding became Air Member for Research and Development in 1930, and when Mitchell's S.6B won the Schneider Trophy in 1931, the Air Defence of Great Britain (ADGB) was entirely dependent upon biplanes, such as the Bristol Bulldog, Hawker Fury and Demon fighters. These lightly armed fighters, however, were already being outpaced by new biplane bomber variants. For example, the Bulldog's top speed was 174 mph – but the Hawker Hart light bomber, introduced in 1929, was 10 mph faster. Bombers were also of an increasingly substantial construction. The problem, then, was that in the first instance RAF biplane fighters were increasingly unlikely to catch and intercept high-performance enemy bombers, or, indeed, shoot them down, owing to inadequate, rifle-calibre, armament. Dowding quickly realised that drastic advances were required to both airframes and aero-engines – particularly where fighters were concerned. The major improvement evident to him at that time was the monoplane.

Experts, however, advised him that biplanes were superior – to which argument Dowding countered that if that was so, why had Mitchell chosen to develop a monoplane to win the Schneider Trophy? The use of more metal parts in his designs was also noted by Dowding. Hitherto, biplanes had largely been constructed from seasoned wood and fabric. Dowding feared that in the event of war, it would no longer be possible to import sufficient quantities of such timber, favouring, therefore, the elimination of as much wood in aircraft manufacture as possible. From this point onwards, therefore, Mitchell's influence on the development of military aviation can clearly be seen.

Dowding's belief that the experience gained by designers during the Schneider Trophy races should be applied to military land-based aircraft led to the Air Ministry issuing Specification F.7/30 on 1 October 1931. The intention was for British aircraft designers to produce a new single-seat day and night-fighter intended to replace the Bristol Bulldog. The actual specification required was documented in detail by the Air Ministry's Directorate of Technical Development. The main requirements were:

1. Highest possible rate of climb.
2. Highest possible speed at 15,000ft.
3. Fighting view.
4. Manoeuvrability.
5. Capability of ease and rapid production in quantity.
6. Ease of maintenance.

The machine had to be armed with four machine-guns, carry four twenty-pound bombs and powered by any British produced engine. The Air Ministry required that the new fighter achieved a speed of at least 250 mph. Over the next three years, eight very different designs were submitted, five of which were biplanes. Among these was the Hawker PV 3, a direct development of the existing Hawker Fury, also designed by Sydney Camm, but with a Goshawk engine and four machine-guns grouped together in the nose.

The Bristol Aircraft Company, however, produced an unusual monoplane with a pusher Mercury engine. The Westland tender – also a monoplane – was never seriously considered with a top speed of only 185 mph. Although not accepted for production, according to Francis K. Mason 'the most direct and significant end product of the F.7/30 venture was R.J. Mitchell's Goshawk-powered Supermarine Type 224 monoplane'. This, he wrote, 'formed an essential link between the successful Schneider Trophy racing seaplanes and the Spitfire'. That may be so, but Gordon Mitchell described his father's Type 224 as 'a near disaster – with a maximum speed of only 230 mph, its performance in general fell short of what had been considered an "easy to achieve" specification'.

R.J. Mitchell himself was never happy with the Type 224, a low-winged monoplane completely constructed of metal – an innovation described by Alfred Price as 'a considerable novelty at that time'. The aircraft's main failing, in fact, was that the Goshawk engine was prone to overheating and the overall performance was poor: with a top speed of 238 mph it took eight minutes to reach 15,000ft. Gloster Aircraft won the competition with a radial engine biplane, the SS37, developed from the existing Gauntlet. The winning machine's top speed was 242 mph and reached 15,000ft in six-and-a-half minutes. This further delayed, however, the RAF's entry into the monoplane age. Nonetheless, it was an unexpected turning point so far as fighter development was concerned.

Although the SS37 was the winning tender it failed to enter production. The Air Ministry realised that its edge in performance was insufficient to warrant an order because it would doubtless soon be obsolete. An aircraft was required that had a considerably greater margin of superiority. Mitchell, it has been argued, had found Specification F.7/30 'too restrictive and insufficiently advanced in concept to produce an aircraft of the highest possible performance'.

The Air Ministry, however, wanted Supermarine to replace the problematic Goshawk with a Napier Dagger engine, but both Sir Robert McLean, Chairman of the Vickers (Aviation) Board which owned Supermarine, and Mitchell were convinced that the Type 224 could be developed no further. On 6 November 1934, the Air Ministry's proposal was therefore turned down. Sir Robert and his opposite number at Rolls-Royce, A.F Sidgreaves, decided that their companies would be better advised to collaborate not on F.7/30, but on 'a real killer fighter'.

Sir Robert later wrote that 'The Air Ministry was informed of this decision, and were told that under no circumstances would any technical member of the Air Ministry be consulted or allowed to interfere with the designer.' In November 1934, Mitchell was given permission to begin work on his Type 300 fighter. Concurrently, Rolls-Royce continued improving its new PV XII engine – later called Merlin.

It is a little-known fact the initial design and development work on both the Spitfire aircraft and Merlin engine began as a privately funded venture. The Air Ministry has been blamed for a lack of foresight regarding the new fighter's specification. This is not entirely justified. Sir Robert McClean made it formally quite clear that this was a private venture and that Air Ministry involvement was unwelcome.

On that basis, the Air Ministry was unable to do anything other than permit Vickers-Armstrong (Aviation) and Rolls-Royce to privately fund their new project. It could perhaps be argued that had the Air Staff been properly familiar with the developments in single-seat and single-engine performance wrought by the Schneider Trophy, it would have issued an appropriate requirement from the outset in 1931.

Clearly, however, the Air Staff were prepared to listen and learn. McClean's actions, though, obviously represented a lack of confidence in the Air Staff's ability to write an appropriate specification. Just one month later, however, the Air Ministry – stimulated by news of the Type 300 and PV XII combination – commissioned Supermarine to produce an 'improved F.7/30' design. From that point onwards, therefore, the venture was no longer privately funded. The reason it was ever privately funded appears to have been due to the attitude of Vickers-Armstrong (Aviation) and Rolls-Royce – not any reluctance or antipathy on behalf of the Air Ministry – which was quick off the mark to recognise the potential of the new design and provide government funding.

On 3 January 1935, the Supermarine Aviation Works sent the Air Ministry details of the new 'Experimental High-Speed Single Seat Fighter'. The document confirmed that the Supermarine submission would 'conform to all the requirements stated in Specification F.7/30'. Furthermore, a tail wheel (as opposed to the traditional skid) was to be fitted and the four machine-guns wing-mounted to fire beyond the propeller arc. This was progress indeed.

In April 1935, the Air Ministry issued its 'Requirements for Single-Engine Single-Seater Day and Night Fighter (F.10/35)'. The main points were that the new fighter:

1. Had to be at least 40 mph faster than contemporary bombers at 15,000ft.
2. 'Have a number of forward firing machine-guns that can produce the maximum hitting power possible in the shortest space of time available for one attack.' The Air Ministry 'considered that eight guns should be provided'.
3. Had to achieve 'the maximum possible and not less than 310 mph at 15,000ft at maximum power with the highest speed possible between 5,000 and 15,000ft'.
4. Have the best possible climbing performance to 20,000ft, although this was considered of secondary importance to 'speed and hitting power'.
5. Be armed with at least six, but preferably eight, machine-guns, all forward firing and wing-mounted outside the propeller arc. These were to be fired by 'electrical means'. In the event of six guns being used, 400 rounds per gun was necessary, 300 if eight were fitted.
6. Had to be 'a steady firing platform'.
7. Had to include the following 'special features' and equipment:
    a) Enclosed cockpit.
    b) Cockpit heating.
    c) Night flying equipment.
    d) Radio Telephony (R/T).
    e) Oxygen for two-and-a-half hours.

f) Easily accessed and maintained guns.
g) Retractable undercarriage and tailwheel.
h) Wheel brakes.

Such an aircraft would indeed be a 'real killer fighter'. Interestingly, however, the Air Staff did not dictate that it must be a monoplane. This indicated that monoplanes were not yet considered supreme in the corridors of Whitehall – although thanks to both R.J. Mitchell and Sydney Camm that would soon change.

The requirement for eight machine-guns – and situating these beyond the propeller arc – was significant. Existing fighters' guns were nose-mounted and fired through the propeller arc via an interrupter gear. A study in 1932 suggested that more guns were required to destroy a modern bomber, and that interrupter gear should be dispensed with to both save weight and permit the guns to fire at their own rate. Eight machine-guns were decided upon because it was believed that a fast monoplane would provide its pilot with only one high speed attack – and as much lead as possible had to be delivered in that limited time.

Dowding, however, knew that most pilots were poor shots, frequently opening fire at far too great a range. Moreover, tiny rifle calibre bullets were not always sufficient to bring down an enemy aircraft – even at close range. The answer was exploding 20mm cannon shells, but although such a cannon – the Hispano-Suiza – was available but it remained unreliable and experimental even by the forthcoming Battle of Britain. As will be explained later, this would prove significant.

Nonetheless, with rearmament now underway at last and both Hawker and Supermarine working on new fighters, prospects for Britain's air defence were more optimistic now than at any time since 1918. It was just in time. Adolf Hitler and the Nazis came to power in Germany in 1933, the clouds of war thickening rapidly thereafter. Significantly, in 1934 the RAF's annual air exercise had been, according to Orange, 'a fiasco'. Only two of the five bombers used in the mock air attack were successfully intercepted. Incredibly the air defences at that time were only capable of intercepting a total of five raiders simultaneously. The new 'real killer fighter' was needed desperately – and in numbers.

While the 1934 air exercise highlighted the great deficiencies in Britain's aerial defences, Winston Churchill was becoming increasingly concerned and vociferous regarding the threat posed by Nazi Germany. In November 1934 Churchill criticised the government's efforts in respect of air rearmament. This programme was intended purely to preserve parity with Germany. In Churchill's view this was not enough. His information suggested that within a year the Luftwaffe would be equal to the RAF, and two years later would be twice as strong. The Prime Minister, Stanley Baldwin, rejected Churchill's assertions while confirming that his government would 'not accept any position of inferiority with regard to what air force may be raised in Germany in the future'.

The threat from across the Channel, however, was clearly growing and no longer being ignored. The 1934 air exercises indicated the importance of improving both the systems and aircraft involved. Work by British designers on new monoplane fighters was now of crucial importance.

Two of Camm's designs were already in service with the RAF: the Hart light bomber and Fury fighter. The latter provided the RAF's first fighter with a speed over 200 mph – but monoplanes were needed now. Although the Fury arguably represented the ultimate biplane fighter, nothing could be done to significantly improve its performance. Camm knew this. He was also inspired by Mitchell's Schneider Trophy success, recognising that monoplanes represented the future. Inevitably, therefore, Camm responded by designing the 'Hawker Interceptor Monoplane'. This was just in time.

A one-tenth scale model of Camm's proposed fighter was built in June 1934, and began wind tunnel tests. By August the model had withstood speeds of up to 350 mph. A proposal for the new machine, armed with eight machine-guns, was then put to the Air Ministry, which consequently issued Specification F.36/34. This required a top speed of 320 mph in level flight at 15,000ft. By November, Hawker's Experimental Shop was producing the jigs required to build the new fighter's fuselage. In the past, Camm's fuselages had been of a fabric-covered tubular-metal framework.

The Interceptor Monoplane was no different in that respect, although the undercarriage was retractable and the pilot's cockpit enclosed. The weight of eight Browning machine-guns also dictated that the wings not be covered in fabric, as was traditional, but with stressed metal. This would prove significant. By now the Rolls-Royce PV XII engine had been renamed 'Merlin', in the tradition of naming the company's aero-engines after birds of prey. The Merlin was to become the most famous engine of all time and Camm designed his fighter around it. On 21 February 1935 the Air Ministry received detailed performance calculations from Hawker, resulting in a contract being issued for the production of a prototype: K5083.

On 6 November 1935, the company's chief test pilot, P.W.S. 'George' Bulman, complete with trilby and watched by an anxious Sydney Camm, made the Hawker Hurricane's first flight from Brooklands. Pulled along by a comparatively basic Watts Z33 fixed-pitch, two-bladed wooden propeller, Camm's Hurricane revealed no major deficiency. After this historic flight, the Hawker team began the hard work of rigorously testing every aspect of their creation. Bulman soon initiated minor improvements, but after his flight on 7 February 1936, declared K5083 ready for evaluation by the Aeroplane and Armament Experimental Establishment (A&AEE) at Martlesham Heath.

These brief trials largely concerned performance and handling. A maximum speed of 315 mph was recorded at 16,200ft at 2,960 rpm and six pounds boost. The silver fighter soared from the runway to 15,000ft in just 5.7 minutes. The pilots concerned were generally satisfied with K5083, other than reporting heavy aileron and rudder controls at high speed. The enclosed cockpit was popular and the retractable undercarriage commended. Having passed these initial service trials, Camm's proto-type returned to Brooklands for further development.

On 3 June 1936, the Air Ministry issued Contract 527112/36 for 600 aircraft – later that month officially approving the name 'Hurricane' – the largest production order ever placed for a military aircraft in Britain during peacetime, indicative of the Air Ministry's growing concerns with events in Germany.

In November 1937, 111 Squadron at Northolt received the first production Hurricane, L1547. By Christmas, the Squadron boasted four of the new monoplanes. One by one the Squadron's Gloster Gauntlet biplanes were replaced and under the command of Squadron Leader John Gillan, 111's pilots converted to the Hurricane. They found the Hurricane extremely fast, being nearly 100 mph faster than the Gauntlet. The monoplane increased visibility enormously without compromising manoeuvrability. In sum, the Hurricane was a revelation. Nonetheless the conversion was sadly not without incident: during the first few weeks there were several accidents, one of them fatal.

On 14 January 1938, by which time 111 Squadron had been equipped with the Hurricane for four weeks, Gillan reported comprehensively on the new fighter's 'operational characteristics':

Flying Characteristics
 (i) The Hurricane is completely manoeuvrable throughout its whole range, though slow at speeds between 65 mph and 200 mph controls feel a bit slack.

   Owing to its weight and speed, some time is taken in coming out of a dive and at high speed the turning circle is large.

   On the ground the Hurricane is as manoeuvrable as is possible and has the additional advantage of feeling secure across wind or a strong wind due to its high wing loading.
 (ii) Cross-wind landings are particularly easy in the Hurricane. Simplicity in cross-wind landings is a characteristic of aircraft with a high wing loading.
 (iii)
  (a) Taxiing with the seat full up and the hood back is exceptionally good all round, far better in front and above than the fighter aircraft before in the service, and just as good in all other directions.
  (b) Taking-off. The view is considerably better than the Gauntlet and better than the Demon, both individually and in formation.
  (c) Landing. The view is considerably better than the Gauntlet and better than the Demon both individually and in formation.

(d) Flying in Formation. The view is better than the Gauntlet or Demon with the hood open or closed, though at present no experience is available of flying in formation, in bad rain or damp cloud when it is thought the hood may fog or ice up.

(e) The view is better than the Gauntlet or Demon.

(iv) Formation flying at height at speeds in excess of 200 mph is very simple. It is thought the reason being that air resistance at this speed is considerable and that the power used by the engine at this speed means the pilot can slow his aeroplane up or accelerate it very quickly indeed.

At slow speeds in the neighbourhood of 100 mph when only a small proportion of the engine power is in use and the resistance to the air of this clean aeroplane is comparatively small, some difficulty is found in decelerating the aircraft, though no difficulty is found in accelerating.

Landing in formation is similar to landing in formation in any other type of aircraft.

Taking off in formation is simple, but immediately after leaving the ground when pilots retract their undercarriages and flaps, aircraft cannot keep good formation as undercarriage and flaps retract at different speeds in each aircraft. It is recommended, therefore, that take-off should be done individually, in succession.

(v) The Hurricane is a simple aircraft to fly at night. There is no glare in the cockpit, either open or closed, from the cockpit lamps or luminous instruments.

The steady steep glide at slow speed, which is characteristic of this type, makes landing extremely simple.

The take-off run being longer than has been experienced in the past, it is recommended that the landing light should be at least 600 yards away from the beginning of the run, instead of the normal 250 yards on ordinary flare paths.

(vi) The minimum size of aerodrome from which the Hurricane can be operated in still air in England must depend on obstructions surrounding the aerodrome. With good approaches and inexperienced pilots the Hurricane could be operated from an aerodrome 800 x 800 yards and with experience could probably be reduced to 600 yards.

(vii) The Hurricane without its engine running has a very steep glide and to the pilot inexperienced on this type, judging the flattening may be difficult. Therefore it is recommended for initial training that pilots should come in with their engines running. After they have become accustomed to an aeroplane of high wing loading and steep glide, they should be able to land efficiently off the glide in the Hurricane as in any other aircraft. It follows that landing with an engine lengthens the period of holding off, making landing easier, and in the event of flattening out too high gives the pilot time to stop the aeroplane falling heavily on the ground as speed falls off.

(viii) The cockpit is large and comfortable and there is room for the largest man inside with the hood shut, and by using the adaptable seat the smallest man can see everything comfortably.

It is thought that from an operational point of view, the system of having a selector box and a lever which must be operated to move either the undercarriage or the flaps is unsatisfactory and furthermore it occupies for a period of perhaps half a minute the right hand of the pilot while he flies with his left and neglects the throttle. Should it be essential to take-off in formation or in conditions of bad visibility the difficulties of the system are obvious, and it is recommended that two simple controls, one which moves the flaps to full up and full down position, and the other which would move the undercarriage from full down to full up and vice versa could well be substituted.

All other controls are easily accessible and efficient and the instrument layout is good and not complicated.

Operational Characteristics
With more experience on this type of aeroplane further figures will be submitted, but as far as can be seen at present the indicated airspeed at 2,000ft is 270 mph, at 10,000ft indicated airspeed 260 mph and at 15,000ft indicated airspeed 240 mph.

The petrol consumption at 15,000ft and economical cruising speed of 160 mph indicated correcting to 200 mph is 25.08 gallons per hour. At + 2½ lbs boost is the maximum permissible cruising speed-petrol consumption approaches 60 gallons per hour.

At 2,000ft an indicated air speed of 200 mph petrol consumption is 30 gallons per hour at an indicated boost of +1lb.

The remaining operational characteristics have yet to be investigated, but as yet the windscreen has shown no sign of oiling up and the cockpit is weather-proof so far as can be seen at present.

It was a good start; Gillan's report revealed no major problems.

On 10 February 1938, Gillan took off from Northolt, bound for Turnhouse near Edinburgh. Having experienced high winds while outward bound, after refuelling the pilot decided to use those 80 mph winds to his advantage and return south at maximum speed. He took off shortly after 17.00 hrs, climbed to 17,000ft – the altitude most favourable to the performance of his machine.

Forty-eight minutes later he landed at Northolt – having covered 327 miles with an average ground speed of 408.75 mph. The feat was publicised, it being conveniently forgotten that a considerable downwind had significantly helped Gillan achieve his colossal speed. Nonetheless, in air force circles Gillan was forever after known as 'Downwind'.

On 3 May 1938, the Hurricane was displayed to a delighted public for the first time at the Hendon Air Pageant. *The Times* subsequently described the aircraft as 'the fastest plane in service anywhere in the world ... outstanding in its class in respect of duration as well as speed'. This was an impressive reaction, and one with which Camm and Hawkers were no doubt well pleased.

Understandably, rearmament in Britain accelerated after the Munich Crisis over Czechoslovakia in September 1938. On 5 October, Churchill told the House of Commons that 'We are in the presence of a disaster of the first magnitude. And do not suppose that this is the end. It is only the beginning of the reckoning.' Top priority was at last given to producing defensive fighters. Peter Townsend had flown Hawker Fury biplanes with 43 Squadron at Tangmere; in November 1939 he found himself converting to the new Hurricane:

> By mid-December we had our full initial equipment of sixteen aircraft. The Fury had been a delightful play-thing; the Hurricane was a thoroughly war-like machine, rock solid as a platform for its eight Browning machine-guns, highly manoeuvrable despite its large proportions and with an excellent view from the cockpit ...
>
> At first the Hurricane earned a bad reputation. The change from the light and agile Fury caught some pilots unaware. The Hurricane was far less tolerant of faulty handling, and a mistake at low altitude could be fatal.
>
> One day a sergeant pilot glided back to Tangmere with a faulty engine. We watched him as with plenty of height he turned in – too slowly – to land. The Hurricane fell out of his hands and before our eyes he dived headlong into the ground. The unfortunate pilot died as the ambulance arrived.

Nonetheless conversion from biplane to the new monoplane continued apace. Townsend wrote:

> And so we came to know ourselves and our Hurricanes better. There grew in us a trust and an affection for them and their splendid Merlin engines, thoroughbreds and stayers which changed our fearful doubts of the Munich period into the certainty that it would beat all comers.

'REAL KILLER FIGHTERS'

Peter Brothers was another experienced pre-war fighter pilot who found himself flying Hurricanes in 1938:

> We were shown over the aircraft. We then familiarised ourselves with the controls and instruments – no Pilot's Notes were available at that time! Then it was start-up and taxi over the grass to the boundary fence and take off. These Mk I Hurricanes had a fixed-pitch two-bladed propeller which gave rapid acceleration. It was the first type I had ever flown with a retractable undercart and closed canopy – both great improvements. On my first flight I performed a few aerobatics and was impressed by the aircraft's immediate and smooth response. I knew straightaway that going to war in this machine was preferable to doing so in a biplane which – as the record of the Polish Air Force in 1939 would show – would have been suicidal.

The fixed-pitch propeller, however, required improvement. This did not just concern the Hurricane but applied to every service aircraft. German aircraft designers had recognised the benefits of the variable-pitch propeller the previous year. The pilot had a control with which he could change the pitch – or angle that the blade bit into the air – while in flight. The effect was similar, in fact, to changing gear in a car and therefore provided more power for certain situations – including take-off and combat.

In August 1938 trials began on the de Havilland two-pitch propeller. This was constructed of duralumin and had three blades. Fitted with the new variable pitch airscrew a marked improvement was recorded in tests on Hurricane L1582. Fine pitch, which is to say 30.5°, was used for take-off, coarse pitch, 42.5°, in flight. Even given a weight increase of 300 lbs, L1582 reduced the time climbing to rated altitude by one minute.

This was, however, only a half-way house. Rotol Ltd had been developing a constant-speed (CS) propeller. Also three-bladed and made of duralumin, the pilot could rotate the blades through 360° and therefore fly in the optimum pitch for any given circumstance. On 24 January 1939, Hurricane L1606, fitted with the experimental CS propeller, achieved 328 mph – 13 mph faster than Bulman's maiden flight in K5083 – and took 6.2 minutes to reach 15,000ft. These improvements would soon be desperately needed on all operational RAF fighters.

Speed was all-important and the most notable difference for pilots converting to the new fighter. Douglas Grice converted from the Gloster Gauntlet biplane to Hurricanes with Peter Brothers on 32 Squadron:

> It meant flying an aircraft which at cruising speed did about 240 mph – about 100 mph faster than you were used to flying. The flaps did not worry me but what was rather worrying was the Merlin engine. It was so powerful that it took a bit of getting used to... What

a thrill to be flying so fast. There were no vices with the Hurricane at all. And it was so rugged. You could virtually fly it into the ground and it would just bounce up and land by itself.

In 1938, it became known that German fighters were armed not just with machine-guns but also with the heavier 20mm cannon. This led to the fitting of more armour plate to British fighters, protecting the pilot and fuel tank. These improvements included a thick armoured glass windscreen. Of course this increased weight decreased performance slightly, but such modifications were essential.

Although metal stressed-skin wings for the Hurricane had been mooted back in 1935, they did not become a reality until 1940. The process to address this deficiency began in April 1939. Existing Hurricanes in service were slowly fitted with new metal wings, but the factories were still producing fabric-covered wings until March 1940. Eventually, all Hurricanes enjoyed the benefits of metal wings, bringing the Hurricane in-line with both the Supermarine Spitfire and Me 109 – both of which much more later.

It has often been argued that because the Hurricane relied upon traditional construction techniques with which the Hawker workforce was familiar, it was easy to produce and henceforth why the Air Ministry initially ordered Camm's fighter in larger numbers than the Spitfire. That may be so, but the lack of a metal covered wing was a design deficiency. Moreover, the reason that it took so long to rectify was because construction of all-metal wings required the workforce to learn new construction techniques. This slowed production, in fact. Fortunately, by the time the shooting began, all operational Hurricanes enjoyed the benefits of metal skinned wings. This is an early indication, however, that the Hurricane was technically inferior to the other two principal single-engine single-seat fighters of the day.

By the outbreak of war on 3 September 1939, 400 Hurricanes had been delivered to the RAF, equipping eighteen fighter squadrons. At the time of Munich, just a year before, Fighter Command mustered a total of 759 fighters – only ninety-three of which were Hurricanes. Although the RAF received its first production Spitfire one month before Munich, the first Spitfire squadron would not be fully operational for another three months. Had Britain gone to war over Czechoslovakia in 1938, therefore, the outcome would have been disastrous.

The British Prime Minister of the day, Neville Chamberlain, is often condemned by history for his policy of appeasing Hitler during the late 1930s. But had Chamberlain not bought time for Britain to prepare for war, the country's weak aerial defences of 1938 would have been exposed. Indeed, as Calder wrote, 'the day of the bombers, Armageddon, was palpably at hand'. One year later – largely thanks to the Hawker Hurricane – the situation was rapidly changing – albeit at the eleventh hour.

After the experience of producing the Type 224, with which Mitchell was dissatisfied, Supermarine was soon hard at work producing the new Type 300 fighter to meet Air Ministry Specification F37/34. Mitchell's Type 224 failure is the principal reason that the Hurricane flew before the Spitfire and was therefore available in larger numbers by the summer of 1940. Had there been no Type 224 but a Type 300 from the outset, things would have been very different. Nonetheless the experience gained in producing the Type 224 was useful to Mitchell when he retired to his drawing board to design an infinitely better aircraft.

Hitherto, it must be remembered, that unlike Hawker's Sydney Camm, Mitchell had no previous experience creating fighter aircraft. Excepting the Schneider Trophy winning machines, his work had largely revolved around the production of biplane flying boats. Now Supermarine's Chief Designer faced the greatest challenge of his career. Time, he knew, was running out for two reasons. Firstly the threat from a revitalised and jingoistic Nazi Germany was clear. Secondly, Mitchell was dying.

In August 1933, while working on the Type 224, his doctors diagnosed rectal cancer. An operation saved him but left a permanent legacy: a colostomy. Advised that the cancer could well return – and that should it do so nothing could save him – Mitchell briefly convalesced in Bournemouth with his wife and nurse before returning to work. As Gordon Mitchell wrote, 'He could not and would not accept the life of a semi-invalid or think of retiring for the rest of what years he might have left.'

Mitchell returned to work and even began learning to fly himself. Throughout 1935, never knowing whether fate would grant him sufficient time to complete the project, he worked on the Type 300. Mitchell did not, of course, create the Spitfire single-handedly. His work was supported by one of the best and most experienced teams of aeronautical engineers in the world, including the likes of Supermarine's Chief Draughtsman, Joe Smith, and aerodynamicist, Alan Clifton.

The Air Ministry, A&AEE and the Royal Aircraft Establishment (RAE) at Farnborough were also involved. Mitchell was, though, the Chief Designer from whose genius the Spitfire was born. Supermarine's new fighter was immediately striking with an elliptical wing and, like the Hurricane, had retractable undercarriage and a sliding cockpit hood. Another similarity was that the Spitfire – so-called after Sir Robert McLean's nickname for his daughter – was also powered by the Rolls-Royce Merlin engine.

By March 1936 the new fighter was ready to fly. The prototype – K5054 – was transported by road to Eastleigh airfield near Southampton and reassembled. The historic flight was made on 5 March 1936 by the Vickers Chief Test Pilot, Captain Joseph 'Mutt' Summers. The Assistant Test Pilot, Jeffrey Quill, was present and recalled that:

> 'Mutt' did not retract the undercarriage for the first flight on, I believe, Mitchell's instructions. The take-off run was short because the aircraft was fitted with a special fine pitch propeller specifically for the first flight. 'Mutt' took the aeroplane up to about 3,000ft, checked the low speed handling and then came straight back to land.

After this successful first flight of some twenty minutes, Summers famously said 'I don't want anything touched.' This remark has passed into legend. Quill later wrote:

> Some of those present, misunderstood his meaning and thought that he had said that the aircraft was absolutely right as it then stood. As I know well that was not the case. 'Mutt' simply meant that he had found no major snag, the thing was functioning all right as a piece of machinery and he didn't want the controls or anything else altered before the next flight ... nevertheless everyone was elated by his comment.

So it was that Mitchell's Spitfire flew at last.

On 3 June 1936, the Air Ministry ordered 310 Spitfires at a cost of £4,500 each (excluding engine, guns, instruments and radios). It was expected that the first production aircraft would be delivered in October 1937, but it soon became apparent that Supermarine – a small company of 500 employees – lacked the capacity to fulfil this large order. By the time those Spitfires were ready, the individual cost had risen to £6,033. In 1937, a further order was placed for another 200 Spitfires. Jeffrey Quill remembered that the cause of problems in mass producing the Spitfire:

> lay in the years of neglect of the aircraft industry by successive governments up to 1936. At the last possible moment they initiated the rearmament programme and expected an industry starved of orders since 1919 suddenly to increase production capacity by four or five times, and change over to building far more complex types of aircraft, all within a space of just two or three years.
>
> Of course there were going to be enormous problems and with the best will in the world mistakes were going to be made. It was all very well for the Air Ministry to say to Supermarine 'What you can't do yourselves you must sub-contract.' But where were the sub-contractors to be found with the necessary experience, on the fringes of an industry which hitherto had hardly sufficient orders to keep itself alive.

These observations put into perspective the old accusations that the Spitfire, being technically advanced, required the workforce to learn new production techniques and hence the delay in delivery to the RAF. More accurately, the problem lay in a simple lack of resources. Nonetheless, as Richard Overy commented, 'a Spitfire did take two and a half times the man hours that it took to produce a Hurricane fighter'. The first Spitfire, K9788, was eventually delivered to the RAF on 19 July 1938.

On 4 August 1938, Jeffrey Quill delivered the first operational Spitfire, K9789, to 19 Squadron at Duxford – nearly a year later than was originally anticipated. By then the Spitfire had been extensively tested with various improvements made. In September 1936, for example, service test pilots at the A&AEE put K5054 through its paces, reporting in detail on every aspect of the new fighter. It was recorded that 'Loops, half rolls off loops, slow rolls and stall turns have been done. The aeroplane is very easy and pleasant to handle in all aerobatics.' In sum the report concluded that:

> The aeroplane is simple and easy to fly and has no vices. All controls are entirely satisfactory for this type and no modification to them is required, except that the elevator control might be improved by reducing the gear ratio between the control column and elevator. The controls are well harmonised and appear to give an excellent compromise between manoeuvrability and steadiness for shooting. Take-off and landing are straightforward and easy.
>
> The aeroplane has a rather flat glide, even when the undercarriage and flaps are down and has a considerable float if the approach is made a little too fast. This defect could be remedied by fitting higher drag flaps.
>
> In general the handling of this aeroplane is such that it could be flown without risk by the average fully trained fighter pilot, but there can be no doubt that it would be improved by having flaps giving a higher drag.

Tragically, Mitchell did not live to see the Spitfire taken on charge by the RAF: the cancer returned and he died on 11 June 1937, aged 42. Joe Smith succeeded Mitchell as Supermarine's Chief Designer and was subsequently responsible for the Spitfire's development for many years to come. *The Aeroplane* of 12 April 1940 rather summed things up:

> True, it all seems simple enough, now that it is done, but it needed the genius of Mitchell to visualise without precise knowledge what had to be done, to reach out into the unknown for something nearer perfection than any other man had been able to reach.

The Spitfire was thus described in *The Aeroplane*:

> From the mediocrity of the F7/30 came the brilliance of the Spitfire, a much smaller aeroplane with greater power ... Structurally, the Spitfire is a straightforward stressed-skin design. The elliptical cantilever low wing, which tapers in thickness, is built up on a single spar with tubular flanges and a plate web. Forward of the spar the wing is covered with a heavy-gauge light aluminium sheet which forms the torsion box with the spar. Aft of the spar the covering is

of thinner gauge sheet with light-alloy girder ribs. The wing tips are detachable for ease of maintenance and repair. Split flaps are between the ailerons and the fuselage.

The fuselage is an all-metal monocoque, built on four longerons with transverse frames and a flush-riveted light-alloy skin. The front frame forms the fireproof bulkhead and is built as an integral part with the centre portion of the main wing spar. To help in maintenance the tail portion of the fuselage with fin and tailplane is detachable.

The tail unit is of the cantilever monoplane type. The fin is integral with the rear fuselage. The tailplane is of metal with smooth metal covering. The elevator and rudders have light alloy frames and fabric covering. There are trimming tabs on elevator and rudder.

The undercarriage is fully retractable outwards into the undersurface of the wings. There are two Vickers cantilever oleo-pneumatic shock absorber legs which are retracted hydraulically. An emergency hand system is fitted to lower the wheels should the hydraulic system be damaged.

The rather uneven spacing of the guns is explained by the fact that the Spitfire was originally designed for only four guns, and not until it was in an advanced stage were eight guns decided upon. If it had not been for this then the installation would have been neater.

Probably the Spitfire could never have come to life had it not been for the relative failure of the F.7/30. For the Spitfire's thin wing we thank the F.7/30's thick wing. For the Spitfire's smoothness, the F.7/30's corrugations and roughness. For the Spitfire's sweet lines the F.7/30's angularities. For the Spitfire's simple basic structure, the F.7/30's complex structure of tubes and stressed skin.

The Spitfire was undoubtedly stunning in appearance, like a flying bullet. Its elliptical wings provided a unique signature, and the Spitfire soon excited the general public as its inspirational shape and sound was seen and heard in British skies.

According to Gordon Mitchell, however, his father 'was heard to say on a number of occasions that "A Spitfire without a pilot was a lump of metal", which was meant to show the high regard and respect he had for the pilots whose job it was to fly his "lump of metal".' The first service pilots to fly Mitchell's 'lump of metal' were those of 19 Squadron, commanded by Squadron Leader Henry Cozens and based at Duxford. Among them was Flight Sergeant George Unwin:

> Before the Spitfire arrived we flew Gloster Gauntlet biplanes, which were good so far as biplanes went. But of course the Spitfire was in a completely different league. We were naturally very proud to have been chosen to be the RAF's first Spitfire squadron and it was our job to learn to fly it operationally and iron out any teething troubles along

the way. There were a few accidents. Flight Lieutenant Clouston and Pilot Officer Ball collided, but neither was hurt. Clouston forced-landed on Newmarket racecourse, causing quite a stir!

On 9 March 1939 I had to make a forced-landing at Sudbury in Essex due to a broken coolant pipe, which caused the engine to partially seize up. I decided to land on a large playing field and was doing fine with undercarriage down until the schoolchildren who were playing on the various pitches saw me descending – I was apparently on fire and trailing smoke. They ran towards me and on to the path I had selected for a landing.

I was then at less than 100ft and decided to stuff the Spitfire into the thick hawthorn hedge in front of me. The impact broke my straps and I gashed my right eyebrow on the windscreen but was otherwise unhurt. For this I received an Air Officer Commanding's Commendation.

It was the first of many an exciting adventure flying Spitfires – the speed and power after our old Gauntlets was quite something to behold, and the aircraft's aerobatic ability was excellent. This was the fighter that we wanted to go to war in.

Although late in the day, the superiority of the monoplane had at last been recognised. The RAF now had not one but two fast modern interceptors – which, in spite of production difficulties, were quickly replacing obsolete biplanes on the front line. This salvation was due to various factors, not least the technical advances achieved by Mitchell in the Schneider Trophy contest, which both he and Hawker's Sydney Camm subsequently applied to the design of fighters. The Camm's Hurricane was good and available in greater numbers than the Spitfire – but Mitchell's fighter was better, having the ability to fight at high-altitude – which would soon prove crucial. Not all pilots, surprisingly, were overly impressed with the Spitfire; Pilot Officer Michael Wainwright, 64 Squadron:

> On 30 March 1940, I flew a Spitfire Mk I for the first time at Church Fenton, after twenty minutes dual in a Miles Master. To be honest I didn't think that much of the Spitfire on that first occasion: you have to control the throttle with your left hand, but on those early Spitfires the undercarriage had to be pumped up by hand – which made things difficult. They also had a primitive ring and bead gunsight. Also, the machine-guns were harmonised to converge at 400 yards – which is too far, it needed to be 200 – 250 yards, but because we had no combat experience on these new monoplanes no one knew that then.
>
> Anyway, I had no intention of being a hero fighter pilot, I can tell you, I was just there to do my bit. Over the next few weeks we continued to practise on Spitfires while still flying Blenheims

operationally, while the latter was replaced by the Spits. It didn't really bother me what I flew. Geoffrey Wellum and countless other fighter pilots fell in love with the Spitfire, but for me it was just another aircraft.

We did a bit of night-flying too. I didn't think the Spitfire was that bad an aircraft to fly at night, although others did. Because of the long nose you couldn't see anything forward when landing in the daytime anyway! Although I didn't fight in one, I did fly the Hurricane and actually preferred it to the Spitfire, because visibility was better and it had a variable flap control, whereas the Spitfire was simply either 'up' or 'down'.

I actually developed my own technique of landing a Spitfire: with the undercarriage down and flaps up, she didn't stall until sixty knots, so I'd make a gentle approach and at that speed apply the flaps – the Spitfire would then just flop down. The best thing was that you didn't then have such a long run across the ground before stopping. The Spitfire was certainly a nice aeroplane, although I felt no emotional attachment to it, as others did, and, of course, it flew higher than the Hurricane.

The third single-engine fighter in service with Fighter Command was the Boulton-Paul Defiant, powered by the same Rolls-Royce Merlin engine propelling the lighter Spitfire and Hurricane into battle – but having an air gunner occupying an in-line turret behind the pilot. The turret weighed-in at an extra 361lbs, the four machine-guns adding a further 88lbs, ammunition 106lbs, plus 35lbs for the gunner's oxygen system and then, the gunner himself. This extra weight gave the Defiant a top speed of 259 mph at 15,000ft, which was too slow for a modern fighter, and a maximum service ceiling of 30,350ft. The biggest drawback, however, would prove to be the lack of fixed, wing-mounted, armament. The idea was that the Defiant pilot, without having to personally worry about firing, could concentrate on positioning his fighter below and slightly in front of any target, providing his gunner an unmissable shot. Moreover, operating in concert, a formation of Defiants could bring multiple guns to bear.

In 1935, the Air Ministry's specification F.9/35 invited aircraft designers' tenders for a two-seater day and night-fighter turreted fighter, with a top speed of at least 290 mph. The powered turret was to provide a 360° field of fire – but only in the upper hemisphere, the gunner unable to shoot forwards, straight and level, owing to the propeller arc. This meant that when firing forward, the angle was always elevated at 19°. Cutting a long story short, on 28 April 1937, the Air Ministry ordered eighty-seven Defiants straight off Boulton-Paul's drawing board, the proto-type not actually making its maiden flight until 11 August 1937.

When the Bristol Blenheim, a twin-engine monoplane, first flew in 1936, it was faster than the biplanes equipping the RAF's frontline squadrons, and hailed as a major success. With a maximum cruising speed of 278 mph at 15,000ft, it was substantially slower than the German single-engine Me 109E (348 mph at 14,560ft), and the twin-engine Me 110 reached 336 mph at 19,685ft. By the time war broke out, therefore, the Blenheim was already obsolete. Nonetheless, what the Mk IF, the fighter variant, did have was four .303 Browning machine-guns firing forward, situated in a belly-mounted battery fired by the pilot, another forward-firing machine-gun in the wing, and a single Vickers 'K' gun in a hydraulically-operated dorsal turret.

Like the Defiant, the Blenheim Mk IF proved unsuitable for day-fighting but the type, again like the Defiant, would provide an essential resource in the nocturnal battle, until the arrival of dedicated night-fighting aircraft such as the robust Bristol Beaufighter. During the Battle of Britain, the Blenheim Mk IF equipped six of Fighter Command's squadrons in addition to being used, among other types, by the Fighter Interception Unit (FIU), and three Coastal Command squadrons which also contributed to the daylight defence of Britain in 1940.

Up in the Orkneys at Hatston, near Kirkwall, 804 Squadron of the Fleet Air Arm (FAA) provided aerial defence for the famous RN anchorage at Scapa Flow with obsolete Gloster Sea Gladiator biplanes and a small number of American Grumman Martlet monoplane fighters; 247 Squadron of Fighter Command also operated the Gladiator, in Devon, and 808 Squadron FAA flew the Fairey Fulmar, another obsolete, single-engine monoplane. Fighter Command's 263 Squadron exchanged its Hurricanes for the new twin-engine Westland Whirlwind, armed with four 20mm cannons. None of these units, perhaps fortunately, were engaged in the actual daylight combats of summer 1940.

These were the aircraft available with which to defend Britain in 1940 – but the matter of air parity with Germany had been a vexing matter of great concern for some time. As we have seen, RAF expansion began in earnest with Scheme 'F' in 1936, but the appetite and enthusiasm for rearmament remained lukewarm. Economics also influenced thinking and policy at the time. Britain, an island nation with an Empire, enjoyed flourishing trade, so the wisdom of diverting resources from that positive, lucrative and peaceful endeavour for warlike purposes were hotly debated.

The benefit of hindsight, of course, is a wonderful thing, but in 1936 it remained uncertain as to whether war would actually happen. The policy that rearmament must not interfere with trade, however, was rapidly abandoned by the government in 1938, after Hitler's troops marched into Austria and reunited the two nations, which had been prohibited by Versailles. The development of Expansion Scheme 'L' was no longer based upon aerial parity with Germany, but to exceed it and be ready for a fight.

The output of the British aircraft industry, working double-shifts, was estimated at 4,000 machines by April 1939, and 8,000 more over the next year – this from an industry starved of orders after the First World War and therefore running on a much-reduced basis in terms of both manpower and facilities. Nonetheless,

Scheme 'L' predicted the provision of seventy-three bomber and thirty-eight fighter squadrons by spring 1940.

The continued disparity between bomber and fighter strength further evidences that the bomber still held sway in strategic thinking. Moreover, even this output would provide, in two years, only about 75 per cent of the fighter squadrons considered necessary to defend Britain.

Scheme 'M', however, was introduced in November 1938, in the wake of the Munich Crisis, providing for fifty fighter squadrons, with a frontline strength of 800 fighters, predominantly the new Hurricanes and Spitfires, as opposed to the thirty-eight and 608 respectively of Scheme 'L'. It was impossible, however, for those two advanced single-engine fighter types to equip all squadrons, because that would have consumed the entire output of those aircraft, leaving no margin for reserves. This is why some Fighter Command squadrons during the battle ahead were equipped with Blenheims and Defiants, and it must be said that before the war there were high hopes for both types. It is significant, though, that on 26 September 1938, Germany was already ahead, with 883 fighters. Clearly, air parity with Germany had been lost, and hence why, after Munich, Chamberlain's government invested millions in expanding the RAF – and Munich is something we must explore further.

One of the major flaws with Versailles was that the map of Europe was redrawn, meaning that new states inevitably contained ethnic minorities. The population of the new Czechoslovakia, for example, was 24 per cent German, the majority of which lived in a border region known as the Sudetenland. Hitler insisted that this area be returned to Germany. The Czechs refused.

There then followed a series of meetings with escalating stakes between Chamberlain and Hitler, between 15 and 22 September. No agreement was reached. On 26 September, all of 19 Squadron's pilots were recalled from leave and the Squadron remained 'available at two hours' notice' throughout what remained of the crisis. Things came to a head three days later with the Munich Conference, involving Britain, France, Germany and Italy.

The Czechs were not invited to the discussion concerning their country's fate. The Sudetenland was ceded to Germany in return for Hitler's signature on the so-called 'Munich Agreement' guaranteeing the remainder of Czechoslovakia's independence. Chamberlain flew home to Heston, brandishing this piece of paper bearing the Führer's signature, which he considered a guarantee for 'peace in our time'. In the short-term, although the Czechs would not agree, Munich was a victory for appeasement. Churchill and other politicians were angered, however, at this further capitulation to dictatorship, viewing this as a step towards, not back, from war. The Under-Secretary of State for Air, Harold Balfour, had a different view, though, considering the RAF's unpreparedness for war in September 1938:

> In September 1938, the *Luftwaffe* could have shot the RAF out of the skies ... This, from a purely air defence of Britain view, is why

I am a man of Munich ... If you accept, as any student of modern warfare must, that mastery in the air is essential to any victory, then the year Munich gave us saved us from probable defeat ... So far as the air is concerned there can be no doubt that the 'breathing space' saved Britain.

In the House of Commons in September 1938, Churchill said, 'England has been offered a choice between war and shame. She has chosen shame and will get war.' True: we got war, but also final victory whereas war in 1938 could have meant not victory but defeat. What, I ask, is the merit of being the bravest hero of a defeated country?

Together with other Ministers I met Chamberlain at Heston Airport on his return from Germany. I saw him wave that piece of paper and read the declaration that he and Hitler had that day signed, resolving to settle peacefully all future differences between our two countries. Why he said what he did I shall never know. Did he believe it? Was it emotional fatigue and reaction in a man of advancing years who had flown half across Europe in air travel conditions very different to those of today? Did he believe the words 'peace with honour'? Did he regret and distrust almost at once? All this will never be answered with certainty.

What I do know is that none of this can be reconciled with the urgent drive over the next twelve months to prepare the RAF for war and to build up quick expansion of our aircraft industry. Never from No 10 did any order come to slow up anything. On the contrary, we were encouraged and supported to double our efforts. We did our best in the year left to us and for the air, I repeat, 'Thank God for Munich'.

Beyond doubt, the events of 1937–39 haunted Mr Chamberlain to his grave and bighted his reputation. While Churchill undoubtedly mobilised the English language and pitched it righteously into battle, it is impossible to argue against Balfour's appreciation of Munich so far as air was concerned – and it was air, as the Minister rightly said, that mattered. For sure, between the wars Churchill had made many speeches in the House of Commons warning of the aerial disparity between Britain and Germany – and the far-reaching consequences unless this was urgently addressed. But what could Chamberlain to do? Go to war against the lethal new Me 109 with obsolete biplanes?

Although it could be argued that Chamberlain failed to grasp Hitler's mendacity and true intentions, Appeasement bought time for Britain to rearm, and paradoxically rearmament ran concurrently with Chamberlain's naïve efforts to negotiate with dictators. In recent times, Chamberlain's reputation has not been assisted by myth-pedalling popular films such as *Darkest Hour* (2017), but the evidence confirms that the essential time he bought through Appeasement, flawed a policy though it was, actually marks him as one of the unsung architects of victory in the forthcoming Battle of Britain.

In 1943, Squadron Leader Edward George Alford GM, a public relations officer serving at the 11 Group Uxbridge depot, was invited by the Air Ministry to recount his early war experiences for use in training manuals; of this period he wrote that:

> As an introduction the writer would like to express his appreciation of the sound basic training received on entry into the Royal Air Force as an Aircraft Apprentice at the RAF Station Cranwell, from 1920–1923. The subjects covered by the instructors both at school and in the technical workshops, basic and specialist trades, laid the foundation on which service experience built a sound knowledge of service armaments and explosives. The physical and disciplinary training received during that period, although not appreciated at the time, has since been extremely useful and beneficial.
>
> In 1938, I returned from abroad to spend three months leave in an England enjoying a prosperous peace, despite the warning murmur that rumbled over Europe.
>
> On return from leave I joined the RAF Station at Hawkinge, Kent, and immediately found myself engaged in installing Browning guns in the Gloster Gladiators of a leading fighter squadron, and at the time of the Munich Crisis became conversant with anti-gas respirators, both service and civilian.

Gloster Gladiator biplanes, however, would have been no match for Me 109s had Britain gone to war in September 1938.

The effect of Munich did create a sense of urgency however, and the output of Spitfires and Hurricanes rose substantially towards the end of 1938 and New Year 1939; indeed, production exceeded predictions by a quarter, to the great credit of the factories concerned. It had also been decided that fifty-three fighter squadrons were needed to guarantee Britain's security, and the race was on to provide them – especially when Hitler's seizure of Bohemia and Moravia in March 1939 indicated that the Führer had no intention of abiding by the promises for peace made at Munich. Britain and France committed themselves to fight in the event Hitler attacked Poland.

The British feverishly began ensuring that its army of volunteer Territorials was at strength and doubled in size to twenty-four divisions – and introduced conscription. The surprise signing of the Russo-German Non-Aggression Pact on 23 August 1939, prompted a stern reminder to Hitler that Britain and France would stand by Poland. Any hopes of peace were now clearly forlorn.

How, though, was Britain to be defended in the air?

Chapter 3

Dowding, Park, Fighter Command and 'The System'

Hugh Caswell Tremenheere Dowding was born at Moffat, some fifty miles South of Edinburgh, of English school-teacher parents, on 24 April 1882. Hugh's father, Arthur, had founded St Ninian's, a preparatory school in Moffat, in 1879, marrying Maud Tremenheere a year later. Hugh was the eldest of their four children, a daughter and three sons, all brought up in a dutiful middle-class family with Christian, Victorian, values. Educated at St Ninian's and Winchester, in 1899, the eldest Dowding entered the Royal Military Academy at Woolwich, receiving a commission as a Second Lieutenant in the Garrison Artillery.

In 1912, by which time Lieutenant Dowding had served in Ceylon, Hong Kong and India, he attended the Military Staff College at Camberley. In an exercise there, Dowding found himself commanding six imaginary aeroplanes which he despatched together, on a flight of fancy from Camberley, to establish whether the Lincolnshire town of Grantham was in enemy hands. The instructor queried this decision, inquiring as to how the pilots would find their way. Dowding's response was simple: they would follow the railway lines, which to him appeared to be common-sense.

This the instructor also disputed, arguing that the pilots would collide. Dowding knew little or nothing about aviation at this time but could not accept this. Consequently, to expand his experience, having recognised that aviation would play a significant part in future conflicts, Dowding learned to fly, privately, at Brooklands. This was typical of the man.

Dowding once recalled that as a child he had 'never accepted ideas because they were orthodox, and consequently I have frequently found myself in opposition to generally accepted views... perhaps in retrospect this has not been altogether a bad thing'. In his thirties he had acquired the nickname 'Stuffy', on account of his Victorian primness. Described by contemporary Air Chief Marshal Sir Philip Joubert de la Ferté as 'an extremely entertaining companion out of office hours', this sense of fun 'did not, as a rule, extend to his work, and he could be extremely exacting and tiresome to his subordinates. He had, however, a great sense of justice which earned him the respect of all who worked with him.'

Dowding's opposition to conventional opinion, however, underpins many of his clashes with authority. He was an individual, unorthodox, a free-thinker, and would advance his own opinions unflinchingly. Indeed, Dowding's biographer, the superb historian Vincent Orange, writes of Dowding's difficulty in accepting the need to persuade others that he was right about something, and compromise was not in his dictionary. To a degree, later in his career, this was understandable; as the RAF's most senior serving officer, he objected to criticism or resistance to his ideas and decisions from Air Ministry staff – all very much junior to him in age, rank and length of service.

Having gained his private pilot's licence, Dowding was able to take a three-month course provided by the RFC at the Central Flying School (CFS), at Upavon in Wiltshire. Passing the course on 29 April 1914, Dowding received his coveted service pilot's flying brevet, or 'wings', then returned to soldiering. At the CFS, however, his instructor was one John Salmond, who would serve as Chief of the Air Staff (CAS) 1930–33; at Upavon, Dowding also met the CFS Adjutant, Trenchard – soon to become 'Father of the Royal Air Force'. In future, both these highly influential and well-connected men would become, according to Orange, 'bitter, secret and devious critics of Dowding's'.

When the First World War broke out, as a trained pilot Major Hugh Dowding was required to serve in France with the RFC, and appointed to command 16 Squadron at Merville, engaged in artillery observation work. Major-General Trenchard was by then General Officer Commanding (GOC) the RFC, to whom Dowding complained that his squadron had received a batch of wrong-sized propellers. Trenchard objected to Dowding's 'pernickety primness' and ordered him to fit the aircrews as delivered. Dowding did as he was ordered, making the first, disastrous, test flight himself – and was nearly killed in the process. To Trenchard, the incident emphasised Dowding's 'self-righteous stubbornness'. Dowding considered it an outcome of 'Trenchard's technical stupidity'. Worse followed.

On 18 June 1916, Lieutenant-Colonel Dowding was given command of No 9 (HQ) Wing, comprising four squadrons, at Fienvillers, near Doullens, ready for the infamous Battle of the Somme, which began on 1 July. From August 1915 until early 1916, the RFC suffered heavy losses due to the 'Fokker scourge', caused by the superiority of the German Fokker Eindecker monoplane fighter. Trenchard, however, insisted that the offensive be maintained – and, incredibly, forbade his aircrews to wear parachutes in the bizarre belief that the life-saving silk canopies were 'bad for morale'.

The heavy casualties deeply troubled Dowding, who, after further differences with the GOC, was sent home on New Year's Day 1917. It would only later become significant that Dowding's replacement in France was Temporary Lieutenant-Colonel Cyril Newall. By the Armistice, both Dowding and Newall were Temporary Brigadier Generals – but the latter was Trenchard's deputy and therefore in a position of great influence.

The RAF was born on 1 April 1918, with Major-General Trenchard the first CAS – which may explain why Dowding was not given a Permanent Commission, as a group captain, in Trenchard's junior service until 1 August 1919. Nevertheless, after various appointments, on 1 September 1930, Dowding was appointed Air

Member for Supply and Research. Arguably, it was from that point onwards that 'Stuffy' Dowding began preparing for the Battle of Britain.

The RAF air exercises in August 1934, had shown the weakness of the existing 'early warning system', which depended largely upon the Observer Corps' reports, meaning that enemy aircraft could only be detected if they ventured within sight and earshot. Even when practicing with the ancient Vickers Virginia, which plodded through the sky at just 80 mph at 7,000ft, the warning provided was inadequate. Acoustic locators had proved of little use, and the Chandler-Adcock system of radio-direction, which allowed aircraft to be plotted and controlled from the ground, relied upon the 'target' aircraft sending regular transmissions – hostile aircraft, however, were unlikely to be so obliging.

A more general means of detection was therefore required, but had yet to be discovered, and this became of increasing concern: Mr A.P. Rowe, the Air Ministry's Assistant Director of Scientific Research, reported to his chief, Harry Wimperis, that 'unless science finds a new method of assisting air defence, any war within ten years will be lost'.

In 1932, work by the Post Office indicated that aircraft reflected radio signals, this prompted further research by Robert Watson-Watt who, in 1935, submitted his report on the subject. This inspired memorandum identified three areas of research: the re-radiation of aircraft waves (to detect aircraft), radio-telephone communications between fighters and ground controller, and a means of transmitting coded signals from aircraft (so as to identify friend from foe). Immediately recognising the significance of this detailed study, Wimperis requested £10,000 for further experimental work.

Dowding advised caution and requested a practical demonstration. 'Let us first see if the system works,' he said. A month later Dowding was sufficiently impressed by the scientists and the research went ahead, in great secrecy, on the Suffolk coast. This new technology, together with the new eight-gun monoplane fighters, would soon form the cornerstone of the Radar-Based System of Early Warning, Interception & Control. This was one crucial respect in which Britain was far ahead of Germany's scientists. Radar, in fact, concluded any chance whatsoever that the 'bomber will always get through'. A new chapter in aerial warfare had quietly begun, in which Dowding was playing a key part and was best-placed to learn about and understand the various technical and scientific developments involved. This knowledge would prove invaluable.

For more than a decade, all functions of air defence had been overseen by the Air Defence of Great Britain, although the Commander-in-Chief of which was responsible for both fighter and bomber forces, a matter which Dowding felt 'ponderous'. With Germany clearly rearming, the British Expansion Programme of 1936, saw the creation of five separate commands: Fighter, Bomber, Coastal, Training and Maintenance.

Dowding's personal first-hand experience as a fighter pilot during the First World War, together with his involvement in commissioning the Spitfire and

Hurricane, and knowledge of radar, marked him as the perfect choice for RAF Fighter Command's first Air Officer Commander-in-Chief (AOC-in-C). Now he could really get to grips with his vision to ensure 'security of base'. Air Marshal Dowding was 54 when he took up his new appointment on 14 July 1936.

The new Fighter Command's headquarters was located at Bentley Priory, a large country house situated to the north of London, at Stanmore. There, the new AOC-in-C discovered some 'lamentable deficiencies to be made good', his immediate task being to create the 'ideal Air Defence System', and his experience to date uniquely equipped him to do so. Dowding's belief that ensuring security of the home base 'overrides all considerations' now rose to the fore, his unshakeable belief in this leading to an obstinate insistence that his demands for improvements and resources be met.

Consequently, from hereon in Dowding would find himself in almost constant dispute with the Air Staff, where, he later wrote, his name 'stank'. When he became AOC-in-C of Fighter Command, Dowding's aspirations were to ultimately succeed Marshal of the RAF (MRAF) Sir Edward Ellington as CAS, unaware that Air Vice-Marshal Newall was already being groomed to take over the top job. Newall, who had taken Dowding's place in France twenty years before and was junior to him in rank and service, was the preferred choice of Lord Swinton, the Secretary of State for Air, and became CAS in 1937. Dowding was cut to the quick – but had he left Fighter Command at that juncture, arguably the outcome for Britain, just three years later, would have been disastrous.

Upon formation in 1936, Fighter Command comprised two groups, 11 and 12, and for administrative purposes, both 22 Army Co-Operation Group and the civilian Observer Corps. Formed in June 1936, the primary function of 11 Group, was the defence of London and the south-east, while 12 Group, created in May 1937, protected eastern England. It is vitally important to understand that at this time any air attacks made by Germany were expected to approach from the East, across the North Sea, and due to the range involved, such raids were assumed not to involve a fighter escort.

At that time, therefore, 12 Group, defending the industrial Midlands and the north, represented a crucial responsibility. Nonetheless, 11 Group, as it included the capital, was always seen as the primary area. On New Year's Day 1937, Dowding was promoted to Air Chief Marshal, and entrusted the prestigious 11 Group to Air Marshal Leslie Gossage. On 14 December 1937, Air Commodore Trafford Leigh-Mallory became AOC 12 Group – which would have far-reaching consequences for Dowding and, ultimately, Fighter Command, as we will later explore.

Trafford Leigh-Mallory was born on 11 July 1892 at Mobberley, Cheshire; his father, Herbert, was rector of the Anglican church there. The younger brother of George Leigh-Mallory, the celebrated mountaineer Trafford Leigh-Mallory, was educated at Haileybury, winning an Exhibition Scholarship to Cambridge's prestigious Magdalene College in 1926. It was while a member of the Literary Club there, in fact, that he first became acquainted with one Arthur Tedder – later

MRAF, Deputy Supreme Allied Commander for Operation OVERLORD, and CAS 1946–50. Having achieved a degree in law, Leigh-Mallory applied to the Inner Temple to become a barrister, but was thwarted in his ambition when the First World War broke out in 1914. Commissioned into the King's Liverpool Regiment, Lieutenant Leigh-Mallory served in France, suffering a leg wound in June 1915. While recuperating, Leigh-Mallory volunteered for the RFC and was soon flying BE2d observation aircraft with 5 Squadron at Droglandt.

At this time, the RFC's role was largely to act as scouts for the army, providing information regarding German troop movements and spotting for the artillery. On 10 May 1917, Temporary Major Leigh-Mallory became OC (Officer Commanding) of 15 Squadron, and six months later took over 8 Squadron, continuing to fly army co-operation sorties. Leigh-Mallory was an unpopular squadron commander, being aloof and snobbish, and more concerned with logistics than men's lives.

With 8 Squadron, Leigh-Mallory increased his experience of army co-operation, his unit carrying out the first air-to-tank liaison. For his wartime service, Leigh-Mallory was appointed to the DSO, his leadership of 8 Squadron and extensive experience of army co-operation laying the foundation of his subsequent RAF career.

Unlike Hugh Dowding, Leigh-Mallory's name appeared in the first 200 Permanent Commissions for the peacetime RAF, published on 1 August 1919. After training and staff appointments, in 1933 Group Captain Leigh-Mallory began a year-long course at the Imperial Defence College – the most senior of all service staff colleges. In 1937, Air Commodore Leigh-Mallory became AOC 12 (Fighter) Group, setting up home with his wife, Doris, at Woodborough Hall, Hucknall, Nottinghamshire. So it was that an army co-operation expert, with significant experience of training and administration – but not one of fighters – became entrusted with the aerial defence of the industrial Midlands and the North.

It was impractical, however, for Britain to be covered by two such large and unwieldy groups, and so 13 Group was created with responsibility for the north of England and Northern Ireland. In due course, No 10 Group would be formed to defend the West Country and South Wales (although 10 Group did not become operational until 8 July 1940, just two days before the Battle of Britain officially began). Each group was sub-divided into sectors, the main fighter station in each being known as the 'Sector Station'.

Radar had made great progress, and RDF stations were constructed around southern England: by the summer of 1940, there would be twenty-two 'Chain Home' stations supplemented by thirty 'Chain Home Low' stations. Each was positioned, in theory at least, to ensure that every aircraft approaching Britain from the east or south would be detected by a minimum of two stations.

The Germans, of course, knew about the RDF stations, with their 350ft lattice masts, but believed that the operators of this equipment, in times of stress, would be unable to distinguish between large and small formations, and that the whole system would break down if large numbers of aircraft approached simultaneously. In due course the enemy would find itself much mistaken, and likewise that the greatest value of RDF was to direct fighters against specific attacks as they developed, rather than dissipate effort in flying constant standing patrols awaiting the enemy.

RDF now became the keystone of Dowding's System of Air Defence, into which he also absorbed Observer Corps posts and centres, sector operations rooms, radio-telephony transmitters, landlines and ancillary devices.

The 'System' was, in fact, as perfect as technology and resources permitted. At Stanmore's underground filter room, RDF information was sifted by filterers and filter officers, displayed on a gridded map and passed by tellers through closed speech circuits to both the adjacent Command Operations Room and to the appropriate groups and sectors. It took just four minutes between an RDF operator identifying a plot, to this information appearing in the operations rooms. The Sector Controller would then guide his fighters by radio telephone to intercept the enemy. Dowding believed that tactical control, especially during periods of hectic action, should not be exercised by either Fighter Command or group, but by the sector controllers themselves.

After incoming aircraft had crossed the coast, the Observer Corps was responsible for tracking their progress. Observer posts reported to observer centres, which were connected by landline to the Command Operations Room. From the latter, instructions were issued to local authorities as to when sirens should be sounded, warning the local populace of impending attack. The Gun Operations Room tied anti-aircraft guns into the System, making a cohesive whole.

The Observer Corps, in fact, was crucial, because RDF looked outwards towards France, so once an enemy formation crossed the English coast, it could not be traced by radar – which is where the Observer Corps came in, providing reports tracking a raid's progress through physical sightings. This, however, was difficult when the enemy flew at heights above 15,000ft, or when there was cloud cover. Nonetheless, owing to the limitations of the technology at the time, it was the only practical option available – and, in due course, the Observer Corps would provide sterling service.

In each group operations room there was always at least one controller on duty. He scrutinised the large gridded map of his group area. Aircraft approaching or passing over were represented by coloured plaques, manipulated by WAAFs, armed with magnetised wands and headphones linked to a teller at an observer centre or filter room. Facing the Controller was a 'Totalisator', showing the location and readiness state of squadrons available. The Group Controller's job was to decide how to meet each threat: his responsibility was clearly a heavy one.

Sector operations rooms were places where great drama would be played out before too long. Linked by landlines and loudspeakers directly to the aircraft dispersal points, where pilots and aircraft waited to fly, it was also linked to one or more radio-telephony transmitters, placed far enough away to ensure that intercepted transmissions did not reveal its whereabouts. The Sector Controller brought his squadrons to 'readiness', or sent them off to intercept in accordance with orders received from Group.

Once the squadrons were airborne, he was responsible for giving them orders and information with the express intention of placing them in a favourable position to attack the enemy. Controllers and formation leaders used a special code: 'Scramble' meant take off urgently; 'Pancake' was the order to land; 'Angels' corresponded to height measured in thousands of feet, and while 'Bandits' were definitely hostile aircraft, 'Bogeys' were as yet unidentified plots. Pilots were directed by the provision of a compass heading, or 'Vector', expressed in degrees, or by reference to landmarks given codenames. 'Buster' was the instruction for fighters to travel at top speed, and 'Liner' was to do so at cruising speed.

When the formation leader cried 'Tally Ho', the Controller knew that the formation leader had sighted the enemy and was about to attack. After that, tactical control was passed to the formation leader in the air, while those in control rooms anxiously awaited the combat's outcome.

Having enhanced the existing System of aerial defence, Dowding believed more than ever that 'security of base' was paramount, indeed that it 'overrides all considerations'.

In 1937, Dowding found a powerful political ally in Sir Thomas Inskip, the Minister for the Co-ordination of Defence, who asked him to state how many squadrons were required to defend Britain. A committee, chaired by Dowding, decided upon forty-five. It was not until a year later, though, that priority was at last given to the production of fighters. Like Dowding, Inskip believed that the RAF's priority was not the deliverance of a 'knock-out' blow, but to defend Britain from such an attack, permitting the build-up of resources necessary to counter-attack. This made the RAF, in fact, the only air service to place such confidence in the fighter force.

Those fighters Dowding coveted and ensured that his Hurricanes and Spitfires received all the latest technology: armoured glass windscreens, armour plate to protect the pilot, first the two-pitch then CS. airscrews, self-sealing fuel tanks and Identification Friend or Foe (IFF), which prevented Controllers from mistaking friendly for enemy fighters. Exactly how the new fighters would be used once war broke out, however, was still guesswork. Dowding knew exactly where he stood on the issue of an appropriate doctrine, however:

> The best defence of the country is fear of the fighter. If we were strong in fighters we should probably never be attacked in force. If we are moderately strong we shall probably be attacked and the attacks will gradually be brought to a standstill ... If we are weak in fighter strength, the attacks will not be brought to a standstill and the productive capacity of the country will be virtually destroyed.

In 1938, another key player enters our stage: Air Vice-Marshal Sholto Douglas. Born at Headington on 23 December 1893, Douglas was the son of an academic, and educated at Emanuel and Tonbridge Schools before going up to Lincoln College,

Oxford, reading 'Greats'. Commissioned into the Royal Field Artillery in 1914, the following year Douglas transferred to the RFC, becoming an observer in 2 Squadron at Merville, before training as a pilot.

Three months later, Lieutenant Douglas returned to France, flying the two-seater Bristol BE2c Fighter during the 'Fokker Scourge'. Awarded the MC, Douglas went on to command 43 Squadron, flying Sopwith 1½ Strutters, then 84 Squadron, operating single-seater SE5s on the Western Front, winning a DFC. After the First World War, however, Douglas left the service, flying as a commercial pilot, but was persuaded by none other than Trenchard himself to rejoin the RAF in 1920.

Having attended the IDC and commanded RAF North Weald, Douglas instructed at the IDC before becoming Director of Staff Duties at the Air Ministry on New Year's Day 1936. Two years later, he was promoted to air vice-marshal and became the Assistant CAS (ACAS). It was now that this Trenchard favourite clashed with Dowding.

In June 1938, Douglas informed Dowding that he must form nine squadrons of Boulton-Paul Defiants for day-fighting. The Defiant was a two-seater, its armament provided by a turret-mounted battery of four .303 Browning machine-guns, fired by an air gunner. While the turret, it was true, could rotate forward, the guns fired electronically by the pilot, they were not synchronised to fire through the propeller arc and so could only fire at an angle of 20°. The Defiant possessed no wing-mounted or other, fixed, forward-firing armament. The turret and gunner, of course, added weight, the aircraft's powerplant being the same Rolls-Royce Merlin engine powering the lighter Spitfire and Hurricane.

Whereas, for example, the Spitfire Mk IA's top speed was 367 mph, and the German Me 109E-3 348 mph, the Defiant lagged behind at 304 mph. The problem, though, was that the lack of practical pilot-fired forward-firing armament meant the Defiant lacked the instant eye-to-hand coordination required in modern-day fighting. The ACAS was clearly basing his support of the Defiant upon his own experience of flying the two-seater Bristol Fighter – the Air Ministry ordering some 450 Defiants in the mistaken belief that the BE2c's success would be emulated.

While Douglas argued that 'for work over enemy territory a two-seater fighter is best', the point missed was that the BE2c's success was in no small part due to its pilot-fired forward-facing armament. Dowding instantly appreciated this and was angry that such an important decision had been made without his consultation. Ever the politician however, Douglas was supported by both Air Vice-Marshals Sir Edgar Ludlow-Hewitt, the AOC-in-C of Bomber Command, and Donald Stevenson, the Deputy Director of Home Operations. It was originally intended, in fact, to have fifteen Defiant squadrons, this being reduced to nine when Stevenson began having doubts about the type. Dowding continued opposing the Defiant, which was commissioned at the expense of more Spitfires and Hurricanes, but his plea that the turret fighter be confined to training was rejected.

Fortunately, in the event, only two Defiant squadrons were raised – but it was tragic indeed that in 1940, Dowding would be proved right only through the virtual annihilation of these gallant squadrons, which saw the aircraft relegated to a stop-gap night-fighting role. Here, though, was another example of antipathy between Dowding and another high commander, and that Dowding, the chief of Fighter Command, was not consulted regarding the Defiant prior to it being ordered, and others making decisions concerning his command, is evidence of the Air Ministry's questionable attitude toward him long before the Battle of Britain.

In July 1938, however, help was at hand for Dowding when his new Senior Air Staff Officer (SASO) arrived at Bentley Priory: Air Commodore Keith Park. In this loyal and tough fighter ace from New Zealand, Dowding was to find the perfect right-hand man.

Keith Rodney Park was born in Thames, Auckland, on 15 June 1892. In 1914, he answered the call and joined the artillery as a lance-bombardier, seeing action on Gallipoli with the ANZAC big guns, where he was commissioned. In August 1915, Park became a regular officer in the British army, continuing to serve in the Dardenelles until Allied forces were evacuated in 1916. That year, Park fought in the Battle of the Somme, until a shell exploded beneath his horse, killing the animal and wounding the man. Invalided back to 'Blighty', Park was declared 'unfit to ride a horse' owing to his wounds – but was accepted for flying training by the RFC.

Having successfully gained his 'wings', by the time Park was posted to 48 Squadron at La Bellevue in 1917, flying the BE2c, his log book recorded 135 flying hours, this experience prepared him well for aerial combat. By now, Park was already a battle-hardened officer who understood the ground situation from a soldier's perspective and knew what was expected of him in the air. An exacting professional, Park even took personal care of his aircraft's armament and sights, in addition to taking a keen interest in the technical aspects of both airframe and engine.

Following a series of successful combats with Albatross scouts, Lieutenant Park and his observer were both awarded the MC on 19 August 1917, for 'dash and tenacity'. Over the next twenty-six days, Park and his observers destroyed seven more enemy aircraft, and damaged a further seven. Recommended for a DSO by his commanding officer, Major-General Trenchard decreed that a Bar to the MC was sufficient. Park had earned respect and learned important lessons regarding the conduct of fighter warfare.

In 1922, reflecting upon his Western Front experiences, Park maintained that in future wars, squadrons should be widely dispersed on the ground; ground strafing would be best undertaken by small, fast, agile scouts with forward-firing armament; close escorts would be ineffective when opposition was encountered, and, finally, tactics must be studied well in advance, rather than 'on the spot'. Here, then, was clearly a forward-thinker and decorated fighter ace of great skill and experience.

Upon return from France, Park received two training commands before attending a course at 2 School of Navigation and Bomb Dropping, where voluntary long-distance flights were encouraged – leading to Captains Park and Stewart flying a 1,880 mile circuit of the British Isles. Only the second time such a journey had been achieved, the flight attracted much media attention. In June 1919, Park was awarded the DFC, ostensibly for this intrepid flight – in reality, the decoration was intended to compensate him for a catalogue of bureaucratic errors preventing well-deserved promotion. The episode infuriated Park, now a married man who had decided on a long-term career in the service, and embittered him towards the Air Ministry, the incompetence of which meant that in the promotion stakes he had been left behind by certain contemporaries.

On 1 August 1919, Park was given a Permanent Commission and became a flight lieutenant, commanding a reserve of surplus aircraft at Hawkinge – where a certain Squadron Leader Sholto Douglas re-enters our story.

When preparing for the 1920 Hendon Air Pageant, Douglas suggested a daring low-level flypast by three Handley Page V/1500 bombers, a type included in Park's reserve. Douglas arranged with Park that they would each fly one, and another colleague the third. The display was expected to be the Hendon highlight, but Trenchard, the CAS, was less impressed and rebuked Douglas, as the senior officer involved, for the low-level stunt – described in *Aeroplane* as 'a terrifying sensation'.

Trenchard's disapproval also reached Park, already concerned about his lack of promotion, leading to Park and Douglas distancing themselves from each other. Indeed, this distance never reduced, and may have been significant twenty years later, as we will see. Park then served in Egypt until June 1926, when appointed by Air Marshal Sir John Salmond, Commander-in-Chief of Fighter Command's predecessor, ADGB, to command 'Operations, Intelligence Mobilisation and Combined Training', based at Uxbridge. As ADGB was then only a year old, Squadron Leader Park was involved with preparing Britain's modern aerial defences almost from the outset.

In November 1927, Park was given command of 111 Squadron, flying Armstrong Whitworth Siskin biplane fighters at Duxford. On New Year's Day 1929, he was promoted to wing commander and left 'Treble One' that March, returning to Uxbridge and undertaking a staff role at HQ Fighting Area. Not for the first time, Park drove himself so hard that he became ill; a medical board in 1930 sent him on leave for a month, insisting on a complete break from work – echoed by Fighting Area's commander: Air Vice-Marshal Hugh Dowding. The association between these two officers, therefore, began over a decade before the Battle of Britain.

The period January 1931 to August 1932 saw Wing Commander Park commanding RAF Northolt, concluding six years' experience in front line home defence. The next five years, however, were spent in appointments away from fighters, as Chief Instructor at the Oxford University Air Squadron, and then, as a 43-year old group captain in 1934, he became the British Air Attaché in South America.

Three years later, in December 1937, Group Captain Park returned to fighters, at last, when he became Station Commander at Tangmere, that famous fighter station on the South Coast, near Chichester. There he enjoyed a last fling flying

Hawker Furies, before promotion to air commodore on 1 July 1938 – and appointed Dowding's SASO at Fighter Command. Unsurprisingly, given his experience, Air Commodore Park immediately grasped the concept of the System of Air Defence – and would help improve it. Fortunately for Britain, these two men, Dowding and Park, knew as much about fighters as anyone else in the world outside of Germany at that time.

In this, the Germans had the edge, though, given that Hitler's support of the fascist General Franco during the Spanish Civil War of the mid-thirties had provided a unique opportunity to test and prove weapons and tactics. The performance of Germany's *Legion Kondor* in Spain also indicated just how dangerous the Luftwaffe was, which, coupled with Hitler's aggressive foreign policy and military expansion, emphasised the urgency of the hour for those working on Britain's aerial defences.

As SASO at Bentley Priory, Air Commodore Park was largely concerned with fighter tactics, the first clash with the Air Ministry arising over the Defiant issue. After the Munich Crisis of September 1938, Park reported upon deficiencies in Britain's preparedness to meet an aerial threat from Germany. Fighter Command, Park stated, was ten squadrons short of the minimum number required for Britain's defence, and only 25 per cent of existing units were equipped with new monoplane fighters; the Sector Control System required expansion in Scotland and south-west England, more airfields were needed, with improvements required to those in use, and there were insufficient RDF stations and manpower. The report was accurate but not well-received at Whitehall – and further evidence of the antipathy toward Dowding and Park, who continued campaigning for more resources for Fighter Command with the era of Bomber Barons. Theirs was, in many ways, an unenviable task – but one both men were devoted to.

The organisation of Fighter Command and the Dowding System was revealed to the public after the Battle of Britain, in an official pamphlet dated 1943; the most relevant sections of that publication are reproduced below:

Fighter Command
At the time of the Battle of Britain, Fighter Command was organised into four Fighter Groups. Each group was, for purposes of tactical control, subdivided geographically into a number of sectors. A sector consisted of a main fighter station and airfield, sector headquarters and operations room, also one or more satellite or forward airfields upon which were based a number of squadrons varying in accordance with the situation and the need for good dispersal.

No. 11 Group's area covered South-East England and, consequently, it was this group which bore the brunt of the fighting, although other groups extensively reinforced the air battle from time to time and, in addition, fed into No. 11 Group a regular supply of fresh squadrons to relieve those worn down by intensive air fighting.

Operations Rooms

The heart of each headquarters at command, groups, and sectors, was its operations room. This varied somewhat in size and complexity depending upon the scope and function of the headquarters and upon the amount of detail regarding our own squadrons that it was necessary for the commander to have before him; but the ultimate object of all operations rooms remained the same, namely, to ensure the utmost rapidity in the issue of orders. For time was the essence of the problem; with machines of war moving at the rate of 5 miles a minute, the issue of written orders was out of the question and the only possible course was to cut the length of orders to a minimum and to use direct telephone, whether landline or radio.

To effect this, the operations room had, first, to portray physically the movements of enemy aircraft and, where necessary, of our own fighters, over the whole country and the sea approaches thereto (or such part as was appropriate to the headquarters concerned); secondly, to show how soon and in what strength our own squadrons could leave the ground; and, thirdly, to provide an adequate and reasonably secure network of communications both by landline and radio telephony.

Air Raid Intelligence

The essential basis of any air defence system is, of course, a good air-raid intelligence system. In this country, during the Battle of Britain, as now, such a system comprised a chain of radio location stations sited around our coasts. The function of these stations was the detection of all aircraft approaching this country over the sea. This early warning was vital since the German Air Force was in occupation of airfields just the other side of the Straits of Dover, which could be crossed in four or five minutes. It was supplemented over the land by the Observer Corps, whose function was to take over and 'tell on' the tracks of all aircraft as they crossed our coasts and proceeded inland to their targets.

During the Battle of Britain, information received by radio location was transmitted to Fighter Command headquarters and after passing through a 'filter room' was telephoned direct to one of the plotters in the Command operations room and simultaneously to those at the group and sectors affected. Information received from the Observer Corps followed the reverse course, being passed through observer centres to fighter groups and sectors and repeated by the group tellers to Fighter Command and adjacent groups.

Display of Information

In all Fighter Command operation rooms was a large table map upon which this air-raid intelligence could be accurately plotted as tracks, after such tracks had been identified as hostile, friendly or doubtful. Seated round the table map were a number of plotters, each one connected by a landline to the appropriate reporting centre. From these centres the plotters received minute-to-minute information of the progress of enemy aircraft towards and over this country, together with their numbers and height. The plotter displayed, on the table map suitable symbols indicating the identity, numbers, height and track of the aircraft concerned.

Thus each RAF commander, from the Commander-in-Chief in his operations room at Fighter Command down to the sector commander in his operations room at a fighter station or airfield, had continually before him the same moving picture of the enemy as the situation continually changed at the speed of modern flight. Naturally the area that had to be covered by the picture presented to a Sector Commander was much smaller than the area required for the command or group operations room, but in so far as their responsibilities were severally affected, it was the same picture.

During the heavy attacks in September it was found that in No. 11 Group Headquarters operations room the table got too congested, so all detail regarding enemy raids and the fighter squadrons detailed to intercept was transferred to a slotted black-board on the wall known as the Totalisator, leaving the map clear except for the raid numbers and symbols for our squadrons in the air.

Each operations room contained an elevated dais which might extend much of the way round the room; a gallery was sometimes added between the dais and the floor of the room. On the wall was shown complete meteorological information including wind and clouds and, at groups and sectors, the strength and degree of readiness of our own squadrons. In sector operations rooms arrangements existed whereby the minute-to-minute position of our own fighters was also plotted on the table map.

Transmission of Information and Orders
In the centre of the dais sat the controller with his assistants responsible for the issue of orders. In the gallery or on the dais sat the tellers who passed on the information appearing on the table map to plotters in other operations rooms. Accommodation on the dais was provided for representatives of the Observer Corps, A.A. guns and searchlights and the Ministry of Home Security. Very complete intercommunication was provided; for instance, the controller in a group operations room could, by moving a switch, speak directly to any of his sectors, and the controller in a sector operations room could speak through R/T with any of his squadrons in the air or at their dispersal points on the ground.

At Fighter Command headquarters was the main operations room. In addition to the Commander-in-Chief Fighter Command and his staff, it contained the Commander-in-Chief A.A. Defences and the Observer Corps Commandant, or their representatives, liaison officers from the Admiralty, Bomber and Coastal Commands, as well as a Home Security official. It fulfilled many functions. Information from the various sources was coordinated and analysed and the reported formation identified as friendly or hostile and, if the latter, was allotted a number. Where any doubt existed as to the responsibility, raids were allotted to groups.

The air raid warning system was operated through certain trunk exchanges in direct telephone communication. The Commander-in-Chief Fighter Command exercised general control over the opening of A.A. gunfire and the exposure of searchlights, through the Commander-in-Chief, A.A. Command. He also controlled the balloon barrage through his group commanders. Group commanders decided which sector should meet any specified raid and the strength of the fighter force to be employed. Sector Commanders detailed the fighter units.

Responsibility of Commanders

This system enabled RAF commanders at each different level immediately to dispose their air forces to meet any situation as it could be seen threatening or developing before his eyes on the table map. It enabled the Commander-in-Chief to reinforce groups with fighters from an adjacent group as and when he saw where the weight of the enemy's attack was likely to fall. It enabled a group commander to organise his squadrons in the various sectors at the appropriate states of preparedness to leave the ground and to order his readiness squadrons off the ground at a moment's notice. It enabled a sector commander to carry out interceptions with incoming raids; since he could see on his table map the minute-to-minute position, course and height both of the incoming enemy formation and of his own outgoing intercepting fighters. He could thus, by R/T, issue orders to his formation leaders in the air, giving the compass course to steer and height at which to fly so as to ensure the best chance of interception.

When once visual contact in the air with the enemy raid had been made, the executive control of the fighters passed automatically from the sector commander in the operations room to the man on the spot, the leader of the fighters, who, in turn, issued to his pilots by radio telephony his executive orders for the conduct of the ensuing air battle. Interception depended finally on being able to see the enemy, so although the system worked well by day, it was not sufficiently accurate to effect interception at night against raiders not illuminated by searchlights.

When the battle was joined, it was the function of the sector commander or his representative in his operations room to 'listen-in' and observe radio silence during the fighting, unless it appeared that other enemy fighters or bombers were approaching the area, when the formation leaders were duly informed. Immediately the battle was over, it became the function again of the sector commander to take control and assist his pilots to regain their home base or nearest airfield if necessary, particularly when, as often happened, squadrons became much split up during a dog-fight or when bad weather intervened and petrol was low.

Group, and, in a less degree, sector commanders had many factors to keep in mind: the necessity for holding some squadrons in reserve to meet further attacks that might develop at short notice; recalling squadrons at the right moment to land for refuelling and rearming; petrol endurance; probable expenditure of ammunition. All these had constantly to be weighed up and decisions made very rapidly.

The whole technique of operating fighters in defence of Great Britain and the facilities provided in Fighter Command operations rooms were the result of a steady process of development over many years. Arrangements are never static. Improvements in methods, in layout and in equipment of operations rooms, are constantly being introduced. However, the existing arrangements today are, in their essentials, the same as they were in the days of the Battle of Britain.

A.A. Guns

The anti-aircraft guns, under the Command of General Sir Frederick Pile, took no small toll of enemy aircraft, and during the heavy attacks on London rendered great service in turning them back, both by day and night, through the weight of their barrage. On some nights as many as 60 per cent, of the enemy aircraft approaching London from the South, dropped their bombs in open country or on the fringe of the barrage, and then went home. They also rendered direct service to our fighter aircraft, first by breaking up enemy formations, thus rendering them more vulnerable to fighter attacks, and secondly by indicating to our pilots in the air the position of enemy aircraft by shell bursts. On the dais are the tellers, passing on plots as they appear on the centre table to fighter group and sector operations rooms and adjacent observer centres.

Where conditions permit, posts are spaced so that all aircraft flying over the country are within sight or sound of at least one post and continuous tracks are therefore obtained at the centres. Each track is given a separate symbol to maintain its identity, and when 'seen' the height and number of aircraft are reported and 'told' forward. The Observer Corps organisation was the sole method of tracking enemy aircraft overland during the battle, and its efficiency enabled many successful interceptions to be made and this contributed in no small degree to the result. It was also essential for the air raid warning systems.

In addition to the work in connection with Air Defence the organisation was of great value in enabling our own aircraft, lost in thick weather or at night, to be grounded. Any aircraft thought to be in difficulty owing to its erratic course, the sound of its engines or distress signals was specially tracked and told forward. In some cases RAF airfields were asked by centres to light their landing lights and fire pyrotechnics to help the aircraft down.

The organisation was a very democratic one, members being drawn from all classes of society, but all were animated by the knowledge that their work was of vital importance to the country and to the Royal Air Force. Their skill at recognition reached an astonishingly high standard. During the severest winter known for half a century, every post and every centre was continuously manned day and night by these civilian volunteers, many of them over sixty years of age. Their motto is *Forewarned is Forearmed*.

During the first years of war, General Pile's gunners would claim the destruction of 444 enemy aircraft (although the actual figure was substantially lower). Nonetheless, the gunners would make a real contribution in the battle ahead, forcing German bombers to fly higher and therefore attack with less accuracy, given the limitations of the bomb-sighting available. Most of the heavy 4.5 and 3.7 inch guns were deployed around key towns and factories in batteries of four, linked to a local Gun Operations Room. Pile's headquarters was actually at Bentley Priory, and he and Dowding worked in perfect accord.

Britain's key population centres were also defended by barrage balloons, or more accurately hydrogen-filled Low Zone (LZ) Kite Balloons. Although designed to fly from a tethered position at 5,000ft, in practice altitudes of 6,500ft were frequently more common. Again, this forced the enemy to attack from higher altitudes with less accuracy – and balloons were a menace on occasions to friend and foe, especially at night.

The Observer Corps (OC) represented an essential link in Britain's defences, visually tracking enemy aircraft which had crossed the British coastline and no longer tracked by radar, which only looked out to sea. Information on the enemy's progress was passed by telephone to Observer Centres, then relayed to the Fighter Command Operations Room at Bentley Priory. There, all incoming information was assessed and if necessary passed to the relevant group controller at sector operations room level. At first, the OC wore civilian dress with a striped armband overprinted in red with 'Observer Corps'. These men were all volunteers, it must be remembered, often contributing twenty-four hours duty per week, in addition to their full-time jobs.

In 1937, the Air Raid Precautions (ARP) service had been formed, when the ARP Act designated local responsibility to county councils. The service's intention was to provide leaders and advisors to supervise air raid shelters, issue gas masks and check black-out precautions. Most ARP wardens were middle-aged or elderly men, although one warden in six was female. The service was controlled by twelve regional commissioners, answerable to the Ministry of Home Security, and did much valuable rescue and warning work while Britain was under air attack.

Britain's police forces continued with their peacetime duties in addition to the many extra tasks wartime imposed upon them. The regular service was assisted by the temporary full-time constables of the Police War Reserve, and part-time volunteers of the Special Constabulary. In the rural areas of south-east England, during the summer of 1940, the local 'bobby' sometimes found himself guarding captured German airmen and crash-sites, and even helping arrange transport back to base for downed British airmen. Indeed, the police stations of 1940 would become clearing houses for all manner of victims and survivors.

In the last years before war broke out, an appeal was also made for volunteers to join the Auxiliary Fire Service (AFS), some 60,000 ultimately bolstering the 6,000 professional firefighters of the National Fire Service (NFS). Often poorly equipped and lacking appropriate training, the auxiliaries nonetheless worked long hours, tirelessly, winning the respect of the NFS.

Each area also had Rescue Squads, being a first-aid unit equipped with a motorised ambulance, crewed by a driver and assistant, which trained and moved as a cohesive team. Somerset, for example, had thirty-nine such Rescue Parties in 1940, with a strength of twenty-one personnel. Like the other voluntary organisations, these humanitarian units made a substantial contribution under difficult conditions.

Then, of course, there were the Local Defence Volunteers (LDV) – renamed the 'Home Guard' later in the summer – for which volunteers were requested in May 1940. Within a week, 250,000 men had stepped forward, and a million by August 1940, overwhelming the authorities' ability to train, organise and arm them. There were precious few rifles available for the Home Guard, which armed itself with privately owned shotguns and other firearms, and even swords, clubs and staves. During the eventual collapse of Nazi Germany, a similar initiative, the Volkssturm, proved of more propaganda than military value, so it is unlikely that in the event of a German invasion the Home Guard would have done much more. The volunteers did, however, take over tedious local guard duties that would otherwise have overburdened the army, and gave every community a sense of direct involvement in the defence of Britain.

Finally, there were the Bomb Disposal Units (BDU), whose job was to make-safe Unexploded Bombs (UXB). BDU teams exclusively comprised volunteers, mostly skilled men of the Royal Engineers (RE). At first, the German bombs in use were designed to explode on impact, although some did malfunction and had to be made safe by having their fuses removed. Then, delayed action bombs appeared, and built-in anti-handling devices, making this an even more hazardous occupation.

Also, across Britain, prefabricated fortifications, 'pill-boxes' sprang up, made of concrete, enabling the siting of machine-guns to defend key targets, and air raid shelters galore, from self-made 'Anderson' shelters in back gardens to large communal, robust, shelters in towns and cities.

Britain, therefore, was in a state of some preparedness to meet an aerial onslaught. Indeed, the System essentially represented the most advanced air defence in the world at that time – but there were vexing issues.

Chapter 4

'We Lacked Experience but were Certainly Keen'

While the System was developed and perfected, the tactics which Fighter Command's pilots would use in battle remained a matter of speculation. This was because the monoplane fighters had appeared so late in the day that the RAF remained inexperienced in their operation. When war eventually broke out on 3 September 1939, for example, the Hurricane had been taken on charge by 111 Squadron less than two years previously and the first Spitfire squadron, 19, had been fully operational for only nine months. Most importantly, however, it was understandably not envisaged that Britain would ever come within range of German single-engine fighters, so this significantly influenced pre-war tactical thinking.

It was believed that only twin-engine bombers, flying from bases in Germany, would have the necessary range to intrude over the British Isles, meaning that RAF fighters would only need to intercept these types. The Hurricane's maximum speed was around 320 mph, the Spitfire's 355 mph. The German Do 17 bomber, however, cruised at 236 mph, the He 111 at 225 mph, and the Ju 88 at 286 mph.

Bombers, therefore, could not out-run a British fighter, and any evasive action possible was in no way comparable to the aerobatic capabilities of either the Hurricane or Spitfire. For defence, bombers had to rely upon armour plate and mutual fire support. Most of the German bombers each had some five machine-guns for defence sited around the aircraft to cover all directions. The two primary RAF fighters, however, each had eight machine-guns, all firing forwards. If these aircraft were operated in sections of three, flying close together in a V-shaped formation called a 'vic', then a total of twenty-four guns would simultaneously be brought to bear upon the target.

This tactic, of course, assumed that the aircraft attacked was taking little or no evasive action – and as it was only expected to encounter bombers, this was given. Fighting Area Attacks, in fact, consisted of six set-piece interceptions with whole squadrons flying in sections of three and therefore attacking with a total of ninety-six guns. So much faith did the Air Ministry invest in these tactics that squadron commanders were officially forbidden to experiment with alternative ideas.

Not all senior RAF officers, though, were satisfied that the Fighting Area Attacks were correct. In July 1938, after being appointed Air Chief Marshal Dowding's SASO at Fighter Command HQ, Air Commodore Keith Park became specifically responsible for the Command's fighting efficiency. In November, he attended a meeting of the Air Fighting Committee at which a report on tactics for the new monoplanes was examined. This emphasised that the vic was the most suitable fighter formation – but Park disagreed.

On 29 December 1938, he sent a written proposal to the commanders of both 11 and 12 Groups to the effect that the officially dictated formations and attacks were too rigid to be practical, imploring that 'some latitude be left to the leader in the air in order to effect surprise'. This was to no avail; the Air Ministry ruled that fighters should only attack from astern or below. Moreover, in 1938, the RAF's *Manual of Air Tactics* stated that 'manoeuvres at high speeds in air fighting are not now practicable because the effect of gravity on the human body during rapid changes of direction at high speed causes a temporary loss of consciousness'. For this reason it was believed that the fast, new, monoplanes would be physically incapable of engaging each other.

On 10 January 1939, Park wrote to the Air Ministry criticising the manual. In total contravention of Air Ministry beliefs, he wrote: 'The possibility of bombers having fighter escorts even in attacks on London should not be overlooked.' The fact of the matter was that Park understood fighter combat and tactics perfectly – probably even more so than Dowding, who concentrated on the System and strategy.

Although Park's views on tactics involving the new monoplanes were also based upon speculation, he, more than any other, grasped the most likely principles – the reality of which would be poles apart from the pre-war manual.

In February 1939, Park issued new instructions: 'Fighter Command Attacks 1939'. Although these still concentrated upon attacks against ponderous bombers, and assumed that combined firepower was advantageous, it was emphasised that these instructions were not a drill to be blindly followed, because formation leaders, having been guided to the interception by ground control, were encouraged to use their own initiative and act accordingly.

Sergeant Reg Johnson:

> Our CO of 222 Squadron, Squadron Leader 'Tubby' Mermagen, was a pre-war aerobatic formation champion, which probably explained his addiction to making us fly our Spitfires in tight squadron formation. We actually flew so tight that our wingtips overlapped. From Kirton he led us off in squadron formation and at times we even landed in squadron formation. We even rolled as a squadron on one occasion! Mermagen was an exceptional pilot, but such training was completely unsuitable for what actually lay ahead.

In March 1939, Dowding responded to a question concerning tactics by Air Vice-Marshal Gossage, then the commander of 11 Group. The Commander-in-Chief explained that if too many fighters were scrambled at once they might be bombed while refuelling and rearming. If insufficient fighters were scrambled to meet a threat, then losses would be too great. The squadron, directed Dowding, would be the largest unit deployed under normal circumstances, although two or more might fight in pairs against a significantly superior enemy force.

Dowding knew that his Command could not even practice or work towards the discovery of ideal tactics because his squadrons were as yet still largely unfamiliar with the new monoplanes, and limited resources dictated the provision of too small a number of 'target' aircraft with which to practice interceptions. Training was, therefore, always undertaken in completely unrealistic conditions. There was no alternative though, and clarity would only be provided through actual combat experience – hardly ideal.

While how best to use formations was carefully considered, so too was the intercepting formation's size. On 3 April 1939, Air Vice-Marshal Gossage sent a memorandum on this subject to his sectors and squadrons:

> The Air Officer Commanding-in-Chief Fighter Command has stated that his policy in regard to the engagement of enemy bomber formations is to match a fighter against each bomber of the enemy formation so far as this is a practical proposition.
>
> In Fighter Command Attacks 1939, it will be noted that this policy does not find its fullest expression in that the largest number of bombers which are simultaneously engaged by fighters is six. This limitation is at present occasioned by the following considerations:-
>
> i) Some squadrons have not had their monoplane fighters long enough to be able to employ them efficiently in formations greater than sections or flights.
> ii) In Air Exercises, the best and most economical use has to be made of the target aircraft which can be obtained for interception practice. For instance, if sixty bombers are available they are best used in flights or sections in order to give the maximum practice to as many fighter flights as possible, as opposed to operating the bombers in two masses of thirty, or five formations of twelve aircraft.
> iii) It is desirable, from the point of view of training junior leaders, that interception exercises shall be carried out by flights or sections, so that the maximum amount of practice, initiative and experience can be obtained.
>
> Thus it will be seen that training in the tactical handling of the formations of squadron strength has not been pursued as it might have been.
>
> The AOC-in-C holds the view that the squadron is likely to be the largest tactical unit employed by the simultaneous attack of a

large enemy formation, and that if two or more squadrons have to be despatched to engage such a raid, squadrons would attack in succession, as individual units, acting upon the initiative of the squadron commanders when interception has been made.

Gossage's memorandum is of interest because it clearly outlines Dowding's thoughts regarding the size of intercepting formations, particularly that it was considered perfectly permissible for two or more squadrons to intercept concurrently, if the size of the enemy formation made this necessary. Clearly, then, Dowding's was not an inflexible insistence that small formations must always be used. It is noteworthy, too, that Gossage writes that multiple squadron formations would not attack as a cohesive whole, but in succession as individual units.

There was one very good reason for this, which also applied during the forthcoming Battle of Britain: the limitations of radio telephony. The radio sets fitted to RAF fighters enabled the pilots of a particular squadron to talk to each other and the ground controller – but not to other airborne squadrons. Until this restriction was overcome, therefore, it was impossible for squadrons to instantly communicate during an interception – something not widely appreciated, even today.

The memorandum also emphasises that because monoplane fighters were so new, with squadrons still converting to, and becoming familiar with, their operation, not all squadrons had actually flown as a single unit, but in flights or sections. That there was more experience and interception training provided to the flight formation, it also followed that this would be the obvious and preferred tactical formation.

In July 1939, 11 Group conducted a simulated defence of southern England against an 'attack' by Bomber Command. A week later, 12 Group did likewise in response to a similar 'raid' on northern England. A de-brief at Bentley Priory noted that 11 Group's interception success rate was a reasonable 60 per cent. 12 Group's was less, but Leigh-Mallory's fighters had begun practising the new interception techniques later than Gossage's, and 12 Group's RDF was found to be less reliable than 11's.

The exercises were unrealistic, however, owing to the small number of bombers provided by the AOC-in-C Bomber Command. Air Chief Marshal Sir Edgar Ludlow-Hewitt. The following month, though, another exercise went ahead involving a larger number of bombers, the results of which were rather embarrassing for Leigh-Mallory. A low-level 'raid' had surprised certain of 12 Group's sectors, forcing the AOC to thereafter mount resource-hungry standing patrols. Indeed, Dowding and Park considered this an overreaction. Moreover, too many 12 Group fighters had been diverted from the primary function of intercepting bombers attacking vital targets, and were instead defending their own bases.

Furthermore, during a night 'attack', the all-important 12 Group Operations Room was evacuated for ten crucial minutes. Dowding consequently directed Leigh-Mallory that in future, neither group nor sector operations rooms were to be

'WE LACKED EXPERIENCE BUT WERE CERTAINLY KEEN'

evacuated unless dictated by damage. These were, of course, the very nerve-centre of the System, without which the whole process broke down. Suffice it to say, the 12 Group AOC's performance in this exercise bode not well.

On 9 August 1939, the Air Ministry wrote to Air Chief Marshal Dowding on the subject of 'Tactics v Massed Bomber Formations':

> On the one hand it is said that the air fighting problem does not really extend beyond the tactical situation involved in combats between units of squadron size, because a massed attack of the type envisaged will, in fact, take the form of a number of squadron formations in quick succession, possibly some hundreds of yards apart.
>
> Furthermore, to meet such an attack it is unlikely that a fighter formation exceeding squadron strength will be mustered and operated as one tactical unit before interception, and the chances of more than one fighter squadron attacking at the same moment are very small. The air fighting problem, therefore, is covered adequately by the investigations of the AFDE by formations of squadron strength.

Wing Commander G.M. Lawson, of Park's Operations staff, provided the following information to inform the AOC-in-C's reply:

> It is considered that a fighter tactical unit consisting of more than one squadron would not be able to carry out the role of interception and attack as efficiently as a squadron formation. It would take longer to climb to the height of the enemy formation, and it could not manoeuvre as quickly into position for the attack. In all probability, unless the enemy was intercepted at very close range, the wing fighter formation would have to split up in order to close quickly with the enemy bombers.
>
> It would probably be necessary in any case for the wing fighter formation to split up into squadrons or flights in order to bring effective fire against the greatest number of bombers at the same time. Attacks in wing formation would be impractical in conditions of heavy cloud, bad visibility or at low height.
>
> The school of thought which is in favour of large formations suggests that the aim should be to concentrate in strength before attacking.
>
> It is considered that time is the important factor in interception and attack. The aim should be to attack the enemy as soon as possible, and not to wait until we have concentrated in strength before attacking.
>
> The Memorandum gives particulars of the area covered by a large bomber formation. It is improbable that this represents a true

war picture. It ignores the probability of dispersion after a long flight over the sea, after heavy AA fire, and after attacks by our fighters. The enemy bomber formation would almost certainly be dispersed over a larger area, and in groups which would be unable to support each other by rear gunfire when the fighters attacked. These dispersed groups of bombers could be dealt with more effectively by fighters operating in flight or squadron strength.

Apart from the operational objections referred to above, it is suggested that peace training must be regulated to war conditions. It might be possible to train our regular fighter squadrons in wing tactics in peace, but it is doubtful whether it would be possible to maintain that high standard in war.

On 19 August 1939, Dowding replied to the Air Ministry:

It is only a year ago since there existed a considerable body of opinion to the effect that high-speed monoplane fighters would not be able to deploy and deliver a simultaneous attack against an enemy formation owing to the danger of collision or shooting one another.

2. These fears, although not groundless, are proving to be exaggerated, and sections and flights are now habitually deployed for attack and we are working toward the habitual deployment of complete squadrons.
3. The training required for these tactics, however, is by no means inconsiderable and, although I am glad to say that no collision has yet occurred in aircraft deployed for straightforward attack following a direct approach, I have observed several instances in which one fighter has flown into the cone of fire of another when the target aircraft have adopted a rotating method of avoiding action.
4. While, therefore, I do not discount the possibility of mass deployment at some future time, I can say without hesitation that even tentative and experimental work in this connection would be premature at present.
5. My own opinion (which I do not want to over stress at the moment), is that the squadron will always be the largest tactical unit which it will be practically expedient to employ.
6. The main object of simultaneous and combined attack is to secure superiority of fire, and each individual fighter has at present so great a superiority of fire against its 'opposite number' that the situation may be considered satisfactory, and we ought not to sacrifice the speed, flexibility and safety of our

deployment for theoretical advantages which are likely to be illusory in practice.

7. I agree that, on the evidence available, the *Geschwader* of twenty-seven or thirty aircraft is the most likely formation in which the Germans would deliver their attacks, but I should propose to operate against such formations at the present moment by flights in succession, and later by squadrons.

8. A further point is that under our present organisation, squadrons use different wavelengths, even when they are in the same sector, and cohesion of attack would be difficult to ensure unless all aircraft were on the same wavelength.

9. I should make it clear that the above remarks apply to the fixed-gun single-seater fighter. If, and when, multi-seater fighters are adopted in the Service, the problem must be reconsidered on its merits.

Clearly, Dowding was receptive to 'mass deployment' in future, if appropriate. In order to ensure a rapid, effective and safe reaction to any threat, however, the AOC-in-C emphasised that the flight, or in time squadron, was the 'largest tactical unit which it will be practically expedient to employ'. One of the main reasons for this, as explained, was that tactical training on the new monoplane fighters revolved around the flight of six aircraft, not, as yet, the whole squadron of twelve operating cohesively.

With squadrons only beginning to learn how to operate as one, there was no question of a multi-squadron wing at this time, purely for practical purposes, taking aside any tactical considerations. Moreover, Dowding confirmed that the limitations of communications made command and control of a large fighter formation impossible. The correspondence, however, sharply evidences the great consideration that had been given to formation size by Dowding, and the very good reasons for his views.

In September 1939, Leigh-Mallory caused further concern at Fighter Command HQ. Dowding had expressly ordered his group commanders not to issue their own local instructions regarding the movement of squadrons, because this was dealt with by Fighter Command battle orders. Local arrangements, therefore, only served to confuse the issue. Dowding, of course, was conscious of the bigger picture, appreciating that in response to a changing military scenario, squadrons may need to move freely about the Command. Despite having been told to cancel his local orders of 5 September 1939, on 26 September Leigh-Mallory wrote further to both his sectors and Dowding:

> In view of the small number of squadrons in any one sector, and taking into consideration the fact that the Germans may deliver large scale raids on such important places as Birmingham, Derby and Sheffield, it is highly desirable that it should be possible to

concentrate aircraft from as many other sectors as possible onto the front of the threatened target.

On 1 October 1939, Dowding responded:

Dear Leigh-Mallory

I have been reading your 12G/S.1292 dated 26 September 1939, on the subject of lateral reinforcement.

2. I find your paragraph 2 very difficult to understand. I take it you mean that in some circumstances Digby would require reinforcements, and in other circumstances Wittering.
3. In the former case you would have five squadrons at Digby, and in the latter no less than seven squadrons at Wittering.
4. Now I have delegated tactical control almost completely to groups and sectors, but I have not delegated strategical control, and the threat to the line must be regarded as a whole and not parochially. The units at Debden and Duxford may be urgently required at short notice for the defence of London and, although they have been put under you to balance the number of stations in groups, this function of theirs must not be overlooked. (You will remember there is an emergency order 'Concentrate on London', which involved action by these two stations).
5. Then again, I do not wish normally to operate more than three squadrons from one aerodrome, or four squadrons under one sector commander. Aerodromes must not become too crowded, and our organisation allows only four wavelengths to each sector. This of course does not prevent formations flying and fighting in another sector, so long as they are operated by their own sector controller.
6. I note that you have made arrangements to operate a fifth wavelength in a sector by means of the R/T Tender, but this was not the purpose for which R/T Tenders were provided.
7. The last part of your letter is difficult to understand. I imagine that the crystals referred to are for ground sets only.
8. Please do not think that I am criticising you in this letter. I admire the energy and foresight which you are bringing to your task. I would only ask you to remember that Fighter Command has to operate as a whole, and reinforcements and readjustments may have to be made between groups and not only within them. We require a simple and flexible system which can be put into effect at short notice and with the minimum of preliminary arrangement.

My idea is that I shall never put more than four squadrons into a sector, that crystal and control arrangements exist for this to be done in such a way that any squadron, and not only a previously selected squadron, can be moved, and that if more than four squadrons have to intercept and fight in any one sector they will do so under the control of neighbouring sector commanders.

Air Chief Marshal Dowding had provided clarity, were any required, to the 12 Group commander regarding Fighter Command's strategy. Significantly, Dowding indicated that there was every intention of using 12 Group squadrons to reinforce 11 Group's over London if necessary (Debden was in 12 Group until August 1940, when absorbed by 11 Group). On 3 October 1939, Air Vice-Marshal Leigh-Mallory replied, acknowledging that his previous letter 'concerning lateral reinforcement cannot have been a very good memorandum as it misled your regarding my intentions', going on to say that:

2. This matter has been frequently discussed by me with my sector commanders, and this type of reinforcement has been practised during some of my Group exercises, so that my sector commanders are fully conversant with my ideas. This is why the whole scheme was not more comprehensively explained in my memorandum.
3. What I have in mind is a German mass attack of say 300–400 aircraft being delivered against one of the important objectives in the Midlands. In any one sector I have only twenty-four aircraft for day operations, and consequently if such an attack develops, I must be able to bring aircraft from adjoining sectors to counter it.
4. I can assure you that there is no intention on my part to upset the strategic situation in the Command, but only to make the greatest tactical use of the units in my Group. This scheme provides purely for air reinforcement, and it is not intended that any aircraft should land at an aerodrome other than their own, so that the times during which squadrons would be away from their parent aerodromes would vary between about forty minutes, in the case of Digby reinforcing Wittering, and Wittering reinforcing Digby, and about an hour and a half for Duxford reinforcing Digby.
5. As it is purely an air reinforcement, the Duxford squadrons would be in R/T touch with either their own ground station or with one working their wavelength at Digby, by which it would be possible to recall them in the event of a threat developing further South.
6. You will see from the above remarks that I have no intention of departing from what you say in paragraph 5.

7. In regard to paragraph 6 of your letter, if you remember, last autumn when it was laid down how the R/T Tenders should be allotted, they were sited so that sectors could operate on the front of adjoining sectors. With this end in view, the R/T tenders in the Wittering Sector, for instance, were sited at: Wainfleet All Saints, from which aircraft from Wittering could fly up as far as Dona Nook, and West Raynham, from which it is possible to operate as far as Great Yarmouth and Honington into the Duxford Sector.
8. To take a concentrated attack on Rolls-Royce at Derby, as an example, as how I was proposing to carry out this type of reinforcement. Digby would carry out the first interception about Skegness. Wittering then intercept about Horncastle, working with their R/T Tender at Wainfleet All Saints. Digby would carry out a third interception in the neighbourhood of Digby; the Duxford squadrons, as they have furthest to come, would intercept in the area Newark, Bottesford. The Germans might very easily direct a mass attack of 300–400 aircraft against Derby, and even with this method of reinforcing I would only bring sixty fighters into action against them.
9. With regard to paragraph 7 of your letter, the crystals referred to are for ground sets only, as with this type of reinforcement there would not be time for aircraft to land and change crystals as the opportunity would be lost.
10. I can assure you that in any operations of this nature I shall always be watching the situation to the South of me most carefully, as I realise the reinforcement of London may, in certain circumstances, become my primary task. With this end in view I have arranged not only to concentrate the Duxford or Debden squadrons for that purpose but for Debden to hold a crystal for No 213 Squadron, which they could operate on their fourth R/T set, and 213 Squadron could thus be utilised to operate in the vicinity of Harlow.

Leigh-Mallory's letter certainly helps us appreciate the limitations of airborne communications in use at the time. The letter appears to have reassured Dowding, who replied a week later, acknowledging that he had 'misunderstood' Leigh-Mallory's original letter, adding that,

> if one sector controller does not try to handle more than four squadrons, the plan ought to work all right.
>
> The chief difficulty might be from jamming between wavelengths of units in adjoining sectors, but I see that you intend to

> operate units one after the other and not simultaneously. In the example you give in paragraph 8, do not overlook the possibility of some of the earlier squadrons being able to land and rearm quickly so as to be able to have a second go on the return journey.

At the time, however, Dowding had more pressing matters at hand, not least grave concerns regarding Fighter Command's overall strength, which was eighteen squadrons below the fifty-two considered necessary to defend Britain. Indeed, Dowding was steadfastly resisting the Air Ministry's efforts to send more fighter squadrons to France and reduce his strength to a mere twenty-six squadrons.

In a letter to the Under-Secretary of State for Air on 16 September 1939, Dowding rightly described this as 'a grim prospect – the number is exactly half that laid down by the Air Council as necessary for the defence of the country'.

The letter was both detailed and lengthy, concluding that his concerns were,

> written as much from the offensive as the defensive aspect. Presumably the time will come sooner or later when we will have to take offensive action with our bomber striking force. When the time comes it will be necessary to be strong at home, so that we may not be diverted from our aim for fear of reprisals.

Repeatedly, Dowding's was the voice of both experience and reason resisting foolhardy decisions by the Air Ministry. It would not, however, win him many friends at Whitehall.

Leigh-Mallory was concerned about the strength of 12 Group, and wrote to Dowding on 24 October 1939:

> I feel most uneasy about the number of squadrons at present in 12 Group. I have, up to the present, lost three squadrons to the Field Force; No 616 permanently to 13 Group, and now No 19 sent North to reinforce 13 Group.
>
> In the last Command Battle Order, no less than four of the squadrons shown under No 12 Group are non-effective as far as I am concerned. They are:
>
> 19 Squadron – attached to 13 Group.
> 616 Squadron – now belonging to 13 Group.
> 229 and 222 Squadrons – neither of which has any aircraft.
> In addition, 46 Squadron is standing by to go out to France.
>
> 2. We have recently been faced with a phase in which the Germans have been attacking coastal objectives. It seems to me from watching the international situation that we may be

approaching very near the time when Hitler resorts to entirely different methods and begins to bomb military objectives in Great Britain itself, such as Rolls-Royce at Derby and various shadow factories and aero-engine factories in the Birmingham, Wolverhampton and Coventry areas. If such an attack develops, my position is a most precarious one.

3. I only have seven day-fighter squadrons at the present moment. Of those, 610 and 611 cannot be regarded as more than 50 per cent efficient when compared to the regular squadrons. They are a very different proposition to 602, 603 and 607 Squadrons, which were all in a very much more advanced state of training. That leaves me five reasonably well-trained squadrons with which to meet a really intensive attack on the Midlands. If one counts 610 and 611 together as one squadron, it gives me a total of six.

4. With the big area I have to defend and the weight of attack which may be delivered against me, I wish to place on record that I think this inadequate.

Leigh-Mallory's letter would not have told Dowding anything he did not already know, which is why his horns were locked with the Air Ministry over the issue of Fighter Command's overall strength. Moreover, paragraph 4 was clearly an unashamed back-covering proviso. Air Commodore Park, Dowding's SASO, noted, though, that the AOC 12 Group's report was inaccurate: both 264 and 266 squadrons were at Sutton Bridge, and the Gladiator biplane-equipped 141 Squadron was in the process of converting to Blenheims. Also, 19 Squadron was actually returning to Duxford, its home station, after a brief deployment to Catterick.

In March 1940, Dowding gave Leigh-Mallory an interview at Bentley Priory, after which the latter stopped off at Park's office before leaving. The loyal SASO was later to recall that 'Leigh-Mallory was very angry and said that he would move heaven and earth to get Dowding sacked'. Park himself was consequently 'greatly annoyed', recalling that as a result of this incident his 'peacetime friendship for Leigh-Mallory drained very rapidly'. It is not known what the interview between Dowding and Leigh-Mallory was about, but the timing of it suggests that it may have had a significant outcome.

In February 1940, Air Marshal Sir William Welsh had succeeded Air Marshal Sir Leslie Gossage as AOC 11 Group. As explained, although German air attacks at this time were expected to be coming in over the east coast, making 12 Group Britain's aerial frontline, as 11 Group included London, it was still considered the primary group command. That being so, with the experience of having commanded 12 Group since December 1937 behind him, Leigh-Mallory might have naturally expected to be next in line to command 11 Group, as and when the job became available.

On 13 April 1940, however, Park was informed of his promotion to air vice-marshal and appointment to succeed Welsh in command of the prestigious 11 Group.

In view of Leigh-Mallory's performance to date, however, it is hardly surprising that Dowding passed him over for this primary command, instead appointing his able former SASO. Dowding was not, though, personally aware of Leigh-Mallory's hostility towards him, this only being revealed by Park in 1968, during the making of the 1969 film *Battle of Britain*. Had Dowding been aware, he would have sought Leigh-Mallory's replacement immediately. Long after the war, Dowding told Robert Wright, his one-time personal assistant, that he should have been much 'stricter with Leigh-Mallory', who 'was not prepared to follow my orders, and I should have got rid of him'. As AOC 11 Group, Air Vice-Marshal Park would also soon have to 'endure', wrote Wright, 'this curious enmity of Leigh-Mallory's'.

For all of Leigh-Mallory's 'curious enmity', the fact remains that Keith Park, a warrior born and bred, was the perfect choice for the key command. Having spent two years working closely with Dowding as his SASO, Park fully understood the System and the overall strategy. Dowding's delegation of local tactical control to group commanders, however, meant that the role and importance of group AOCs was a vital one. Park was able to think in terms of handling 11 Group tactically in-line with the overall Fighter Command strategy, which was essentially preserving limited resources while executing the greatest possible damage to the enemy. It would soon be largely Park's responsibility to fight the forthcoming tactical battle.

Another issue of concern was pilot training. Before the war, pilots went straight from Flying Training School (FTS) to their squadron, where they were trained on the fighter type with which their squadron was equipped, and made combat ready. With the advent of war, it was clear that this could not continue, because hard-pressed squadrons had neither the time nor resources to provide such operational training.

The Air Ministry, therefore, revealed plans to create special units which would train fledgling fighter pilots to operational standard prior to them reaching their actual units. Three training 'pools' were proposed, the first of which was the 11 Group Pool at St Athan, which had eleven Fairey Battles (single-engine light-bombers, soon replaced by the North American Harvard monoplane trainer) and twenty-two Hurricanes on strength. Shortly after the outbreak of war, the course length was halved to four weeks, and syllabus hours were reduced from forty-five to thirty hours per pupil. It was hoped that 300 pilots would be trained to operational standard, per pool, per annum.

In March 1940, the group pools were renamed Operational Training Units (OTU), and a third such unit was added. Nonetheless, during the forthcoming Battle of France, their combined output was barely sufficient to make good the losses of squadrons fighting on the Continent, where the standard of training was harshly criticised: new pilots often had only ten hours' flying time on Spitfires or Hurricanes, with no high altitude or fighter attack experience.

Sergeant Bill Green:

In October 1939, I was posted to the Elementary Flying Training School (EFTS) at Hanworth, at what is now Heathrow airport, and Heston, and started training on Miles Magisters. I remember with some pleasure my first solo, which was a wonderful day for me. We were housed in the Hanworth Airport Hotel, which was in the centre of the airfield and which, for me, was absolute luxury – I'd never had such food, or enjoyed such comfort in accommodation. I successfully completed my elementary flying training, and after about sixty flying hours I was posted to the Flying Training School (FTS) at South Cerney in Gloucestershire. This was in March 1940, and there I was trained on Hawker Harts, a beautiful aircraft to fly.

Our training included night flying, which was quite a thrill, and after another fifty hours we began advanced training, on Harts or the Audax – the same aeroplane but with a gunnery platform. My promotion from Leading Aircraftman (LAC) under Pilot Training to corporal then came through. Then, they gathered us all together in this so-called advanced training school and said 'Here's your "wings". You are now sergeants.'

I was then posted back to 501 'County of Gloucester' Squadron of the AAF, which had returned from the Battle of France via Jersey, reassembled at Croydon and immediately posted to Middle Wallop, which is where I rejoined them.

I well recall arriving at Middle Wallop with brand new sergeant's stripes and wings, and presenting myself to the CO, Squadron Leader Hogan. He inquired as to who I was, where I'd been and what I'd done, and asked if I'd fired any guns, used oxygen or a radio, which I hadn't. He asked if I had flown an aircraft with a variable pitch airscrew, retractable undercarriage, flaps and enclosed cockpit, which I hadn't. He said 'Oh, you're no use to me. Look, they are starting some things called OTUs, and there's going to be one at Aston Down, near Bristol. You go home, and in due course you'll receive a telegram telling you to report.' So, off I eagerly and happily wended my way to my mother-in-law's house, where my wife, Bertha, and I were staying.

When I arrived, there was already a telegram waiting, telling me to report to RAF Uxbridge. Well, I knew enough about Uxbridge to know that there was no airfield there and that it was a recruiting station. However, I decided that I wasn't going to be denied a night with my wife, so I used a call box to phone Uxbridge and asked if I could report the following day.

The voice on the other end said 'Oh, you don't want me, you want the BBC.' I didn't know what he was talking about, so put the phone down in disgust and called again. The next person gave me the same answer, so I said to my wife, 'To hell with it, I'll go tomorrow anyway.' So I went the next day and reported to the Guard Room, where the sergeant said 'Oh, you don't want me, you want the PDC, the Personnel Despatch Centre.' So, off I went to the PDC, hence the confusion with 'BBC'.

When I got there, there was some newly uniformed pilot officer sat there, who said 'What did you do before you became a pilot?' I answered that I had been a fitter, and he replied 'Oh, you'll be for Takoradi, on the Gold Coast. Go over to stores and get overseas kit, and be back here by two o'clock to go into town and be inoculated for Yellow Fever.' So, I was a bit bewildered by all of this, thinking I was going to an OTU, and suddenly I'm on my way to Takoradi, overseas kit piled high, until eventually it finished up with a pith helmet on the top, and the Corporal said, 'Sign here, Sergeant.'

I said, 'Well, I don't know that I'm going to sign it.'

He said, 'What's the matter with you, don't you want to go to Africa, Sergeant?'

I said, 'No, I don't!'

He said, 'Oh, it's wonderful! You'll either enjoy wonderful health while you're there, in which case you'll probably die within six weeks of getting back here, or you'll die there!'

Oh,' I said, 'Great!' So, I went back without taking any of the kit or signing for it, to see this acting pilot officer, and told him I wanted to phone my adjutant at Middle Wallop.

'Why?' he said, '*Why*?'

I said, 'Because I don't think that I'm supposed to be going to Takoradi, I'm supposed to be going to an OTU when it's formed.

'I'll phone him,' he said, somewhat bombastically. He disappeared and came back. He said, 'You're quite right, report to the football stadium.'

This Uxbridge activity was fast becoming a farce. Firstly, I'm supposed to be going to an OTU, and I'm posted to the middle of London; secondly, I'm on my way to Africa; and now I have to report to the football stadium. Anyway, I wandered down to the football stadium, which is, in fact, a sports track with a football field in the middle of it, went across to the one and only stand and heard voices emanating from the changing room.

I went in there, and there were a number of other fellas, much like me, and there was a huge plotting board, as used by the plotting stations, with a drawing of the south east corner of England on it.

When we had all mustered, we were addressed by someone who I thought was named Professor Lloyd Williams, and he was either of the BBC, or had a person of the same name, perhaps his father, who was well known in the BBC. Anyway, he said that we were there to learn how to make the best use of radar, both by improving our diction and by adopting and getting used to a given jargon. And he then went on to explain why it was necessary.

He said, 'With the rapid increase in numbers of aircraft, the wavelengths are completely overburdened and becoming jammed because people are using an undisciplined form of communication, everybody saying what they think they need to say, and without the person at the other end having the slightest inclination of what to expect he will say.

For instance, one person might say, "Oh, this is Fred Jones, and I'm from so-and-so, so-and-so squadron, and I've just been here, and I've just been there, and I want to come in to land", or whatever. Now I'm going to play a record, and I want you to tell me what it is.' So he put this record on, and it played for about a minute, and it sounded just like a chipmunk. Having stopped, he said, 'Now, does anyone know what it says?' And, of course, we all laughed, because there was no way.

So he said, 'I'm going to play it again.' He duly played it again, and, of course, nobody knew what it was, although one or two had a wild guess. He said, 'Now I'm going to tell you what it says before I play it for the third time: "Mary, Mary, Quite Contrary, How Does Your Garden Grow?"' Then he put the record on at the same speed, and it sounded crystal clear. And it was a wonderful demonstration of how, if the brain is, through the ears, searching for something that is being transmitted, there are a billion items that it might be, whereas if one has some idea of what it might be, then one has a lesser field to cover, and therefore the brain is more likely to interpret the message.

He then went on to say that in selling this idea to the senior echelons of the RAF, he picked up, in their presence, a telephone which had loudspeaker attachments, and a female voice said, 'Number, please!' And he said, 'The gentlemen of Wembley are a motley assembly.' She said, 'I'm sorry, Sir, what was your number?'

He said, 'The gentlemen of Wembley are a motley assembly.'

She said, 'I'm very sorry, Sir, I didn't get your Wembley number.'

He then said, 'I am not saying a number,' repeated it, and then got the answer that he would have got the first time, if she hadn't been trying to identify a number from the words he was using. I thought that was an absolutely wonderful demonstration of the need for a disciplined jargon in communications.

Anyway, this was all quite cleverly done in retrospect, because at one end of the football field were three 'Wall's Ice Cream Stop Me and Buy One' tricycles. Each had a TR9 radio set, identical to those used in fighter aircraft, with a helmet, earphones and plug. And at the other end of the field was a solitary bicycle, of similar type, but with no radio. The field had been marked out in white chalk, with sections like 1, 2, 3, 4, 5, 6, 7, 8, 9, 10 or whatever, and we were asked to participate in an exercise.

One of us would go onto the roof of a little hut with a Verey flare pistol, and three of us would be on a bicycle each at one end, and one at the other end; the rest would be either the controller or plotters in the plotting room. The exercise would begin when the participant on the roof would fire a Verey cartridge, and the controller would 'scramble' the three bicycles by communicating through the cyclists' headphones. When the Verey light had been seen, the person riding the solitary tricycle at the other end had already received instructions that he was to cycle towards the opposite end of the football field, changing course now and again.

The controller would then give the leader of the three bicycles a course, to intercept the intruding 'bomber' tricycle, worked out from information supplied by the rooftop observer.

This would then be plotted on the field, and the whole interception recorded. This was quite ingenious, because it provided participants a complete picture of how the whole radar and interception technique worked, and at the same time enabled Professor Lloyd Jones, Lloyd Williams or whatever his name might have been, to criticise the voices or diction we were using. This lasted for three days, or thereabouts.

So at the end of the three days I returned to Middle Wallop, only to find the squadron had moved to Gravesend, to where I then wound my way. Again I presented myself to Squadron Leader Hogan, and he said 'What's been happening to you?' bearing in mind that probably a week had elapsed since I first met him.

So I told him. And he said, 'Oh well, we're not bothering with the OTU, we'll train you here. Unfortunately, we don't have a Miles Master, but they have one over at Biggin Hill in 32 Squadron, so get over there.' The Master was a low-wing monoplane which pilots flew before soloing on the Spitfire or Hurricane. Biggin Hill was the parent station of Gravesend and one or two other satellites. So, a Pilot Officer Aldridge, of the AAF, and I got into a Magister and flew across to Biggin Hill.

There we presented ourselves to the commander of the training flight, who said, 'Well, unfortunately, our Master's unserviceable, but they've got one over at Hornchurch, so you'd better go over there, tell them who you are, and they'll take you in hand.' Well, away we went to Hornchurch, and eventually Aldridge did two dual and one solo circuit in the Master, and I one dual circuit. So, the training flight commander said, 'Well, there's no time for you to do more tonight, so you'd better get back to Biggin.' So back to Biggin we go in the Magister. And the next morning I presented myself to the training officer and told him that I'd just done the one dual circuit. He said, 'Well, what aeroplanes did you have in 501 then, when you were a fitter?' I said, 'Well, we'd just got *one* Hurricane.'

'Oh,' he said, 'Well then, you know all about them. Look, there's one out there on the tarmac,' which he pointed to; 'Go and sit in it, and when you feel happy, just take it off.' 'Well, just a minute,' I said, 'What speed does it lift off at, and what is the approach speed, and what speed would I need for a loop, etc?' So he told me these things. So I did as I was told, went and sat in it, and familiarised myself with the taps, and off I went. And I thought, 'Right, I'm going up high to do my first loop,' and up I went to about 20,000ft, adding about 50 per cent to the speeds he'd given me, for safety purposes.

Well, bearing in mind I'd only flown Hawker Harts and Magisters, with a top speed of about 110 mph, I dived this Hurricane down to about, 250, 280, 300 mph, pulled back on the stick as I would with a Hawker Hart, and immediately blacked out. And, when I came to, I was hanging in my straps and I looked over the side and saw sky, and realised I was upside down, so put the stick over to the normal position, and spun.

I didn't know much about spinning, having done my spinning training in Magisters and Harts, but I had heard say that with these new-fangled Spitfires and Hurricanes, you didn't get into a spin because, if you did, you couldn't get out. So anyway, away I went, spinning away, doing the corrective action that I'd been taught, and, lo and behold, it worked. The aeroplane came out of the spin, but I was so relieved I forgot to centralise, and off it went again, spinning in the opposite direction!

By the time I managed to resume the normal flying position, I was down in the clag, very humid, hazy weather, with no clear and defined horizon, and all the instruments were going round in the cockpit like hummingbirds. Nobody ever told me that you had to lock the gyroscope of the artificial horizon before you spun, and as a consequence, the gyrations I had been through had toppled the gyroscope – the artificial horizon was going round and round like a washing machine!

Anyway, I felt a little bit nauseous, but managed to get back to Biggin Hill. The air was full of dogfighting activity, warnings and shouting and so on and so forth. I approached Biggin Hill, made my approach, and realised a little bit late in the game that I had overshot, by which time I was holding off well up the runway, probably halfway, so dropped down and realised that I was going to run out of runway – and hurtled towards the Hurricanes of 32 Squadron, or some of them anyway, which were scattered about the place.

Using my brakes judiciously, eventually, and somewhat miraculously, and thankfully, I came to a halt without damaging my aeroplane, any other aeroplane, or myself. I had done over 170 hours at that time, and this first Hurricane flight was on 8 August 1940, in P2549. Anyway, having screamed to a halt, I was sat in my cockpit feeling very relieved, when Squadron Leader Worrall, the CO of 32 Squadron, hurtled out of his office, jumped up onto my wing and gave me the biggest telling off of all time, confining me to camp for two weeks and ordering me to report to his office immediately, which I did. He there tore off a second strip, asked me what on earth I thought I was doing etc; I told him that it was my first flight, and related my lack of experience. At that he relented, and said 'OK, in that case forget about being confined to camp, but for heaven's sake don't ever do such a thing again, you could have written off several aeroplanes and killed yourself, and other people, in the process.'

So, that was that.

An operational fighter squadron comprised twelve aircraft and pilots, excluding reserves, divided into two 'flights': 'A' and 'B', each commanded by a flight lieutenant. The flights were then sub-divided into two sections of three aircraft, each trio of fighters having its own leader and being identified by a colour. 'A' Flight usually consisted of Red and Yellow Sections, while 'B' comprised Blue and Green. Each section was numbered from one to three, one indicating the leader. 'Blue One' would therefore identify the leader of 'B' Flight's Blue Section.

Each squadron was identified by its own two code letters, which were applied to the fighters' fuselages in medium sea grey. Individual aircraft were then further identifiable by a single letter, choosing from A to K for 'A' Flight, and L to Z for 'B'. Each squadron also had its own radio call sign: 'Luton Blue One' therefore identified the leader of 19 Squadron's 'B' Flight. A squadron leader was in overall command, who, in addition to flying duties, was responsible, through his adjutant, for administration, discipline and general day-to-day smooth running of his unit.

In the air, officers and non-commissioned pilots flew together, but on the ground, while off duty, they were segregated in this still very class-conscious society. It should not be forgotten that a fighter squadron also included those in behind-the-scenes, but nonetheless essential, roles: intelligence officers, airframe riggers, engine fitters, instrument fitters, and armourers, firemen, caterers, clerks, guards, to name a few.

The operational centre of the squadron was 'dispersal', usually a wooden hut on the airfield in which was situated the orderly clerk and all-important telephone.

There were also twelve beds on which the pilots rested between sorties. Outside, their aircraft were dispersed as a precaution against bombing, facing the centre of the airfield so that pilots could take off with the minimum of delay.

During the daytime, pilots learned to leave their parachutes, which they sat on, not in their bucket seats but on top of either the port wing or tailplane with the straps hanging down, meaning that they could seize the two shoulder straps, pull the parachute pack off the wing and move towards the cockpit, all without pausing.

Pilots wore a flying helmet made of leather, containing radio-telephony earphones, the leads of which were plugged into a socket in the cockpit, in which the helmet and goggles were left, usually on the reflector gunsight or control column top. Stout leather flying boots were usually worn, lined with sheepskin, to insulate against the cold in what were unheated cockpits, and a life jacket known as a 'Mae West', after the buxom American actress and for obvious reasons.

Oxygen, required at high altitude, was delivered via an oxygen mask, covering the nose, cheeks and mouth, the pilot's eyes being protected by his goggles. With the addition of leather gauntlets, the pilot was thus afforded some protection from fire.

What fighter pilots rarely wore, however, in direct contrast to the movies and due to the tight confines of their tiny cockpits, was the bulky, leather and sheepskin flying jacket. Instead they preferred to wear uniform shirts and tunics, although the brightly coloured silk neck scarf was not altogether a pose but necessary to prevent chafing as the pilot constantly screwed his neck around searching for the enemy. Moreover, neck ties shrank in seawater, another valid reason why their use was discarded on operations over water. On the ground, the fighter pilot famously wore his tunic top button undone.

Most squadrons worked a four-day cycle, on the first day of which pilots would be on 'Stand by', and therefore available to fly within the hour; second day would be 'Available', as in ready to fly in fifteen minutes, and day three would see the stakes upped to 'Readiness', when pilots were ready for immediate take-off. On day four came 'Stand down', when pilots, with their flight commander's permission, could leave the aerodrome. One flight of operational pilots had to remain on the airfield, so this was often used as an opportunity for further training, operational conditions permitting.

In April 1940, Pilot Officer Hubert 'Dizzy' Allen reported to fly Spitfires with 66 'Clickety-Click' Squadron at Duxford:

> I didn't know where Duxford was and nor was I aware of what aircraft 66 Squadron had – they could have been Hurricanes, which did not appeal to me in any way. On the other hand they might be Spitfires, which appealed to me very much. I had seen a Spitfire in flight, had seen many pictures of it, to me it was the very pink of perfection (which, with experience, proved to be the case). When I arrived at Duxford's hangars I could see nothing but Spitfires littering the airfield – not a Hurricane in sight. Whatever Heaven is, St Peter opened the doors to it that day I arrived at Duxford!

'WE LACKED EXPERIENCE BUT WERE CERTAINLY KEEN'

Bob Morris was posted to 'Clickety-Click' a month later:

> In May 1940, I passed out of the RAF Technical School at Halton as an aeronautical engineer, and was posted to 66 Squadron at Coltishall. I knew not where Coltishall was, or what aircraft 'Clickety-Click' had. My first glimpse of Coltishall airfield in Norfolk, and of 66 Squadron, was from the bus, which travelled along the airfield perimeter for a short distance. What an absolute thrill to see Spitfires! Here was every young man's dream!
>
> In 66 Squadron I found that the set-up was two groups of technical people who looked after the aircraft. The trades in the RAF were sub-divided into five, the technical people being the first and we did all the major work on the aircraft. Group two were flight mechanics, the semi-skilled, whose job was to look after the aircraft's daily requirements, like the daily inspection: oil, petrol, tyre-pressures etc.
>
> In our group was a Fitter Engines and a Fitter Airframe, likewise in the second there was a Flight Mechanic Engine and a Flight Mechanic Airframe. The latter two always remained with the same aircraft. The Flight Mechanic Engine would start up the aircraft's engine first thing in the morning, so that when a scramble call came the engine was already nice and warm.
>
> We 'Fitter IIEs', however, never had an aircraft of our own as there were less of us, so we could be called upon to work on any of the Squadron's Spitfires. We used to do thirty, sixty and ninety hour inspections. When each aircraft had done the maximum amount of flying hours per its particular type of engine, it had an engine change, which we would also do.
>
> My first jobs were mainly inspections, as opposed to repair work. I remember a pilot getting into the cockpit and I helped him to get going, pulled the chocks away and set him up to fly. As he taxied out I thought to myself 'I bet he doesn't know that this is my first attempt!' Perhaps he wouldn't have taken off so confidently, had he known!

Pilot Officer William Walker was a pilot of the RAFVR posted as a replacement pilot to the auxiliary 616 'South Yorkshire' Squadron:

> The early days of war were interesting so far as we were unprepared for what was to come. It is my lasting regret that I did not have more operational training – trying to pick it up with the Squadron straight from flying school was a pretty haphazard affair. For instance, I flew my first Spitfire on 23 June 1940, and was declared operational on 1 July ... We lacked experience but were certainly keen.

The Battle of Britain would officially begin nine days later.

Chapter 5

Göring, Hitler and 'Mein Kampf'

According to German history, the First Reich was the Holy Roman Empire; the Second followed the year-long Franco-Prussian conflict, which concluded in 1871 – a most significant date for Germany: for the first time since the medieval era the country's states were finally unified under the German Empire, with the King of Prussia at its head as Kaiser (emperor). Like Britain, the Kaiser's Imperial German Army's first flirtation with aviation concerned balloons.

In 1901, Germany formed a dedicated balloon battalion, while concurrently German aeronautical designers experimented with gas-filled airships, most notably Zeppelin. In 1910, the first aircraft entered service for military purposes in Germany, leading to the far-sighted creation of five aviation battalions in 1913. This, then, was the beginning of German military aviation – which would ultimately have far-reaching consequences for the Western world.

Prior to unification, each of the twenty-six German states involved had autonomy over its own armed forces. Unification led to a single command structure, although the Bavarian army remained independent from this. Despite unification, however, there remained rivalry between the former states and each army involved controlled its own aviation units. This confusing and counter-productive scenario was positively addressed in 1916, when, two-years after the First World War broke out, the Imperial German Air Service (IGAS, or more accurately Der Fliegertruppen des deutschen Kaiserreiches Luftstreitkrüfte) was formed with responsibility for all military aviation including home defence and intelligence, excluding the Imperial German Naval Aviation Service (IGNAS), which remained independent.

While similarities existed between the birth of the British and German air forces, they were bi-polar in terms of the social history concerned. In Britain, as we have seen, Trenchard's vision was that all his pilots would be officers, and officers at that time were exclusively drawn from fee-paying public schools – the domain of the top 5.2 per cent of British society's socio-economic pyramid. In Germany, conversely, flying – which is to say actually piloting an aircraft – was looked down upon socially. Consequently, the first German service pilots were NCOs, while officers – many of which in the IGAS came from cavalry backgrounds, flew as observers. This is also why, unlike in RAF aircraft, the observer, not the pilot, was captain of German aircraft, even during the Second World War.

GÖRING, HITLER AND 'MEIN KAMPF'

Against this backdrop it was Germany which developed the first long-range bombers, and the Zeppelin-equipped IGNAS raided Britain many times during the First World War; this changed the whole concept of warfare. As mentioned previously, Germany recognised long before Britain that the fighter pilot was also a potent weapon in the propaganda war – and immediately set about promoting their exploits, which were eagerly followed by the German public.

Even today, Manfred von Richthofen – better known as the 'Red Baron', owing to his scarlet fighters, remains one of the most celebrated and famous fighter pilots of all time. One particular First World War German fighter ace, though, remains infamous and is reviled the world over: Hermann Wilhelm Göring – who is pivotal to the events with which we are primarily concerned.

Göring was born on 12 January 1893 at Rosenheim, in Bavaria, the second son of Heinrich, a former Prussian cavalry officer turned German consul-general in Haiti. This was Heinrich's second marriage, five children having already been born to his previous spouse, and Hermann was one of four children born to him by his second wife, Franziska. The family, a typical service one, had been on the fringes of the Prussian social elite and royal circles for a couple of centuries or more; in terms of social strata, the Görings occupied a seam between the middle and upper classes.

The young Göring grew up in a small castle, Veldenstein, near Nuremberg, Bavaria's second city in southern Germany. This home had, in fact, been provided for the family by Heinrich's supposed friend and Hermann's godfather, Dr Hermann Epenstein, a wealthy Jewish physician and businessman whose mistress Franziska had become. The dilapidated castle was decorated with medieval imagery and artefacts, inspiring in the impressionable young Hermann a great pride in Germany. These influences would, in due course, generate a version of romantic patriotism and a nationalistic outlook which ultimately proved so dangerous. Influenced by tales of great Teutonic heroes, Göring, however, was nonplussed by his early military service in the declining Second Reich, which failed to provide opportunities for such glory and adventure.

In March 1912, Göring had been commissioned into the 112th Infantry Battalion of the Prinz Wilhelm Regiment at Mülhausen, a German town in Alsace near the French border, where he was serving when war erupted in August 1914. There he saw action for the first time, and was involved in skirmishes with the French. His best friend, *Leutnant* Bruno Lörzer, however, transferred to the flying school situated just outside the garrison town, and learned to fly – his tales of the air sufficiently inspired Göring to attempt a transfer himself; he was rejected, but later literally transferred himself to become an observer, flying with Lörzer in the Fifth Army's 25th Field Air Detachment.

The pair, based in France on Stenay, flew reconnaissance sorties and were so successful that *Krownprinz* Friedrich Wilhelm awarded both airmen the Iron Cross, First Class. Indeed, because the aerial photographs and sketches of enemy positions taken and made by Göring required expert explanation and interpretation, the two airmen attended senior staff conferences, as a result of which Göring became known personally to the Prince. This may have helped the latter eventually transfer to pilot training, which he completed in record time. In October 1915, Göring became a *Jagdflieger*, a fighter pilot – which suited his romantic outlook and heroic ambitions perfectly – with Lörzer in *Jagdstaffel* (*Jasta*, fighter squadron) 5.

Having recorded his first aerial victory on 16 November 1915, Göring was shot-up and badly wounded in combat with a new British Handley-Page bomber and Sopwith Camel fighters that same month. He crash-landed next to a German field hospital, which saved his life. So bad were his injuries that it took a year to recover and return to operational flying, in February 1917 – joining *Jasta* 26, commanded by his old friend Bruno Lörzer.

By May 1917, Göring had achieved seven victories and was given command of *Jasta* 27. His score rose quickly, sixteen by the year's end – one which saw him decorated with the impressive Military Karl-Friedrich Merit Order, the Knight's Cross with Swords of the Royal House Order of Hohenzollern and the Knight's Cross Second Class with Swords of the Baden Order of Zähringer Lion; Hermann Göring was now the hero he had so wanted to be, especially when he was awarded the coveted *Pour le Mérite* in June 1918. Indeed, his status as such was more than adequately confirmed when, on 9 July 1918, he was promoted to *Oberleutnant* and given command of *Jasta* 1 – formerly commanded by none other than Richthofen, the Red Baron, himself, who had fallen in action on 21 April 1918. By the end of the war, Göring had recorded twenty-two kills – marking him as a most successful fighter pilot indeed.

Germany's defeat, although clear-cut, was not wrought by a decisive Allied victory on the battlefield, although by 1918, with America now sided with the Allies, it was clear that the Central Powers would ultimately be overwhelmed, and the ground war was not going well for them. Austria-Hungary was collapsing, and manpower for the Central Powers was becoming limited. Nonetheless, Germany's defeat was ultimately wrought by the Allied blockade, causing acute food shortages, the privations involved arguably pushing the German civilian population too far, leading to strikes, beginning in Vienna, initiated by the Bolsheviks, food riots in Germany, and, worse, the Kriegsmarine mutinying and refusing to mount a forlorn, desperate, attack on the mighty RN. Consequently, what was essentially an internal German revolution and the effect of hunger led to the Kaiser abdicating, bringing the First World War to an end on 11 November 1918. There would not, however, be a happy and lasting peace ahead.

After the Kaiser abdicated, the powers of the Imperial Chancellor were handed to Friedrich Ebert, a moderate socialist, and a democratic republic, based at Weimar, was inaugurated. A split soon developed between the moderates of Ebert's Social Democratic Party and the extreme left, meaning there was no united front against the right-wing threat. Weimar was also weakened by not having the army's full support and loyalty, which saw Ebert's moderate socialism as only marginally more desirable than the extreme left's communism.

Weimar soon faced a communist attempt to seize power, which was defeated in bloody street battles by the Freikorps, a paramilitary organisation comprising disaffected, right-wing, former servicemen bitter at Germany's defeat and who felt a passionate duty to continue defending Germany against foreign influences. And so with a weak republic, seen as a puppet of the victorious Allies, Germany descended into a political vacuum fostering extreme politics, to which, in fact, the birth of the far right can be traced.

Against this backdrop of political unrest came the Versailles Peace Settlement of 1919, which did more to lay the foundations for another world war than ever it did those of a lasting peace. The Treaty's terms were announced on 7 May 1919, but only a year before Germany had been on the brink of victory; when the armistice was announced, the Germans had presumed this to be the start of peace negotiations, not a humiliation.

Versailles was, therefore, a crushing blow to national pride, which many thought too harsh – although noteworthily, the Allies' terms were more lenient than those Germany intended to present to the Western powers had it emerged victorious, and those imposed by Germany on Russia. Infamously, though, Versailles included the 'War Guilt' clause, placing firmly at Germany's door full responsibility for causing the First World War, which Weimar had no choice but to accept, angering the German people. Hefty reparations also placed a substantial financial burden on Germany, intended by France to ensure that the Germans did not recover from the war more quickly than itself.

The Germans were incensed by sanctions such as granting the Poles a strip of land providing access to the Baltic at Danzig, effectively dividing Germany in two; and prohibiting reunification with Austria. These sanctions led to brooding resentment of the hated Versailles *Diktat*. Indeed, the creation of minority groups caused by the redrawing of Europe's map would also contribute to the political unrest and extremism soon to develop. Significantly, so far as this narrative is concerned, Versailles, unsurprisingly considering Germany's record in the field and jingoistic culture, reduced the German army to 100,000 volunteers, permitted the *Kriegsmarine* to become just a coastal defence flotilla – with no submarines – and prohibited Germany from having an air force – more of which in due course.

When the First World War ended, a certain German infantry corporal was recovering in Passewalk hospital from the effects of a gas attack. Like countless other Germans he was angry and intensely bitter about Germany's defeat, which he fervently believed was due to German enemies – especially communists and Jews – undermining the country's will to fight, thereby stabbing in the back the servicemen on the battlefields. His name was Adolf Hitler.

In 1919, Hitler – then an army spy – joined the German Workers' Party, which although anti-Semitic and nationalist managed to appeal to the masses. Hitler's brief was to ascertain whether the GWP was a left-wing movement. He became, however, attracted to the party's nationalistic message and wide appeal, so left the army to become the GDP's fifty-fifth member. Becoming politically engaged, his powers of oratory soon impressed his peers and Hitler rose rapidly up the party's hierarchy, even composing the party's manifesto. This naturally attacked the communists and capitalist big business, while conversely promoting the rights of workers; the programme emphasised that Germany's borders must be restored and German citizenship aligned strictly to German ethnicity. In 1920, the GDP morphed into the National Socialist Workers' Party – the NSDAP (*Nationalsozialistiche Deutsche Arbeiterparte*) – better known as the 'Nazis' – of which Hitler became leader.

Unsurprisingly, Göring similarly embraced the 'stab in the back' concept, bitter at Germany's defeat. In short, he joined the ranks of disaffected former servicemen alienated by Weimar, still fostering his deep feelings of romantic patriotism. He too was attracted to the Nazis, and after hearing him speak in 1922, met Hitler who explained his *Weltanschauung* (World View). Göring was mesmerised, and swore an oath of personal allegiance to Hitler. Hitler, needing a distinguished war hero aboard, gave him command of the *Sturmabteilung* (SA), which at the time was a small party police force. It was the start of a long and sinister association.

In this climate of extremism, hyperinflation, bitterness over Versailles and resentment of Weimar, Germany descended into a turbulent time of political fighting, some of it openly and overtly violent, and a series of attempts to seize power by extremist groups. Indeed, the Nazi *Putsch* on Munich, on 8 November 1923, when Hitler planned to seize power and march on Berlin, failed. Hitler was arrested, tried for treason in 1924 and imprisoned at Lansberg, although he served only five months of his five-year sentence. While there, he dictated two volumes of his political testament, *Mein Kampf* ('My Struggle') – which is also significant to this narrative.

Hitler's political manifesto was published in two volumes, in 1925 and 1927. By 1939, it had been translated into eleven languages and sold 5.2 million copies. It was, in short, a Nazi manual, based upon Hitler's extreme racist ideology, declaring Jews 'parasites', asserting Germans as the Aryan Master Race requiring *Lebensraum* – living space – to be achieved through an aggressive expansionist policy.

The truly significant thing about this is that such expansion was aimed firmly eastwards, with Germany overrunning Slavs, the Baltic states and the despised Russian communists. While *Mein Kampf* trumpeted vengeance against France, as far as the West was concerned, Hitler was clear regarding his stance over Britain: it was pointless challenging Britain's sea power, at least not before Germany's domination of the Continent had been secured, and so the two countries should form an alliance. Indeed, according to Hitler, Germany's only potential allies in Europe were Britain and Italy. Hitler much admired the British Empire, in fact, and saw no benefit in its demolition, which he perceived as being more to the benefit of America and Japan than Germany.

Hitler, who in 1933 was democratically elected Chancellor of Germany, and subsequently became sole Führer and supreme warlord, had no early plans to invade Britain. We will, in due course, investigate how and why this changed.

GÖRING, HITLER AND 'MEIN KAMPF'

After failure of the Munich Putsch, in which Göring was wounded, he was a wanted man and fled into exile, enduring poverty and hardship, drifting towards morphine addiction requiring recovery in a Swedish sanitorium. Returning to Germany in 1927, Göring sought Hitler out and rejoined the NSDAP. In a change of fortunes, Göring was selected as a Nazi candidate in the 1928 elections and subsequently became one of the twelve Nazis elected to the Reichstag.

By 1932, Göring was President of the Reichstag, and the following year played an important part in negotiations leading to Hitler becoming Chancellor in 1933. Indeed, it was he who broadcast to the German people on 30 January that year, announcing Hitler's Chancellorship, heralding the Third Reich. Göring's reward for his industry, commitment and loyalty was being made head of the Air Office, which had overseen the secret rebirth of the German Air Force – the *Luftwaffe*.

Ultimately, he wanted authority over an air force independent of the army, believing that a future war could be won by air power alone, and agreed with Hitler that a strong air arm represented a powerful threat, possibly sufficient to even win diplomatic concessions. Both Hitler and Göring at this time, however, remained loyal to the foreign policy laid out in *Mein Kampf*.

Later, unexpected, developments would alter that perspective, at least where Britain was concerned.

Chapter 6

'The Personnel of the Luftwaffe … Took the Oath of Allegiance to the Führer'

The Air Clauses of the Treaty of Versailles in 1919 were intended to end military aviation in Germany, thereby preventing a resurrection of the IGAS. In accordance with these provisions, in 1918 Germany surrendered over 15,000 aircraft and 27,000 aero engines. The Treaty, however, failed to prevent Germany possessing or manufacturing civil aircraft. The opportunity was immediately seized in Germany, therefore, to develop and expand civil and commercial aviation, including airlines, flying clubs, and schools to train both air and ground crews.

Behind this innocent façade, however, the foundations of a new – illegal – air force were soon being laid. As early as 1920 General von Seeckt, the Chief of the Army Command at the Reichswehr Ministerium (Ministry of Defence), was convinced that German military aviation must be revived. Certain officers whose names were later to become famous as commanders in Hitler's Luftwaffe, including Sperrle, Kesselring and Stumpff, were given responsibility for various aspects of military aviation and secreted away in von Seeckt's ministry. Thus the first cornerstone was laid of a renaissance of German air power.

By 1926, Germany was widely considered the most air-minded nation in Europe. The German society for aviation enthusiasts, the Deutscher Luftsportverband, founded in 1920, exceeded 50,000 by the end of that decade. Again, von Seeckt was behind this, encouraging an interest in gliding to circumvent Versailles. Thus Germany had no shortage of air-minded youngsters eager to aspire to powered flight – and who already had air experience.

Although the Paris Air Agreement of 1926 considerably restricted the number of service personnel permitted to fly, von Seeckt succeeded in creating a secret cadre of trained aircrew. These men were trained in the schools set up for the civilian commercial airline *Deutsche Lufthansa*, and in a top-secret military flying training school at Lipetz in Russia. It is widely believed that Hitler and Göring were responsible for the birth of the *Luftwaffe* between 1933–36, but clearly this is untrue: Von Seeckt was.

Furthermore, as Göring was so preoccupied with politics, it fell to another former First World War fighter pilot, Erhard Milch, to oversee the organisation of the new *Reichsluftfahrt Ministerium* (RLM, the Air Ministry). In 1926, Milch had become Director of *Lufthansa*, and under his leadership had built airfields, influenced the German aircraft industry and established high standards of day, night, and blind flying – leading to the airline being the best equipped and trained in Europe.

By 1928, however, government subsidies were cut by half, but that year Milch met Göring, then a member of the Reichstag, who agreed to support Milch and *Lufthansa*. In February 1933, Milch officially became Göring's deputy at the RLM, when appointed Secretary-of-State for Air. In addition to that role, from February 1939, Milch was also Inspector-General of the *Luftwaffe*. It would be remiss not to mention the contribution made by *Generaloberst* Ernst Udet, a famous First World War fighter ace and commander, test-pilot and aerobatic pilot who joined the new *Luftwaffe* in June 1935.

In February 1936, Udet became inspector of fighters and dive-bombers, and four months later Director of the RLM's technical department, responsible for developing and procuring military aircraft. Considering the excellent modern aircraft Germany produced during this period, Udet has also earned his place in the history of the *Luftwaffe*'s rebirth. Indeed, in addition to Von Seeckt, who had even argued early on for an independent air force, the new air force owed as much to Milch and Udet, and, in reality, substantially less to Hitler and Göring.

The German historian Wilhelm Deist rightly argued:

> Between 1933 and 1939, Germany's neighbouring states regarded the build-up of the *Luftwaffe* as the most dangerous existing threat to their security. The aeroplane even more than the tank was viewed as the offensive weapon of the future, its potential effects seeming to embody both the totality and the brutality of modern warfare.

Indeed, air power was certainly seen as fundamental to the achievement of Hitler's expansionist aims in foreign policy. At first Hitler intended to achieve Lebensraum in the East. Britain, he thought, would either ally itself with him or at least not intervene. It soon became clear, however, that Britain was likely to oppose Hitler's intentions, from which point onwards Hitler had to consider a major war against Britain, and mobilise German resources rapidly. Initially, therefore, the Luftwaffe was conceived as a comparatively short-range force in anticipation of war with Germany's Polish neighbour to the east, and French to the west.

Nonetheless, it was the people of Britain who feared German air attack more than any other nation. This concern was increased when Nazi Germany withdrew from the League of Nations and the disarmament conference in 1933. The following year Baldwin, who had famously endorsed the view that 'the bomber would always get through', told the House of Commons that Germany's progress in military aviation meant that the aerial defence of Britain 'no longer began at the White Cliffs of Dover but at the Rhine'.

In 1935 Hitler was sufficiently confident to blatantly contravene Versailles and reveal to the world his new Luftwaffe – making Göring Commander-in-Chief of what was, at last, an independent force, subordinate only to the Oberkommando der Wehrmacht (OKW, Supreme High Command of the Armed Forces). Immediately, Göring began politicising the new air force's leadership, but it was not until a year later when he created an air staff under a confirmed National Socialist, namely *Oberstleutnant* (later *Feldmarschall*) Albert Kesselring.

A former artillery officer, 'Smiling Albert' had transferred to the Air Ministry in 1933, heading up the administration branch before becoming *Luftwaffe* Chief of Staff and a *Generalleutnant* in 1936. Kesselring wrote:

> The personnel of the Luftwaffe, like all other members of the Wehrmacht, took the oath of allegiance to the Führer; they considered themselves unresolvedly bound by it ... and kept it loyally. Hermann Göring ... a National Socialist and man of grandiose ideas ... though he exacted a great deal he left the generals in the Air Ministry the greatest possible freedom of action and screened us from interference by the politicians.
>
> During my long military career I never felt so free from outside influence as when I was administrative chief of the Air Ministry, Luftwaffe Chief of Staff and a service commander during the formative years of the air force from 1933. As members of the Luftwaffe, enjoying protection of the prodigious personality of the Commander-in-Chief, we were welcomed in every social sphere, including the NSDAP.
>
> Like all prominent Wehrmacht, state and army officials, we went as guests of the Führer to the Nuremberg Party Festival, and the Goslar Harvest Festival in honour of the peasantry. We also appeared at ceremonies in remembrance of the war dead, at the parades on Hitler's birthday, banquets in honour of distinguished foreign visitors and all big Wehrmacht occasions.
>
> I confess much of what I saw made a strong impression on me and I admired their brilliant and smooth-running organisation.

Indeed, it is difficult not to be impressed by the pageantry of the Nuremburg rallies, which Hitler bade the German director Leni Riefenstahl immortalise in her film *Triumph des Willens* ('Triumph of the Will') in 1935 (see Bibliography). This kind of regimented, perfectly choreographed performance appealed perfectly to the orderly German military mind.

Kesselring continued: 'It was possible to ignore the less pleasing things. I had no occasion for criticism, since in the circles in which I moved there was no evidence of serious excesses.'

Nonetheless, there was evidence enough of the Jews in Germany being openly discriminated against and, indeed, violently persecuted and humiliated after the Nazis came to power, so it is difficult to understand what Kesselring means by 'serious excesses'.

Although Kesselring also claimed that 'no attempt was made by leading politicians to bring us into the National Socialist fold', and claimed 'indifference to political events', he was 'obliged to admit' that 'was a mistake'. The point, however, is that, like other branches of the Wehrmacht, the Luftwaffe had sworn a personal oath to the Nazi dictator, Hitler, and clearly senior air force officers like Kesselring were impressed by the Nazis and what was happening in Germany. The new German air force was, therefore, bound directly to the Nazi story – not least considering that on 30 August 1939, Hitler appointed Göring chairman of the new German war cabinet, and on 1 September 1939, after Germany had invaded Poland that morning, announced him as deputy Führer and political successor.

Owing to the Luftwaffe's growth, 1939 also saw a reorganisation of command structure. Milch assumed both offices of Secretary-of-State for Air and Luftwaffe Inspector General. Kesselring had already been replaced as Chief of Staff by General Hans-Jürgen Stumpff in 1937, and in the reshuffle was given command of an air fleet, Luftwaffengruppenkommando 1; 2 went to General Hellmuth Felmy, although he would be replaced by Kesselring in January 1940; under Kesselring, Luftflotte 2, as it had become, would play a primary role in the West. When Kesselring replaced Felmy, his place commanding Luftwaffengruppenkommando 1 was taken by Stumpff, replaced as Chief of Staff by Generaloberst Hans Jeschonnek.

In May 1940, Stumpff would take over Luftflotte 5, based in Norway. Luftwaffengruppenkommando 3, the forerunner of Luftflotte 3, went to Generalmajor Hugo Sperrle, another army officer turned flier. Having served in the *Reichswehr* (the limited armed force permitted by Versailles) during the Weimar period, Sperrle was promoted after Hitler came to power and commanded the 'Condor Legion' – Germany's expeditionary force supporting the fascist General Franco during the Spanish Civil War (much more of which in due course), between 1936 and 1937.

All of these high commanders had Göring and Hitler to thank for their appointments – and would soon play significant parts in the campaign against the West.

Chapter 7

Messerschmitts, Spain and Mölders

At its inception, the new, independent, Luftwaffe's strength stood at 1,888 aircraft of all types and 20,000 personnel, supported by between thirty and forty airframe and engine manufacturers. The *Luftwaffe* immediately began improving its aircraft, testing them in competitions all over Europe and in large-scale air exercises at home. Influenced by the same factors as British aircraft designers, the emphasis on German aircraft development in the mid-1930s revolved around the monoplane.

By 1935, the prototypes of many German aircraft which would become so familiar in the Second World War began appearing. In 1920, Professor Hugo Junkers had opened a factory in Dessau; in 1922, Ernest Heinkel built at aircraft factory at Warnemuende; Claude Dornier began production in Friedrichshafen; in 1924 Heinrich Focke and George Wulf founded the Focke-Wulf aircraft company at Bremen. While all of these would produce bombers and fighters, providing the mainstay of the Luftwaffe throughout 1939–45, most importantly Professor Willy Messerschmitt took over the Bayerische Flugzeugwerke (BFW) at Augsburg and began producing sporting aeroplanes.

By 1934, Messerschmitt had designed a monoplane, the Me 108 Taifun, as an entrant in an international aviation contest, the Challenge International de Tourisme, held in Poland. Although the 108 came fifth, sixth and tenth, its 'overall performance', wrote the German expert Uwe Feist, 'was impressive'. Already though, Messerschmitt was working on a new monoplane fighter incorporating the features found in his Taifun – which was an advanced starting-point for such development.

During 1933, the technical department of the RLM, known as C-*Amt*, reported on the conclusions of research concerning applying modern technology to air combat. C-*Amt* considered that to meet future needs of German air power, four types of military aircraft were needed: a multi-seat medium bomber, a tactical bomber, a single-seat fighter and a two-seater fighter. The single-seater, which would replace the existing He 51 and Ar 68 biplane fighters, was required to have a top speed of at least 250 mph at 19,690ft, achieving that height in seventeen minutes with a maximum operational ceiling of 30,000ft.

Thus far, the German requirement was almost identical to the RAF specifications F.36/34 and F.37/34. Submissions were made by Arado, Focke-Wulf, Heinkel and BFW. Designs by the first two companies were immediately rejected, leaving

Heinkel's He 112 and Messerschmitt's Me 109. Messerschmitt's new fighter first flew in May 1935 – six months before the Hawker Hurricane and nearly a year before the Supermarine Spitfire. Although the He 112 compared favourably to the Me 109, according to Hough and Richards 'a combination of superior salesmanship and swifter development won the day for the Augsburg company'.

Messerschmitt's new monoplane fighter was based entirely upon the principle of producing the smallest and therefore lightest airframe around the most powerful engine – initially a Rolls-Royce Kestrel. The so-called 'Augsburg Eagle' featured a metal-alloy framework, flush-riveted stressed metal covering, leading-edge wing slots in conjunction with slotted trailing-edge flaps which increased the wing area upon demand, retractable main undercarriage, and an enclosed cockpit with a jettisonable canopy – another far-sighted consideration.

As there was no requirement for wing-mounted armament, the 109's wing was extremely thin, the main spar being situated at the mid-chord point. In fact, it became necessary to strengthen the join of the wings and fuselage. Torque also caused landing problems, exacerbated by the narrow track undercarriage. The 109 was initially armed with two nose-mounted 7.92 mm machine-guns and, like the first Hurricanes and Spitfires, a wooden fixed-pitch propeller.

After extensive testing at Tavemünde, the 109 was officially declared the winning design and awarded a production contract. According to Mason, 'no authentic figures have ever been traced relating to the performance of the prototype 109s, it is unlikely that the Kestrel-powered 109V-1 exceeded 280 mph'. The first production model, the B-1, however, was powered by the Junkers Jumo 210D, and achieved 292 mph at 13,100ft, reaching 19,700ft in 9.8 minutes. In April 1937, *Jagdgeschwader Richthofen* became the first unit to replace their obsolete He 51s with the new 109. Messerschmitt's fighter therefore entered operational service before both its British contemporaries.

The development of other German monoplanes used in the forthcoming Battle of Britain must also be examined. The spring of 1937 saw the Ju 87 Stuka, a single-engine crank-winged monoplane dive-bomber enter service. With a crew of two, sitting back-to-back, the Stuka's top speed was only 232 mph – slower than any of the Luftwaffe's medium bombers. Classified as a short-range moderate performance machine, the Ju 87's virtues had nothing to do with its speed, range, or bomb load, but everything to do with the accuracy of bombing made possible by its unique design. The other enemy aircraft were all twin-engine.

In 1935, the Heinkel He 111 medium bomber first flew and was in service by 1937, with a top speed of 255 mph. The Dornier Do 17, another medium bomber, also made its maiden flight in 1935. At an international flying event held at Zurich in 1937, this so-called 'Flying Pencil' outpaced all interceptors present at 265 mph.

The best German medium bomber, the Junkers Ju 88, did not fly until December 1936, though, and when war broke out remained at the pre-production development stage. Rapidly pressed into service, the 88's top speed was 286 mph. These were all comparatively fast and modern warplanes, and what proved a massive advantage when the Second World War began, Hitler was able to test some of these designs in actual combat conditions during the Spanish Civil War. The experience gained was immense, putting the Luftwaffe far ahead of the RAF – which could only evaluate its new fighters in totally inadequate and artificial air exercises, all of which were based upon supposition and perceptions rather than reality.

German intervention in the Spanish Civil War began in August 1936, when twenty Ju 52 transport aircraft and six He 51 fighters were despatched to assist General Franco's fascist forces. More fighters followed, with pilots to fly them. It soon became clear, though, that such a small number of German fighters could make no impression on the conflict's outcome, not least because the He 51 was inferior to the Russian- and American-built fighters flown by the Republicans.

The decision was therefore made to send a powerful German force – the Condor Legion – to Franco's aid. Without doubt, the Spanish Civil War represented a unique opportunity between the wars for the development of modern air power under actual combat conditions. In this conflict the Wehrmacht tested new weapons and tactics.

For the Luftwaffe, Spain became an essential proving ground for the new monoplanes, although these did not arrive in Spain until the early summer of 1937. Air superiority, however, was soon achieved and maintained, thus providing an early indication of the monoplane's superiority.

As the Condor Legion veteran and expert German fighter pilot Adolf Galland wrote, the Me 109s 'were mainly intended to combat the numerous Curtiss and Rata fighters, either as lone wolves or when escorting bombers formations. The Me 109 was definitely superior to them and shot down a great number, the record for "kills" being held by *Leutnant* Harder, until eventually Mölders topped his figure.'

Upon arrival in Spain, Werner Mölders succeeded Galland in command of 3/J 88, which was converting to Me 109s; with a full complement of 109s, Mölders was instrumental in working out the mechanics of combat tactics with the new monoplane fighter – and was uniquely placed to do so, achieving fourteen personal victories over Spain in the process.

Mölders rapidly realised that fighter combat was fast and furious, a cut and thrust affair often lasting but a matter of minutes. Given the high speed and manoeuvrability of the new monoplane fighters it was quickly realised that inflexible formation attacks – such as those being practised and rigidly enforced by Fighter Command – were totally inappropriate. Fluency and fluidity were actually required. Pilots needed to keep a sharp lookout – because enemy fighters could appear and attack in a very short time, owing to the speeds now involved, and be able to break and respond to any given tactical situation – be that from a perspective of defence or attack.

What was required now, Mölders discovered, was a combat formation based upon the fighting pair, not a squadron of twelve aircraft flying cohesively in sections of three and in close formation, as practised by the RAF. Conversely, the fighting pair, or *Rotte*, developed by Mölders, comprised leader and wingman, and before battle was joined the *Rotte* operated as part of a *Schwarm* of two *Rotten*. This section of four cruised in line abreast, each aircraft some 200 yards apart, slightly stepped up, permitting pilots the freedom to search for the enemy instead of concentrating on avoiding collision with their neighbour. When battle commenced the *Schwarm* broke into two *Rotten*, each *Rottenführer*'s (leader of each pair) job was to shoot down the enemy while his tail was protected by his wingman, or *Katschmarek*.

Air Vice-Marshal Johnnie Johnson, officially the top scoring RAF fighter pilot of the Second World War, commented on the *Schwarm*: 'We used to see the 109s flying this loose, flexible, formation, alert, like the four fingers of an outstretched hand. I always thought that they looked aggressive, ready for anything, like a pack of hunting dogs.'

Much later, after bitter experience, the RAF copied the *Schwarm*, calling it the 'Finger Four' or 'Crossover Four'. In 1936 and 1937, however, those days were a long way off.

Mölders' new tactics helped Stumpff's Condor Legion achieve air superiority in 1937, which it never lost over Spain. The balance sheet indicated seventy-two German combat losses against 327 Republican aircraft destroyed. Upon return from Spain, Mölders wrote a new manual of fighter tactics for the monoplane, which became standard operating procedure throughout the Luftwaffe – earning for himself the nickname *Vati* – father – of the German *Jagdwaffe* (fighter force).

Spain was also important to the Germans because it was there they developed close-support tactics between the air force and army. According to the official British history, the *Rise and Fall of the German Air Force 1933-45*, this development was the 'only revolutionary' conclusion drawn from the Germans' experience in Spain. Although tactical air-to-ground cooperation would become an essential feature of Germany's new Blitzkrieg tactics, this cannot be considered correct. Mölders work with the new monoplane fighters was equally, if not more, 'revolutionary' – so much so that all these years later his ideas remain the basis of fighter combat.

Given that today's fighters are highly sophisticated and computerised fast jets achieving speeds unimaginable in 1937, this can only be considered remarkable. The understanding of fighter tactics gained in Spain would be a huge advantage to the Luftwaffe in the early stages of the Second World War, although, interestingly the Spanish experience led to the Luftwaffe over-estimating the abilities of their new monoplane bombers. The new He 111 had encountered only slight opposition, inclining the Germans to believe that they could be operated with only light fighter protection. Moreover, the Germans believed that the fast medium-bomber could be used in a devastating strategic role, providing only weak fighter opposition existed.

If RAF fighter tactics would soon be found wanting, however, the Luftwaffe's inaccurate perception of its medium bombers would likewise be shot down in flames. Nonetheless, the bomber emerged from Spain confirmed as the most feared weapon so far created by man. This was because of one word: Guernica.

Guernica was a Basque village with a population of around 5,000. Standing between Franco's forces and the capture of Bilbao, it became crucial to the war in northern Spain. The town had no anti-aircraft guns and defensive sorties by Republican aircraft were not a consideration, due to recent heavy losses. The target was of military importance: the road network and bridge in the suburb of Renteria. The raid was a combined operation between the Germans and Italians, involving twenty-three aircraft carrying twenty-two tons of bombs.

After the bombing, Me 109s and He 51s strafed the roads around the target. The attack failed to confine itself to the intended, legitimate, military target and destroyed most of the defenceless village. At the time, civilian casualties were reported as 1,654, although more recent research indicates a death toll of up to 400. Nonetheless, the raid was perceived as a deliberate terror attack aimed entirely a defenceless civilian population and confirmed the fear of air power prevalent throughout the 1930s. The world's media became virtually hysterical and Guernica's suffering was immortalised in Picasso's stark and emotive rendition of the tortured souls who suffered and died in this unprecedented air attack.

German air doctrine did not, in reality, revolve around terror bombing, however. In fact the indiscriminate bombing of cities was regarded as largely wasted effort and potentially counter-productive. The Italian fascist dictator Benito Mussolini also sent troops to Spain, and in March 1938 his Regia Aeronautica unleashed heavy attacks on Barcelona lasting several days, causing 1,300 casualties.

Although initially the shocked survivors were demoralised, once they recovered the main emotion was anger and defiance. The Germans realised, therefore, that such bombing could actually increase the enemy's will to resist, rather than be completely demoralising, as the Italian air theorist General Douhet believed. Consequently *Luftwaffe* air power doctrine concentrated on supporting land operations, but, nonetheless, in Spain the bomber had, indeed, always got through and the global fear of it appeared completely justified. So far as Dowding was concerned in Britain, events in Spain only served to convince him that a strong fighter force was an absolute priority.

So far as the development of the Me 109 was concerned, the unique opportunity to evaluate and improve the new fighter in actual combat conditions was an immeasurable bonus. The 109 was so clearly the best fighter in Spanish skies that production of it was accelerated, so that it replaced the He 51 biplane well ahead of schedule. Already, in July and August 1937, the Germans had shown off the 109 to the aeronautical world at the Fourth International Flying Meeting held at Zurich. Five 109s were entered by the German team, which out-performed the competition, with Carl Francke setting a new speed record of 254 mph.

On 11 November 1937, an Me 109 V-13 set a new land-speed record at 379.38 mph. This unprecedented speed was made possible because of a new engine: the Daimler-Benz 601, which would become to the German fighter what the Rolls-Royce Merlin was to both the Hurricane and Spitfire. By the end of that year, production problems concerning the new engine had been overcome, so it could from then onwards be fitted to production 109s. So was born the Me 109E variant, known affectionately as the *Emil*, and which entered service in early 1939. It was this aircraft, in fact, which equipped the *Jagdwaffe* during the battles of 1940. Another significant milestone had been reached.

Spitfires and Hurricanes during the Battle of Britain period were powered by the Merlin III, the maximum power of which – 1,310 hp – was achieved at 9,000ft. The DB601A's maximum power was 1,036 hp at 5,250ft. The Merlin III, in fact, was a more powerful engine at all altitudes. The DB601A enjoyed one great advantage over the Merlin, though: it was fuel injected. This meant that the fuel supply was unaffected by gravity – unlike the Merlin's float-type carburettor that was affected by negative-G. Consequently it would be discovered that fuel injection always permitted the 109 to outpace a Spitfire or Hurricane in the dive, because, unlike the RAF fighters, its engine did not momentarily cut out. The DB601A also had the advantage in fuel consumption.

Another improvement to the early 109s was that the original fixed-pitch propeller was soon replaced by the three-bladed VDM 'controllable-pitch' airscrew. This was the equivalent of the British Constant Speed (CS) propeller, permitting rotation of the blades through 360° and therefore enabling the pilot to select optimum pitch for any situation. The British fighters were first updated to the two-pitch propeller which, although better than the original fixed-pitch design, was but a half-way house (although the CS propeller was ultimately fitted as standard to production aircraft, during the Battle of Britain the conversion from two-pitch to CS aircrews was actually undertaken on the fighter stations by de Havilland engineers). The new propeller increased the Spitfire's rate of climb by 730ft per minute. This is another indication that British aircraft designers were actually behind their German counterparts – who, like the air and ground crews involved, learned many lessons from the Spanish Civil War.

The matter of the Me 109's armament is an interesting one. The armament required by a new monoplane fighter was a matter in which the German planners were initially behind the British. In 1932, Wing Commander Arthur Thomson suggested that, in future, fighters should have eight guns capable of firing 1,000 rounds per minute. Thomson's thoughts revolved entirely around the rifle-calibre machine-guns that had been used in the Great War – in which he had flown as a flight commander in Dowding's 16 Squadron. An armament expert, Squadron Leader Ralph Sorley, endorsed this view in 1934, claiming that multiple machine-guns would be necessary to destroy modern bombers – which were now made of metal and enjoyed the benefits of armour plate.

Dowding agreed and included the requirement for eight machine-guns in his specification for the RAF's new fighters. Hitherto, fighters' machine-guns had been mounted in front of the pilot, but it was impossible to locate eight guns this way. The only feature capable of accommodating the guns was the wings. German designers, however, were naturally unaware of this and so the first 109s were designed with two engine-cowl mounted 7.92 mm machine-guns.

Another of these MG 17s was engine-mounted, to fire through the propeller hub, but this was unsuccessful. The news that the British were using eight machine-guns led to a rapid rethink. The problem was that the 109's wings were so thin that they were not strong enough to carry more than two guns, the additional hitting power of which was inconsequential when offset against the technical difficulties involved with fitting them. The answer was to use cannon in the wings rather than machine-guns – one in each wing, in addition to the nose-mounted machine-guns.

The weapon chosen was the MG-FF 20mm cannon made by Oerlikon. The cannon's muzzle velocity, however, was much lower than a machine-gun: eight rounds per second offset against seventeen respectively. Consequently, it was a weapon better suited to an above average shot – the 'spread' of fire from a battery of fast-firing machine-guns being more forgiving, and similar to the effect of a shotgun. Nonetheless, the cannon's destructive power was supreme – just one strike from an explosive 20mm round could be fatal. The Oerlikon carried sixty rounds per cannon, the ammunition drum being accommodated by way of blisters on both wing surfaces.

In the fighting ahead, cannon would provide the 109e with another advantage: the German fighter, having both rapid firing machine-guns and the slower but heavier cannon, enjoyed the best of both worlds. The generally accepted view, however, is that the 109 was cannon-armed because the German designers recognised the great benefits of this weapon whereas the British did not. This is not true. The fitting of cannon arose simply because the Germans underestimated the number of machine-guns that the British would use and, being unable to wing mount a sufficient number of extra rifle calibre guns compromised by using cannon. It was arguably a reactive compromise – but one that would prove a happy one for the *jagdfliegern*.

Cannon also featured in the armament of another fighter produced by Messerschmitt – the twin-engine Me 110 *Zerstörer*. With a crew of two sitting back-to-back, the 110 was intended as an invincible long-range escort fighter able to clear the path ahead for bomber formations. Although first flown in 1936, like the Ju 88 it did not enter production until 1939, and was not, therefore, tested in Spain. It was heavily armed, with four forward-firing machine-guns in addition to two 20mm cannon, and a rearward-firing machine-gun for defence. Capable of 350 mph at 23,000ft, it was faster than the Hurricane but slower than the Spitfire. Ultimately, however, the 110 overall proved unsuccessful in its intended role because it was not manoeuvrable enough to deal with the British single-engine fighters.

As the 1930s began drawing to a close, the *Luftwaffe*'s expansion gathered in momentum. In 1937 the *Luftwaffe*'s front-line strength was between 2,000 and 2,500 aircraft of all types. By August 1938 it had increased to 2,900. That year, Germany produced 5,235 military aircraft – 8,295 in 1939. Britain's figures for the same years were 2,827 and 7,940 respectively. On the eve of war, at the end of August 1939, *Luftwaffe* strength stood at 3,750, of which 850 were Me 109s. According to Air Ministry Pamphlet 248,

> the German conception of the employment of fighter aircraft was not in a very developed stage on the eve of war. The majority of the fighter force was intended for deployment over the battle area ... In support of ground units one of the main functions of the single-engine fighter units was to prevent or hinder activities by enemy reconnaissance aircraft. In addition, single-engine fighter units were intended to protect and escort bomber and dive-bomber formations operating against enemy ground target.

From this it is clear that the *Luftwaffe* had not considered the kind of protracted strategic offensive air operations that became necessary during the summer of 1940. The intention was to fight a series of short, sharp, wars using fast-moving ground forces supported by flying artillery – *Blitzkrieg*. German air policy concentrated on bombing, based upon Douhet. This is evident by the fact that at the outbreak of war, 40 per cent of *Luftwaffe* units were bomber or dive-bomber units, while only 25 per cent were fighters. So although much has rightly been made of the opportunity provided by Spain, not even the Germans had got air power doctrine right as yet.

Even though the *Luftwaffe* had the most up-to-date combat experience, and overall was equipped with excellent aircraft, it was not a flawless foe. Still, from a perspective of day-fighter warfare, regardless of the confusion as to how best to employ fighters generally, in the event of contact with enemy fighters the German pilots had a huge edge: Mölders had rewritten the book of fighter tactics, based upon his experience in Spain, and these tactics were now standard operating procedure throughout the *Jagdwaffe*. Moreover, as the British Air Ministry observed: 'There is no doubt that in 1939 the Me 109 was superior to any Allied fighter except the Spitfire which, however, was then only available to the RAF in small numbers.'

When war eventually broke out and the opposing air forces met head-to-head, however, the importance of the Me 109 and excellence of the German fighter tactics would become all too evident.

Chapter 8

'Barking Creek' and 'A Queer War'

On the night of 31 August 1939, Nazi Germany invaded Poland in an undeclared act of war. Simultaneously, German troops crossed the frontier along its entire length, attacking guards and forward defensive positions. At dawn, the *Luftwaffe* bombed aerodromes and major strategic assets throughout Poland. In spite of all the diplomatic unrest that summer, the German attack achieved complete surprise.

The first day of mobilisation in Poland was, however, 31 August, with reservists reporting to their units and operational squadrons dispersing to various airfields. Few, though, believed that war would actually break out, the reservists expected little but an inconveniently long stay with the colours ahead of them. The Poles trusted that Britain and France would honour their pledge to support Poland in the event of Nazi aggression, and mistakenly believed that this would be sufficient to deter Herr Hitler. Many expected the Soviets to side with the Western Allies, unaware of the secret Non-Aggression Pact signed by the foreign ministers of Germany and Russia on 23 August. On that day, Poland's fate was sealed.

At 11.00 hrs on Sunday, 3 September 1939, Britain and France declared war on Nazi Germany following Hitler ignoring their ultimatum to withdraw from Poland, although in reality the Western powers were not geographically positioned to provide military support. In real terms, Poland was on her own.

Sixty-three German divisions attacked Poland, facing fifty-six Polish. The German attack was spearheaded by fifteen mechanised *panzer* divisions, whereas the Poles only fielded two motorised formations. Indeed, the enemy's superiority of arms was considered 8:1. Moreover, the German *Wehrmacht* was a modern force, equipped and armed to current standards, whereas Poland went to war with the equipment of 1925. Importantly, Germany's diplomatic successes of 1938 and 1939 had secured strategic advantages in that Poland's northern frontier and most of the southern was controlled by Germany, and the attack was made simultaneously from north, south, east and west. Offensives on both flanks and steady pressure in the centre enveloped Poland. Nonetheless, by the campaign's ninth day, German losses were such that it was clear they had overlooked the determined fighting spirit of the Poles – a factor emphasised by the propaganda machine that prepared German public opinion for news of heavy casualties. This fighting spirit, in fact, would define the Polish contribution to the Allied cause throughout the hard-fought Second World War.

'BARKING CREEK' AND 'A QUEER WAR'

In 1939, Poland, even more than Britain and France, was ill-prepared for a war in which air power played a crucial role. The immense capital investment required to create and maintain a modern air force was quite simply beyond the means of a newly independent country. The technical inferiority of its air force made Poland vulnerable – but the bravery of her aircrews was beyond doubt. The first German aircraft to be destroyed during the Second World War were two Do 17s shot down over Olkusz by Lieutenant W. Gnys; the Polish fighter pilots destroyed 126 enemy aircraft in total during the campaign. It would not be enough.

At 11.15 hrs on Sunday 3 September 1939, the British Prime Minister, Neville Chamberlain, spoke to the nation:

> This morning the British Ambassador in Berlin handed the German Government a final note stating that unless we heard from them by 11.00 a.m. that they were prepared at once to withdraw their troops from Poland, a state of war would exist between us. I have to tell you that no such undertaking has been received, and that consequently this country is at war with German.

Lieutenant The Master of Forbes was a platoon commander in the 3rd Battalion, Grenadier Guards, and recalled that fateful morning:

> While the Battalion was engaged in constructing air-raid trenches, we were told that a special announcement was to be broadcast on the wireless at 1115 hrs. All of the officers foregathered in the Officers' Mess, where we heard the Prime Minister announce to the nation that we were at war with Germany. There was no alternative: the chips were down.

Guardsman Percy Nash, also of the 3rd Grenadiers:

> When war was declared I couldn't wait to get some action, that was what I had joined for, after all. I think we were all prepared to do whatever was required of us.

There was, however, none of the popular excitement that had greeted the outbreak of war in 1914; the British attitude was 'Let's get it over with', and in France 'Il faut en finir'.

For some, the war was a welcome release from drudgery and an exciting opportunity for adventure, as Sergeant Ken Wilkinson recalled:

> Soon after my seventeenth birthday, my father asked me if I would like to fly in the RAF. Of course there was only one answer: yes! Applications could only be made at seventeen and three-quarters,

so before that father arranged for me to fly in a service aircraft, to ensure that I was OK with flying. Earlier, I'd had flights in an aircraft of Alan Cobham's Flying Circus, which cost five shillings, but that wasn't really an indication of my suitability, just involving a take-off, straight and level flying, and a landing.

So it was that I went to Brockworth aerodrome to fly with John Summers, brother of Supermarine test pilot 'Mutt', who flew the prototype Spitfire, K5054, on its first flight. We flew in a Hawker Hartebeeste, built for the South African Air Force, which was basically a Hawker Hart light day bomber; I was in the rear gunner's seat, facing backwards. The flight was certainly thrilling – even looking backwards. John carried out aerobatics, which were part of the test. After a while we landed and I expressed gratitude for the great favour I had received. Sometime later I discovered that John had been grateful to have someone in the back, as ballast, otherwise he would have flown with a sack!

In due course I was unsuccessful in my application for a SSC. That was just as well, as it turned out, because during the war I met a successful candidate who had been poorly paid during peacetime and miserable not to go into it with the rest of us when the balloon went up in 1939. The next option for me was joining the RAFVR, but as I was travelling around the country for various jobs, opportunities were limited until I was told that there were vacancies at Staverton, near my home in Cheltenham. I was then working in Birmingham, so I gave my notice, got a job in Cheltenham, and applied to the VR: again, an interview and another medical. I was surrounded by big, beefy, fellows who positively exuded fitness – while I had been out dancing the previous night! Strangely, I passed, they didn't; I was attested the same day.

The following morning, I went to Staverton airfield, made myself known to the instructors, and had my first flight in a Tiger Moth – thus properly starting my flying career. Within a day or so, I was told that there was a vacancy for the fifteen days of annual training, so I applied to go. Once more I gave in my notice and started full-time flying training. Obviously, as a result, I went solo fairly quickly. When we were flying, pupils sat outside, watching those in the air, and listening to the instructors and others. The days passed thus: cycle to Staverton, flying training, cycle home, then ground training at night school.

Then I got a job with the test flight department at Rotol, at Staverton, working for the test pilot. My social life became Aircraft 2, Girls 0, and the girl I intended to marry ditched me and went off with a chap who worked for Cheltenham council. At that time,

'BARKING CREEK' AND 'A QUEER WAR'

I had decided to become a curate, and in order to raise the necessary money for theological college, I had agreed with said girl that I should join the RAF for four to six years, after which I would have both the money and the ability to fly and navigate aircraft. Despite that agreement I was ditched, but that meant I could concentrate on flying training and ground school – which I did.

I passed the elementary flying on Tiger Moths, and went on to fly Hawker Harts. While working at Rotol, I got in quite a few hours flying time, including odd things like ferrying new aircraft to RAF aerodromes – where the sight of a pilot in 'civvies' was rare. Then came 1 September 1939: we were all called into the test pilot's office and told that we were in reserved occupations. When my turn came to speak, I said that I hadn't joined the RAFVR for that – and took my leave of Rotol. On 3 September 1939, war began – and I was gainfully employed again.

Having been a small peacetime air force, general mobilisation at the end of August and beginning of September 1939 literally expanded and changed the RAF's composition virtually overnight. The RAFVR was called to full-time service, and the AAF was placed on a war footing.

Sergeant Ken Wilkinson:

When the VR reported for duty at Cheltenham headquarters, one of the pilots was called Perkins. He was the MP for Stroud and told us that he had been talking to Neville Chamberlain, the Prime Minister, who thought war would be over by Christmas; how wrong he was. During the summer of 1939, pupil pilots would go off to the Severn, generally Wainlodes, drink beer, have bread and cheese, which allowed us to carry on drinking until 11 pm. We'd then strip off, swim the Severn and go back.

Some of us then had to get on our bikes and cycle twelve miles to Cheltenham. Other VR members were posted off, to continue their service flying training, but I stayed at VR HQ, assembling equipment and packing it up in cases. You get to know what makes a Rolls-Royce Kestrel engine when you have to put it back together again. Once or twice I had to take parties to places like Cambridge, for them to continue training, then return to Cheltenham. All comparatively dull, until December, when I was about the last to be posted, and went to the Initial Training Wing (ITW) at Marine Court, on the sea front at Hastings: my RAF career had finally begun.

The ITW was really intended to occupy us with Physical Training (PT), drill and sport, but there were also exams in various subjects. Marine Court was a block of luxury flats, which had been cleared out and requisitioned by the RAF. We were on the top floor (no lifts). We discovered that if we failed we would be re-mustered as air gunners. The majority passed everything. Although we were not actually flying, we were treated very well and a lot of famous people came to see us.

In RAF terms, the most important was Billy Bishop, a Canadian VC and Great War fighter pilot. I was in charge of the guard, and asked him if he wished to inspect us; he took one look and declined! Len Harvey, the lightweight champion boxer, gave us lessons on the stage, and we were entertained by stars including Marlene Dietrich.

On the day Germany invaded Poland, 3,000 reservists of the British Army Reserve were recalled to the colours; two days later, by the declaration of war, the British Army numbered 1,065,000 men, of which 160,000 were allocated to the BEF, commanded by General The Viscount Gort VC. Britain had maintained a comparatively small regular army between the wars, and so a significant proportion of Gort's force comprised reservists and units of the recently expanded Territorial Army (TA), all mobilised for service on the continent.

The BEF's move to France began on 10 September 1939, it being believed that Britain's battles would again be fought in France. There the BEF dug in along the Franco-Belgian border, having been denied access to Belgium itself, the Belgian king determined to remain neutral. The Allied strategy was one of static defence, there being little or no question of an offensive being launched against Germany.

The key to this Allied strategy was the heavily fortified Maginot Line, but this was incomplete, extending northwards only as far as the Franco-Belgian border at Longwy. Aware of this, the Allies were haunted by traumatic memories of the German Schlieffen Plan of 1914: a massive sweeping thrust through Belgium, aimed at Paris. While Allied plans, however, were based around those of 1918, German generals were making plans based upon modern weapons and fast moving troops closely supported by aircraft. It was to the vulnerable northern flank of the Allied position that the BEF was deployed, and there Gort's men settled down to the so-called 'Sitzkrieg', as both sides sat out the winter in anticipation of campaigning weather the following spring.

The Advanced Air Striking Force (AASF) also went to France, initially envisaged as a Bomber Command commitment rather than to support the BEF. The BEF comprised squadrons of light-bombers, army cooperation units and four fighter squadrons. This, however, provided Air Chief Marshal Dowding a dilemma. As the Commander-in-Chief of Fighter Command, his priority was, of course, home defence. The figure of four AASF fighter squadrons had been included in the final peacetime air defence plan, which perceived forty-six squadrons being required and provided for air defence, three for the defence of Scapa Flow and Northern Ireland, and four each for trade protection and the AASF.

'BARKING CREEK' AND 'A QUEER WAR'

The intention was that the four fighter squadrons bound for France would be Blenheim-equipped, but Dowding argued that a fighter operating close to and over a battlefield needed a high rate of climb and speed. Consequently the Air Staff decided to send Hurricanes instead, thereby depleting Dowding's limited Home Defence force by four precious single-engine fighter squadrons. In addition to those four squadrons, Dowding also faced losing replacement aircraft needed to make good their losses in France. Myth has it that Dowding sent Hurricanes to France instead of the superior Spitfire, which were fewer in number, preserving Mitchell's precious fighter for the defence of Britain. While Dowding must surely have been anxious even at this early stage to preserve his Spitfires, it was the Air Staff which decided to send Hurricanes alone, not Dowding – and that Hurricanes went at all was actually because of Dowding's memorandum. It was probably the one-time Fighter Command's stoic chief wished he had kept quiet counsel.

When war broke out, following years of Germany propagandising the destructive power of its air force, Britain fully expected the dreaded 'knockout blow'. Indeed, Londoners believed that Armageddon had arrived when the sirens wailed at 11.27 hrs that Sunday morning. It was a false alarm, the first of many, caused by an unannounced French aircraft. Duxford's Spitfire squadrons reacted to this perceived threat, however, as Fred Roberts remembered:

> Shortly after the declaration of war the local air raid sirens were screaming and from the station yard we saw 19 and 66 Squadron aircraft scramble, circle round then land. I remember one of the lads saying 'I don't know what good they can do except ram any Germans – there's no ammo in them Spitfires, we have it all here!'

In the early hours of 4 September 1939, the capital's air raid sirens wailed again, sending Londoners scurrying for shelter. The writer and journalist Hector Bolitho was unimpressed: 'It all seemed such a bore, waiting, with the humiliating gas mask: a snout of rubber in a brown carboard box. There was no air raid.'

That afternoon, Bolitho, who was a house-guest of the Romanian Minister Viorel Tilea in Belgravia, 'went onto the roof to look at the balloon barrage. The hundreds of silver monsters caught the sunlight as they rode below the clouds. They were magnificent: they gave London a sort of carnival look, and had no apparent relationship with bombers or death.'

Squadron Leader Edward Alford:

> As the shadows of the inevitable war darkened in early 1939, we pushed ahead with training of both air and ground personnel, and struggled to overcome the ravages of time on old G.3 Camera Guns to further ground training while the cine cameras fitted to aircraft often disappointed both pilots and ground staff. Perseverance, however, gave us good results and it was while the fighter squadron was at

Armament Practice Camp that war was declared and they moved direct to the defence of London instead of returning to the station. Defence crews were posted with Light AA guns on the drome and made ready to put into practice all they had learned during training.

The declaration of war, though, prompted many to reflect on life in general, because clearly nothing was ever going to be the same again, the future – if there was one – uncertain. Indeed, that Britain was at war lacked the public displays of enthusiasm that had greeted war in 1914. After the First World War people were less naïve, and knew what to expect from modern warfare. On 4 September 1939, Flight Lieutenant Adolph Gysbert 'Sailor' Malan, a South African and former mercantile marine officer turned fighter pilot flying Spitfires with 74 Squadron at Hornchurch, wrote a rare letter home to his parents:

> I started to write this letter to you over a week ago. But the same day we were ordered to readiness and war stations and I hadn't another chance. I suppose I am in the prime of life and yet have a lot to be thankful for. I have had quite a good fling for one. But the biggest factor is that I have had eighteen months of complete happiness and blissful contentment with one of the sweetest women in the world, and thank God for that. It probably seems a strange thing to say but I am more than ready to enter the conflict having had those glorious eighteen months.

Clearly, Malan was ready for a fight and had no regrets. Sadly, he was about to be consumed by particularly tragic events – confirming just how taught nerves were stretched.

Shortly after 06.00 hrs on 6 September 1939, a searchlight battery reported high-flying aircraft over the Essex coast at West Mersea to the Sector Operations Room at North Weald. Having passed the information to the Observer Corps, the Sector Controller scrambled 151 Squadron's Hurricanes, and those of 56, both based at North Weald, to patrol between Harwich and Colchester at 11,000ft in response to the 'X-Raid'. Already, there are important facts to consider.

Firstly, squadrons were still gaining experience of the new monoplane fighters. By way of an example, 56 Squadron had only converted from biplanes to the Hawker Hurricane in May 1938, and 151 Squadron in December 1938. How RAF tactics for the new fighters would work in practice remained an uncertain. Moreover, German bombers being escorted by single-engine fighters was unanticipated, the assumption being that any attack would be launched from bases in Germany, and therefore beyond the Me 109's range. Consequently, tactics had been formulated on the basis that only ponderous German bombers would be engaged, the proposed and practised tactics involved revolving around the squadron or flight, flying in sub-sections of three aircraft.

'BARKING CREEK' AND 'A QUEER WAR'

Indeed, on 3 April 1939, Air Vice-Marshal Gossage, AOC 11 Group, had sent a memorandum to his sectors and squadrons emphasising that, 'Some squadrons have not had their monoplane fighters long enough to be able to employ them efficiently in formations greater than sections or flights', and that 'interception exercises shall be carried out by flights or sections'. This is significant. Until the enemy was sighted that fateful morning, the North Weald Controller, Group Captain D.F. Lucking, possessed of all the latest incoming information via the 'System', was solely responsible for deploying and directing defending fighters at sector level (not Fighter Command HQ).

At 06.30 hrs, Lucking began scrambling whole squadrons, not 'flights or sections', to meet the perceived threat. The wisdom of this, considering how little training had been undertaken by squadrons operating both as a cohesive unit or in conjunction with other squadrons, can only be considered questionable – but in fairness to Lucking, there was no precedent for him to follow.

At 06.30 hrs, Squadron Leader 'Teddy' Donaldson led the whole of his 151 Squadron up from North Weald. Previous accounts have claimed that the CO of 56 Squadron, Squadron Leader Knowles, ignored the order to scramble a single flight, and instead took off with his whole squadron. This, however, cannot be true, because were that the case, and given the tragic end result of this interception, Squadron Leader Knowles would undoubtedly have found himself the subject of a Court of Inquiry. The fact of the matter is that 56 Squadron's 'A' Flight, led by Flight Lieutenant Soden, scrambled from North Weald at 06.40 hrs, a total of eight Hurricanes, significantly including Pilot Officer Montague Hulton-Harrop and Pilot Officer Frank Rose.

Ten minutes later, Squadron Leader Knowles followed with 'B' Flight, adding a further six fighters to those already airborne. With incoming reports from radar plots and the OC suggesting that a hostile force of over fifty aircraft was approaching London via Southend, the understandably flustered Sector Controller then scrambled the whole of 74 Squadron at 06.45 hrs, along with further Spitfires from 54 and 65 squadrons, both also Hornchurch-based, between 06.55 hrs and 07.10 hrs.

It was a unique moment in time, highly charged with excitement and tension, everyone involved braced for the 'knockout blow'. The RAF fighters, their pilots' senses acutely alert, were converging on each other and all expecting to see the enemy for the first time – and none of the RAF pilots involved had any previous combat experience. Ahead and just west of Ipswich, Flight Lieutenant Malan sighted a formation of twelve aircraft, which were not flying the prescribed Fighter Command close-formation vics of three, but spread out more loosely, with two, what appeared to be, covering fighters following behind and below. Given the information available to him, and in the heat of the moment, Sailor shouted 'Tally Ho!', meaning enemy sighted, and ordered 'A' Flight to execute a Fighter Command No 1 Attack by sections.

Tragically, as things turned out, it was not the enemy in sight but 56 Squadron's Hurricanes. According to his subsequent testimony, realising seconds later that the 'bandits' were in fact friendly fighters, Sailor claimed to have immediately issued a follow-up verbal order over the radio, cancelling the previously ordered attack. Yellow Section of 'A' Flight still attacked however, Flying Officer Paddy Byrne and Pilot Officer John Freeborn opened fire, shooting down the two trailing Hurricanes of Pilot Officers Hulton-Harrop and Rose. Tragically, the former was killed while the latter safely force-landed his damaged machine.

Group Captain Lucking was immediately removed from office and both Pilot Officers Byrne and Freeborn arrested; a Court of Inquiry was convened. Neither pilot claimed to have heard their Flight Commander's second order cancelling the attack. At the subsequent hearing, held at Hendon on 17 October 1939, Flight Lieutenant Malan appeared as witness for the prosecution, stating under oath that he had cancelled the attack – but that Yellow Section had pressed on.

The defence barrister, Sir Patrick Hastings, called Malan 'a bare-faced liar!' seeking only to protect himself, which some have cited as evidence that this was the case. Being called a 'liar' by the defence, however, is absolutely no proof whatsoever, because such an accusation is standard practice, in order to discredit a witness and plant doubt in the court's mind. Sailor Malan, however, is remembered as a consummate and mature professional, and even at that early time was a pilot and leader of some experience. Reserved by nature, a man of impeccable integrity with the heart and courage of a lion, to lie would have been out of character and contrary to everything we know about the man – who was strongly opposed to any kind of injustice. Moreover, had there been any case for him to answer, Flight Lieutenant Malan would also have been charged and been in the dock alongside his two errant pilots.

This, then, suggests that the investigators were satisfied with Malan's conduct and clearly felt that the blame lay with Freeborn and Byrne. Wing Commander John Freeborn, as he became, however, maintained to his dying day that Malan never gave a cancellation order. So what is the explanation?

This question is impossible to answer definitively, on account of the Court of Inquiry report being closed for 100 years, and what became known as 'Barking Creek' remains an emotive issue, still vexing historians years later. To my mind, the most likely explanation for the tragedy lies in the comparatively primitive, and often unreliable, in-aircraft radio telephony involved – and of course, unlike today, there was no onboard radar or heads-up display. RAF fighters used the TR9D High Frequency radio, enabling communication between pilots of a squadron with each other and the ground controller. What the TR9D did not provide for, however, was for airborne squadrons to communicate directly with each other. Had that been possible, then clearly the whole sorry mess could perhaps have been avoided. Moreover, a small number of aircraft in each unit were also fitted with a navigational aid called 'Pip-squeak', on account of the high-pitched 'pip' it emitted.

The problem was that for fourteen seconds of every minute, the TR9D of the 'Pip-squeak' aircraft automatically switched channel to transmit a homing signal to ground direction-finding stations, enabling the exact position of friendly formations to be plotted. During those fourteen seconds when the radio channel switched to 'Pip-squeak', the pilot in the transmitting aircraft could neither hear others nor communicate via the TR9D. As the Flight Commander and formation leader, it is highly likely that Sailor's Spitfire carried a 'Pip-squeak' device, and the fourteen second automatic channel-switch could well explain why his cancellation order was not heard. This is certainly the view of academic researcher Nick Black, who forensically deconstructed the events involved (see bibliography), concluding that,

> It is difficult to believe that this man, who would go on to become one of the most celebrated aces of the Second World War, would lie to cover his own back, as Freeborn suggested ... it is highly possible that Malan was not a liar and that that the device known as 'Pip-squeak', designed to assist in locating RAF aircraft while airborne, interfered with his radio transmission and caused his countermanding order to not be heard by the pilots of 74 Squadron 'A' Flight'.

Clearly, Freeborn and Byrne had not deliberately ignored an order, and had not taken to the skies that day to destroy friendly aircraft, and were rightly acquitted in what was simply a tragic accident. John Freeborn, however, later also a decorated ace and one of the Few, survived the war but never forgave Malan for what he steadfastly maintained until his dying day was a 'bare-faced lie'. Conversely, Group Captain Malan, as he became, maintained a life-long and dignified silence on what became known as the 'Battle of Barking Creek'.

Whatever the truth, the incident certainly highlighted the crucial importance of correctly identifying radar plots and accurately reporting sightings of aircraft. Given the background to this early interception and state of high tension, it was, arguably, an inevitable tragedy. Interestingly, over time, 'Pip-squeak' was found to be problematic on account of monopolising one of the TR9D's two channels, meaning that all transmissions were restricted to a single frequency, and because of the constant interruption for fourteen seconds of every minute. By the Battle of Britain, a new system, 'Identification Friend or Foe' (IFF) had been developed, involving the radar network and which did not interrupt radio communication, although it was impossible to replace 'Pip-squeak' with IFF until after the battle.

It was perhaps an ironic twist of fate that on the afternoon of 'Barking Creek', and the following day, 74 Squadron's 'B' Flight, led by Flight Lieutenant 'Treacle' Treacy, provided Spitfires to fly for the making of *The Lion Has Wings*, a feature film intended to reassure the public 'of the power of the Royal Air Force' and its ability to defend Britain from aerial bombardment.

Given the fear of German air attack, this was a vitally important propaganda film, which again emphasises the fearful atmosphere of the time. Starring Ralph Richardson, Merle Oberon, June Duprez, Anthony Bushell, and, interestingly, Ronald Adam – a First World War RFC veteran who in 1939 was commissioned in the RAF as a wing commander and became Sector Controller at Hornchurch –

the film firmly held Hitler responsible for causing the war, while emphasising that Britain's industry was prepared for war production, the excellence of our own bomber force, and, most importantly, that the RAF could defeat any German bomber attack. Indeed, this underpins the entire film, the destruction of a German bomber (in this case a Focke-Wulf Condor long-range reconnaissance bomber) by Spitfires provides a climatic conclusion. The film was the top cinema attraction of November 1939, the British Film Institute reporting that the movie 'admirably fulfils its object – to inspire quiet confidence in the hearts of those who see it'. Indeed, the evidence available from Mass-Observation surveys indicates that the film definitely helped to assuage public anxiety, at least temporarily, until the bombs began to rain down on Britain.

So concerned was the British Government about the threat of a German aerial attack, in fact, that when war broke out 'Plan Yellow' was activated, in which certain Government offices, comprising 25,000 civil servants, were relocated from London to the provinces. Under a further plan, 'Black Move', if the worst happened the primary Government departments were also to leave London. Private industry and commerce followed suit; 5,600 prisoners were freed and 140,000 hospital patients were sent home to make space for projected air raid casualties. Upon their own initiative, 2 million people left cities for the countryside in the West Country, Wales, Scotland and elsewhere.

From the summer of 1938 onwards, the Government had been planning a massive operation in anticipation of evacuating millions of Londoners and other city dwellers to the countryside. This was believed to be a military necessity, because German air attack was expected to demoralise civilian populations, and the Government wished to avoid a disorganised and chaotic ad hoc exodus to the rural areas in such an event. Local authorities audited potential billets for evacuees, and had powers to requisition them. Britain was divided into 'evacuation', 'neutral' and 'reception' zones – respectively, cities which were likely to be attacked, areas which would neither require evacuation or be needed to accept evacuees, and the places where evacuees would be received and accommodated.

After Munich, when fear of bombing in Britain was especially endemic, 80 per cent of parents in London expressed a desire for their children to be evacuated. Surprisingly, by August 1939, that figure had dropped by around 30 per cent. When war came, less than 50 per cent of London's children were evacuated to the country, and only 48 per cent of all English schoolchildren became evacuees, along with 37 per cent from Scotland. In total, 3.5 million people were evacuated to safer areas, the majority of whom were expectant mothers and children. The US Committee for the Evacuation of European Children also arranged for many British children to cross the Atlantic, while thousands more went to Britain's dominions. Also, since 1938, Britain had received an influx of European refugees fleeing Hitler's Germany – many of them German-Jews, who were already being openly persecuted by the Nazis. The peace-loving, philanthropic and compassionate Quakers, and other organisations, cooperated to set up the *Kindertransport* system,

'BARKING CREEK' AND 'A QUEER WAR'

a humanitarian operation which saw trainloads of Jewish children leave Germany for Britain between 1 December 1938 and the outbreak of war.

By that time, there were over 60,000 German and Austrian nationals living in Britain, a large number being arrested by the police and interned as 'Enemy Aliens', along with, as of 22 May 1940, anyone the Home Secretary believed to threaten national security. The following day, Sir Oswald Mosley, leader of the British Union of Fascists, was arrested, his party dissolved and its publications banned. By August 1940, in fact, 1,600 British subjects were being detained without trial. In many cases, 'Fifth Column Fever' was to blame, with people convinced that 'Fifth Columnists', spies, saboteurs and Nazi sympathisers were embedded in British society ready to disrupt defences and assist the enemy. Certainly there were some, but the small number was disproportionate to the fears and rumours spread. Indeed, rumours frequently concerned German spies and supposed landings by enemy parachutists.

This became such a concern that in June 1940, an Emergency Regulation made it an offence, punishable by a fine of up to £50, to spread any story about the war 'likely to cause alarm or despondency'. Slightly tongue in cheek, Alan Herbert, the independent MP for Oxford University advised the readers of the satirical magazine *Punch*:

> Do not believe the tale the milkman tells;
> No troops have mutinied at Potters Bar.
> Nor are there submarines at Tunbridge Wells.
> The BBC will warn us when there are.

Hector Bolitho:

> The refugees in the village turned out to be unwashed illiterates from Whitechapel. Stanley, the village carter, found six fleas in his clothes after bringing their paraphernalia of luggage from the station. The radio told us that the evacuation of the London children had been made without a hitch. Well, it is an unholy mess here. There is bitterness already.
>
> Today the villagers are full of friendliness for me. Some months ago it was a different story. Rodney Wilkinson [Squadron Leader R.L. Wilkinson, who would be killed in action flying Spitfires with 266 Squadron on 16 August 1940] came to stay for the weekend and, on Monday morning, rose early and left for his RAF station, taking my shaving brush by mistake. He telephoned me from Duxford and said that he would fly over the house and drop the brush on the lawn. It sailed down, from the aircraft, in a brightly coloured linen bag, in time for me to shave.
>
> There was a lot of busy gossip in the village: the ultimate story was a) As my name ended in a vowel, I must be an Italian;

b) As I had been to Italy for my last holidays I was obviously a spy, and c) The aircraft was obviously Italian, dropping messages to me from Mussolini!

Bolitho offered his services to the Air Ministry, asking for 'Any job. Any place'. He duly became an intelligence officer with the rank of squadron leader on 10 September 1939.

The lack of an early German effort to deliver the expected 'knockout blow', however, made it, as Flight Lieutenant Brian Lane, a Spitfire pilot with 19 Squadron, wrote, 'a queer war':

> Everybody said so ... The *Luftwaffe's* expected blows on this island did not fall. Göring contended himself instead with raids by single aircraft against the convoys round the coasts. So for month after month we patrolled the shipping, no doubt frightening many Huns but never so much as catching sight of one.

The lack of the dreaded knockout-blow, in fact, led to a feeling in the autumn of 1939 that the Government had, according to that great British social historian Angus Calder, 'grossly over-prepared for air attack'. Indeed, by October 1939, a poll confirmed that half of the working-classes doubted there would be any air raids, and of those who did, only a small percentage expected any serious attacks. This, then, was a clear shift away from pre-war fears – because not only had there so far been no knockout-blow, there was absolutely no sign of one.

Journalist Edward Bishop:

> The people had braced themselves and nothing had happened. They found time to sit down and write grieved letters to the newspapers about the situation. There were complaints of 'Too much war news in the press and on the air'.

The *Church Times* rebuked the BBC:

> Its perpetual news bulletins, largely repetitious, pander to a nervous craving on the part of people without sufficient control to wait a few hours for information, and it allows comedians to demoralise taste by making silly jokes. We quite realise that the BBC finds it difficult to find comedians who are funny. But we regret that it seems to find that object less attainable when the subject is vulgar.

Vi Farrant was a volunteer member of the Women's Land Army, which recruited women from urban areas to undertake agricultural work in rural areas, replacing men now in the services:

'BARKING CREEK' AND 'A QUEER WAR'

The outbreak of war and first few months of it was a strange time. After all those years of tension, everyone expecting an immediate, possibly overwhelming, German attack, but nothing seemed to happen. We also called it the 'Bore War' or the '*Sitzkrieg*', and there was a famous song at the time, 'We're going to hang out the washing on the Siegfried Line', suggesting that there would be no action and all the military preparations and defences would go unused by their intended purpose.

In Poland, however, the war was all too real. In total, the Polish fighter squadrons, including the Fighter Brigade and Army Cooperation units lost fifty pilots and 114 aircraft during the campaign, while the bomber force suffered 90 per cent casualties in aircrew and aircraft.

By 14 September 1939, losses were such that the Polish Air Force was unable to continue operations. Some squadrons lost their last aircraft on that day, others, threatened with being overrun, destroyed their remaining machines. On 17 September, fittingly in a violent thunderstorm, the few remaining Polish aircraft crossed the Romanian border, ending the air fighting over Poland. On the same day, in another undeclared act of war and a real shock, Russia invaded eastern Poland. Polish Air Force flying schools, experimental and maintenance units evacuated their personnel to Romania and Hungary.

On 1 October 1939, German troops entered Warsaw. Six says later, Polish resistance finally ceased – although the Polish Home Army would continue fighting a partisan war until the Germans were finally defeated five years later. From a Polish viewpoint the short, tragic, campaign was a consequence of unpreparedness, the outcome, against ruthless and efficient aggression, inevitable. Nonetheless, Poland's defiant spirit, refusing to surrender without a fight, no matter what the odds, set a benchmark of courage that would resonate throughout the Second World War.

It is important to understand the Polish character, fundamental to which is a powerful sense of duty and love of country. For five hundred years, Poland fought two or three defensive wars every generation. Poles know full-well that material possessions, even the family home, can be lost – instantly. Anything that the enemy can use must be destroyed, so therefore not valued highly. Polish soil, however, cannot be destroyed, and neither can national solidarity, an iron will to endure whatever the odds. Consequently, the Polish nation has survived even when forced into exile. It is this long history of suffering and its profound effect on the Polish psyche. This, more than anything, explains why, when Poland had fallen, the Polish Armed Forces trekked west, to continue the fight. It explains why, when the call was made for the Polish Air Force to reassemble in France and later Britain, only the dead, those who were prisoners or ordered to remain in Poland, did not respond. For others, not continuing the fight and ultimately liberating Poland was unthinkable.

Organising the evacuation of the Polish Air Force was a huge task. First, crossing into neighbouring states such as Romania, Hungary, Latvia and Lithuania the Poles were interned. In Romania, where the majority of air force personnel were interned, officers and 'other ranks' were immediately segregated. Unsurprisingly, Romania was unprepared for this influx of personnel, and things were chaotic. When the news was received that General Sikorski had re-formed the Polish government in France and was assembling the Polish armed forces there, this chaos worked to the Poles' advantage; many staged individual escapes, the majority travelling by boat via Constanza, Beirut, Malta and Marseilles.

On 25 October 1939, British, Polish and French delegates met at the French Air Ministry to decide the best way forward. The Poles argued that their air force should be re-formed in Britain, given their familiarity with British aero-engines but ignorance of French equipment. The French countered that the Poles should be equally divided between Britain and France, believing that Polish squadrons could be quickly formed and would be welcome reinforcements on both sides of the Channel. Finally, it was decided that 300 Polish aircrew and 2,000 ground staff would be stationed in Britain, the rest in France. This now meant that a large-scale evacuation had to be organised from the internment camps.

Interned in Romania was the young Polish officer and fighter pilot Boleslaw Henryk Drobinski, more commonly known as 'Gandi' on account of being so thin:

> I had toothache so obtained a pass to leave the camp and visit the local dentist. On producing my pass for inspection, the Romanian guard asked where the others were, 'Boleslaw, Henryk and Drobinski'! Immediately I grabbed two others, and off we went to France!

Eventually, the Poles reached France and were passed from camp to camp until Lyon became the central collecting area. On 25 October 1939, British, Polish and French delegates met at the French Air Ministry to decide the best way forward.

The Poles argued that their air force should be re-formed in Britain, given their familiarity with British aero-engines but ignorance of French equipment. The French countered that the Poles should be equally divided between Britain and France, believing that Polish squadrons could be quickly formed and would be welcome reinforcements on both sides of the Channel. Finally, it was decided that 300 Polish aircrew and 2,000 ground staff would be stationed in Britain, the rest in France. And there the Poles eagerly awaited the chance to meet Germany on the battlefield again.

Squadron Leader Edward Alford:

> The Army Cooperation Squadron at the Station (Hawkinge) hastily prepared to move to France with the AASF and took off one afternoon in early October to earn a splendid reputation in the first phases of the war.
>
> A few days after their departure I was posted to RAF Kenley in Surrey to take over as Station Armament Officer. On arrival there

I found that things were very much the same, except that I had several dispersal aerodromes to cater for besides the home station.

Commanded by the late Group Captain Moore, I would pay tribute to the excellent training and leadership he showed, which brought the station to a fine pitch of efficiency, which was maintained by his successor, Group Captain Prickman OBE, in readiness for the gruelling time which followed during the Battle of Britain.

Training was continued at even greater pressure than before, constant practice being carried out by pilots and ground crews with cine cameras in Air to Air and Ground to Air Firing. Results were projected and analysed as soon as possible afterwards to point out mistakes which had been made, in deflection allowed and range at which fire was opened, the latter being the most prevalent error. To overcome this, due stress was made of Wellington's words to the British troops at the battle of Waterloo, being 'Din't shoot until you see the whites of their eyes,' and this brought better results.

The point was explained to ground gunners that to open fire too early, when the enemy aircraft was out of range, revealed the position of the posts and decreased the element of surprise, besides lessening the chances of hitting.

At first it was strange to service aircraft at dispersal points and to maintain dispersed stocks of SAA but the difficulties were overcome and the discomfort and long hours which the aircraft ground crews endured remains to their everlasting credit.

On 16 October 1939, thirty Ju 88s of I/KG 30 attacked shipping in the Firth of Forth, damaging several ships of the RN. It was the first air attack on Britain during the Second World War. The Germans would also suffer their first losses to the guns of Spitfire pilots: at 14.45 hrs, Flight Lieutenant George Pinkerton of 602 Squadron shot down a Ju 88 that crashed into the sea off Crail, and at 15.30 hrs Red Section of 603 Squadron sent another raider crashing into the 'drink' near Port Seton. Other Spitfires of the same squadron damaged another Ju 88, but this aircraft was more fortunate and returned safely to Westerland.

From that point onwards similar attacks on the RN at their Scottish bases continued, as did Spitfire victories. The following day, Gladiators of 607 Squadron destroyed a Do 18 reconnaissance machine. On 21 October, a Hurricane scored its first kill in the defence of Britain when three mine-laying He 115 seaplanes were sent plunging into the sea off Yorkshire by 46 Squadron. This was hardly an august feat, however.

On 30 October, Pilot Officer P.W. 'Boy' Mould of 1 Squadron scored the RAF's first kill over France since the First World War, a Do 17 destroyed near Toul. Then, on 29 November, Squadron Leader Harry Broadhurst, the CO of 111 Squadron, destroyed a lone He 111 off the Northumbrian coast. These sporadic actions, however, were not fought against great air fleets bent on delivering a heavyweight punch – and there appeared no sign of one. Indeed, the 60,000 British hospital beds set aside for the first casualties remained unused. In spite of its fearsome reputation, the fact was that the *Luftwaffe* was not equipped to defeat an enemy through strategic bombing alone.

President Roosevelt of the United States appealed to the belligerents that there should be no aerial bombardment 'of civilian populations or unfortified cities'. Hitler's response claimed that German soldiers had been victims of atrocities committed by Polish civilians, and emphasised that the British blockade was indirectly a war waged against German civilians, including children – but he did undertake that Germany would wage a humane and chivalrous war.

Indeed, neither side wished to be responsible for unleashing unrestricted warfare, and on the evening of 4 September 1939, Bomber Command's first raid on Germany dropped not bombs, but tons of propaganda leaflets. In any case, after the departure of ten Battle bomber squadrons to France, and with twenty squadrons non-operational, Bomber Command's strength had shrunk to just twenty-three squadrons, or 350 aircraft – against Germany's 1,200 bombers.

The question was how to best use such a comparatively small force, while balancing avoiding enemy civilian casualties and provoking the stronger *Luftwaffe*. There was, however, virtually no reserve. Had an all-out aerial offensive been launched by Britain, it is likely that Bomber Command would have only lasted a month. Bombing was also notoriously inaccurate, especially when it came to hitting specific targets, and none of the sophisticated radar and radio beam navigation aids effective later in the war were available to either side. Bomber Command's twenty-three squadrons were equipped with the twin-engine Blenheim, Wellington, Hampden and Whitley bombers. The bomb-loads of all were medium at best and incomparable to those of the later four-engine 'heavies' like the Lancaster, Sterling and Halifax. This, then, was a force, like its opponent, incapable of delivering a decisive attack, and so Bomber Command's initial strategy, therefore, was to target German ships at sea, thus avoiding civilian casualties, and pursue a leaflet dropping campaign.

Bomber Command's twenty-three home squadrons were deployed in four groups – Nos. 2, 3, 4 and 5, with a fifth, No 1, in France with the AASF. These groups were situated in eastern England, from Dishforth in North Yorkshire to Bassingbourn in South Cambridgeshire – facing out towards the North Sea and Germany. All of Bomber Command's machines, however, achieved maximum speeds of between 222 and 266 mph – whereas the Me 109 reached 350 mph.

As we have seen, air-power thinking between the wars revolved around the belief that the bomber was invincible, so it was not perceived before the war that these offensive aircraft required escorting and protecting by friendly fighters, which could then engage enemy interceptors on equal terms. In any case, Germany lay well beyond the limited range of single-engine RAF fighters, and the fighter variant of the twin-engine Blenheim, which did have the range, was no match for the lethal

109. Daylight raids by unprotected bombers were perilous, but just how so had yet to be grasped. On 29 September 1939, this came into sharp focus.

On that day, eleven unescorted Hampdens, in two formations, were despatched to search for German warships in the Heligoland Bight, a bay in the North Sea at the mouth of the Elbe. Emphasising the inaccuracy of pinpoint bombing, six aircraft dropped bombs on two enemy destroyers without scoring a single hit. According to German propaganda, the second formation, of five 144 Squadron aircraft, were intercepted by 'a hornet's nest of fighters', and destroyed.

What became known as the 'Battle of the Heligoland Bight' (3 September 1939 – 17 December 1939) saw Bomber Command suffer twelve bombers destroyed and three damaged at a cost of fifty-seven aircrew killed. Conversely, only two Me 109s were destroyed, with a handful of 109s and Me 110s damaged; just two German pilots were killed and two more wounded.

This, the first named air battle in history, was a stark warning to any aerial commander of the folly of sending bombers to attack enemy territory in daylight without fighter escort. In fact, this experience led to Bomber Command changing tack and electing to attack by night. Clearly, the bomber would not 'always get through', and the fighter was clearly much more important than Trenchard and the between-the-wars 'Bomber Barons' believed. That no thought had been given to a long-range, single-engine, fighter by Britain would later have significant consequences.

Essential lessons were being learned – the hard way and at a cost in men's lives.

Chapter 9

Operation Weserübung: The German Invasion of Norway

After the defeat of Poland, the *Wehrmacht* rested. The participating *Luftwaffe* units were withdrawn to refit in Germany, hunkering down for a winter of rest and expansion before the forthcoming assault on the west. The few German fighter units facing westwards were forbidden from seeking combat, and aerial activity over Britain was confined to the reconnaissance of ports and naval installations, and occasional attacks on RN targets.

Clearly, the RN was feared, and considered a high priority target. However, when the aircraft carriers *Ark Royal*, *Courageous* and *Glorious* patrolled and flew Britannia's proud flag in the Western Approaches on 14 September 1939, the former only narrowly avoided being sunk by the German Type VII submarine U-36; three days later *Courageous* was sent to the bottom by *U-36*. Then, on the night of 13/14 October 1939, the Revenge-class battleship HMS *Royal Oak* – was sunk by *U-47* in home waters – with great loss of life and in what was an especial blow to British national and maritime pride.

When the First World War ended, the German High Seas Fleet, commanded by Rear-Admiral Ludwig von Reuter, surrendered to the RN, the seventy-four ships of which were interned at the famous RN anchorage at Scapa Flow, in the Orkneys. Cutting a long story short, on Midsummer's Day 1919, Reuter signalled from the cruiser *Emden* that the fleet was to be scuttled. So it was that these once proud ships, the pride of the Germany navy, ended up at the bottom of the Flow – in what was a further humiliation for Germany.

Between the wars, the name of Scapa Flow, home of the hated British Grand Fleet, was a painful thorn in the side of every German naval officer bent upon revenge. Among them was one Karl Dönitz, who, in 1935, took command of Nazi Germany's first U-Flotilla, submarines actually having been prohibited by Versailles. Within days of the Second World War breaking out, *Kommodore* Dönitz began planning 'the boldest of bold enterprises': getting a U-boat into Scapa Flow, to wreak havoc among the British ships at anchor. The submarine commander chosen for the job was *Kapitänleutnant* Gunther Prien of *U-47*.

Ironically, given subsequent events, the British Home Fleet in September 1939 was confident that it was safe from submarine and surface attack at

OPERATION WESERÜBUNG: THE GERMAN INVASION OF NORWAY

Scapa Flow – the last enemy submarine attempting to penetrate the anchorage having been destroyed in 1918.

On 8 October 1939, however, the German Fleet Commander, Admiral Hermann Bohm, made a clever sortie up the Norwegian coast with his flagship, *Gneisenau*, the cruiser *Köln* and nine destroyers, the purpose of which was to divert attention away from the surface raiders *Graf Spee* and *Deutschland*, which were heading for the South Atlantic, and secondly to entice the Home Fleet out of Scapa Flow to be attacked by the *Luftwaffe*.

Admiral Sir Charles Forbes, commanding the Home Fleet, was ordered to intercept Bohm, his Humber Force sailing from Rosyth and the Home Fleet out of Scapa Flow. RAF Wellingtons failed to find Bohm's ships, and similarly, the *Luftwaffe* missed the Home Fleet while unsuccessfully attacking Humber Force, and U-Boats made no contact with either of Forbes' forces. Forbes then returned to Scotland, fearful of air attack dispersing his ships; by 13 October 1939, only HMS *Royal Oak* remained in the north-east corner of the Flow, a mile offshore, together with just the aged aircraft carrier HMS *Pegasus*.

At 04.37 hrs that day, *U-47* settled on the seabed in 90 metres of water, just off the Orkneys – there awaiting their moment to attack. At 19.15 hrs the submarine surfaced in Holm Sound, pressing ahead, negotiating sunken blockships and strong currents – achieving the impossible and getting inside the anchorage. At 00.14 hrs, Prien's first torpedo hit the starboard bow of *Royal Oak*, tearing a 50ft hole beneath the waterline. The ship's captain, Captain William Benn, was advised that an internal explosion in the paint store was most likely responsible: that an enemy torpedo had caused the damage was unthinkable.

Two more torpedoes were fired but failed to explode – then three more, the effect of which was catastrophic.

Able Seaman Arthur Smith:

> Hardly had I resumed my position as aircraft lookout after the first explosion than the ship rocked to three more, again from the starboard side. Almost immediately, the ship listed to starboard and I was pretty sure she was finished. When the order to 'Abandon Ship' was piped, I immediately ran down to the four-inch gun deck, which I intended to jump off, and one of my most vivid memories of that night was struggling to release the toggles of my duffel coat with cold fingers. By the time this was accomplished, there was no time to divest myself of boots and uniform, so into the sea I went, fully clothed.

Boy Sailor Kenneth Toop:

> The ship was listing so much to starboard that I was able to lean over the port-side, sliding down and stepping on the slight ledge

where the anti-torpedo blisters joined the ship's side. By clambering and crawling, I managed to make my way aft along the side towards the stern, where the drifter, *Daisy II*, attached to the ship as a harbour tender, was tied up alongside – but at this time the ship was turning over onto its starboard side and so the Daisy had to be cast off, or she would have floundered. I was left with no option but to move up the side towards the keel, until sliding into the sea was unavoidable. I entered into a thick covering of oil fuel on a freezing sea.

Boy Seaman Bert Pocock also ended up in the water:

They say you can get sucked back into the ship when one goes down, so once in the sea I swam like mad away from the ship.

Able Seaman Stanley Cole had also abandoned ship:

I could smell the oil-fuel but could not avoid getting some in the mouth, nose and ears. I kept my eyes closed until I surfaced. Coughing and spluttering, I became aware that my right foot and leg seemed to be hanging in the water as I began to swim away from the ship's side, along with some others. It was like trying to swim through liquid tar, and I was convinced that I wasn't going to make it.

The water was bitterly cold, and from all around me in the darkness I could hear cries for help from injured, burned and despairing bodies. Kicking out as best I could with my good leg, I was sure that I could feel the bodies of drowned shipmates underfoot. Then my hand caught something: a piece of wood about two foot long by six inches wide, so I hung onto it in the blind faith that it would keep me afloat – I would have killed anyone who tried to take it from me! Then, another stroke of luck: what I took to be a five-gallon oil drum came within range and I tried to hold my arm over it, as it slipped and rolled with the oil. Finally, after what seemed like ages, I made out three or four bobbing heads paddling slowly along a length of timber, which I suppose could have been one of the 'deals' we adapted for seating a church serves etc. I let go of my drum but not my small scrap of wood, and joined up with the lads paddling the deal. We tried shouting and singing, our throats hoarse, but without success, growing colder and more exhausted. One of our number slipped off the plank and we never saw him again.

My last view of *Royal Oak* was of her keel, silhouetted against the dark skyline. She appeared to have turned right over. Then, just as I had all but given up the struggle, along came a ship's whaler and

OPERATION WESERÜBUNG: THE GERMAN INVASION OF NORWAY

I felt myself lifted over the boat's side, with two or three other lads dumped on top of me in a cold, sodden, oily heap.

While the individual bodies were being taken from the water, the crew of the drifter *Daisy II*, under the command of skipper John Gatt, were valiantly picking men up until *Daisy* herself was in danger of capsizing under sheer weight of numbers.

With both engines running at high speed, *U-47* withdrew, Prien believing he had destroyed one battleship and damaged another. In his wake was left destruction and misery.

The once-proud HMS *Royal Oak* now lay on the bottom of the Flow in 32 metres of water, along with 833 members of her crew. The survivors were grateful to be alive, but in shock.

When news of Prien's audacious success was broadcast in Germany there was a frenzy of popular enthusiasm throughout the Fatherland. *U-47* had expunged the humiliation of the High Seas Fleet, and was welcomed home to Wilhelmshaven by cheering crowds and bands playing. Dönitz himself arrived to personally confer upon Prien the Iron Cross 1st Class, and 2nd Class for the crew. Then, at Hitler's invitation, 'The Bull of Scapa Flow' and his crew were summonsed to Berlin, Templehof airport being packed with people awaiting the U-Boat men's arrival. The streets to the Kaiserhof Hotel, to which the party travelled, were lined with tens of thousands of cheering people. At the Reich Chancellery the crew paraded and were presented to the *Führer*, who hung the covered Ritterkreuz (Knight's Cross) around '*Kaleun*' Prien's neck. If the mood in Germany was euphoric, however, that was far from the case in Britain.

The British were stunned. On 17 October 1939, the First Lord of the Admiralty, Winston Churchill, paid tribute, however, to Prien, telling the House that 'this entry by a U-Boat must be considered as a remarkable exploit of professional skill and daring'. It was indeed, but tragic though the incident was, the loss of an obsolete battleship would have no influence on the overall war at sea. Nonetheless, Prien had exorcised the ghosts of the Kaiser's naval defeat in 1918 and the 'Grand Scuttle' of 1919 – which increased Hitler's confidence in the U-*bootwaffe* (submarine arm) sufficiently to lift all restrictions on U-Boat operations: from now on, all enemy ships, including liners in convoy, could be attacked on sight. For the first time, the German nation embraced the idea that the mighty RN could be beaten by the *Kriegsmarine*. Certainly, with the loss of both *Courageous* and *Royal Oak* so early on, it was hardly an auspicious start to the British navy's war.

RN resources, however, were widely dispersed, and *U-47*'s success, and a subsequent aerial attack on the venerable HMS *Iron Duke*, confirmed that the famous Scapa Flow anchorage was insecure and also vulnerable to air attack. Consequently, the Home Fleet was forced to use anchorages on the west coast of Scotland, on the wrong side of the coast; reconnaissance of the North Sea had proved inadequate and aerial attacks on German shipping there had been unsuccessful. Britannia did not, therefore, rule the North Sea, control of which had been temporarily lost.

These factors led the British War Cabinet to conclude that a seaborne invasion of Britain by Germany had to be considered as a real possibility. The Chiefs of Staff agreed that raids were certainly possible, and a full-blown invasion not impossible, but did not consider these threats of sufficient gravity to justify tying down resources needed more urgently elsewhere. Nonetheless, troops were deployed within easy reach of the East coast, any invasion expected to approach across the North Sea and land there, and port and aerodrome defences were bolstered.

At home, civilians were starting to feel the pinch. In January 1940, the Ministry of Food introduced food rationing, to ensure a fair distribution of essential foodstuffs at a time of national shortage. Everyone, men, women and children, were issued with ration books and coupons confirming eligibility to purchase rationed items, including meat, sugar, fats and cheese. Other foodstuffs, such as tinned goods and biscuits, were rationed by a points system governed by availability and need – priority being accorded to expectant mothers and children for, say, eggs and milk.

This further privation would cause disruption for daily living, long queues for food becoming commonplace as shortages increased. Fruit and vegetables were never rationed, though, as the Government encouraged civilians to grow their own in the 'Dig For Victory' campaign, which saw public spaces turned over as allotments. At Wimbledon, the world-famous home of the All England Tennis Club, voluntarily became a pig farm for the duration; 'There is little tennis and we must do something' the secretary told the papers. All serious sporting competitions had in any case been suspended. So far as cricket was concerned, the West Indian tour and test series was prematurely concluded in August 1939, and first-class cricket was suspended; both the Oval and the hallowed ground of Lords were fitted out as prisoner of war camps (although not, in the event, so used). Football stadiums and grounds were commandeered by the army, and the Home Guard drilled between goalposts.

Journalist Edward Bishop:

> They had volunteered for a citizen Home Guard with such zeal that in one gallant company six retired generals marched as privates. They had mined the seaside holiday resorts, blocked the coast roads and evacuated the donkeys from the beaches. In the Invasion Corner of south-east England they had uprooted the village signposts. A double-edged brainwave, as it turned out. British defending troops, unfamiliar with the area, becoming almost as lost as the guttural enemy was expected to be.
>
> In London, Boer War veterans living near one big square had given the lead for a Square by Square defence of the capital. Jingoistically they called themselves 'The Boys of the Bedford Square Brigade'.

In the provincial cities members of the Auxiliary Fire Service built home-made fire engines. One rickety machine was fashioned from a Grimsby fish carter's truck.

Near London there had been opened a school of guerrilla warfare where clerks practised the fine art of garrotting with piano wire and shuddered as the instructor barked 'Any man found leaving dead Germans lying in a mess in the middle of the road will cop it. Give 'em a decent burial in a ditch and for Gawd's sake clear up the blood so the next Jerry won't get suspicious.'

The daily newspapers provided tips for the new Local Defence Volunteers: How to turn shot-guns into deadlier weapons. How to load with bicycle ball-bearings. How to turn ordinary shot cartridge into a miniature shell; 'nick it with a penknife'. How to kill Germans with bullets originally manufactured for tiger shooting!

The entire output of the Thompson Automatic Gun Company – 5,000 'Tommy guns' a month – was on the way from the United States in weekly shipments. In the meantime the new citizen army must shoulder whatever arms it could pick up. Some bore pikes.

These were the men to whom the new War Minister, Sir Edwards Grigg, was to broadcast: 'You are now more than 500,000 strong, and the time is close at hand when you can render yeoman service to the country...'

They were 'Civilian snipers and rifle-wenches trained by criminals released from prisons,' the Germans were told.

Squadron Leader Edward Alford:

The early months of 1940 brought climatic, besides technical, troubles, and 'All hands' were required to keep the runways clear of snow, while a constant watch had to be maintained to ensure that liberal minded armourers did not extend their generosity to an extreme when lubricating Aircraft Browning Guns.

Despite the issue of technical instructions regarding over-oiling of these guns and the danger of them freezing up at altitudes, cases were found where a well-meaning but mis-guided armourer had applied a thin coating of anti-freezing grease to the Breech Blocks of Aircraft guns.

The squadrons patrolled the spring months away but few of Göring's much vaunted *Luftwaffe* were seen, though we had many 'Preliminary Air Raid Warnings' over the 'Tannoy', and one day were treated to 'lurid discussion' over the air, by two airmen who had inadvertently left the 'Mike' live after an announcement, from the control shelter at Croydon.

At this period some squadrons were still equipped with Gloster Gladiator aircraft, which had two synchronised Browning guns firing through the arc of the airscrew, and this necessitated special care being taken with the ammunition which was then classified as 'red label' for use with synchronised guns, to ensure that at no time did belts of ammunition become mixed and non-synchronised ammunition be used for firing through the airscrew.

Storage regulations were such that when a sealed box of ammunition containing special 'red label' ammunition had been opened it was necessary to relegate this ammunition for use in non-Synchronised Guns after the period of fourteen days. This meant that huge stocks of ammunition were relegated every fortnight, besides the extra work of involved of opening up fresh boxes of 'Red Label' ammunition and making it up into belts to replace that which had to be changed from the synchronised gun tanks when the safe period of its life as special ammunition had expired.

This problem, however, disappeared when the Gladiator aircraft were taken out from home operational service and substituted by the eight-gun Hurricane and Spitfire monoplane fighters, whose guns, being outside the aircrew's arc, did not need 'red label' ammunition.

Until spring 1940, Britain's land-based defences came under the auspices of the so-called 'Julius Caesar Plan'. This assumed that the Germans would focus upon the early capture of a deep-water port, and that airborne forces would play a part in such an enterprise. It was believed that a German division would require transporting across the North Sea in at least twenty ships of 4,000–5,000 tons, taking twenty hours to cross the water, escorted by twenty-five to thirty destroyers. In reality, up to sixty such transports would actually have been needed, the crossing would have taken at least thirty-six hours, and Germany only possessed some twenty destroyers – this, though, was not known at the time. It was rightly anticipated that a major air assault on both the RN and RAF would be undertaken prior to, or concurrently with, a seaborne invasion. Should a landing be made, Home Forces were promised the support of two bomber and three army cooperation squadrons, although in all, squadrons would be made available to attack any approaching armada.

On the ground, General Sir Walter Kirke, Commander-in-Chief of the British Home Forces, had nine, albeit weak, divisions, including only one armoured formation, with which to repel an invasion. The land defences were not, therefore, as robust as perhaps they could and should have been.

Hitler, however, was not focused on an invasion of Britain at that time. His policy was one of blockade, endorsed by the *Oberkommando der Kriegsmarine* (OKM), the German Navy High Command. In early 1939, the OKM's plan was to secure naval bases on the North Sea and Atlantic, providing Germany access to the world's oceans, so thus the strategic priority was seizing ports in Norway and on France's Atlantic coast – not in Britain. Indeed, possession of ports along France's northern coast were considered of limited value to the *Kriegsmarine*, although the area would clearly be advantageous to an aerial campaign against Britain.

In fact, the use of this northern French coastline as a launch-pad for an invasion of south-east England was not even considered at that time. After the defeat of Poland, Hitler and his generals began planning for their offensive against the West – but the *Führer*'s strategy towards Britain remained the same. The objective of any attack on the West was clearly defined as acquisition of a large area of land with potential for waging air and sea warfare against Britain – by, according to Grand Admiral Raeder, Commander-in-Chief of the *Kriegsmarine* on 25 November 1939, 'submarines, mines and aircraft'. *Korvettenkapitän* Hansjürgen Reinicke, a staff officer serving on the OKM, was nonetheless tasked with researching and producing a feasibility study regarding an invasion of Britain by sea, sharing his conclusions in November 1939. The report revolved around a North Sea crossing, favouring capturing harbours rather than landing troops on open beaches. Furthermore, Reinicke believed that if all the conditions for a landing were met, the British would be so demoralised as to make an assault unnecessary.

Hitler remained unmoved, if, indeed, he ever even saw Reinicke's report. The *Führer*'s War Directive No 9, of 29 November 1939, acknowledged that 'England has shown herself to be the animator of the fighting spirit of the enemy and leading enemy power. The defeat of England is essential to final victory', but also that the 'most effective means of ensuring this is to cripple the English economy at decisive points'. No mention was made of invasion. This German strategy would remain in place until the following summer – which included commerce raiding against British merchantmen.

On 21 August 1939, the Deutschland-class *Admiral Graf Spee* – a *Panzerschiff* (armoured ship) to the *Kriegsmarine*, a 'pocket battleship' to the British – had left Wilhelmshaven bound for the South Atlantic. There, its captain, *Kapitän-zur-See* Hans Langsdorff was ordered to steadfastly adhere to prize rules, meaning that enemy ships had to be stopped, searched and their crews safely evacuated before they were sunk. Langsdorff was also ordered to avoid combat, all of this further evidence of Hitler's reluctance to antagonise the British, whom he hoped would accept terms once Poland had been invaded and defeated.

Graf Spee rendezvoused with its supply ship, *Altmark*, south of the Canaries on 1 September 1939. Ten days later, HMS *Cumberland* was reported as approaching, so the two German ships left at speed, evading interception. On 26 September 1939, with Britain having shown no enthusiasm for terms, Hitler ordered attacks on British shipping.

Four days later *Graf Spee* sank the British freighter *Clement*, leading to Britain and France creating eight task groups to find, sink and destroy the German raider – which was becoming an increasing menace. On 15 December 1939, Langsdorff engaged HMS *Exeter*, which returned fire, as did HMS *Ajax* and *Achilles*. *Exeter* was hit three times and forced to withdraw, badly damaged, before returning to the fray for more punishment. *Graf Spee* hit *Exeter* again, forcing it to withdraw once more, and badly damaged *Ajax* before both sides broke off the engagement. Langsdorff took refuge at Montevideo, in the River Plate estuary, to make good his own repairs, while *Exeter*, *Ajax* and *Achilles* took station on the open sea, awaiting *Graf Spee*'s reappearance on the high sea.

Cleverly, the Admiralty began broadcasting signals convincing Langsdorff that a great force of British ships awaited him, so Berlin ordered him to either break-out and see his ship interned at Buenos Aires, or scuttle *Graf Spee* in the Plate. His dilemma was that although Uruguay was neutral, it was pro-British, and therefore British naval experts would very likely be allowed aboard his ship if interned in Montevideo. The Argentinians, however, were pro-German. But, with such an apparently large British force waiting to engage him, could Langsdorff reach Buenos Aires?

Unwilling to risk the lives of his crew, the gallant German captain decided to scuttle his ship – which sank below the waves at 20.55 hrs on 17 December 1939. Seen as a victory for the RN, the Battle of the River Plate did much to restore British maritime morale in the wake of losing *Courageous* and *Royal Oak*.

Naval blockades were certainly attractive as this avoided the bloodshed of land-based battles and distanced the action from civilian populations – while indirectly damaging the enemy through cutting off essential supplies. One crucial commodity to German industry was Swedish iron-ore, and as the majority of this was exported via the Norwegian port of Narvik, control of the Norwegian coast and North Sea would be essential for Britain in the event of war with Germany. Raeder realised this and in October 1939 urged Hitler to consider violating Norwegian neutrality and seizing the country's key ports.

Hitler's strategy at that time, however, was focused upon attacking the Netherlands, Belgium, Luxembourg and France in the spring of 1940, and using favourably located ports to effectively wage war against the British economy. No heed, therefore, was taken by OKW of Raeder's pleas.

The following month, Winston Churchill, First Lord of the Admiralty, proposed Operation *Wilfred*, the mining of Norwegian waters to force Hitler's iron-ore cargoes out into the North Sea where the RN could intercept them. Anticipating a violent German response, Churchill also proposed implementation of Plan R4, the British occupation of Norway.

The Prime Minister Neville Chamberlain, and Foreign Secretary Lord Halifax, rejected all of this, concerned that such a violation of Norway's neutrality could anger other neutral states – not least the United States, which steadfastly continued isolating itself from events in Europe. In November 1939, however, the Soviet invasion of Finland caused alarm, changing the strategic canvas. The following month, Britain and France prepared to send aid to Finland, via Norway. This again entailed violating Norwegian neutrality through landing a force at Narvik, seizing the main railway used for transporting iron-ore from Sweden, and occupying the mining area of neutral Sweden.

OPERATION WESERÜBUNG: THE GERMAN INVASION OF NORWAY

Perhaps surprisingly, Chamberlain approved this plan, possibly hoping that Norway and Sweden would cooperate with the Allies – but such hopes were shattered when Germany made clear the consequences to the two Scandinavian states. In the event, the Winter War in Finland concluded with the Moscow Peace Treaty in March 1940, so R4, which involved the serious matter of disrespecting neutrality, could not be justified and was therefore abandoned.

Hitler was now fully aware of the threat posed by Britain to his precious iron ore supplies, and in December 1939 ordered preparations to be made for the invasion of Denmark and Norway, the occupation of which would safeguard both iron ore and Germany's northern flank, in addition to providing naval bases in Norway, advantageous to the campaign against Britain. If Germany attacked on land, the Polish experience suggested that the Danes would be quickly overwhelmed by the use of *Blitzkrieg* tactics.

The problem was that Norway was separated from Denmark by the Skagerrak, a 700-metre-deep strait between the Danish Jutland peninsula, south-eastern Norway and western Sweden. So as not to disrupt iron ore supplies, Hitler respected the Swedes' neutrality, meaning that Norway could not be attacked from land via that route. Either way, such attacks on Denmark or Sweden would alert the Norwegians, providing time for their defences to be prepared. There was only one answer: a seaborne invasion of Norway.

On 16 February 1940, a Lockheed Hudson of Coastal Command's 233 Squadron reported a sighting in Jossing Fjord – in Norwegian waters – of the German tanker *Altmark*. Aboard *Altmark* were some 300 British sailors, survivors of ships sunk by the pocket battleship *Graf Spee* – prisoners of war who should have been released immediately *Altmark* entered a neutral zone. HMS *Cossack* then intercepted *Altmark* and released the prisoners. Both *Cossack*'s intervention and *Altmark* carrying prisoners of war in Norwegian waters were violations of neutrality. This incident served only to embolden Hitler, it being clear that Norway was of sufficient interest to the Allies that Britain was prepared to violate international law.

Germany's invasion plan for Denmark and Norway – Operation *Weserübung* – involved a simultaneous surprise attack on both neutral states, investing major ports and airfields before the Allies could send reinforcements. Hitler's problem was landing his own reinforcements and resupply quickly, before the RN's inevitable mining operations in the Skagerrak rendered this impossible. Now came a significant departure from conventional military thinking: paratroops would drop and seize all vital locations, they would then be supplied by an unprecedented aerial transport operation. This was the Second World War's first major combined operation, requiring the close cooperation of all three services. From the *Luftwaffe* perspective, General Hans-Ferdinand Geisler was made air commander, his *Fliegerkorps* 10 having been formed specifically for anti-shipping operations. The swarms of transport aircraft involved in this massive resupply project were the responsibility of a new post, the *Transportchef Land*, under Geisler's overall command.

Weser provided for a dawn landing of army troops in the ports of Oslo, Arendal, Kristiansand, Egersbund, Stavanger, Bergen, Trondheim and Narvik. Simultaneously, Denmark was to be attacked by land forces, and troops landed by sea at Copenhagen and the Danish Islands.

The *Luftwaffe*'s role was envisaged mainly as providing air support to the land troops invading Denmark, and simply frighten the Scandinavians into submission by demonstrations of aerial might. The whole plan, however, relied entirely upon surprise – and was not without risk. One consideration was Norway's small air force, although this could be destroyed on the ground. Another consideration was the RAF – although owing to the distance involved, by the time British aircraft appeared overhead, German fighters and flak units would be established at Stavanger and Oslo.

On 4 April 1940, Bomber Command reported two German capital ships at Wilhelmshaven, the primary *Kriegsmarine* base on the North Sea. Then the presence of the battle cruisers *Scharnhorst* and *Gneisenau* were confirmed among other warships. More ominous enemy shipping was sighted at sea – the battle cruiser *Hipper* and fourteen destroyers, all en-route to Norway.

What the Germans were up to, however, was unknown – in spite of intelligence reports emanating from the Baltic that some kind of invasion fleet was being assembled. Whatever the Germans were doing clearly represented some kind of substantial threat, and so the commander of the Home Fleet, Admiral Sir Charles Forbes, sallied forth from Scapa Flow with the capital ships *Repulse*, *Valiant* and *Rodney*, two cruisers and ten destroyers, while four more destroyers steamed from Rosyth to bolster the force. Already, another capital ship, *Renown*, was at sea along with fourteen destroyers, engaged on an operation to mine the sea lanes used to transport Swedish iron ore to Germany.

Collectively, this represented the bulk of the Home Fleet – with which Forbes intended to engage the enemy ships, should they make for the Atlantic. This, however, left much of the North Sea open, and after an action between a RN destroyer, HMS *Glowworm*, and *Hipper* on 8 April 1940, it was clear that the enemy's objective lay north of the Skagerrak. While the Home Fleet and aircraft of Coastal Command searched the North Sea, the German flotilla was able to sail in safety further south – to southern Norway – achieving the crucial element of surprise.

At dawn on 9 April 1940 – *Wesertag* – German troops disembarked and invaded Norway concurrently with German forces crossing into Denmark and seizing the Danes' primary airfields. By nightfall Denmark was defeated.

Several hours after the German landings in Norway, the *Luftwaffe* surprised the Norwegian air force, destroying it on the ground at Stavanger/Sola and Oslo/Fornebu airfields as expected. German airborne landings were successful, and by midday, when Oslo/Kjellar airfield was also taken, the first German transport aircraft arrived carrying cargoes of reinforcing troops and supplies. These forward airfields were then used to accommodate two squadrons of crank-winged *Stuka* dive-bombers, and fighters ready to confront any counter-attack by the RAF.

OPERATION WESERÜBUNG: THE GERMAN INVASION OF NORWAY

On that first day, some 180 German aircraft landed at Stavanger/Sola alone. On that first day, Narvik had been captured without loss to the Germans, who had captured 600 Norwegian soldiers and sailors in addition to seizing a large army base, five British merchantmen and their crews. The following day, the RN successfully counter-attacked at Narvik, sinking two German destroyers, an ammunition supply ship and six freighters, and damaging four destroyers, offset against two destroyers sunk and one damaged.

Three days later, the RN attacked again, this time finding the enemy ships lacking fuel and ammunition. In this battle, the Germans lost eight destroyers sunk or scuttled, and a U-boat sunk by a Fairey Swordfish from HMS *Warspite*, while British losses amounted to just three destroyers damaged. The port of Narvik, however, remained in German hands. A British Expeditionary Force was despatched to Norway, setting up headquarters in Harstad on 14 April 1940, reinforced by French units a fortnight later. The Allies, however, were ill-equipped, untrained in mountain warfare, and their plans changed virtually hourly.

From an aerial perspective, the Allies troops' air cover was hardly even minimal. Squadron Leader Jack Donaldson's 263 Squadron, equipped with obsolete Gloster Gladiator biplanes, joined the aircraft carrier HMS *Furious*, subsequently flying off and operating from a frozen Norwegian lake, Lesjaskog. The squadron engaged and destroyed several He 111s on 25 April 1940, although pilots later lamented the Gladiator fighter's 'inability to overtake the He 111'. That day, however, the *Luftwaffe* responded by destroying virtually all of the Gladiators by bombing them on the ground, forcing 263 home to re-equip.

Back home, Squadron Leader Donaldson and one of his flight commanders, Flight Lieutenant Stuart Mills, reported to the Air Ministry on 28 April. Mills later recalled that when his CO pointed out that the Squadron had been sent to Norway with the wrong fuel and oil, unserviceable starter batteries, no maps, limited ammunition and other unsuitable ammunition, they were told that the Squadron was only sent to Norway as a 'token sacrifice'. Before an interview with Sir Samuel Hoare, Chamberlain's Secretary-of-State for Air, the pair were warned not to give the Minister the actual facts but simply present a positive description of the fighting in Norway. Afterwards, Air Chief Marshal Dowding received his two officers for lunch at Bentley Priory celebrating good news: for Donaldson a DSO, a DFC for Mills. Both were well-earned decorations.

By mid-May 1940, Donaldson's men were back in theatre, fighting bravely, but by 24 May both pilots and groundcrews were 'showing signs of tiring', according to the unit's Operations Record Book (ORB). That month, the old Gladiators were reinforced by the modern Hurricanes of 46 Squadron, which flew off the carrier *Glorious* on 26 May to operate from the Norwegian airfield at Skaanland. Two days later, Pilot Officer J.W. Lydall of 46 Squadron destroyed a Ju 88 over Ofotfjord – which a Gladiator could never have caught. Sadly, the following day the Hurricanes were in action against 'superior forces', losing two pilots – one of then Lydall.

A handful of Gladiators and Hurricanes, no matter how bravely the pilots fought, were no match for the enemy's overwhelming numbers: in early May, the *Luftwaffe* strength in Norway amounted to 710 aircraft, including fifty single-engine and seventy twin-engine fighters. During the campaign, 263 Squadron lost twenty-three Gladiators to enemy action and six more were ultimately abandoned when Lake Lesjaskog was evacuated; 46 Squadron lost six Hurricanes. In response, the RAF fighters were credited with thirty-nine twin-engine German bombers and *Stukas* destroyed, and eight damaged – but not one single or twin-engine enemy fighter appeared in the RAF combat reports. During the Norwegian campaign, Bomber Command had flown 882 sorties and lost thirty-one aircraft in action, claiming eleven German aircraft destroyed. Command of the air over Norway, however, undoubtedly belonged to the Germans.

On 24 May, however, the British War Cabinet had secretly decided to evacuate British troops from Norway, at a point in time when the land battle actually looked optimistic for the Allies. The Norwegians were pushing northwards, the French from the west and Poles from the south-west. On 10 May 1940, as we will see, Germany had invaded the Netherlands, Belgium, Luxembourg and France, and was currently in the process of achieving a lightning advance to the Channel coast and an unprecedented victory.

Those events, closer to home, suddenly became much more important than Norway, and the resources deployed there could soon be needed to join Britain's Home Forces or reinforce those on the Continent. The Norwegians received news of the proposed evacuation with dismay at the beginning of June 1940, but on 7 June, King Haakon and his government left Norway for exile in Britain. The British evacuation went ahead between 4 and 8 June 1940, and on 10 June, Norway surrendered.

On 8 June 1940, surviving pilots of 46 and 263 squadrons returned to the flight-deck of *Glorious*. The captain of *Glorious* was permitted to proceed independently to Scapa Flow. The German battle-cruisers *Scharnhorst* and *Gneisenau* were at large, however, and spotted the carrier. Shortly afterwards, *Glorious* became aware of the German ships' presence but failed to change tack or speed. Although five Fleet Air Arm (FAA) Fairey Swordfish were brought up to the flight deck, no aerial reconnaissance or defensive patrol was ordered however, and nor were any aircraft available for immediate take-off. The destroyer HMS *Ardent* bravely approached the German capital ships, scoring a hit on *Scharnhorst* before being pulverised and sunk.

At 16.38 hrs, *Scharnhorst*'s third salvo hit *Glorious*, holing the flight deck and rendering it inoperative. After further, grave, hits, *Glorious* sank at 18.10 hrs. Some 900 men abandoned ship, but only forty-three were rescued (by a Norwegian vessel). The German ships were unaware that *Glorious* was not part of a larger force and so they beat a hasty retreat, not staying to rescue survivors. This was yet another embarrassment for the RN, which only learned of the loss when trumpeted on German radio.

OPERATION WESERÜBUNG: THE GERMAN INVASION OF NORWAY

The gallant Squadron Leader Donaldson and all nine of his pilots aboard *Glorious* were lost, and eight pilots of 46 Squadron. Only Squadron Leader Cross and Flight Lieutenant Jameson of the latter survived, rescued from the sea, still clinging grimly to life rafts three days later. It was a tragic final curtain on an ill-fated campaign. As Dowding later wrote in his Battle of Britain Despatch, 'I trust that the epic fight of 263 Squadron, under Squadron Leader J.W. Donaldson DSO, near Aandalsnes, may not be lost to history'.

The Norwegian campaign was significant for many reasons. Germany had introduced a whole new dimension into warfare through the shocking use of paratroopers dropping behind the lines, achieving complete surprise, capturing key installations, and the massive air transport operation delivering troops and supplies. This was visionary, providing unique operational experience. Hitler had secured his iron ore supply and gained important bases to continue the war with Britain and later disrupt Allied supplies bound for Murmansk, and of benefit to his plans to invade Russia. Germany suffered 5,296 men killed, wounded or missing in Norway, Britain 1,869, and France and Poland collectively 533; Norwegian losses are estimated at 860. *Luftwaffe* losses, according to official German sources, were ninety aircraft against the RAF's 112. German air superiority was the deciding factor in the campaign's ultimate outcome – evidencing the fact that fleet operations without air cover were a thing of the past and emphasising that in modern warfare, to send troops into battle without adequate air cover was suicidal.

The importance of accurate and reliable intelligence was also clear, the British having failed to take heed of reports concerning German fleet and troop movements. The German invasion of Norway also represented the first major amphibious operation harnessing air, sea and land – but those elements had not necessarily always worked harmoniously together, and there was certainly work to be done there. For any observer, however, it was obvious that such an ambitious and complex operation required the utmost cooperation between the three services – which in time would become known as 'combined operations'. Operation *Weserübung* was, all things considered, far-sighted indeed, and the operational experience gained of great benefit to the OKW.

The *Kriegsmarine*, though, had lost half its strength in Norway. Numerically weaker, it would not have been up to defending an invasion fleet in the English Channel before suffering those losses – and certainly was not afterwards, leading Churchill to conclude that in the 'supreme issue' of an invasion of Britain, the German navy was 'no issue'. Dowding, however, was far from sure, and was understandably concerned that the mighty RN had failed to prevent the *Kriegsmarine* stealing a march and successfully landing troops on Norway. The vexing question, of course, was whether the RN could now deter or defeat a German invasion fleet bound for Britain.

Time would tell.

Chapter 10

Fall Gelb: Blitzkrieg in the West

By now, a dark and sinister shadow was enveloping Europe, the barbarity of which was already evident in Poland. According to Martin Gilbert, since Germany's victory there, 'torture and killing had continued without abatement'. Two hundred and twenty Poles, including women and children, were shot near Serokomla on 14 April 1940 alone. On 1 May, Lodz's 160,000 Jews were forbidden to leave what had become an overcrowded area, and German police were ordered to shoot any Jew approaching the barbed wire fence enclosing the ghetto. In Poland, then, an unspeakable horror had already begun to unfold, the 'cumulative radicalisation' ultimately leading to the virtual destruction of European Jewry and mass murder of countless other 'undesirables'.

A 'queer war' to Brian Lane and 'Phoney' to others it may well have been, but to those in the occupied lands, the grim realisation of Hitler's racial policies was already beyond terrifying – providing an indication of what lay in store if Britain was invaded.

Hitler, however, was confident that having witnessed the *Wehrmacht*'s might during Germany's victorious campaign in Poland, the Western democracies would come to terms. After all, Britain and France had done nothing to physically assist Poland, so perhaps now those two powers would back down, accept a peace deal, return Germany's former overseas territories and not interfere with his eastward expansion plans.

The British War Cabinet made it known that it was preparing for a war lasting at least three years. Wisely, Hitler concluded that the Allies would wish to delay a decision on the battlefield until expansion and rearmament programmes were complete. Then, there was also the possibility that America would intervene on the Western Allies' side. The sooner, therefore, the West was attacked and defeated, the better. To his generals' consternation, even before the Polish campaign was over, Hitler ordered preparations for a Western campaign – in the autumn of 1939. Given the exertions in Poland, it was unthinkable that the *Wehrmacht* would be ready to undertake an even more ambitious assault so quickly. Even Göring, Hitler's right-hand man, the so-called 'Iron Man' of Germany, was surprised. So it was that the planning began for *Fall Gelb* (Case Yellow): Hitler's long-awaited attack on the West.

On 6 October 1939, Hitler addressed the Reichstag, outlining his plans for an international conference attended by the leading powers to resolve Europe's problems – with the strict proviso that there would be no restoration of Versailles or concession of any territory won to date by Germany and the Soviets. In the event of the Western powers rejecting this offer, they would be annihilated. Nonetheless, on 12 October Chamberlain did reject the offer. In anticipation of this, Hitler had issued Directive No 6 three days earlier, provisionally ordering *Fall Gelb*, with supplementary instructions following on the 'prosecution of the war against the Western enemy'. 'The English', Hitler said, 'would have to learn the hard way'. The service chiefs, though, knew full-well that an attack so soon was impossible.

The euphoria following the victory in Poland had all but evaporated in Germany, with most people simply wanting the war to be over. Despite an unsuccessful attempt to assassinate Hitler in January 1940 by George Esler, a 36-year-old German opposed to the war, Hitler still resolved to attack the West, although he postponed *Fall Gelb* until the spring of 1940. In the meantime, as we have seen, Hitler's attention was turned to Norway and Denmark, which were invaded on 9 April 1940. A month later, while the fighting in Scandinavia continued, the hammer-blow fell.

At 04.05 hrs on Friday 10 May 1940, disbelieving Belgian sentries saw, in the dawn half-light, troop-carrying German gliders silently approaching their huge concrete fortress at Eben-Emael (commanding the Albert Canal's all-important bridges and considered the strongest defensive position in existence). Confused, the Belgians failed to react until 04.20 hrs – by which time it was too late.

Achieving complete surprise, at 04.35 hrs on Friday, 10 May 1940, 136 German divisions crashed into Belgium and Holland. Overhead, 2,500 German aircraft streamed westwards to attack Allied airfields, while 16,000 German paratroopers seized Rotterdam, Leiden and The Hague. At 07.00 hrs, the British government received desperate pleas for help from both the Dutch and Belgians: the great and long-awaited storm had at last broken.

In the British sector, Lord Gort, the BEF commander, now left carefully prepared defences along the Franco-Belgique border, pivoting forward sixty miles into previously neutral Belgium across unreconnoitered ground and without prepared supply dumps. Serving with the 3rd Grenadier Guards, Guardsman Bert Middleton remembered that shocking day 'vividly': 'Major West lined us of 4 Company up in front of a barn. "We're going to give 'em hell", he said. We were all quite confident that we would.'

To some extent there was a party atmosphere west of the front line, with Belgian civilians cheering on their British champions, showering the advancing troops with flowers and pressing refreshment upon them. The reality of *Blitzkrieg* had literally yet to hit home – it rapidly would – because the calculated process of completely dislocating and unhinging the Allied defences and command was already well underway.

While the Allies' attention was diverted by events on the Belgian-German border, the way was clear for XIX *Panzer Korps* to negotiate the supposedly 'impassable' Ardennes and deliver the *Schwehrpunkt* (point of main effort), some forty miles further South. This was a military masterstroke. Believing the main attack to be coming through the Netherlands and Belgium, as it had in the First World War, the Allies focused their attention in that direction – completely missing this cleverly disguised armoured sickle-cut, which would by-pass the Maginot Line and race for the Channel ports.

At home, the House of Commons had assembled on 7 May 1940 for a debate on the government's conduct of the campaign in Norway. Passions ran high and many a fierce speech ensued, with Prime Minister Chamberlain robustly defending his position. He faced a lack of confidence, the mood summed up by former minister Leo Amery who quoted Oliver Cromwell, having decided that the Long Parliament was no longer competent: 'In the name of God, go!'

On 10 May 1940, the same day that Hitler attacked the West, Chamberlain resigned. The popular myth has it that this was owing to appeasement having been an unpopular policy, its failure culminating in the German invasion of Holland, Belgium, Luxembourg and France – but this is not so. Chamberlain's removal owed more to the 'Norway debate', and the fact that he had an insufficient endorsement from members of his own party to govern in time of war. After rapid political manoeuvrings, on the same day Churchill – who ironically, as First Lord of the Admiralty, had been more responsible for the Norwegian failure than Chamberlain – was invited to form a coalition government. Churchill was a man made to be a war leader, a man of fire and steel – and Hitler's fiercest opponent.

Flight Sergeant George Unwin was a regular pre-war airman who had been lucky enough to be selected for pilot training under Trenchard's expansion plans, and in May 1940 was flying Spitfires with 19 Squadron at Duxford:

> I suppose looking back it was as if the world we knew was being turned upside down, but at the time we didn't think about things in any depth, we just thought "Right, now we can have a crack at 'em at last."

Pilot Officer Peter Parrott had joined 607 'County of Durham' Squadron of the AAF, at Vitry-en-Artois, near Arras and Douai, in Northern France on 28 January 1940:

> On 10 May 1940, the real war started at about 0415 hrs – when He 111s streamed over the airfield returning to base after bombing the British Army and RAF HQ at and around Arras. After a hectic seven days, there were far too many pilots, including reinforcements, for the amount of Hurricanes still serviceable; the previous evening, on 16 May, the Germans were reportedly just thirty miles away.

What Parrott, with typical modesty, fails to mention is that on that fateful day he was credited with the destruction of two He 111s, and two probables; three days later he safely returned his shot-up Hurricane to base after being bounced by 109s over Louvain.

Flight Lieutenant Peter Brothers, 32 Squadron:

> I was at Biggin Hill when things were hotting up in France. Went over there in our Hurricanes half an hour before first light, landed in France, operated there and went back to Biggin Hill for the night. The object was to help stem the German advance. But the Allied organisation was so chaotic that we really operated almost independently. We went over to Merville, refuelled – which we had to do ourselves, from jerry cans – starting our aircraft with handles – we started each other's Hurricanes, left them ticking over and went down the line to the next one – then took-off and just roamed around looking for German aircraft.
>
> One of our first actions was strafing the airfield at Ypenburg near Rotterdam, which had just been captured by the Germans. When we strafed the German planes on the ground it turned out they'd already been burnt out, apart from one which I found tucked between the corners of the hangars. I set that one on fire. We discovered some months later that some Dutchmen had been saving it to escape in to England.

At Westminster, Churchill organised his new administration, speaking to the House on Monday, 13 May. Mobilising the English language (and recycling certain historical rhetoric from Garibaldi, Clemenceau and a previous speech of his own), Churchill made clear that at this stage he had 'nothing to offer but blood, toil, tears and sweat' in what was 'an ordeal of the most grievous kind' – but the 'aim', he vowed, was clear: 'Victory at all costs, victory in spite of all terror, victory however hard and long the road may be; for without victory, there is no survival'. And in France there certainly was 'terror' from the air.

Eric Wylam, Royal Engineers:

> On we went, after ascertaining that the coast was clear, and eventually reached the top of the 'Mont-du-Chats' [Mount of Cats] without further interruptions and able to indulge in a short rest. This brief spell was soon broken by the ominous drone of many planes in the distance. Anti-aircraft fire soon warned us that these were enemy planes.
>
> We dived into the thickly wooded hillside more for camouflage than for shelter. These visitors evidently meant business for there were about thirty of them and the tactics they used were pretty frightening: the first five to ten planes released all their bombs at once, at least ten more dived and dropped their missiles singly – literally combing the

hill with bombs. More and more arrived, and closer came the bombs. It seemed as though the raid would never end. The twelve and a half minutes they were bombing us seemed like an eternity, but once again we were relieved to hear of no casualties ...

The planes were on their way: the ominous drone filled the sky. There was obviously a large number as the drone grew louder and louder. The wounded were moved against the walls of the building to afford them a little protection from the expected bombs that would be falling in a matter of minutes – poor devils.

Ten, twenty, thirty – forty – fifty planes in all we counted, consisting of twenty-five Messerschmitts and twenty-five Heinkels – and more coming. Page, Jennings and myself were in the midst of making some tea and eats for the lads and we decided to carry on to the last minute, or until 'bombs were dropping'. This we did, and when they did start falling, we were too late to get any substantial shelter, so we parked ourselves under the lintel of a door leading to the cellar. There were women in that shelter ...

The first concussions of the bombs were soon felt, and they weren't far away. They appeared to be fairly small high-explosive bombs, but quite capable of causing a fair amount of damage should they have dropped closer. Fires clearly indicated where incendiary bombs had fallen.

We clustered, somewhat scared and certainly with tense anticipation, expecting the very roof to collapse on us at any moment. CRASH! One heavy high-explosive bomb had landed in the garden, not thirty yards from us. Every pane of glass on that side of the building was blown into the room. The impact was horrifying. The very building shook from its foundations and we could see large cracks running the length of the room we were in. But alas! No masonry fell and the monastery remained erect – Thank God! Other high-explosive bombs crashed in the vicinity of the monastery. The building withstood the concussion and remained steady, much to our relief.

The *Messerschmitts* were now fiercely attacking us with their machine guns: peppering the walls for all they were worth. They dived and turned with the most hair-raising stunts in accompaniment, and we could not help but marvel at the skill at which the German pilots handled their planes. What can we do? We were <u>helpless</u> against such 'bloody' warfare! Again and again the fighters dived and splattered machine-gun fire at the building with even greater viciousness. But still everyone on the staff was unharmed. Once again it seemed as if we were all being protected by some invisible hand.

FALL GELB: BLITZKRIEG IN THE WEST

On 12 May 1940, 'A' Flight of 12 Group's Defiant-equipped 264 Squadron, led by Squadron Leader Hunter, flew to Horsham St Faith to refuel and rendezvous with six Spitfires of 65 Squadron's 'B' Flight.

Taking off at 13.10 hrs, in vic sections of three, each section of Defiants following one of Spitfires, by 13.55 hrs the formation had crossed the North Sea and was patrolling The Hague. The 264 Squadron ORB reported that:

> An aircraft, afterwards recognised as a Ju 88, was seen approaching and dropped one bomb near three destroyers at 1410 hrs. Red Section cut him off as he turned to port (inland) and dived almost to ground level. An overtaking attack was commenced, then each machine made a 'cross-over' attack in turn. Tracer bullets could be seen entering the *Junkers*, smoke poured from its port engine and it crashed in the middle of a field full of cows and surrounded by dykes. Meanwhile, Yellow Section, with a section of Spitfires, had sighted a He 111 at 3,000ft, which promptly dived to ground-level. While three Spitfires attacked from behind, Yellow 1 carried out a cross-over attack from the starboard side, when smoke immediately issued from both engines ... the machine crashed in a field, ending up against a hedge.

This was, of course, exactly the kind of combat envisaged for the Defiant – unescorted bombers, and Squadron Leader Hunter's team had not disappointed. The following day, however, came a reality check.

This time, it was the turn of 264 Squadron's 'B' Flight and the Spitfires of 66 Squadron's 'A' Flight, the fighters taking off at 04.30 hrs and heading over the North Sea to harass enemy transport aircraft ten miles north of The Hague. At 05.15 hrs, the Dutch coast was crossed, the RAF formation proceeding inland on a northerly course when Dutch AA fire opened up, forcing the fighters to take evasive action. Then, a number of Ju 87s dive-bombing a railway line were spotted by the leading Spitfire pilots, who led the whole formation into attack. Four of the dive-bombers, from 12(St)/LG1, were destroyed. Then ... disaster.

High above, keeping a watchful eye on the *Stukas*, lurked the Me 109s of 5/JG26, which lost no time in surprising the British fighters. Within a matter of seconds, five of the six Defiants were shot down – one spectacularly exploding in mid-air. Three 264 Squadron aircrew were killed; five wounded and/or captured; two crash-landed and evaded. Only one aircraft, flown by Pilot Officer H.S. Kay, survived the encounter. In response, 264 Squadron shot down just one of their assailants, *Leutnant* Karl Boris, who baled out west of Dordrecht. The Spitfires fared somewhat better, with just one of their number being damaged.

Ironically, on the day 'B' Flight was massacred over the Dutch coast, the Defiant's manufacturer telegrammed 264 Squadron, referring to the previous day's success: 'Squadron Leader Hunter and Squadron. Congratulations on first blood.'

The following signal was received from Air Vice-Marshal Leigh-Mallory on 15 May:

> I want to congratulate 264 Squadron most heartily on the success of their operations over Holland which have proved the success of the Defiant as a fighter. I much regret the loss that 'B' Flight suffered in the second operation. The courage and determination displayed were of the highest order and create for 264 Squadron a tradition that any squadron might well be proud of.

And from the CAS himself: 'You have done magnificent work during the last 48 hours in Holland and Belgium and fully justify the confidence placed in you. Keep it up.'

While the bravery of the crews in the somewhat quirky aircraft are beyond reproach and can only be admired, considering the balance sheet, it is difficult to see anything 'magnificent' about it.

> Flying Officer Christopher Foxley-Norris, 13 Army Co-operation Squadron: I went over to France with an army cooperation squadron equipped with Lysanders – we lost the lot, all twelve. Some men baled out but others were killed. We finished up stuck over there without aircraft.

On 12 May 1940, Liege had fallen, and panzers crossed the Meuse at Dinant and Sedan. The BEF, advancing into Belgium, expected to meet the German *Schwerpunkt* – point of main effort – which was expected to follow the same route, through Holland and Belgium, as in the First World War. It did not. The Netherlands was certainly attacked – the Dutch Air Force being wiped out on the first day – but the main enemy thrust was cleverly disguised.

As Allied eyes were firmly focused on the Belgian-Dutch border, *Panzergruppe* von Kleist achieved the supposedly impossible and successfully negotiated the Ardennes, much further South. German armour poured out of the forest, by-passing the Maginot Line, rendering its concrete forts useless. The panzers then punched upwards, towards the Channel coast – ten days later the Germans had reached Laon, Cambrai, Arras, Amiens and even Abbeville. Indeed, Erwin Rommel's 7th *Panzer* covered ground so quickly that it became known as the 'Ghost Division'.

The effect on the Allies was virtual paralysis, so shocking was the assault, unprecedented in speed and fury. Civilians in Britain were equally shocked – not least after the bombing of Rotterdam on 14 May 1940, reportedly caused 30,000 civilian fatalities (although post-war estimates put the death toll at nearer 3,000). Hard on the heels of Guernica and Warsaw, Rotterdam's fate was terrifying news indeed.

FALL GELB: BLITZKRIEG IN THE WEST

Lance-Sergeant Charles Constantine, 3rd Grenadier Guards:

> Very soon we could hear the sound of aircraft and civilians were running for cover and shouting to each other ... Seconds afterwards we looked up at the sky and saw a *Stuka* dive-bomber diving and releasing its bombs. I remember throwing myself to the ground beside a low brick wall as the bombs exploded just twenty-five yards from us. To say that I was not frightened would be a lie ... We were already beginning to develop a hatred of the pilots who flew those gull-winged planes ... a low-flying *Messerschmitt* riddled the road with bullets, a second followed its leader's example.
>
> This time we managed to get off a single shot with our rifles and our Bren gunner fired a short burst of automatic fire, but they came in so fast nobody had time to get their sights on properly. Several of the refugees had been hit, some very severely, and there was no hope for a few of them, including women and children. As we marched along I am sure all of us were rather shocked and feeling very bitter towards the enemy aircrews concerned. These attacks and casualties made us resolve not to show much sympathy towards the enemy once we made contact.

Private Ernie Leggett, 2nd Royal Norfolks:

> We went up to the river Dyle but gradually moved back, fighting little skirmishes ... The *Stuka* dive-bombers were more of a nuisance for splitting our ear drums with the shriek from the sirens fitted to their aircraft and bombs. Some of them were shot down. The towns and villages through which we passed were flattened to the ground, buildings still smouldering. Water cascaded everywhere from burst mains. The desolation and eerie atmosphere were most distressing. The smells of death were obnoxious.

When the AASF had flown to France on 2 September 1939, Fairey Battle light-bombers went first, followed by Blenheims and Hurricanes – but no Spitfires. And Dowding only spared Hurricanes for two reasons: first, due to political pressure, he had no choice but to support the French by providing a certain number of his precious fighters; second, that being so, he wisely decided only to send Hurricanes, which he knew were inferior to the Spitfire. Moreover, there were precious few Spitfires available in any case – certainly insufficient to send to France, thereby weakening Britain's defences for – as Dowding would later see it – no good purpose.

On 10 May 1940, though, there were six squadrons of Hurricanes in France. One week later the equivalent of six more squadrons had crossed the Channel, and another four were operating from bases on the south-east coast of England, hopping over the Channel on a daily basis but returning to England – if they could – at the end of each day. Losses in France rapidly stacked up. The Air Ministry acted as though these casualties were a complete surprise. Dowding's sharp riposte was 'What do you expect? When you get into a war you have to lose things, including precious aircraft. That's exactly what I've been warning you about!' His fears regarding the wastage of fighters were now being realised.

The crux of the problem was that the more fighters Dowding was forced to send to France, the further he weakened Britain's defences. Although Churchill later wrote that Dowding agreed with him the figure of twenty-five squadrons to defend Britain, the latter dismissed this statement as 'absurd'. With the French constantly clamouring for more fighters, and putting Churchill's War Cabinet under increasing pressure, things came to a head on 15 May.

On that day, Dowding joined Newall, the CAS, at a Cabinet meeting. Both men spoke out against sending more fighters across the Channel. These could not, however, be entirely denied, as elements of the BEF were poised to attack enemy communications near Brussels. Dowding was dissatisfied and later commented that:

> There had already been serious casualties in France, and they alone had been worrying me a very great deal. I had to know how much longer the drain was going on, and I had to ask for a figure at which they would shut the stable door and say no more squadrons would be sent to France.

Unable to request an interview with the Cabinet every time a new demand for fighters was received, on 16 May Dowding sat and composed the strongest case he could to prevent further fighters being drained away in a battle already lost. The following is extracted from that letter, which Robert Wright described as 'one of the most important documents of the early part of the Second World War':

> I must therefore request that as a matter of paramount urgency the Air Ministry will consider and decide what level of strength is to be left to the Fighter Command for the defence of this country, and will assure me that when this level has been reached not one fighter will be sent across the Channel however urgent and insistent appeals for help may be.
>
> I believe that, if an adequate fighter force is kept in this country, if the fleets remain in being, and if the Home Forces are suitably organised to resist invasion, we should be able to carry on the war single-handed for some time, if not indefinitely. But, if the Home Defence force is drained away in desperate attempts to remedy the situation in France, defeat in France will involve the final, complete and irremediable defeat of this country.

FALL GELB: BLITZKRIEG IN THE WEST

The CAS endorsed Dowding's view, and no further Hurricane squadrons were sent across the Channel. Most importantly, squadrons of the superior Spitfire were being preserved for Home Defence. By 19 May, the situation on the Continent had deteriorated further still. On that day the War Office and Admiralty began facing the possibility of evacuating the BEF from France.

Churchill finally saw sense: the Prime Minister's decision was recorded in a minute: 'No more squadrons of fighters will leave the country whatever the need of France.'

By the following day, only three of Dowding's squadrons remained on the Continent. He considered that this 'converted a desperate into a serious situation', or, as Wright put it, he was now 'able to mend some fences'. The importance of this change in policy cannot be overlooked: yet again, the defence of Britain had occasion to thank 'Stuffy' Dowding.

While Dowding awaited the Prime Minister's decision, the situation across the Channel deteriorated further still.

Squadron Leader 'Teddy' Donaldson was in action over France:

> The French bolted, including their air force. I have never seen so many people running so fast anywhere, as long as it were west. The British Tommies were marvellous, however, and fought their way to the sand dunes of Dunkirk. I was in command of 151 Squadron, and our Hurricanes were sent to reinforce the AASF, flying from Manston to France on a daily basis.
>
> In some respects, the Germans were grossly over confident in the air, and so didn't have it all their own way. But every day we had damaged Hurricanes and no ground crews to mend them, dictating that we had to return to Manston every evening. In any event, our airfields in France were being heavily bombed, so had we stayed, although pilots could have got off the airfield to sleep, our aircraft would have taking a beating. 151 Squadron would fly up to seven sorties a day, against overwhelming odds, and on one occasion even stayed on patrol after expending our ammunition so as to prevent the *Luftwaffe* attacking defenceless British troops on the ground.

At 08.30 hrs on 17 May, Pilot Officer Jack Hamar was among Donaldson's pilots landing at Abbeville, near the Somme estuary. At 10.00 hrs, 151 Squadron took off on an offensive patrol of the Lille/Valenciennes areas.

An hour later, two *Stukas* were sighted at 12,000ft, a considerable distance to the south-east. Ordering Blue and Yellow Sections to provide top cover, Donaldson and Red Section gave chase. Twenty *Stukas* of III/StG51 were found, the whole squadron participating in the interception over Valenciennes, which occurred at low altitude. Six *Stukas* were subsequently destroyed, including one of 9/StG51, by Pilot Officer Hamar. Jack's first brush with the *Luftwaffe*, however, could easily have been his last: upon landing, he counted ten bullet holes in his Hurricane.

Pilot Officer Peter Parrott, 607 Squadron:

On 17 May 1940, I had been granted a rest day, but was awoken by Pilot Officer Peter Dixon, telling me that he and I were going on leave, and that an Air Transport Auxiliary (ATA) Avro Ensign was waiting to take us back to England – but didn't intend hanging around for very long.

We started with a low-level cross-country flight to the Channel, where the captain felt brave enough to climb from 500ft to 2,000ft, before arriving at Hendon. This flight was, in fact, a very risky one. The ATA lost five out of their seven ex-Imperial Airways Ensigns in France (there were half-a-dozen pilots from other squadrons also aboard).

We had not been given time to pack our kit, so I arrived back in England with just an overnight bag, which was barely adequate for a weekend; I never saw my kit again. I still feel resentful that I lost £64 of clothes, but the Air Ministry allowed me only £24; £3 per month to Burberry's went on for a long time thereafter! The Station Adjutant at Hendon rang the Air Ministry and the Staff Officer who answered told him to give us ten days leave. I was staying with family when, on Sunday morning, 19 May, I received a telegram ordering me to report to 145 Squadron at Tangmere – immediately.

Squadron Leader Jack Satchell:

I was sent to France to be Fighter Controller at Merville – but I'd never controlled a bloody fighter in my life! We set up an operations room there in a requisitioned part of a farmhouse. They fixed us up with telephones all over the place, which all had the same ring, so it was hard to make out which one was ringing! It was hopeless. Anyway, the Huns turned up before we could get started. Somebody reported motorbikes approaching – it was the bloody Krauts. So we left Mills bombs inside the house, primed to go off when anyone touched a telephone. Then we climbed out through the loo window and took to the fields.

Although Spitfire squadrons were not sent to operate from France, by this time some of these precious squadrons were patrolling over the French and Belgian coast. On 17 May 1940, for example, 65 'East India' Squadron was up from Hornchurch to patrol Flushing, via Ostend. The ORB describes the ensuing action:

Offensive patrol over Flushing consisting of four sections led by Red Section – Squadron Leader Cooke; Yellow Section – Flight Lieutenant Olive; Blue Section – Flight Lieutenant Saunders; Green Section –

Flying Officer Kingcome. Left Hornchurch and followed a course to Ostend and there up coast, arriving over objective approximately 0755 hrs. One enemy plane (Ju 88) was seen by Red Section and Flying Officer Welford was ordered to attack. Attacking from astern, Flying Officer Welford brought the aircraft down, causing it to crash on the beach below. The Squadron saw no other machines. The coastline was followed at heights between 9,000–11,000ft, but no movements of any description could be seen All our aircraft returned safely after a patrol lasting two hours. Flying Officer Welford had bullet holes in his wings. Formation adopted three sections in vic line astern, with one section astern and above.

Welford's victim was a Ju 88A of *Stab*/III/KG30 on anti-shipping sortie over Flushing and which crash-landed on the beach at Renesse, Schouwen Island. Strangely, *Oberleutnant* Wagner and crew remain missing.

At 14.00 hrs on 18 May, 151 Squadron flew to Vitry, and were again in action at 15.30 hrs. The 151 Squadron ORB documents that 'A colossal dogfight took place above the aerodrome in which about twenty Me 109s came out of the sun and attacked a squadron of Hurricanes taking over escort duties.'

At 18.45 hrs, 151 scrambled from Vitry to intercept several 109s seen over the aerodrome; three miles north-west of Vitry, Pilot Officer Hamar caught an Me 110:

I climbed to 7,000ft and attacked two Me 110s, succeeding in getting onto the tail of one enemy aircraft (E/A). I opened fire at 300 yards with a burst of five seconds. While closing in I noticed tracer passing over my head, from behind, and looking around discovered the other E/A on my tail. I immediately half-rolled away and noticed two Hurricanes chasing another E/A, which was diving to ground level.

I followed down after the Hurricanes, and, as they broke away, I continued the chase, hedge-hopping, but did not seem to gain on the E/A. I got within 500 yards and put in a five second burst. I saw my tracer entering both wings, but did not observe any damage. As my windscreen was by this time covered in oil from my own airscrew, making sighting impossible, I broke away and returned to Vitry.

On 19 May, Sir Alexander Cadogan, the Permanent Under-Secretary at the Foreign Office, wrote the following in his diary:

News pretty bad. Germans now driving NW to cut through to Channel ports between us and French. French army not fighting. We must fight on, whatever happens. I should count it a privilege to be dead if Hitler rules England. I had not thought I should have to live through such awful days.

Pilot Officer Peter Parrott:

> On 20 May 1940 I arrived at Tangmere. The following day I was busy getting a new helmet, parachute, Irvin flying suit, flying boots etc. I was glad to find that Peter Dixon, who had been a good friend in 607, was also posted to 145, although he was in 'A' Flight, commanded by Roy Dutton, and I was in 'B', led by Adrian Boyd (known to all as 'Boydy').
>
> Our squadron CO was 'Dusty' Miller. He had formed the squadron in October 1939, firstly equipped with Blenheims, but in spring 1940 converted to Hurricanes. He was older by some years than his flight commanders, let alone we young, nineteen, twenty and twenty-one-year-old, junior pilots. He had led the squadron on a couple of sweeps over Northern France, but had not pleased the flight commanders, who persuaded him not to do so any more.
>
> Before the war, squadron commanders had been administrators rather than operational, flying, leaders, and were not then expected to lead their squadrons in the air, or even fly at all, which was their choice. Our Squadron Leader Miller was of that ilk. In effect, therefore, our flight commanders grounded the CO, who shortly afterwards was promoted and posted to Jersey as a Wing Commander.
>
> 145 Squadron was dispersed on the south-west side of Tangmere Sector Station. Each flight had two Nissen huts, one for the pilots, the other for 'Chiefy' and his groundcrews. To the east of us was 601 Squadron, with similar accommodation. Most of the pilots had been with the squadron from its formation, so knew each other well. They had all flown sweeps over France and had combat experience. Apart from the flight commanders, we were all pilot officers or NCOs, and got on well together.
>
> I did my first operation with 145 Squadron on 22 May 1940, a sweep of the Arras/Bethune area.

On that day, having returned to Manston, three sections of 151 Squadron escorted Ensign transport aircraft to Merville. On the return journey, twenty-four *Stukas* were seen dive-bombing St Omer. Donaldson's pilots attacked, their resulting 'bag' being four confirmed destroyed and two unconfirmed. Pilot Officer Hamar was again successful:

> The leader ordered Red Section to attack and we dived towards the *Junkers* 87s. I lost sight of my leader and circled to select a target. I closed on one which was diving, but failed to attack before the E/A dropped its bombs onto a village.
>
> As the E/A pulled up, I attacked, giving a five second burst at 200 yards, which killed the rear gunner. I closed to 100 yards and after

a seven second burst the E/A turned on its side with smoke pouring from its engine. It went into a steep dive and crashed in a field.

I attacked another E/A at which I fired a short burst from 200 yards, after which I experienced no further fire from the rear. I closed to 100 yards and opened fire, which tore off the side of the fuselage and top of port wing. I was forced to break away without observing what happened to this E/A because I ran into another five Ju 87s. I did not see any further E/A crash but saw a parachute descending. Having turned the petrol supply onto the gravity tank, and having fifteen rounds per gun remaining, I returned to base.

One of Jack's targets was possibly a Ju 87B of 4/StG77, which crash-landed back at Rocroi, having been badly shot-up by a Hurricane during an attack on a crossroads east of St Omer.

The Spitfires of 65 Squadron were also in action again that afternoon: 'Squadron led by Squadron Leader Cooke patrolled Calais – Boulogne, Blue Section, led by Flight Lieutenant Saunders, attacked Ju 88, Pilot Officer Smart killing the air gunner. The starboard engine was put out of action, and machine was last seen entering a cloud emitting black smoke.'

The following morning, Squadron Leader Cooke again led his Spitfires over the French coast, wherein another hazard was encountered: 'Fired at by destroyers of the Royal Navy on way home, some shots being uncomfortably near.'

Flight Lieutenant Gerry Edge was a flight commander with 605 Squadron, also flying Hurricanes above what was developing into a military catastrophe for the Western Allies:

> After the German offensive began, the roads below were full of columns of civilians and soldiers, all progressing westwards. Once we came upon a *Stuka* that was strafing a column of refugees. It was plain to anyone, especially from that low altitude, that this was a civilian, as opposed to a military column. I am pleased to say that I shot this *Boche* down. There were no survivors. Does that concern me? Not at all. Of all the enemy aircraft I shot down, that one gave me great pleasure.

While Dowding was fighting the political battle to preserve fighters and especially retain Spitfires for the defence of Britain itself, Air Vice-Marshal Leigh-Mallory was trying to get his 12 Group into the war. Operating from Martlesham Heath on the East Coast, shortly after first light on Easter Monday, 13 May 1940, six Defiants of 264 Squadron took off, escorted by six Spitfires of 66 Squadron's 'A' Flight, bound for the Dutch coast.

While patrolling off The Hague, a formation of 12/LG 1 Stukas dive-bombing a railroad was attacked. Unfortunately, the Ju 87s had fighter escort: Me 109s of

5/JG 26. In the subsequent action *five* of the six Defiants were destroyed by the German fighters, and a Spitfire was also despatched, the pilot of which crash-landed and returned home safely. This was a pointless sortie that cost the lives of good men. It was also contrary to Dowding's policy of preserving fighters for Home Defence.

This appears to be an early indication of just how wrong Leigh-Mallory's offensive outlook and desire to see 12 Group at the forefront of battle was. On 18 May, as Dowding agonised over the Battle for France bleeding away his precious fighters, Leigh-Mallory, incredibly, visited 19 Squadron at Duxford, arranging for the Spitfire-equipped squadron's proposed move to France – another indicator of his inability to think beyond his own interests. Fortunately, however, there was no repetition of the suicidal sortie to Holland and no 12 Group Spitfire squadrons ever went to France.

On 21 May 1940, the news from France was alarming; incredibly, German troops had reached the seaside resort of Le Crotoy, on the Channel coast, at the mouth of the Somme – cutting the Allied armies in half. That day, the BEF, aligned division by division, had fought off the enemy's attempts to cross the river Escaut, to the East of the French city of Lille, just across the Belgian border. It was a valiant effort which saw two Victoria Crosses awarded. The German thrust to the Channel, however, changed everything. The BEF was now in grave danger of being driven back against the North Sea coast, enveloped and destroyed. Although under political pressure to counter-attack to the South, the crumbling Belgian front to the North dictated no option for Lord Gort but to withdraw behind the Ypres-Comines canal.

So hard-pressed had the Hurricane squadrons been in France that, for the first time, Spitfires were committed to battle over the French coast on 21 May 1940. Off Dunkirk and Calais, 11 Group's 54 and 74 squadrons claimed a number of enemy bombers destroyed. Two Spitfires were lost, both of 74 Squadron; one pilot returned to England but the other was captured. Shortly after 17.00 hrs that day, Flight Lieutenant 'Sailor' Malan had led 'A' Flight of 74 Squadron to patrol Dover at 20,000ft. Sailor described the ensuing action in a subsequent interview with the American journalist Quentin Reynolds:

> There wasn't much hope of finding the enemy formation we had been sent up to intercept in these broken clouds. It was just another patrol by the look of it. I felt mad because I knew we were a good flight, but how good or bad we couldn't say. We'd never been tried. We'd been reading what Hurricanes could do in France against Messerschmitt 109s and Heinkels. We thought we had something better still in the Spit. But that still had to be *proved*...
>
> Anyhow, we came out of the clouds at 17,000ft. There were six of us all told, and we came out in perfect formation. Johnny's [Pilot Officer Freeborn's] wing was tucked right inside mine, and on the

left Bertie Aubert, who was half-American, had his wing-tip nestling close. I said through my intercom disc 'Nice flying, boys', and then I looked towards France and saw something else.

France was still our ally then, remember. I saw black puffs about 15,000ft over Calais. The ack-ack guns kept firing and that meant there were Jerries about. I yelled 'Tally Ho over Calais. Let's cut some cake!'

We opened up fast, A Spit can cross the Channel about as quick as you can cross the street. There were more clouds between us and Calais. I was flying across the top of a great hummock when I nearly flew into a He 111. What happened next was done mainly by instinct. I was moving so fast that only by pulling the stick back and a quick swerve did I avoid ramming him. I was so afraid the German might drop down into the cloud a hundred feet below that I began firing as I did a steep banking turn on his tail. The bullets ripped into him from tail to nose. Pieces flew off. He belched heavy smoke, his undercart fell out and he dropped helplessly into the cloud. As I saw it breaking up I yelled through the intercom 'Re-form, re-form'.

The historic moment was dramatically recorded by Sailor's cine-gun camera. The enemy aircraft of 1/LG1 force-landed at Groede, the crew of four being captured, one of whom died in hospital from wounds. Sailor continues:

I'd tasted blood at last. The release from tension was terrific, the thrill enormous. I'd been wondering for so long – too long, how I'd react in my first show. Now I knew. Everything I had learnt had come right. There was hardly any time to feel even scared. After that I found a Ju 88. That was a much slower-moving target. It seemed easy, even though it carried rear-gunners.

I got on its tail and fired when I was about 500 yards off. That was more or less according to regulations. It wasn't quite so simple, although I saw my bullets hammering against his starboard wing-root, where the wing meets the fuselage. In the next few moments I was more into position. At 150 yards my bullets burst all over him. There was no return fire. Then he fell into a dive, with flames showing. I turned to look for the other two in my flight.

During the attack on the Ju 88, Pilot Officer Freeborn was immediately behind Malan, also attacking the same target successfully. Of Pilot Officer Aubert, however, there was no trace.

On 22 May 1940, German armour continued advancing northwards, threatening Boulogne. Home-based Spitfire and Hurricane squadrons provided air cover for that port, Calais and Dunkirk, flying a total of 198 patrols. At dawn, Flight Lieutenant

Malan and 'A' Flight were at Rochford on readiness, and scrambled shortly after 05.00 hrs. Sailor's combat report describes events:

> I was leading three sections off Dover at 12,000ft when I sighted a Ju 88 steering NE in a clearing in the clouds. Formed line astern with Red Section and cut enemy aircraft off from cloud. He dived for sea very steeply ay 400 mph, IAS (Indicated Air Speed) and jettisoned four bombs. I delivered No 1 Attack at 250 yards range.
>
> After second two-second burst, rear gunner stopped firing from twin guns in top blister. Enemy aircraft took avoiding action by skidding and turning. I saw incendiary entering port engine and all-around fuselage, while white vapour was emitted by both motors. At commencement of action IAS was 280 mph, but after my fifth burst speed suddenly reduced, and as my windscreen was covered in white vapour I broke off to port and observed results of action.
>
> No 3 [Sergeant Mould], whose R/T had failed, then attacked from 200 yards and expended all his ammunition and broke off. No 2 [Pilot Officer Freeborn] then attacked but after his first burst enemy aircraft suddenly lost height, as though both engines had stopped and broken up. There was nothing left after two seconds except the dinghy. Searched for crew but found none.

The Ju 88 had been engaged at 05.45 hrs, 'ten miles north of Calais', at 'sea level'. During this combat Flight Lieutenant Malan closed to 200 yards. This machine, which went down in the Channel, was an aircraft of 3/KG30 engaged on a reconnaissance sortie at first light – all aboard were lost. From Malan's perspective, it was a perfect example of team work.

It was 74 Squadron's only engagement that day, the remainder of which was largely spent providing aerial protection to coastal convoys.

With an armoured wedge driven firmly between the Allied armies, those in the north were now focused on retiring to the Channel coast. By 23 May, however, Boulogne was besieged and Calais isolated, leaving Dunkirk as the only option. On this day, Fighter Command would fly 250 sorties providing air cover over the French coast; at 06.00 hrs 74 Squadron was up from Rochford, the CO, Squadron Leader Laurie White, and Flying Officer Measures shooting down an Hs 126 reconnaissance aircraft of 1(H)/14 over Guines, killing the pilot and wounding the observer. The German observer's return fire, however, damaged White's radiator, forcing the CO to land at Calais-Marck airfield.

Hornchurch's other Spitfire squadron, 54, had preceded 74 on patrol that morning but returned after yet another uneventful sortie, enviously eyeing the Tigers's lead section returning with gun patches blown. Pilot Officer Al Deere, of 54 Squadron, immediately drove over to 74 Squadron's dispersal to get the 'form'.

First to land was Sailor. Air Commodore Deere, as he later became, recalled the conversation with Sailor:

> 'Hello, Al, I might have known you'd be sniffing around to find out the form. I always said that the "Tigers" would be first to get among them; aren't you envious?'
> 'You bet I am, Sailor! Tell me more...'
> 'Sorry, haven't got time. All I can say is that we were jumped, and all because some bloody fool would keep nattering on the R/T with the result that when Paddy Treacy gave a sighting report only one or two of the chaps heard it. On top of that the CO had engine trouble, and all in all it was a confusing and frustrating engagement. I think he finally made Calais/Marck airfield where he landed successfully.'

Little did he know it, but Al Deere would soon be caught up in high drama owing to Squadron Leader White's predicament.

Having force-landed, Squadron Leader White hitch-hiked to Calais, presented himself to the nearest Army Transport Officer and telephoned Fighter Command HQ requesting that a new engine be sent over for his Spitfire, which was a new aircraft and repairable, and an aircraft to collect him. The Hornchurch Station Commander was informed, and he, Group Captain 'Daddy' Bouchier, aware that 54 Squadron possessed a two-seater Miles Master, ordered Flight Lieutenant 'Prof' Leathart of that unit to fly over to Calais, escorted by two Spitfires, and collect 'Droguer' White.

Understandably, when Sailor was told about the plan he insisted that the Tigers were perfectly capable of rescuing their own CO, and requested that Sergeant Skinner of 74 Squadron should fly the Master, which he had once instructed on. For some unknown reason Bouchier refused – for which, according to Ira Jones, 'Malan never forgave him'.

So Leathart flew to Calais-Marck, closely escorted by two 54 Squadron Spitfires, flown by Pilot Officers Al Deere and Johnny Allen, while Flight Lieutenant Malan – honour slightly restored – and 74 Squadron provided high cover. Over the French airfield, the Master was attacked by Me 109s of 1/JG1, Deere and Allen joining the fray and claiming three confirmed destroyed and three unconfirmed between them. Flight Lieutenant Leathart was then able to safely extract Squadron Leader White, for which feat 'Prof' received the DSO, while Deere and Allen were both awarded DFCs.

On 23 May, the first big air battle between the opposing fighters took place over Calais. Spitfires of 54 Squadron claimed three Me 109s destroyed, while 92 claimed two in addition to seven Me 110s shot down. Both squadrons claimed various enemy aircraft as probably destroyed or damaged. I/JG 27, however, lost four 109s while no 110s are recorded as having been destroyed or damaged that day – one which saw the Spitfire's first victory over the Me 109. This was actually recorded by 54 Squadron's Pilot Officer Al Deere, a New Zealander, who later wrote:

> In my written report on the combat I stated that in my opinion the Spitfire was superior overall to the Me 109, except in the initial climb and dive; however this was an opinion contrary to the belief of the so-called experts. Their judgement was of course based on intelligence assessments and the performance of the 109 in combat with the Hurricane in France. In fact, the Hurricane, though vastly more manoeuvrable than either the Spitfire or the Me 109, was so sadly lacking in speed and rate of climb, that its too-short combat experience against the 109 was not a valid yardstick for comparison.
>
> The Spitfire, however, possessed these two attributes to such a degree that, coupled with a better rate of turn than the Me 109, it had the edge overall in combat. There may have been scepticism by some about my claim for the Spitfire, but I had no doubts on the score; nor did my fellow pilots in 54 Squadron. Later events, particularly in the Battle of Britain, were to prove me right.

Interestingly, the Spitfire Deere flew that day, N3180, the 416th of the type so far produced, was one of a small number fitted with the Rotol Constant Speed propeller, which was superior in performance to the de Havilland variable pitch aircrew fitted to RAF fighters at that time. Although the de Havilland propeller was a great improvement on the original mahogany two-bladed fixed-pitch propeller, it still only offered the pilot two settings: coarse and fine pitch, whereas the German VDM propeller provided the facility for the pilot to select the optimum setting for any combat scenario. This was another technical area, in addition to armament, the 109's cannon was found to be most effective, where RAF fighters lagged behind.

The overall balance sheet on 23 May 1940 was not favourable to Fighter Command: 74 Squadron lost two Spitfires, 92 Squadron five. The total of sorties flown by 11 Group on that day was 250; ten pilots were lost. The action was even greater on 24 May, 54, 65, 74 and 92 squadrons, all being engaged. At this time Park's squadrons were patrolling singly. The *Luftwaffe* fighters, however, were sweeping the Channel coast in *gruppe* strength – some thirty-six aircraft. The airspace above the French coast was rapidly becoming a killing ground.

Flying Officer Richard Gayner, 615 Squadron:

> Terror and exhaustion dominate my recollections of that period over France and Belgium – terror because of all the bloody Huns. There were so many more of them than us, they had better aeroplanes, they were trying to kill us, and they were better at it than we were. They liked war and most of us didn't like it at all.

FALL GELB: BLITZKRIEG IN THE WEST

Flight Lieutenant Peter Brothers:

> While operating over France as a flight commander in 32 Squadron, I naturally took our latest replacement under my wing to fly as my Number Two. Suddenly I had that feeling we all experience at some time that I was being watched. Glancing in my rear-view mirror I was startled to see, immediately behind me and between my Number Two and me, the biggest and fattest Me 109 – ever! As I instantly took evasive action his front end lit up as he fired.
>
> I escaped unscathed, the 109 climbed and vanished as I did a tight turn, looking for my Number Two. There he was, good man, cutting the corner to get back in position, as I thought, until he opened fire on me! Suggesting on the radio that his action was unpopular, as there were no other aircraft in sight we wended our way home. Not only had he not warned me of the 109's presence or fired at it, he had had such an easy shot but missed.
>
> I dealt a blow to his jauntiness by removing him from operations for two days' intensive gunnery training; sadly it did not help him survive.

Significantly, on 24 May 1940, Hitler – who believed that the war would be over in six weeks and the way clear for an agreement with Britain – consented to General von Rundstedt's request that the German advance be halted east of the Lens-Bethune-St Omer-Gravelines line, in order to preserve armour for operations against the French further south. Indeed, both Hitler and von Rundstedt were confident that the Allied forces now within what had become the Dunkirk perimeter, could be destroyed from the air, given that the *Luftwaffe* enjoyed complete aerial supremacy over France.

This, in fact, had been the primary deciding factor in the campaign and achieved by the German fighters, especially the Me 109. This aerial umbrella provided for the German ground forces to advance and fight unimpeded by Allied air attack, and without substantial fighter opposition, *Stuka* dive-bombers were able to wreak havoc.

It has been argued by various historians that Hitler gave this infamous 'Halt Order' because he was sympathetic to the British and foresaw both Britain soon coming to terms with Germany and perhaps even joining the forthcoming fight against the Soviets. In truth, Hitler had nothing to gain by allowing the BEF to escape destruction in France, and needed to deliver the British a grievous blow to make Churchill even consider terms. The following day, Generals Brauchitsch and Franz Halder (the OKH Chief of Staff), who both assumed that the *panzers* would press on, made representation against the decision to stop, but Hitler left the final decision to Von Rundstedt. So the *panzers* stopped. Hitler was unconcerned, having total confidence in the *Luftwaffe* to finish the job while the *panzers* rested and firmly believed only a handful of Gort's men would get away.

While the Germans paused, however, the evacuation of British troops started – a thousand embarked from Boulogne on the day that Hitler's air assault began. It was now clear to Lord Gort that evacuation was the only option to prevent the BEF's destruction, even if that meant losing all transport and heavy weapons. The situation in France was becoming graver by the minute. That afternoon, a substantial German force bypassed Calais, heading towards the Belgian coastline, cutting off the gallant British garrison. Again, Fighter Command was heavily committed patrolling the coast and Pas-de-Calais inland to St Omer, losing ten aircraft and six pilots.

Still operating out of Rochford, Flight Lieutenant Malan's combat report takes up the story of the mid-morning patrol:

> The Squadron was on offensive patrol of Calais. Sighted Do 17 five miles out to sea, below 8/10th cumulus. E/A made off towards cloud at very high speed. Delivered short bursts at E/A whenever opportunities occurred, i.e. when he emerged into clear air between clouds. Most of my bursts were delivered at 4-500 yards owing to difficulty of closing up quickly. Broke away after E/A dived below cloud-base and I had expended my remaining ammunition and had his starboard engine on fire. I then saw Red 2 and 3 firing from astern. The E/A burst into flames and crashed. I filmed the crash and wreck with my cine-gun. The pilot got out and dragged a wounded crew-member out. At one time I saw what appeared to be flaps falling off when I was firing.

The Do 17 was very likely a machine of 1/KG77, which crashed near Fruges killing one crew-member. Unteroffizier Heilmann is known to have been wounded and was possibly the man Sailor saw dragged from the wreck. The victory was shared by Sailor with the two other members of Red Section. Another Do 17 was claimed by Flight Lieutenant Treacy and Pilot Officer Derek Dowding (son of Air Chief Marshal Dowding).

The afternoon patrol was hectic. Sailor's combat report:

> I was leading Yellow Section of four aircraft on offensive patrol Dunkirk – Calais – Boulogne. Spotted AA fire at 12,000ft over Dunkirk when at 500ft off coast west of Dunkirk. Climbed in line astern to investigate and saw three vics of mixed bombers (approx. 9 -12 – 9). Intercepted second vic at 12,000ft and passed through very heavy and accurate AA barrage. Attacked starboard flank in echelon port from astern as Me 109 and Me 110 were observed above and into sun, turning onto our flank to attack.
>
> Observed about eight of these but probably many more about. Delivered three one second bursts at both engines and fuselage

Above left: Winston Spencer Churchill, who succeeded Neville Chamberlain as Britain's Prime Minister on 10 May 1940 – and became the war time leader the country so badly needed.

Above right: In 1936, Air Chief Marshal Sir Hugh CT Dowding (pictured here earlier in service) became Commander-in-Chief of Fighter Command. Totally committed to the concept of 'security of base', Dowding, who understood technology in addition to having been a fighter pilot in the First World Wear, immediately set about improving the System of Fighter Control with which he would one day defend the British Isles.

Below left: Dowding's Senior Air Staff Officer before the war was the tough First World War fighter ace, Keith Park, a New Zealander, who perfectly understood modern air strategy and tactics. On 13 April 1940, Park was promoted air vice-marshal and given command of the prestigious 11 Group, Fighter Command, defending London and the south-east; there was no better choice. Park is pictured here later in the war whilst commanding Malta's aerial defence.

Below right: Air Vice-Marshal Sir Trafford Leigh-Mallory, commander of 12 Group, Fighter Command, defending the Midlands and industrial North. An ambitious man, unlike Dowding and Park, Leigh-Mallory had no personal experience of fighters and the evidence confirms his inability to grasp the required strategy – which later caused major problems as the Battle of Britain progressed.

Fighter Command's group boundaries, sector airfields and radar coverage, and Luftwaffe deployment for the Battle of Britain.

Adolf Hitler, leader of the Nazis, Führer and supreme German warlord with Reichsmarschall Hermann Göring, another First World War fighter ace and chief of the *Luftwaffe*. Hitler's policy for prosecuting the war against Britain after the Fall of France was initially blockade, not invasion, although Göring was totally confident in his air force's ability to defeat the RAF.

Had Britain gone to war over the Munich Crisis in September 1938, this obsolete fighter, the Gloster Gauntlet, equipped the majority of Fighter Command's frontline units; the Luftwaffe's primary fighter, however, was the Me 109 – an incomparable, modern, monoplane of infinitely superior performance.

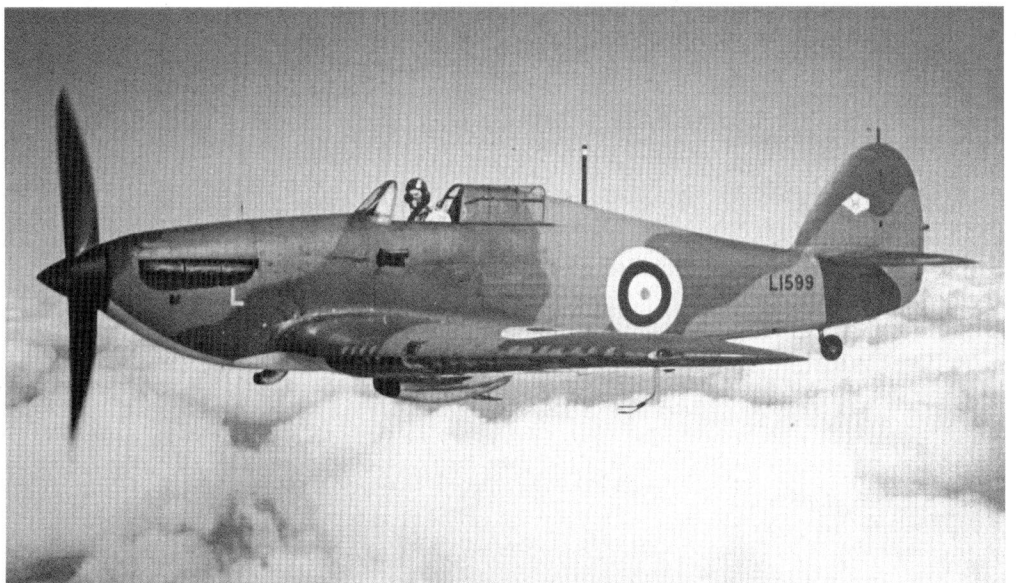

Fortunately, from November 1937 onwards, the new Hawker Hurricane monoplane fighter, designed by Sydney Camm. This is Pilot Officer Maurice Mounsden of North Weald's 56 Squadron airborne in an early Hurricane Mk I, circa 1938 (Paul Weaver).

Above left: Two 56 Squadron Hurricane pilots at North Weald in 1938 (Paul Weaver).

Above right: On 4 August 1938, 19 Squadron received the first Supermarine Spitfire delivered to Fighter Command, and three months later was operational on type by both day and night. The Spitfire's performance was superior to the Hurricane, and although available in smaller numbers for the Battle of Britain, with its ability to take on the Me 109 at high-altitude, the outcome may well have been very different. These are those first Spitfire Mk Is of 19 Squadron, arrayed for the camera at Duxford in 1938.

Below: Wishful thinking: a spurious tactical diagram published in the Air Ministry's 1941 morale-boosting account of the Battle of Britain. Anyone believing that Me 109s either flew in the same suicidal formation as the RAF, or would take no evasive action upon being attacked, would find themselves much mistaken.

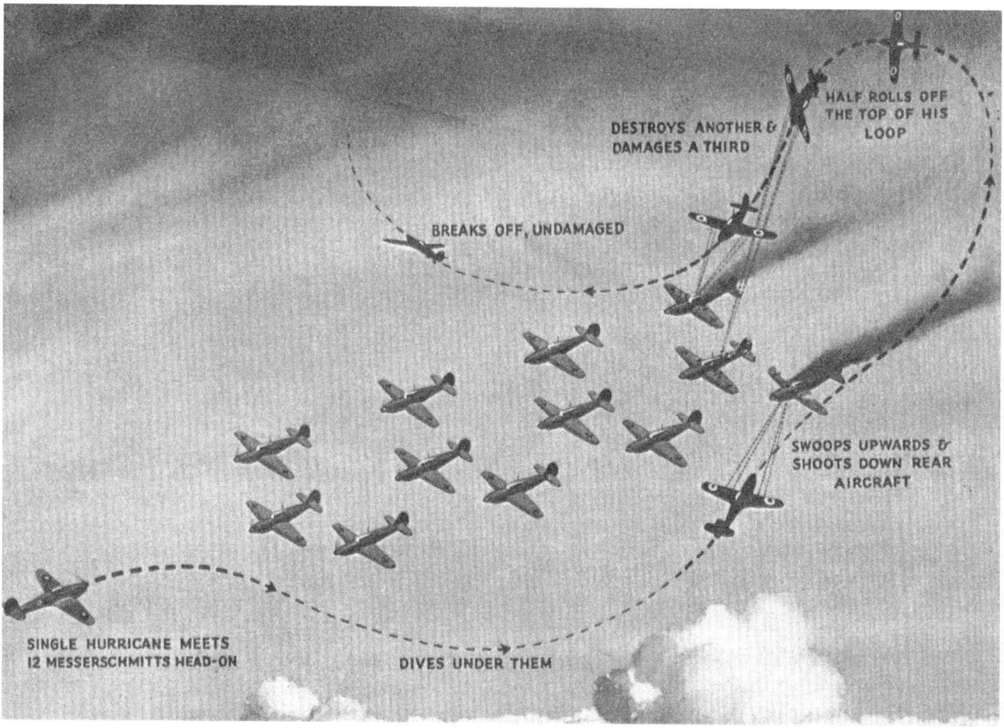

Above left: A Spitfire squadron flying in tight sections, or 'vics' of three – an inflexible formation requiring too much time concentrating on formation flying and insufficient looking out for the enemy.

Above right: A flight of two sections of Hurricanes in 'vic' formation.

Right: The System of Fighter Control, as illustrated in a wartime publication.

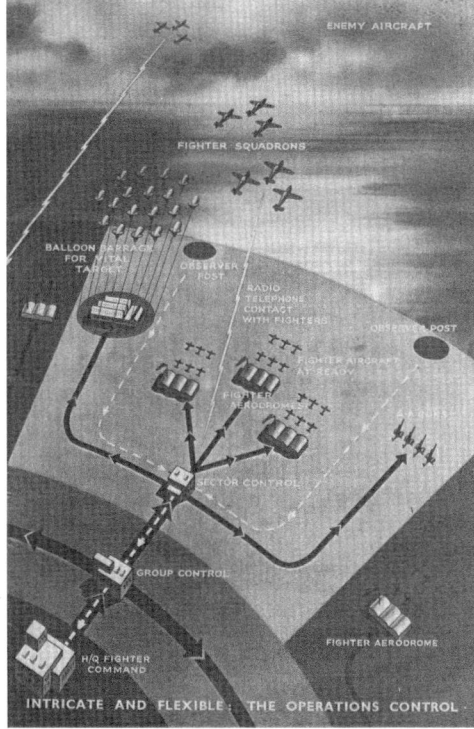

Flight Lieutenant Peter Townsend whilst serving with 43 Squadron at Wick, pictured with his Flight Rigger, Duxbury (left) and Engine Fitter, Hacking.

Above left: The first German aircraft, a He 111, to fall on English soil since 1918, destroyed by Flight Lieutenant Townsend's Blue Section on 3 February 1940. The enemy bomber crashed near Whitby.

Above right: Flight Lieutenant Townsend enemy rear gunner, Unteroffizier Karl Missy, who had lost a leg, in hospital. Missy's pilot also survived, but both the observer and flight engineer were killed. Many years later, Group Captain Townsend, as he became, and Herr Missy met again, at the latter's home in Germany: 'He bore me no ill-will and welcomed me as a friend', the RAF fighter ace recalled.

The bombardier and front gunner of a He 111 in the bomber's highly vulnerable glazed nose.

The best German bomber: a Ju 88 of KG51 Edelwiess.

In addition to Spitfires and Hurricanes, Fighter Command was also equipped with the fighter version of the twin-engined Bristol Blenheim. Found to be unsuitable for daylight operations against the lethal Me 109, the Blenheim would do sterling service as a stop-gap night-fighter whilst the arrival of dedicated night-fighting types was eagerly awaited (Neil Hutchinson).

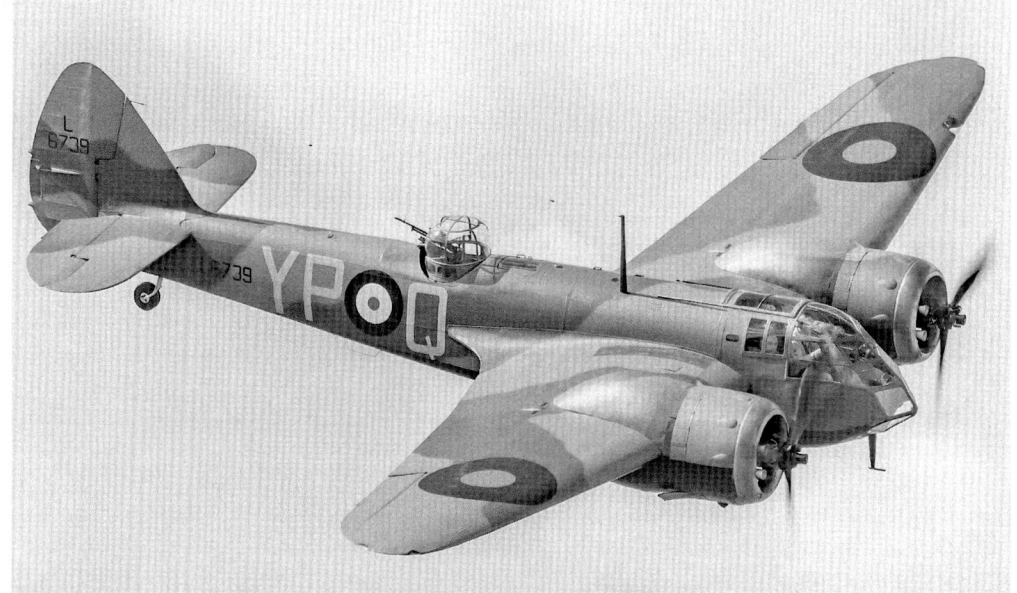

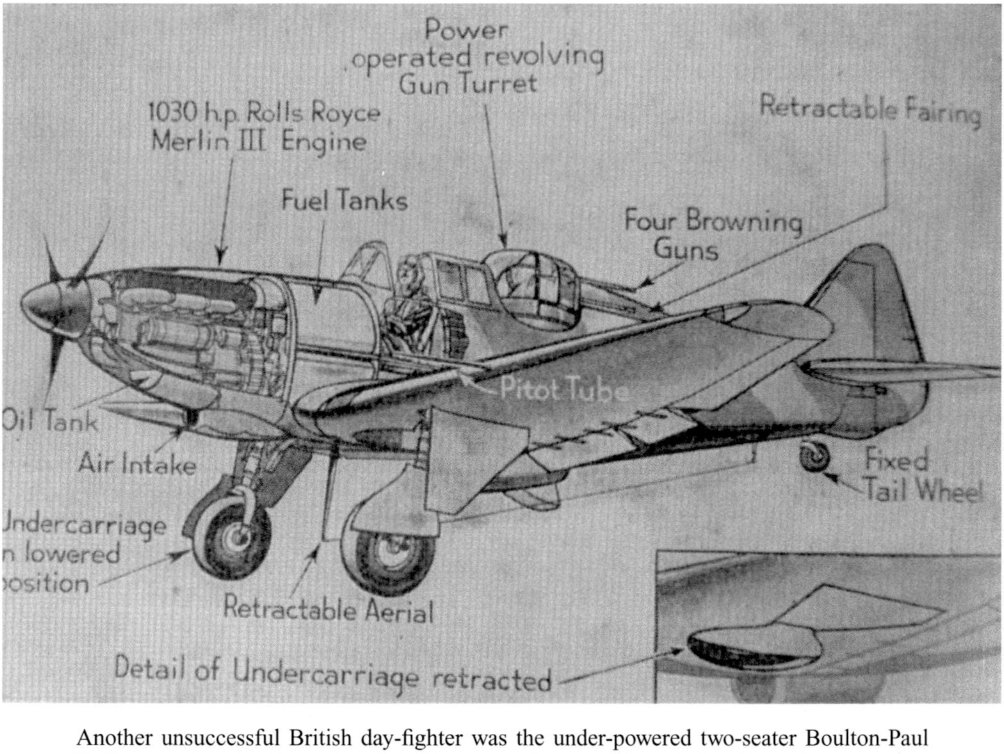

Another unsuccessful British day-fighter was the under-powered two-seater Boulton-Paul Defiant, equipped with an electronically operated turret and carried a pilot and air gunner.

Above left: The Defiant turret-fighter was armed with four .303 Browning machine-guns but without fixed and forward-firing armament operated by the pilot lacked the immediate hand-to-hand coordination necessary in fast-moving modern air combat (Andy Long).

Above right: David Scott-Malden, a Cambridge scholar who flew Spitfires during the Battle of Britain, surviving to became a highly decorated ace and ultimately retire from the post-war service as an air vice-marshal. David's handful of diary entries during the period immediately preceding the Battle of Britain perfectly capture the uncertainty and anxiety of those desperate days.

Below: Hurricane pilots of 56 Squadron at North Weald in 1939 – including Pilot Officer Montague Hulton-Harrop (second right), tragically killed in the so-called 'Battle of Barking Creek': a 'friendly fire' incident involving 74 Squadron's Spitfires on 6 September 1939 Paul Weaver).

A sergeant of the Women's Auxiliary Air Force on duty in the Duxford Operations Room during the Battle of Britain.

Above: With only Hurricanes deployed to the continent during the Fall of France, the Spitfire and Me 109 met for the first time over the French coast during the Dunkirk evacuation. Central to this snapshot, taken at that time, is the legless fighter ace Douglas Bader, at the time a flight lieutenant in 222 Squadron, which was operating out of Hornchurch with 92 Squadron. Also pictured, second right, is Flight Lieutenant Robert Stanford Tuck of the latter unit, who, like Bader, would become an ace and prisoner of war.

Right: Without doubt, the most outstanding Fighter Command personality to emerge from the early war period was the South African Adolph Gysbert Malan of 74 Squadron, known universally as 'Sailor' on account of previous service in the merchant navy.

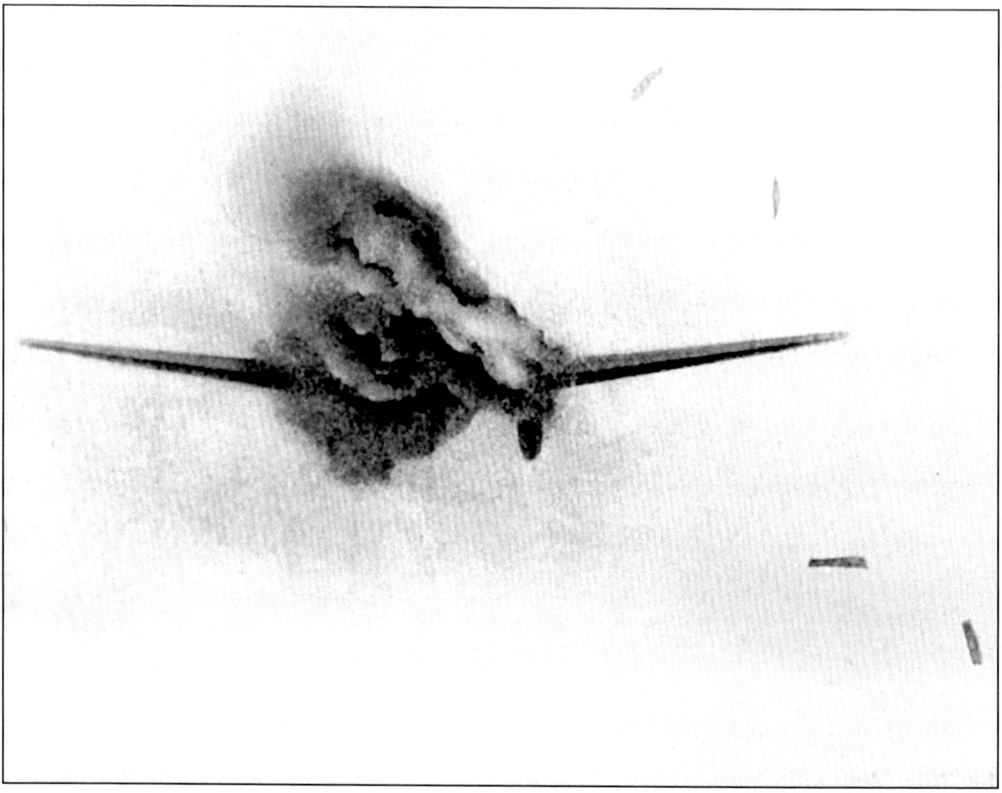

Above: Like many other Spitfire pilots, including Bader, Malan recorded his first aerial victories over Dunkirk – this combat footage showing a He 111 under fire from his guns.

Left: On the night of 18/19 June 1940, the lull after Dunkirk broke when over seventy German bombers ranged over England, attacking various targets. At 0020 hrs on 19 June 1940, Flight Lieutenant Malan destroyed a He 111 of Stab/KG4 'General Wever' off Foulness, recording what was the Spitfire's first nocturnal kill. The bomber crashed at Chelmsford, the scene envisioned here by a war artist.

Above: The German Me 109 'Emil', which enjoyed a number of technical advantages over the Hurricane and Spitfire to begin with, including fuel-injection, a constant speed propeller, and a pair of 20mm Oerlikon cannon. This section of 109s, off the French coast, is flying in the classic Schwarm formation: four aircraft stepped up in line abreast, each projecting the other and separated by a couple of hundred metres (thereby allowing pilots to concentrate on searching for the enemy, rather than formation flying). When battle was joined, the section broke into two Rotten, or fighting pairs, each comprising the leader, whose job it was to take the shot, whilst his tail was protected by a wingman, thereby enabling the leader to concentrate on the target.

Below left: During the early war period the Luftwaffe reaped the benefits of having tried and tested its new weapons and tactics in the Spanish Civil War. It was there that Werner Mölders rose to prominence and worked out the basis of modern air fighting. Dubbed 'Vatti', the 'Father of German Air Fighting' would prove a formidable opponent in the Battle of Britain ahead.

Below right: Another 'Spaniard' who rose to prominence, and later great office, was Adolf Galland, pictured here describing his latest aerial victory at the birthday party held in Le Touquet on 15 April 1941 for General Theo Osterkamp (extreme left), an ace in both World Wars and responsible for the German fighter force in the Battle of Britain. Next to Galland is his friend, Mölders.

Above left: Generalfeldmarschall Albert Kesselring, commander of Luftflotte 2, visiting Major Mölders' field headquarters in the Pas-de-Calais.

Above right: Generalfeldmarschall Hugo Sperrle, former commander of the 'Legion Kondor', Hitler's expeditionary force supporting General Franco in the Spanish Civil War, commanding Luftflotte 3.

Below left: Göring's intelligence chief, Oberst 'Beppo' Schmid – who failed to provide accurate information concerning the RAF's strength and deployment throughout the Battle of Britain – with disastrous consequences for the enemy.

Below right: The feared Ju 87 'Stuka' dive-bomber – which did so much damage during the Blitzkrieg years.

The hallowed grounds of the All-England Lawn Tennis Club at Wimbledon became a pig farm to support the war effort – desperate times indeed.

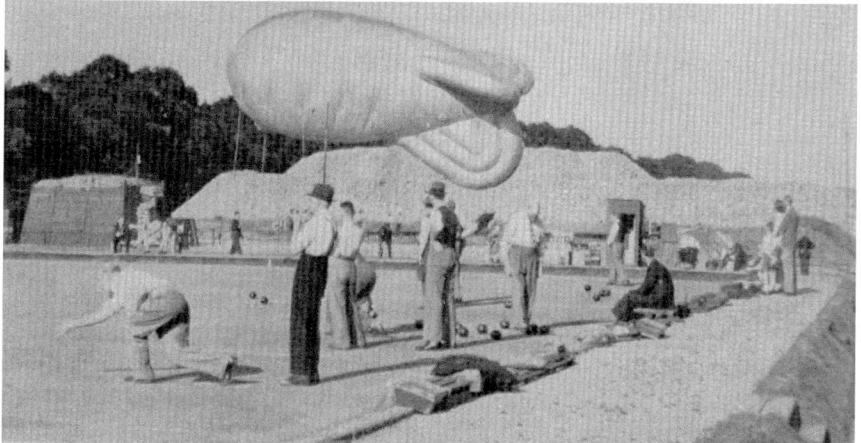

Above: It could only be an English summer: a barrage balloon hovers above bowlers in a London park.

Right: Dr Jocelin Perkins, Sacrist of Westminster Abbey, training with his Local Defence Volunteer unit – better known as the 'Home Guard'.

Above: The Second World War would be reported like no other previous conflict: here Robin Duff, as BBC Observer, and two members of recording staff report on a Channel air battle from the Dover sea front – their vehicle reinforced with nothing more than an old mattress.

Below left: To confuse and confound an advancing enemy in the event of a German landing on the South coast, street signs and place names were deliberately altered or removed.

Below right: Lord Beaverbrook, the dynamic minister responsible for aircraft production, with his fighter pilot son, Max Aitkin.

To prevent glider landings, open spaces in south-east England were festooned with abandoned motor vehicles and all kinds of contraptions.

Above: In it together: Princess Elizabeth, accompanied by her younger sister, Princess Margaret Rose, broadcasts to the children of the Commonwealth.

Right: The great masts of a Chain Home Radio Direction Finding station.

Below: The map table of Air Vice-Marshal Park's 11 Group underground Operations Room at Uxbridge.

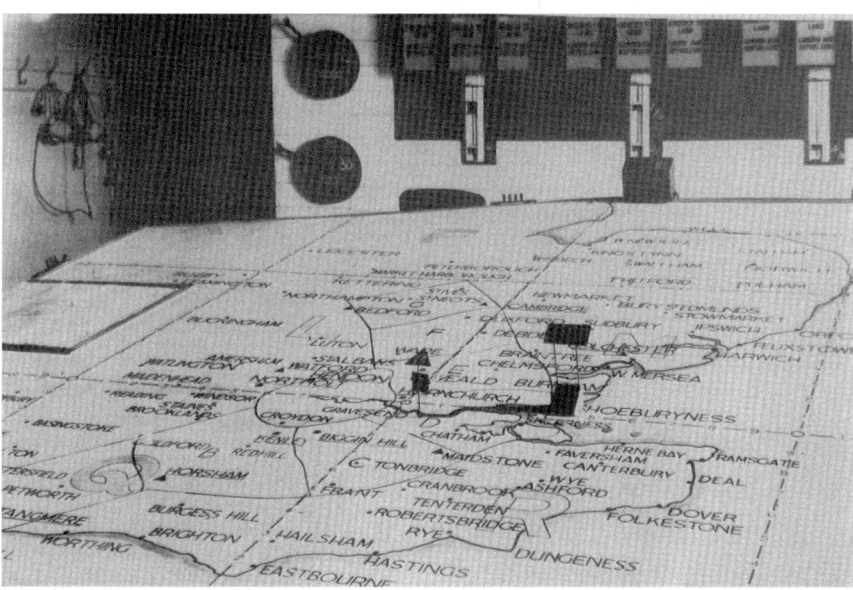

German air sea rescue provisions were superior to the RAF's. This He 59 seaplane of the Seenotdienst (air sea rescue service) was forced down on the Goodwin Sands by 54 Squadron Spitfires on 9 July 1940, and later towed ashore by the Walmer lifeboat. Fighter Command considered these Red Cross seaplanes fair game.

Above left: The Battle of Britain, Lord Dowding 'somewhat arbitrarily' decided began on 10 July 1940, lasting sixteen weeks, until 31 October 1940. In reality, the fighting began, the record shows, on 2 July 1940, but those pilots who saw action, including those killed or maimed, up to and including 9 July 1940 will not be found amongst the names of the fabled 'Few' – those entitled to wear the Battle of Britain Clasp to the 1939-45 Star. This is Sergeant Patrick Sherlock Hayes, a Spitfire pilot at Hornchurch with 65 Squadron, reported missing over the Channel on 7 July 1940 (Michael Taylor).

Above right: A classic RAF recruiting poster appearing during the Battle of France – whilst the featured pilot, Pilot Officer Peter Parrott, was embroiled in the fighting, flying Hurricane fighters.

His Majesty King George VI energetically visited fighter stations, providing encouragement, and is seen here meeting Spitfire pilots of 64 Squadron early in the Battle of Britain.

All photographs Dilip Sarkar Archive unless otherwise acknowledged.

of He 111 on starboard flank, 250 – 150 yards. I was then hit on starboard mainplane and through fuselage by AA fire which severed electrical leads near my seat and extinguished reflector sight.

As I broke off I observed one Me 110 coming up on starboard quarter and one 109 astern. I executed some very steep turns into sun and lost sight of the other two fighters. I changed bulb in reflector sight but as it failed to function I concluded that wiring had been cut and chipped spare ring for ring and bead sight. By this time the battle had gone out of sight and I hadn't enough petrol to give chase. While climbing into sun I observed crew of He 111 I had shot take to parachutes and aircraft gradually lose height on zig-zag course. While climbing up to the attack, I observed one bomber badly hit (presumably by AA) with port engine stopped and left wing well down, dropping out of formation.

This is incredible; while under attack from two German fighters and executing violent evasive manoeuvres, Flight Lieutenant Malan – cool as you like – *changes the bulb in his gunsight – and even tries to replace the unserviceable electric unit with the spare ring and bead sight in his locker*! If ever evidence was required of the man's professionalism and self-control in a combat situation, this surely provides it in spades.

The He 111 was claimed destroyed. During his interview with Quentin Reynolds, Sailor added more detail:

They were the first parachutes I had seen open in the air ... Bertie Aubert was killed, Johnny Freeborn was hit. Mungo-Park got one in the arm, and Paddy Treacy got it bad. At least his plane did. His engine was on fire, but he kept going till a bullet went through his windshield and he got a mouthful of glass.

Then he baled out. On his way down a Messerschmitt kept circling and taking pot shots that peppered his 'chute and hastened his descent. As he got near the ground – it was just outside Dunkirk – French troops fired at him. He landed in a pigpen deep in mud. He didn't mind the mud, it broke his fall. He did mind the owner of the pen, a large boar which charged and caused him to twist his ankle!

Flight Lieutenant Treacy had been shot down by Leutnant Hillecke, an Me 109 pilot of Stab II/JG26. Sergeant Tony 'Boy' Mould was also shot down in flames and baled out; both Tigers returned home via Dunkirk. Also, Flying Officer D.S. Hoare's glycol system was hit, forcing him to land, as had Squadron Leader White the previous day, at Calais-Marck.

Unfortunately, unlike his lucky CO, Hoare was captured. Finally, as Sailor mentioned, Pilot Officer R.D. Aubert – who only returned to 74 Squadron that morning after his previous escapade – was killed, shot down by *Hauptmann* Karl Ebbighausen, the *Gruppenkommandeur* of II/JG26. As Sailor said, for the outnumbered Tigers 'it was a rough trip home'.

Malan's combat report mentions leading a section of four Spitfires in line astern, rather than the usual vic of three, is noteworthy. Al Deere, also to become a great ace, remembered:

> Sailor Malan was the first [RAF] fighter leader to appreciate the advantage of basing squadron tactics on sections of four aircraft, spaced in such a way that each of the three sections, although an integral part of the squadron, had freedom of action in combat. The element of two, on which this formation was based, was a direct copy of the tactics so effectively employed by the German fighter formations whose leaders must be given full credit for their foresight in introducing the pair as the best fighting unit.

This development was an early indication of Malan's exceptional tactical ability and 'foresight'.

These combats were also highlighting issues such as the point at which machine guns needed to be 'harmonised', which is to say the point at which rounds from all eight guns should converge for maximum destructive effect. Deere remembered that Malan – who he considered 'probably the best shot in Fighter Command' – believed 250 yards to be the optimum distance, and this was adopted as standard throughout the Command. Malan also immediately recognised the advantage to sighting provided by De Wilde ammunition, an incendiary bullet which, unlike other varieties in use, did not generate a trace of smoke or flame in its wake but simply a flash upon impact.

Consequently, with De Wilde rounds included at intervals in belts of bullets, the pilot could see by flashes on his target whether or not his rounds were hitting their mark or not. Malan realised that if De Wilde was adopted as standard, Fighter Command's kill ratio would increase, and Deere also recalled Malan encouraging other squadron commanders and fighter pilots to argue this point. Eventually the Command Armament Officer was persuaded and De Wilde ammunition was widely distributed. Clearly, Malan's thinking was far broader than the accumulation of a high personal score and reputation; he was thinking about tactics and other operational issues of benefit to the whole of Fighter Command, and sharing his experience and ideas.

On 25 May 1940, Pilot Officer Jack Hamar and 151 Squadron's Hurricanes were in action again over France:

> While flying as Red Two with Yellow and Blue Section carrying out a general sweep in the Calais – Boulogne district, a Ju 88 suddenly appeared out of the clouds, passing slightly across and above our

formation. The leader ordered a No 1 Attack. The E/A dived for sea-level and after Red One, Squadron Leader Donaldson, broke away, I attacked ... I used full throttle and gradually closed, opening fire at 300 yards. The slipstream effect was noticed and keeping the sights dead on, I fired two long bursts, finishing at fifty yards, using all of my ammunition. I then broke away. During the attack, I noticed three large pieces drop from the port side of the E/A, which may have been a bomb. No other damage was noticed.

AC1 Fred Roberts was an armourer on 19 Squadron:

On 25 May 1940, the 'balloon went up'. French, British and Belgian forces were in full retreat and so the Squadron was to help cover the troops withdrawing to Calais and Dunkirk. We were to operate from Hornchurch, North of the Thames estuary in Essex, an 11 Group Sector Station. We groundcrew made the journey from Duxford by road, arriving at Hornchurch that evening when the pilots arrived with our Spitfires.

Among 19 Squadron's pilots was Pilot Officer Michael Lyne:

To us the Mess [at Hornchurch] had a new atmosphere, people clearing kit from the rooms belonging to casualties and the Station Commander insisting on closing the bar and sending us to bed early to be ready for the battles awaiting us.

By 26 May it was clear that the Battle for France was lost. On this day, it was also clear to both Churchill and Gort that there was only one option: the BEF must be evacuated via Dunkirk.

The unthinkable had become reality.

Chapter 11

Dunkirk: Operation Dynamo

Operation *Dynamo* was implemented by Vice-Admiral Bertram Ramsay, Flag Officer Commanding Dover, the intention of which was to return home up to 45,000 of Gort's troops within two days – by which time the rescue mission was expected to be halted by enemy intervention.

Ramsay was to be responsible for embarkation, Air Vice-Marshal Keith Park, the commander of 11 Group, for tactical control of covering fighters. Park had already decided on these tactics, which he explained to 11 Group's controllers. Some squadrons had been brought south to make up the sixteen squadrons assigned for the task. These would operate from airfields near the coast, such as Hornchurch, Biggin Hill and Manston. After their first patrol, however, squadrons would land at forward stations such as Hawkinge and Lympne, where the fighters would be quickly rearmed and refuelled before returning to their patrol lines. The force would be divided so that half worked mornings, the other half afternoons.

After the day's second patrol, unless, as Orange wrote, 'the crisis was great', the squadrons were permitted to return to their home or adopted home base as appropriate. Dunkirk, however, was further from Park's coastal airfields than Calais or Boulogne, and therefore a difficult location to cover with short-range defensive fighters. As Flight Lieutenant Malan said, 'The only way we could fly to Dunkirk and have enough juice to spend a few minutes over the battle area was by coasting and flying at sea-level from Boulogne.' Moreover, it would not be possible to patrol the French coast from dawn to dusk, because the quantity of fighters available made it impossible to meet the demands of both continuity and strength. This is why, until now, Dowding had insisted upon squadrons patrolling individually, so as to extend the length of coverage provided. Experience, however, had already indicated the vulnerability of weak patrols.

At this time Fighter Command's pilots were given a performance advantage with the introduction of 100 octane fuel. Of this development, the Supermarine test pilot Jeffrey Quill wrote that:

> I think it virtually certain that the Hurricane operated in France on 87 octane, because it was only shortly before the Battle of Britain that we changed over to 100 octane. It had the effect of increasing the combat rating of the Merlin from 3,000 rpm at 6½ lb or 9 lbs boost

to 3,000 rpm at 12 lbs boost. This, of course, had a significant effect on the rate of climb.

The Merlin III's capacity for a maximum emergency boost of +12 lbs per square inch, was useful for increasing speed for a short time-span. Boost was obtained by pushing a knob on the throttle quadrant, called 'going through the gate', or 'Buster' in correct radio parlance – meaning 'make all haste'. Although the improvements of 12 lbs of extra boost were really only evident up to 15,000ft, it was another step towards achieving an edge over the 109. Emergency boost, though, could only be used for a few minutes at a time, so as not to damage the engine, and any use of it, in fact, had to be recorded by the pilot in the engine's log.

Pilots would use this facility to catch up and intercept an enemy aircraft or, indeed, to escape from a tactically disadvantageous situation. Pilots fighting over Dunkirk would soon find occasion to be thankful of this extra power – among them 74 Squadron's Pilot Officer John Freeborn, who reported the following on 24 May 1940:

> As I broke away two Me 109s got onto my tail. I dived steeply with the two e/a following me, one was on my tail the other on my port quarter. As I dived to ground level I throttled back slightly and the e/a on my tail overshot me and I was able to get a three seconds burst at a range of about fifty to 100 yards. He seemed to break away slowly to the right as though he was badly hit and I think he crashed. The second Me 109 then got on my tail but I got away from it using the boost cut-out.

In the same action, Pilot Officer Colin Gray, a New Zealander, of 54 Squadron, destroyed a 109 but his own aircraft was damaged. Again, emergency boost got him out of trouble:

> I decided the best course of action was to set off for home as speedily as possible. I pressed the emergency tit, which poured on the fuel, but was only for use in dire emergency as it could overstress the engine. I considered this was justifiable under the circumstances, since I was still inside France and could not see anyone coming to my assistance.

The positive effect of extra boost in combat was becoming obvious.
Pilot Officer Peter 'Sneezy' Brown, 611 Squadron:

> Suddenly the sky over the French coast was full of aircraft bearing black crosses. It was frightening. I realised for the first time that someone up there really was trying to kill me. It was a moment

of truth. It was the first time we had met the enemy. I had a tough time with one of those Me 109s. I dived away, into the smoke of the blazing Dunkirk oil tanks and virtually down to zero feet, and lost him. But then I found some courage and, I would like to think, because the 'mouse that roared'.

I climbed up to about 15,000ft alone, which was a really stupid thing to do, inviting trouble. But I had to do it, to prove something to myself. I stayed up there for quarter of an hour before turning to England – where I found twenty-nine bullet-holes in my Spitfire.

Pilot Officer Peter Parrott, 145 Squadron:

On 26 May 1940, we were patrolling near Dunkirk, where the evacuation was in full-swing. Roy Dutton, who was leading, spotted a possible bandit, and led the squadron to the west and down towards it. I was flying as No 2, in the rearmost vic of three, and saw another possible bandit flying to the north of Dunkirk. I called on the radio but got no response, so went ahead of my Section Leader and rocked my wings. I was hoping he would follow me as I peeled off to the north – but he didn't. I gave chase to the 'possible', which I soon identified as a He 111.

I closed to firing range and loosed off several bursts, and hit his port engine, which emitted a thick trail of black smoke, his starboard undercarriage extended. Suddenly, I found myself in thick fog, engulfing my cockpit. I could only see one instrument, the oil pressure gauge in the top right corner of my instrument panel.

The *Heinkel*'s rear gunner had obviously hit my radiator. I had limited, misty, vision through the windscreen. I broke off and turned 180°, heading for England, home and security. The fog continued, but opening the canopy failed to disperse it. I was half way across the Channel, when the rest of the squadron joined me, having seen the white plume I was trailing behind. I had no idea how long the engine would run, but decided to keep going and ditch when it stopped. I was at 4,000ft and Roy kept me on course. The fog finally cleared, but the engine, surprisingly, continued running for a few seconds – then stopped dead as I crossed the beach at Deal; I made a wheels-up landing on the Downs, about a mile-and-a-half from the shore.

The time was about 2000 hrs on a cloudless, warm, summer evening. There were quite a number of people out for a Sunday evening stroll, but no one approached me. I was in the middle of a large field with footpaths on either side, and was thinking of walking to a house about a third of a mile away, for help. Then I saw the local bobby approaching on his bicycle, so explained my presence to him. I was just asking said PC to guard the aircraft while I went to telephone Manston for help, when we saw the farmer approaching in his horse and trap.

Unfortunately, the Hurricane's wings had killed two sheep. The farmer's words to me were 'Who's going to pay for them sheep?' I responded that the Air Ministry would, at which he about-turned and went back to his nearby house. I then asked the constable where the nearest telephone was: the farmer's house! He did allow me to use his phone, but not to share a very handsome ham salad supper. I spent the night at Manston, and Michael Adderley, who had been a fellow pupil at FTS, flew me back to Tangmere in a Tiger Moth being used for radio control of aircraft experiments.

Pilot Officer Michael Lyne:

On 26 May 1940 we of 12 Group's 19 Squadron, temporarily based at Hornchurch and under 11 Group control, were called upon to patrol over the beaches as a single squadron. I will always remember heading off to the east and seeing the columns of black smoke from the Dunkirk oil storage tanks. We patrolled for some time without seeing any aircraft. We received no information from British radar. We had received excellent VHF radios shortly before, but they were only of use between ourselves, we could not communicate with other squadrons should the need arise.

Suddenly we saw ahead, going towards Calais where the Rifle Brigade was holding out, about forty German aircraft. We were twelve. Squadron Leader Geoffrey Stephenson aligned us for an attack in sections of three on the formations of Ju 87s. As a former CFS A1 Flying Instructor he was a precise flier and obedient to the book, which stipulated an overtaking speed of 30 mph. What the book never foresaw was that we would attack Ju 87s at just 130 mph.

The CO led his Section, Pilot Officer Watson No 2 and me No. 3, straight up behind the *Stukas* which looked very relaxed. They thought we were their fighter escort, but the leader had been very clever and had pulled his formation away towards England, so that when they turned in towards Calais he would protect their rear. Alas for him we were coming, by sheer chance, from Dunkirk rather than Ramsgate.

Meanwhile Stephenson realised that we were closing far too fast. I remember his call 'Number 19 Squadron! Prepare to attack!' then to us 'Red Section, throttling back, throttling back.' We were virtually formating on the last section of Ju 87s – at an incredibly dangerous speed in the presence of enemy fighters – and behind us the rest of 19 Squadron staggered along at a similar speed. Of course, the Ju 87s could not imagine that we were a threat. Then Stephenson told us to take a target each and fire. As far as I know we got the last three, we could hardly have done otherwise, then we broke away and saw nothing of the work by the rest of the Squadron – but it must have been dodgy as the 109s started to come round.

As I was looking round for friends after the break I came under fire from the rear for the first time – and did not at first know it. The first signs were mysterious little corkscrews of smoke passing my starboard wing. Then I heard a slow 'thump, thump', and realised that I was being attacked by a 109 firing machine-guns with tracer and its cannon banging away. I broke away sharpish – and lost him.

I made a wide sweep and came back to the Calais area to find about five *Stukas* going around in a tight defensive circle. The German fighters had disappeared so I flew to take the circle at the head-on position and gave it a long squirt. It must have been at this stage that I was hit by return fire, for when I got back to Hornchurch I found bullet holes in the wings which had punctured a tyre.

Alas my friend Watson was never seen again. Stephenson forced-landed on the beach and was taken prisoner.

Back at Hornchurch, there was great excitement as the Spitfires returned and groundcrews clamoured around their pilots demanding news of the fight. Two Spitfires were missing: Squadron Leader Stephenson's N3200 and Pilot Officer Watson's N3237. Flight Lieutenant Lane had seen a pilot clad in black overalls bale out over the sea, so it was agreed that this was 'Watty' and not the CO, who was wearing white overalls. In his combat report, Pilot Officer Michael Lyne described having seen 'one Spitfire hit by a cannon shell near the cockpit, on the port side'. This was undoubtedly Michael's friend, Peter Watson, who although seen to bale out, did not survive; his body was later washed up on the French coast.

Given that the German 20mm round hit 'Watty's' Spitfire close to the cockpit, there is every possibility, of course, that the 20-year-old pilot was wounded and unable to survive immersion in the cold sea. Pilot Officer Lyne also saw 'another Spitfire going gently down with glycol vapour pouring from the starboard side of the engine', which would have been Squadron Leader Stephenson, who forced-landed on the beach at Sandgatte before beginning a whole new adventure – which would end in captivity and ultimately incarceration at the infamous Colditz Castle (more recently, Stephenson's Spitfire, which became something of a tourist landmark for sight-seeing German troops on the beach, was recovered, restored to flying condition and is once more based at Duxford).

The Me 109s which 'bounced' 19 Squadron that day, were elements of JG1 and JG2, both of which claimed Spitfires destroyed over Calais; 1/JG2 and 1/JG2 both lost 109s in that morning's engagement. The *Stukas* were from 3/StG76, which, according to German records, lost four Ju 87s destroyed. 19 Squadron, however, claimed seven Ju 87s and three Me 109s destroyed, and another 109 as a 'probable'.

At 14.45 hrs, it fell to Flight Lieutenant Brian Lane, the senior flight commander and now Acting CO, to lead ten 19 Squadron Spitfires off from Hornchurch back towards France. In his log book, Brian wrote:

> Leading Squadron on patrol of Dunkirk and Calais. Green Section reported eight Me 109s just above us off Calais. Observed Me 109 chasing Sinclair into cloud. Hun pulled up and gave me a sitting target from below. Gave him a good burst which he ran straight into, lurched and went straight down. I followed him but he hadn't pulled out at 3,000ft and must have gone straight in. Blacked out completely but pulled out in time. Landed at Manston and stayed for tea. Lovely near the coast in this weather.

Flying Officers Petre and Sinclair were also each credited with an Me 109 destroyed – but two pilots were missing. Of 24-year old Sergeant Charles Albert Irwin, a married man from Midhurst, Sussex, and Spitfire P9305, nothing was ever seen again (remembered on the Runnymede Memorial, the Commonwealth War Graves Commission had incorrectly recorded Irwin's death as occurring two days later, but accepted the author's evidence that this was on 26 May 1940, and corrected their records accordingly).

The other missing pilot was Pilot Officer Michael Lyne:

> In the afternoon Brian Lane led us on our second patrol over the evacuation beaches. Suddenly we were attacked by a squadron of 109s. As before we were flying in the inflexible and outdated formation of 'Vics of three'.
>
> Later the basic unit became the pair, or two pairs in what became known as the 'Finger Four'. Such a formation, as the Germans were already using, could turn very quickly, with each aircraft turning on its own, but the formation automatically re-formed in full contact at the end of the manoeuvre.
>
> Because of our formation we quickly lost contact with each other after the 109s attacked. I found myself alone, but with a pair of 109s circling above me left-handed while I was going right-handed. The leader dropped his nose as I pulled up mine and fired. He hit me in the engine, knee, radio and rear fuselage. I was in a spin and was streaming glycol. He must have thought I was gone for good. So did I. But for a short time the engine kept going as I straightened out and dived into cloud, setting compass course shortly before the cockpit filled with white smoke which blotted out everything.

> In a few seconds the engine seized and I became an efficient glider. On breaking cloud I saw Deal some way off, but remembered the advice to hold an efficient speed. So with 200ft to spare, I crossed the surf and crash-landed on the beach. That adventure ended my flying until 19 February 1941.

From evidence available, it appears that 19 Squadron had been attacked by the Me 109s of I/JG2, four pilots of which claimed to have destroyed Spitfires over Calais. Flight Sergeant George 'Grumpy' Unwin, 19 Squadron:

> The tacticians who wrote the book really believed that in the event of war it would be fighter versus bomber only. Our tight formations were all very well for the Hendon Air Pageant but useless in combat. Geoffrey Stephenson was a prime example: without modern combat experience he flew exactly by the book – and was in effect shot down by it.

Over Dunkirk and Calais, the misconceptions regarding modern fighter tactics were fatally exposed. Nonetheless, the RAF squadrons gave a determined account, rapidly gaining in experience.

From the German perspective on 26 May 1940, the *Luftwaffe War Diaries* state that:

> The *Luftwaffe* was having to operate at an ever-increasing distance from most of its bases. The *Stukas* of VIII Air Corps were now based on airfields east of St Quentin, but even from there the Channel coast – Boulogne, Calais, Dunkirk – represented the limits of their range ... Two weeks of gruelling operations had sapped much of the *Luftwaffe's* strength. Many of the bomber *gruppen* could only put some fifteen aircraft out of thirty into the air. But they went in, raining down bombs on the quays and sheds of Dunkirk harbour. Around noon on the 26 May the great oil tanks on the western edge of the town went up in flames. In a precision raid *Stukas* destroyed the lock gates leading to the inner harbour. Bombs tore up the tracks of the marshalling yard; ships were set on fire; a freighter sank slowly to the bed of the battered harbour basin.

It was also on this day that Hitler realised his mistake in halting the *panzers*, thereby allowing *Dynamo* to be launched. Comparatively few Allied troops had been evacuated by then, but Park's Spitfires entering the fray for the first time had shifted the balance of power in the air. Clearly, the days of the *Luftwaffe* encountering and sweeping aside inferior fighters were over. Hitler ordered the tanks to roll again – destination Dunkirk.

DUNKIRK: OPERATION DYNAMO

At 07.45 hrs on 27 May 1940, Flight Lieutenant Malan led 74 Squadron back to the French coast, clashing with Me 109s of JG1 at 09.00 hrs:

> I was Red 1. 74 Squadron [eleven aircraft] on offensive patrol over Calais – Dunkirk at varying heights, 2,000–15,000ft, owing to cloud formation. AA fire was observed at 5,000ft south of Dunkirk. Investigated round cumulus cloud but no E/A seen. On returning towards Dunkirk at 2,000ft, various Me 109s were sighted above and behind. Red 1 and 3 attacked one E/A which was above Red 2. I ordered sections to break up into pairs. Red 3 and I climbed and observed one Me 109 directly above, pulled up my nose and gave two full deflection bursts at 100 yards range.
>
> E/A immediately dived towards cumulus. I followed and gave about four two second bursts at approximately 300 yards range, owing to difficulty of closing range in the time. Just before he entered cloud, heavy smoke poured out of the starboard side of engine, and I concluded he had been badly hit. I followed into cloud but lost him. Red 3 saw my tail was safe and attacked other 109s as stated in his combat report.

This report is of interest. Previously we have read how Sailor was operating sections of four – not the usual three aircraft, and now advanced that concept further by instructing pilots to break into fighting pairs – remarkably similar to the enemy's *Schwarm* of four and *Rotte* tactic of leader and wingman.

This is clear evidence that already Sailor Malan had recognised that the inflexible set-piece attacks and right formations recommended by the manual were impractical, especially when engaging similarly fast-moving and highly manoeuvrable fighters. Moreover, to conserve ammunition the optimum firing time is two-seconds a time – and consistently this is repeated in this air-fighting master's reports.

After the combat, Flight Lieutenant Malan paired up with Red 4, Pilot Officer P.C.F. 'Paddy' Stevenson, for the return flight to Rochford:

> Both aircraft very short of petrol. Sighted eight Do 215s in two vics (five and three). Attacked rear vic of three, leader right flank, No 4, left flank. Enemy opened fire at 800 yards and dived for cumulous layer and towards German AA fire. As we couldn't afford a long chase we closed rather rapidly and delivered four one second bursts from 300–100 yards at port engine and fuselage. I broke off to right and observed smoke from tail and port engine and fuselage. As I was returning for second quick attack from astern, I observed that Red 4 (whose first contact it was) had apparently been hit in the glycol feeder tank and would have to land very soon. I followed him up and

called him on R/T with no reply. He suddenly changed his course from cross-Channel and dived towards direction of Dunkirk and I presumed he would attempt a landing on the beach there. I then had to return and landed with two gallons of petrol. Firing seen from E/A appeared to come from one top gun only.

During the combat with the Me 109s, Pilot Officer Stevenson had fought alongside Pilot Officer Freeborn, firing at a 109 that attacked his comrade, leaving the enemy fighter in an 'obviously distressed condition'. Still covered by Stephenson, Freeborn also destroyed a 109. Stephenson later safely alighted on Dunkirk beach, returning home and to 74 Squadron a few days later.

Other Tigers were also successful in this combat: 40-year-old Warrant Officer Ernie Mayne blasted a 109 out of the sky from just fifty yards, and Pilot Officer H.M. 'Steve' Stephen and Flight Lieutenant 'Treacle' Tracey also despatched Messerschmitts.

On 27 May, 65 Squadron patrolled over the French coast between 06.45 and 08.40 hrs. Sergeant Patrick Hayes reported that:

> The Squadron of eleven machines, led by Squadron Leader Cooke, patrolled Calais. Very few enemy aircraft were seen but on return two Do 17s were sighted. Squadron Leader Cooke and Flight Sergeant McPherson attacked from astern and though they emptied their guns into the machine it did not, at that time, appear badly damaged for it made off into the clouds, though evidently experiencing a little trouble.
>
> Later, however, this machine was confirmed by Pilot Officer Deere of 54 Squadron, who had earlier been shot down and was on the beach at Calais at the time. In this sortie, Flying Officer Proudman also sighted a Do 17 and managed to get in a burst of very long duration and it was seen to make for the clouds with smoke pouring from its engines, and it is very improbable that it ever reached its aerodrome.
>
> Flying Officer Proudman was wounded in the left leg, the bullet entering from the rear and then going through the rudder bar, then entering his leg and finally finished in his parachute.

Although not mentioned by the ORB, Sergeant Hayes also attacked a Do 17, at 07.45 hrs, at 7,000ft, north of Dunkirk:

> On the above patrol I was Green Three when we sighted twelve Do 17 bombers about 2,000ft below us. I attacked one of a formation of three from astern with no apparent effect. I broke away and attacked another enemy aircraft with Green Two, firing about a nine

second burst from 400 to 300 yards. The enemy aircraft had dropped back from the formation and white smoke was seen coming from the port engine.

Green Two, Pilot Officer Stan Grant, reported that:

> I was Number Two in Green Section when we sighted twelve Do 17s in for vics of three. I attacked number two of one section from astern, firing bursts totalling about eight seconds with no apparent effect. I broke away and attacked number two of another section from below with a burst of four seconds, which silenced the lower rear gun. I broke away to the right and keeping the same level as enemy aircraft came in again and fired the remaining ammunition in an astern attack, by which time the enemy aircraft had dropped back from his formation considerably, with smoke coming from his engine.

Green Two and Three were awarded an equal share of the Do 17 jointly attacked, which was considered a 'probable'. Like many other Spitfire pilots fighting over the French coast, Patrick Hayes had opened his account.

Between 13.00 and 14.35 hrs, 65 Squadron was back over the French coast again, Sergeant Hayes once more included in the 'B' Flight formation:

> The Squadron, led by Squadron Leader Cooke, patrolled Calais–Dunkirk, encountering *Messerschmitts* and eighteen mixed bombers in formations and sections. In the general dogfight that ensued, Flight Sergeant Phillips sent one Do 17 crashing. Blue Section, led by Flight Lieutenant Saunders, saw a further one go down in flames. Red Section, led by Squadron Leader Cooke, saw two Do 215s descend in flames and Sergeant Franklin on his way home shot down a further Ju 88. In addition, two Do 215s and two Me 110s were engaged but managed to escape into clouds with smoke pouring from their engines.

That afternoon, Flight Lieutenant Malan was leading 74 Squadron over France once more, reporting that at 16.00 hrs, 8,000ft over St Omer:

> Sighted German bomber vics of five and three. Red Section broke up into pairs and approached a wide vic of five, which split up and dived on a SE course. Red 3 and 4 delivered No 1 Attacks on Do 17 at high speed from 250–50 yards range. Red 3 delivered last attack at *twenty-five feet height* and E/A had burning port engine and smoking tail. We experienced very severe and accurate light flak and returned to coast through continuous AA fire.

The Do 17, probably from KG3, was claimed as 'badly crippled'. Having initially been ordered to patrol at a much higher altitude, finding no 'trade', Sailor had descended to a lower height, finding the enemy formation. Again, this is further evidence of his tactical intelligence and willingness to seek, locate and destroy the enemy. Pilot Officer Dowding also damaged a Dornier, Flight Lieutenant Measures and Pilot Officer St John sharing another.

Flight Lieutenant Treacy and Pilot Officer Stephen pursued three bombers inland, setting both engines of one ablaze. Treacy, however, was hit by a German gunner, force-landing near Gravelines where he was captured. Although the pilots were not to know it, it would be the Tigers last patrol during Operation *Dynamo*.

By this time, since 21 May 1940, 74 Squadron had lost four pilots, three of whom were prisoners, and another wounded. With fresh squadrons reinforcing 11 Group, it was time for the Tigers to be withdrawn, to rebuild back to strength. According to Ira Jones:

> Both men and machines were fatigued. Malan told me that on one or two occasions, when making the last landings of the day on 27 May, his eyes were so tired that the aerodrome was in a sort of haze and he just "threw the old Spitfire on the ground". He said he did not know why he had not crashed.

Pilot Officer Peter Parrott, 145 Squadron:

> We continued patrolling over Dunkirk – and casualties mounted. On 27 May 1940, three pilots went missing; they had, in fact, been killed in action on their first patrol. Three more, Forde, Wakenham and Ashton, were also shot down but returned by sea. On 31 May, my friend Peter Dixon was killed. In all, we lost four pilots and eight Hurricanes.

Providing continuous fighter patrols from dawn to dusk using what were actually short-range defensive fighters was impossible, and this would have required every single one of Dowding's aircraft – leaving Britain itself vulnerable to attack. Another hugely significant factor in the fighting over Dunkirk would be that the British fighters were unassisted by radar. The System of Fighter Control only provided a radar network for the defence of Britain, its stations incapable of gathering data from as far away as Dunkirk and beyond. This is why Dowding knew how exhausting the battle ahead would be for his pilots: as they could not predict or have early warning of an enemy attack it would be necessary to fly as many standing patrols as possible.

Even so, Dowding also knew that given the size of the force he was able to make available – sixteen squadrons – there would be times, howsoever brief, that cover would be unavailable. Indeed, given that these fighters were actually intended to be short-range interceptors with limited range, the RAF fighters would only have fuel for a maximum of forty minutes actual patrolling.

On 27 May 1940, Defiant pilot Squadron Leader Hunter of 264 Squadron personally came into contact with the Me 109 for the first time. Espying eight 109s, Hunter ordered his aircraft into line astern – so the 109s, assuming their prey to be Spitfires or Hurricanes, got a nasty shock when they attacked from the rear: two German fighters, of I/JG1, were shot down.

With the German fighters patrolling in large formations, Park repeatedly requested that his squadrons should at least patrol in pairs, to which Dowding eventually agreed. On 28 May, Park's Spitfire squadrons flew in pairs for the first time.

At 03.00 hrs that day, Flight Lieutenant Douglas Bader – an RAF aerobatic legend who had lost both legs in a blameworthy low-flying accident in 1931 – was awakened by his batman at Kirton-in-Lindsey in 12 Group; he was told that at 04.00 hrs, 222 Squadron (in which Bader was a flight commander) was to fly to, and operate from, Martlesham Heath in 11 Group. Air Vice-Marshal Park was concentrating even more Spitfire squadrons in the south-east, ready to operate across the Channel during Operation *Dynamo*.

Squadron Leader H.W. 'Tubby' Mermagen, 222's CO, and his pilots did not know this, however, as they took off, bleary eyed, and flew to their destination, near Felixstowe in Suffolk. Biggin Hill's 92 Squadron was already there and had seen action – losing their CO, Squadron Leader Roger Bushell, on the second patrol of 23 May.

Born to a wealthy English family which emigrated to South Africa, Bushell had been educated in England at Wellington College before reading law at Cambridge and becoming a barrister at London's Lincoln's Inn. It was Bushell, in fact, who had successfully defended Pilot Officers Freeborn and Byrne following the 'Barking Creek' fiasco. His social credentials, and sporting achievements in rugby, cricket and skiing, provided admission to the socially-elite 601 Squadron of the AAF, the fabled 'Millionaire's Mob', with which he flew Blenheims.

In October 1939, Bushell was given command of 92 Squadron, but, like 19 Squadron's CO, Squadron Leader Geoffrey Stephenson, he had been shot down, probably by *Oberleutnant* Gunther Specht, the adjutant of the Me 110 equipped I/ZG26, in the Squadron's first clash with enemy fighters over Calais. Captured, Bushell would prove a problematic prisoner, making various escape attempts until murdered by the Gestapo on 29 March 1944, having been recaptured after masterminding the 'Great Escape' from *Stalag Luft* III at Sagan. It was a sad end to a gallant and brave officer.

Returning to the events of 28 May 1940, 92 and 222 squadrons flew together that day, with Flight Lieutenant Robert Stanford Tuck in temporary command of and leading the former squadron. Squadron Leader Mermagen's pilots flew in the stipulated vics of three, while Tuck led 92 in loose well-spaced pairs. It was clear by now that Fighter Command's tacticians really had got it wrong.

The presence of the German single-seater fighter, the Me 109, had changed everything. Although the Spitfire, hitherto preserved by Dowding for home defence, was only now meeting the Me 109 for the first time, the RAF pilots were learning quickly.

Of that first patrol, Squadron Leader Mermagen remembered that 'The sortie lasted two hours and forty-five minutes, a long flight in a Spitfire.'

Yet again, the lack of a long-range fighter was all too apparent. No Me 109s, or indeed any other enemy aircraft, were encountered on that patrol over the French coast. During the return flight, 222 Squadron was diverted to the Kentish coastal station at Manston. After refuelling it was off to Duxford, from where Mermagen was ordered to take his pilots to Hornchurch. From that sector station the Spitfire pilots of 54 and 65 squadrons had already been in action for several days, their place in the line now being taken by 222 and 41 squadrons.

In the Mess that night, Bader, fascinated by air fighting tactics and who had long considered the official Fighter Command tactics useless, spoke to some of the outgoing pilots of their experiences – and learned that all, without exception, totally agreed with his assessment of the area attacks insisted upon by Fighter Command. The suicidal impracticality of these had become immediately apparent, leading to their instant rejection. The problem now faced, though, was that new formations and tactics literally had to be worked out on the job – and a very dangerous one it was, considering the massive advantage in combat experience enjoyed by the enemy's fighter pilots.

Flight Lieutenant Bob Stanford Tuck, 92 Squadron:

> We started over Dunkirk with very poor tactics. We were flying over the beaches in formations which were much too tight. Manoeuvring was cumbersome. You had to concentrate on formation flying, not searching for the Germans who were flying much looser formations. They bounced us on our first encounter over Dunkirk and we lost a pilot, Pat Learmond, who went down in flames. Then we lost our CO, Roger Bushell, and as senior flight commander I found myself in charge. I told the boys that tomorrow we were flying in pairs, in a more open formation. But in those two days of fighting we had already lost five pilots and Spitfires.

On this day, the Defiant-equipped 264 Squadron was engaged by twenty-seven Me 109s over the Channel, Squadron Leader Hunter ordered his men to form a defensive circle. In the ensuing combat, the Defiants claimed six Me 109s destroyed – but lost three of their number of the process.

On 29 May, 222 Squadron was up again, running head-on into a gaggle of twin-engine Me 110s, which broke for cloud out of the Spitfires' guns' range. Mermagen, however, managed to hit one, chalking up 222's first combat victory. The next two days saw Mermagen's pilots patrol uneventfully.

DUNKIRK: OPERATION DYNAMO

Of events on 1 June 1940, Flight Lieutenant Douglas Bader wrote that:

> We were all flying around up and down the coast near Dunkirk, looking for enemy aircraft which seemed also to be milling around with no particular cohesion. The sea from Dunkirk to Dover during those days of the evacuation looked like any coastal road in England on a bank holiday. It was solid with shipping. One felt one could walk across it without getting one's feet wet, or that's what it looked like from the air. There were naval escort vessels, sailing dinghies, rowing-boats, paddle-steamers, indeed every floating device known in this country. They were all taking British soldiers from Dunkirk back home.
>
> The oil-tanks just inside the harbour were ablaze, and you could identify Dunkirk from the Thames estuary by this huge pall of black smoke rising straight up in a windless sky. Our ships were being bombed by enemy aeroplanes up to about half way across the Channel and troops on the beaches were suffering the same attention. There were also German aircraft inland, strafing the remnants of the BEF fighting their way to the port.
>
> I was flying along at 3,000ft when an Me 109 appeared straight in front of me at about the same speed and going in the same direction. Like me, he must have been a beginner, because he stayed there while I shot him down, and I didn't get him with the first burst.

Squadron Leader Mermagen recalled their return from this particular sortie:

> When we landed, Douglas stomped over to me and enthused 'I got five for certain, Tubby, old boy!' Now this was the first time we had met Me 109s, which were damn good aeroplanes, and everything happened very quickly indeed. To be certain of having destroyed five enemy aircraft in such circumstances was impossible. I said 'You're a bloody liar, Bader!' We credited him with one destroyed. Nevertheless, Bader was generally easy to keep in order, as it were, and had already proved to be an excellent flight commander.

The exuberant Bader was also credited, in fact, with damaging an Me 110. With no respite, 222 Squadron was up again later that day. Of that sortie, Douglas wrote: 'Attacked two He 111s. Killed one rear gunner and damaged machine.' Of this operation, Bader wrote:

> A day or two later I saw a Dornier bombing one of our ships. He was about a mile away and I rushed at him with the throttle wide open, giving myself just enough time for a hurried burst which silenced

the rear-gunner. I had to pull up very quickly to avoid a collision. Thinking about it later that evening I got the message which every fighter pilot assimilates early in his career – if he hopes for a career at all. It is this: overtake your target slowly and relax before you start shooting; you will never get him in a hurry.

From 29 May 1940, Air Vice-Marshal Park employed his squadrons in wings of four. The loss ratio was not reduced, however, as fresh squadrons arrived without any combat experience of this kind, and suffered accordingly. On that day, three out of five raids were intercepted, but those that got through caused great execution among the soldiers queuing on the beaches below.

On that day, 151 Squadron escorted a formation of Defiants on patrol, when a fierce combat took place with Me 109s; a Ju 88, believed to be a decoy, was destroyed by Squadron Leader Donaldson and Pilot Officer Hamar, as the latter reported:

> While flying as Red Two on a high escort patrol over Dunkirk, a Ju 88 was seen flying approximately due east at 7,000ft. The leader ordered Red Section into line astern and delivered a No 1 Fighter Attack. The leader also ordered Yellow One to take over and remain above on guard. As I followed the leader into attack, I also saw a large formation of Me 109s high above.
>
> As the leader broke away, I saw white smoke pouring from the E/A's port engine, and it started flying crab-like. Think that this may be a ruse, I decided to attack again, aiming at the port engine. I opened fire at approximately 150 yards and continued the burst until about twenty yards. Large pieces of the port engine were seen to drop off.
>
> I did not experience any fire from the rear of E/A, which neither executed any evasive actions other than a fast dive towards cloud, nearly on its side. I then re-joined Red One.

The Ju 88 was that of *Oberleutnant* Alfred von Oelhaven, *Staffelkapitän* of 6/LG1, who crash-landed his damaged bomber on Nieuport beach at 08.30 hrs. Von Oelhaven and *Feldwebel* W. Notzke were captured unhurt, but both *Oberfeldwebel* F Stobbe and *Flieger* S. Tessmann were killed.

On 29 May, in addition to claiming two further 109s destroyed, 264 Squadron's Defiants were attacked by twenty-one Me 110s – fifteen of which Squadron Leader Hunter and his pilots claimed destroyed. That evening, 264 Squadron claimed eighteen Ju 87s and an 88 destroyed, generating a further congratulatory signal from Air Vice-Marshal Leigh-Mallory. This success 264 Squadron partially ascribed to the enemy having again mistaken their Defiants for 'Hurricanes', attacking from the rear and paying the price.

DUNKIRK: OPERATION DYNAMO

Pilot Officer Michael Wainwright, 64 Squadron:

> On 29 May 1940, we flew a squadron patrol over Calais and Boulogne. We flew in tight vics of three, in perfect formation, as if we were performing a fly past over Buckingham Palace. It was ridiculous. We couldn't search for the enemy because we were concentrating so hard on formation flying. Inevitably we got well and truly bounced by Me 109s, losing three aircraft – including our Commanding Officer – and four were damaged. My Section was 'Arse End Charlie' at the back, so we saw what was happening in front of us.
>
> I immediately shouted over the R/T 'Break! Every man for himself!' and went into a tight right-turn. That gave me more time to see what was going on, and to think. Short of fuel, we had to break off anyway and get home.
>
> It was appalling. Back at Gravesend, the Air Officer Commanding 11 Group, Air Vice-Marshal Sir Keith Park, flew his personal Hurricane in and asked us what had gone wrong; 'Everything!' I said, and told him what I thought of the stupid vic formation.

In his pilot's flying log book, Wainwright wrote: 'Patrol Dunkirk evacuation of BEF. Enemy engaged. Squadron Leader Rogers, Flying Officer George and Pilot Officer Hackney lost.' He described those violent events as 'A terrific engagement, in which we lost our CO and two brave officers. Had a near shave myself. One Me 109 spun in while chasing me around.'

Of tactics, he added that:

> After that our squadron arranged to fly in pairs, copying the Germans, with one aircraft slightly ahead, looking for a target, while the other covered the leader's tail. From time-to-time we'd swap over. That worked much better. Next time I was in action, I once more found myself taking evasive action in a tight right-hand turn. No German aircraft could out-turn a Spitfire, so you couldn't be shot at in such a manoeuvre. A 109 tried to follow me, but lost control; I last saw it spinning towards the sea but don't know what ultimately happened to it. We hadn't really got feelings of hatred against the German aircrews, we just thought that they were 'chaps' like us, it was the machine we wanted to destroy, not the man inside.

Poor flying weather hindered both sides the following day, but heavy German attacks over the next two ensured that the beleaguered troops suffered accordingly. The army asked 'Where was the RAF?' Those being bombed on the beaches were unable to see that Park's fighters were engaged above the low cloud and attempting to prevent enemy bombers reaching Dunkirk. In spite of Fighter Command's best efforts, the beaches were so badly hit that on 2 June, the evacuation was switched to night-time.

Two days later, Operation *Dynamo* was all over. It had been hoped to evacuate up to 45,000 troops; the total actually rescued was 340,000.

The evacuation had been an immense undertaking, involving not just the RN but also those brave civilian craft, the 'Little Ships'. On 30 May, the Admiralty had ordered all self-propelled civilian pleasure craft of over 30ft in length to Southend Pier. From there, tugs towed the boats to Sheerness for refuelling, provisioning and taking over by RN crews, although a small number were taken across the Channel by their civilian owners – brave men indeed.

Among them was Allan Barrell, Master of the coastal pleasure steamer *Shamrock*:

> We stared and stared at what looked like thousands of sticks on the beach and were amazed to see them turn into moving masses of humanity. I thought quickly of going in, picking up seventy to eighty and clearing off. With the sun behind me I calculated I should find some east coast town. We got our freight ... when I realised it would be selfish to clear off when several destroyers and large vessels were waiting in deep water to be fed by small craft, so I decided what our job was to be. We could seat sixty men and with those standing we had about eighty weary and hungry British troops, some without boots, some only in their underwear, but enough life left in them to clamber aboard the destroyers with the helping hands of every seaman available. Again and again we brought our cargo to this ship until she was full.
>
> Navigation was extremely difficult owing to the various wreckage, up-turned boats, floating torpedoes, and soldiers in the water trying to be sailors for the first time. They paddled their collapsible little boats out to me with the butts of their rifles, and that shouted that they were sinking. I was inshore as close as I dared. 'Stop shouting and save your breath, and bail out with your steel helmets,' was the only command suitable for the occasion. Scores offered me cash and personal belongings, which I refused, saying 'My name is Barrell, Canvey Island, send me a postcard if you get home all right.'

It is the contribution of civilian sailors like Alan Barrell and their 'Little Ships' that personify the 'Miracle of Dunkirk'; 850 civilian pleasure craft sailed from Ramsgate to the Dunkirk beaches – 250 were lost. Nonetheless, the BEF's evacuation was humiliating, and the Fall of France a catastrophe for the Western democracies. Left behind in France were Lord Gort's armour and heavy weapons, in addition to 41,338 men missing or captured.

DUNKIRK: OPERATION DYNAMO

The BEF – the first fully motorised army – had taken 68,618 vehicles to France – and left 63,879 on the Continent, either destroyed, disabled, abandoned or captured. This was a disaster, but that 340,000 men were rescued was a deliverance indeed, a miracle amid a raft of despair. While this victory within a defeat was trumpeted by British propaganda as personifying the British fighting spirit and a triumph over adversity, Churchill warned that 'wars are not won by evacuations'.

The successful evacuation of the BEF had arguably been made possible owing to the infamous 'Halt Order' of 24 May 1940, when the panzers rolled to a stop and held back from finishing off the BEF. Allowing the boastful Göring an opportunity for the *Luftwaffe* to finish the job made sense, thereby resting the army, but there is another explanation: Hitler told his entourage that smashing the British army would mean the end of Britain's Empire, and Hitler neither wanted to destroy nor inherit the responsibility of it. Hitler's most recent biographer, Ian Kershaw, however, argues that such a claim by Hitler was simply to justify what was a huge military blunder – for which the *Führer* was ultimately responsible.

Pilot Officer Peter Parrott, 145 Squadron:

> We flew patrols on 1, 2 and 3 June 1940, over Dunkirk, then South along the French coast and over the Channel ports. By then, we were down to only seven serviceable Hurricanes, although we still had fourteen pilots; on at least two occasions, we made up a composite squadron with 601. These final patrols were partly, I think, to see if there were any further soldiers requiring rescue; the *Luftwaffe* did not show up at all. We continued this uneventful patrolling until at least 15 June.

Squadron Leader 'Teddy' Donaldson, 151 Squadron:

> During the Battle of France and Operation DYNAMO 151 Squadron flew as many as seven sorties a day against overwhelming odds. At Dunkirk we even stayed on patrol after running out of ammunition to complete a one-hour patrol. This hindered the *Luftwaffe* from attacking the defenceless troops on the ground. When we finally returned to North Weald, we were involved in escorting RAF bombers attacking German communications and the thousands of invasion barges massing along the Pas-de-Calais beaches, rivers and canals. Most, if not all, of the Hurricane squadrons which had operated from French airfields had by this time been rested, except 151. Basil Embry, a man without fear, was commanding a bomber squadron in those days and always asked for 151 as escort because we always stayed close.
>
> One of the pilots we lost at Dunkirk was Flight Lieutenant Allen Ives, a friend of Jack Hamar's. He was partially trained as a doctor,

so I gave my permission for him to remain on the beaches to help treat badly wounded soldiers. He put up a marvellous show before getting on a boat. This was sunk and 'Ivy' was swimming in the water when shot through the head by a German soldier lying on the deck of an E-Boat. An eye-witness account of the incident was given to me by another 151 Squadron pilot, a New Zealander, also shot down over Dunkirk.

Essential to the evacuation's success was the contribution made by Air Vice-Marshal Park and his fighter squadrons – but the RAF effort was much criticised at the time. Admiral Ramsay, Flag Officer Dover in overall charge of the naval side, complained that efforts to provide air cover were 'puny'. Clearly there was no appreciation of the Fighter Command strength available for the operation, or the limitations due to aircraft performance. While some German bombers had got through to the beaches, without Fighter Command's presence many more would actually have been able to wreak havoc upon the virtually defenceless troops below. Indeed, more than half of Dowding's fighters had been lost fighting over France – 453 fighters destroyed or abandoned and 435 pilots had failed to come home – before the evacuation began. Fighter Command then lost 106 fighters and eighty pilots over Dunkirk, the Germans 130 aircraft during those bitter battles above the beaches.

Upon conclusion of *Dynamo*, Dowding's squadrons were exhausted – with only 331 Spitfires and Hurricanes left; indeed, as Churchill wrote to the French Prime Minister on 5 June, 'British fighter aviation has been worn to a shred and frightfully mixed up by the demands of Dunkirk'. The RAF had lost 106 precious fighters and eighty even more valuable pilots over Dunkirk (*Luftwaffe* losses were heavier but benefited from the release of 400 captured aircrew after France surrendered).

The Home Intelligence Report dated 3 June 1940 stated that:

> The return of our soldiers from Flanders and their dissemination throughout the country has everywhere stiffened morale, but it has brought to the forefront certain critical discussions. In particular, the BEF are found to be stating on all sides that the RAF was not in evidence during the retreat. These first-hand stories are throwing some doubt on the truthfulness of the broadcast news reports of RAF exploits.

This was not good news for the RAF, neither was it fair. Churchill spoke to the House of Commons on 4 June 1940, and made clear:

> This was a great trial of strength between the British and German air forces. Can you conceive a greater objective for the Germans in the air than to make evacuation from these beaches impossible, and to sink all these ships which were displayed, almost to the extent of thousands? Could there have been an objective of greater military

importance and significance for the whole purpose of the war than this? They tried hard, and were beaten back; they were frustrated in their task. We got the Army away; and they have paid fourfold for any losses they have inflicted.

Very large formations of German aeroplanes – and we know that they are a very brave race – have turned on several occasions from the attack of one-quarter of their number of the Royal Air Force, and have dispersed in different directions. Twelve aeroplanes have been hunted by two. One aeroplane was driven into the water and cast away, by the mere charge of a British aeroplane, which had no more ammunition. All of our types – Hurricane, the Spitfire and the new Defiant – and all our pilots have been vindicated as superior to what they have at present to face.

While some of what Churchill said was exaggerated rhetoric, the facts were clear: without the aerial shield provided by Park's aircrews, the evacuation would have been impossible. Any criticism of the RAF's contribution to *Dynamo*, given the limited resources, range and other difficulties, are unfounded – and the experience gained over the bloody beaches would prove significant tactically, technically and strategically, going forward.

After *Dynamo*, Park's personal reputation emerged enhanced, however, and it was over Dunkirk, from the vantage point of his personal Hurricane, 'OK1', that the tough New Zealander formulated the sound principle with which he would soon fight the Battle of Britain: that it was better to spoil the aim of many, rather than just shoot down a few.

The Home Intelligence daily report, 4 June 1940:

> The dominant topic of conversation today is the Paris air raid which has affected people in a special way. Paris, for this purpose, is London and the reality of air raids on London has been brought home. The newspaper reports of the raid were fairly restrained; in fact our reports show that this restraint was often looked at with suspicion. People were puzzled that only seventeen out of 300 planes were brought down: they believed with some confidence that a very large proportion would be brought down in a raid on the capital. They have largely forgotten Baldwin's once familiar tag 'the bomber will always get through'. An important reaction, however, has been the desire for retaliation. Verbatim reports show that there is an active desire for revenge and the fear of consequences is not entering into public calculation.

In addition to proving that the bomber was not invincible, the fighting in France had also confirmed just how wrong pre-war thinking had been about the limited value of fighters. The German success in France was largely owed to aerial superiority over the battlefield, although the enemy did not enjoy quite the same success over Dunkirk – whatever the BEF's perception. In fact, the deployment of Spitfire squadrons, fresh to the battle and with an aircraft capable of more or less meeting the Me 109 on equal terms, the balance shifted in Fighter Command's favour during *Dynamo*.

In his post action report, Air Vice-Marshal Park accredited his squadrons with 'total ascendancy' over the German bombers ... Indeed, the *Luftwaffe* only had the upper hand over Dunkirk on 27 May and 1 June 1940, the RAF having achieved temporary local aerial supremacy. There could now be no doubt of how crucially important fighters were, in both defence and offence, and in supporting ground operations. Little wonder, then, that the far-sighted Dowding fought so hard to preserve his precious fighters – and Spitfires in particular – which he would not see frittered away on a battle already lost – or on foolhardy tactics in the defence of Britain. And fortunately, the experience of France and Dunkirk saw the inappropriate and inadequate pre-war Fighter Command tactics binned – although squadrons now needed to devise more practical and realistic tactics actually on the job.

Nonetheless, the point is that although RAF tactical doctrine, techniques and procedures had been found wanting, important changes could now be made – just in time for the Battle of Britain.

On 4 June 1940, Churchill also paid further tribute to Britain's airmen:

> When we consider how much greater would be our advantage in defending the air above this island against an overseas attack, I must say that I find these facts [see previous Churchillian quote] a sure basis upon which practical and reassuring thoughts may rest. I will pay my tribute to these young airmen. The great French army was very largely, for the time being, cast back and disturbed by the onrush of a few thousands of armoured vehicles. May it not also be that the cause of civilisation itself will be defended by the skill and devotion of a few thousand airmen. There never had been, I suppose, in all the world, in all the history of war, such an opportunity for youth. The Knights of the Round Table, the Crusaders, all fall back into the past: not only distant but prosaic; these young men, going forth every morn to guard their native land and all that we stand for, holding in their hands these instruments of colossal and shattering power, of whom it may be said that,
>
> > *Every morn brought forth a noble chance*
> > *And every chance brought forth a noble knight,*
>
> Deserve our gratitude, as do all of the brave men who, in so many ways and on so many occasions, are ready, and continue ready, to give life and all for their native land.

Across the Channel, however, Hitler was still confident that Britain would be more amenable to seeking terms – but the new British Prime Minister and war leader was a different proposition to Chamberlain and Halifax. Indeed, on 4 June 1940, Churchill, had also made Britain's stance very clear:

> Even though large tracts of Europe and many old and famous states have fallen, or may fall into the grip of the Gestapo and all the odious apparatus of Nazi rule, we shall not flag or fail. We shall go on to the end. We shall fight in France. We shall fight on the seas and oceans, we shall fight with growing confidence and growing strength in the air. We shall fight on the beaches, we shall fight on the landing-grounds, we shall fight in the fields and in the streets, we shall fight in the hills, we shall never surrender.

In June 1940, Pilot Officer David Scott-Malden was converting to Spitfires at 5 OTU, Aston Down, near Stroud in Gloucestershire. On the 12th of that month he recorded in his diary having 'passed successfully into Spitfire flight. First solo an indescribable thrill. Felt a pretty king man.'

Two days later, 'Paris falls ... marvellous days doing aerobatics in Spitfires.' Then, on 17 June, 'The French give up hostilities. Cannot yet conceive the enormity of it all. I suppose it will not be long before we start defending England in earnest.'

On that same day, according to the *Kriegsmarine* staff war diary, the OKW's Deputy Chief of Staff, *Generalmajor* Walter Warlimon, told Admiral Kurt Fricke, the OKM's liaison officer with the *Oberfehlshaber der Luftwaffe* (OdL, *Luftwaffe* High Command) that, 'with regard to a landing in Britain, the *Führer* ... has not up to now expressed such an intention, as he fully appreciates the unusual difficulties of such an operation. Therefore even at this time, no preparatory work of any kind has been carried out in OKW.'

This, of course, was not known in Britain. Just twenty-two miles away, German troops stood on the Channel coast having defeated the great military power that was France in just six weeks. Hitler's *Wehrmacht* appeared invincible, and despite Goring's failure at Dunkirk, his *Luftwaffe* seemed a terrifying and destructive weapon.

On 18 June 1940, Churchill again spoke to the House:

> What General Weygand called the Battle of France is over. I expect that the Battle of Britain is about to begin. Upon this battle depends the survival of Christian civilisation. Upon it depends our own British life, and the long continuity of our institutions and our Empire. The whole fury and might of the enemy must very soon be turned on us. Hitler knows that he will have to break us in this Island or lose the war. If we can stand up to him, all Europe may be free and the life of the world may move forward into broad, sunlit uplands. But if we

fail, then the whole world, including the United States, including all that we have known and cared for, will sink into the abyss of a new Dark Age made more sinister, and perhaps more protracted, by the lights of perverted science. Let us therefore brace ourselves to our duties, and so bear ourselves that, if the British Empire and its Commonwealth last for a thousand years, men will still say, 'This was their finest hour'.

On that day, the last of Dowding's battered squadrons had returned home from France. According to the official history:

> There was, in sum, a gain of eleven squadrons, there being fifty-eight squadrons in Fighter Command on 20 June, compared to forty-seven on 10 May. But this was largely a nominal gain that had yet to be made into a real one; for no less than twelve of these squadrons were unfit for battle and few of the rest had escaped without serious losses. Altogether, 396 Hurricanes and sixty-seven Spitfires were lost outright during the French campaign: and over the same period nearly 280 fighter pilots were killed, missing or made prisoner, and sixty wounded. The result is reflected in the returns of operational strength in Hurricanes and Spitfires at the close of the campaign. On 24 June, for example, nineteen Spitfire squadrons, with an establishment of sixteen initial equipment aircraft and twenty-two pilots each, reported an average operational strength of thirteen aircraft; eighteen Hurricane squadrons, with the same establishment, reported an average of twelve aircraft. The non-operational Hurricane and Spitfire squadrons were in an even worse case. It was to be well into July before all the Command's squadrons were reckoned fit for operations; and, even then, there was still a 20 per cent deficiency in pilots reckoned fit for operations.

As the foregoing narrative concluded, 'the price paid for intervention had thus been high'.

It had indeed – but, if not for Air Chief Marshal Dowding, it could have been much worse, had Spitfire squadrons been sent to France and had the War Cabinet complied with urgent French appeals for more fighters. To Dowding belongs the credit for honing Britain's air defences before the war – and ensuring sufficient fighters existed to meet any threat to home security.

And that threat was coming.

Chapter 12

'We Never Considered Being Beaten. It Was Just Not Possible in Our Eyes'

At a time when the British should have been enjoying their annual summer holidays at such south-east Victorian coastal resorts as Brighton, Eastbourne and Hove, they braced themselves for a German seaborne invasion. At London's railway stations lists appeared of hundreds of coastal locations that could no longer be visited for 'holiday, recreation or pleasure'. Large tracts of the coastline became 'Defence Areas', entry forbidden to those without special permits. Sea-front hotels were requisitioned, beaches were criss-crossed by barbed wire, and machine-guns sprouted from pill boxes everywhere. A curfew was imposed. The great British novelist and broadcaster J.B. Priestley visited Margate, writing that 'The few signs of life only made the place seem more unreal and spectral.' The British were in no mood, perhaps, for holidays.

Whatever lay ahead, the vast majority of Britons had no doubt that the war against Germany should continue – no matter how hopeless that appeared at that time. The traditional narrative of 'Britain alone', however, has been challenged in recent years, historians arguing that Britain was far from alone, given the support and resources of its Commonwealth and Empire. While that is true, the essential point was that it was not India, Canada, Australia, New Zealand, South Africa or the colonies that were within sight of Dunkirk's blazing oil tanks, or within range of German bombers. Moreover, it would take time for those overseas resources to reach Britain.

The threat to Britain, therefore, was immediate and very real – and in that sense Britain, and all those on the island, were both imperilled and alone. For all the dangers so clearly ahead, the British, to their great credit, and that of the men and women of the Empire and Commonwealth, and those from the defeated nations now gravitating towards Britain as the last base from which to continue the fight, did not falter or fail. They were prepared to weather the storm to preserve their chosen way of life and territory. This is not myth. It is fact. The spirit of the British people was supremely defiant and courageous.

After Dunkirk there was a lull in the fighting as both sides retired to repair and take stock. The campaigns fought thus far had proved that an air force with superiority and possessed of the initiative could give powerful and decisive support to rapid armoured thrusts – by preparing the way ahead with concentrated bombing, and then protecting the flanks of friendly forces from enemy counter-attack. The effectiveness of airborne troops, either conveyed by glider or parachute – providing aerial superiority had already been achieved – had also been proven. Norway evidenced how a seaborne landing could be achieved with aerial superiority and surprise – but fleet actions without air cover were doomed to failure.

In France, the Germans had met the Hurricane, which had fought well but in hopeless circumstances. Over Dunkirk the Spitfire had earned the enemy's respect. The *Luftwaffe* now had bases in Northern France, vastly extending the range of its bombers and, most importantly, putting even London within range of the Me 109. That changed everything. The tacticians who had written Fighter Command's Air Fighting Manual between the wars could never have been expected to predict Hitler's unprecedented advance to the Channel coast, making this possible. Air Chief Marshal Dowding garnered his resources and stood firm. Before assaulting Britain, however, the *Luftwaffe* needed to regroup and refit, so a lull followed the Battle of France and Dunkirk evacuation.

On 10 June 1940, during the lull between the Fall of France and the Battle of Britain, the Aeroplane & Armament Experimental Establishment (A&AEE) at Farnborough tested Me 109E-3, *Werk-Nummer* 1304, which had been captured in France and previously used for comparison trials with 1 Squadron's Hurricanes at Orleans. Trials were now flown with Spitfire Mk IA, K9791, fitted with a Rotol CS airscrew. The resulting report is reproduced verbatim:

1. The trial commenced with the two aircraft taking off together, with the Spitfire slightly behind and using +6¼lbs boost and 3,000 rpm.
2. When fully airborne the pilot of the Spitfire reduced his revolutions to 2,650 rpm. and was then able to overtake and outclimb the Me 109. At 4,000ft the Spitfire pilot was 1,000ft above the Me 109, from which position he was able to get on its tail, and remain there within effective range despite all efforts of the pilot of the Me 109 to shake him off.
3. The Spitfire then allowed the Me 109 to get on his tail and attempted the shake him off. This he found quite easy owing to the superior manoeuvrability of his aircraft, particularly in the looping plane and at low speeds between 100 and 140 mph. By executing a steep turn just above stalling speed, he ultimately got back into a position on the tail of the Me 109.
4. Another effective form of evasion with the Spitfire was found to be a steep, climbing spiral at 120 mph, using +6¼lbs boost and 2,650 rpm.; in this manoeuvre the Spitfire gained rapidly on the Me 109, eventually allowing the pilot to execute a half-roll on the tail of his opponent.
5. Comparative speed trials were then carried out, and the Spitfire proved to be considerably the faster of the two, both in acceleration and straight and level flight, without having to make use of the emergency +12 lbs boost. During diving trials, the Spitfire pilot found that, by engaging fully coarse pitch and using -2lbs boost, his aircraft was superior to the Me 109.

WE NEVER CONSIDERED BEING BEATEN

> In general flying qualities the aeroplane is inferior to the Spitfire and the Hurricane at all speeds and in all conditions of flight. It is much inferior at speeds in excess of 250 mph and at 400 mph recovery from a dive is difficult because of the heaviness of the elevator. This heaviness of the elevator makes all manoeuvres in the looping plane above 250 mph difficult including steep climbing turns. No difference was experienced between climbing turns to the right and left. It does not possess the control which allows of good quality flying and this is particularly noticeable in aerobatics.

The content of this report can only be considered surprising. The same 109 had performed extremely well when compared to 1 Squadron's Hurricanes two months before. Having previously been subjected to a forced-landing, however, it is fair to question whether the machine's performance remained at its peak. This is especially important when considering that the RAF aircraft used in the trial was the latest Spitfire and fitted with a CS propeller. Nonetheless, the report would certainly have been morale boosting to Fighter Command's Spitfire pilots.

The previous day, Wing Commander George Stainforth – of Schneider Trophy fame – flew the 109 in a series of comparative trials concerning the turning circles of the 109, Spitfire and Hurricane. Stainforth's subsequent report concluded that the Hurricane out-turned the 109 'within about one complete turn', and that 'The *Messerschmitt* appears to be only slightly faster than the Hurricane.' The Spitfire, he continued, 'out-turned the *Messerschmitt* almost as easily as the Hurricane'.

The 109, however, was considered to have a 'large turning circle' and be 'generally extremely unmanoeuvrable'. Finally, 'the pilot of the Spitfire reports that he had no difficulty in sitting on the *Messerschmitt*'s tail, and could, in fact, have tightened up his turn quite a lot more and got well on the inside. He was at +5 boost – almost full throttle.'

Stainforth's report clearly erred on the side of the Spitfire as to which of the three was overall best performer. In Germany similar trials had also been undertaken and reported upon accordingly:

> In the following performance and air combat comparison that has been performed at the *E-Stelle Reclin* between Me 109E and Me 110C and the captured enemy fighters Spitfire, Hurricane and Curtiss, shall be brought to notice. The results of the comparison are to be announced immediately to all *Jagd* (Fighter) and *Zestörer* (destroyer) units, to guarantee appropriate air combat behaviour in the engagements on the basis of technical conditions.
>
> The Me 109E type clearly out-performs all foreign aircraft.
> Speed: the Spitfire is at 0 m by ca. 20 km/h, at 4 m by ca. 10 km/h. Hurricane and Curtiss at 0 and 4 km altitude by ca. 60 km/h. A similar superiority of the Me 109E exists in climb performance too. Climb

times to 4 km: Me 109E – 4.4 minutes, Spitfire 5 minutes, Hurricane 5.6 minutes, Curtiss 5.2 minutes.

The Me 110C is inferior speed-wise to the Spitfire, superior to the Curtiss and Hurricane. Regarding the climb performance the Curtiss is equal at ground-level, up to 4 km superior then inferior. Hurricane is inferior up to an altitude of 2 km, then superior up to 6.5 km. The Spitfire is equal at ground level but otherwise superior.

The best climb for Me 109E and Me 110C is achieved with shallow climb angle and higher speeds than the enemy fighters. It is wrong to climb away steeply or climb behind an enemy fighter with the same angle.

Before turning fights with the Me 109E, it must be noted that in every case, that all three foreign planes have significantly smaller turning circles and turning times. An attack on the opponent as well as disengagement can only be accomplished on the basis of existing superiority in performance.

The following suggestions are made:

The Spitfire and Hurricane have two-pitch propellers. Climbing away with the Me 109 and Me 110 must be done with the best climbing speed or even higher speeds of about 280–300 km/h. On aircraft with two-pitch propellers with low blade angle the engine will experience a very high over-revolution, and on the hand with a high blade angle high boost pressure – therefore, in other words, performance loss.

On a sudden push forward on the stick to dive, the carburettor of the enemy fighters cuts out due to negative acceleration. This evasive measure, diving, is also recommended.

The rolling ability of the enemy fighters at high speeds is worse than that of the Me 109. Quick changes of the trajectory along the vertical axis cause, especially with the Spitfire, load changes around the cranial axis, coming from high longitudinal thrust momentum, and significantly disturb aiming.

In summary, it can be said that all three enemy aircraft types are inferior to the German planes regarding flying qualities. The Spitfire has bad elevator and rudder stability on the target approach. In addition, wing-mounted weapons have known shooting-technique disadvantages.

Those trials provided an opportunity for none other than Major *Vati* Mölders to fly and evaluate three of the enemy aircraft types he had been shooting down:

> It was very interesting to carry out the flight trials at Rechlin with the Spitfire and Hurricane. Both types are very simple to fly compared to

our aircraft, and childishly easy to take-off and land. The Hurricane is good natured and turns well, but its performance is decidedly inferior to that of the Me 109. It has strong stick forces and is 'lazy' on the ailerons. The Spitfire is one class better. It handles well, is light on the controls, faultless in the turn and has a performance approaching that of the Me 109. As a fighting aircraft, however, it is miserable. A sudden push on the stick will cause the engine to cut, and because the propeller has only two pitch settings (take-off and cruise), in a rapidly changing air combat situation the engine is either over-speeding or else is not being used to the full.

The foregoing assessment is remarkably fair.

Although CS propellers were on the way to Spitfire and Hurricane squadrons, the Merlin's lack of fuel injection could not be addressed and was something the RAF pilots had to cope with. The experience of the fighting thus far also led to certain improvements being absorbed into the 109 programme, leading to the Me 109E-4. This variant had seat and head armour to protect the pilot, and armour for the fuel tank (on top of which the pilot sat), which had been found vulnerable from an astern attack. The canopy was redesigned, offering better visibility, and armament was finally standardised at two wing-mounted Oerlikon cannons and twin engine-cowl mounted machine-guns.

A certain amount of aircraft, designated Me 109E-4B, were modified to carry a single *Sprengbombe Cylindrisch* (SC) 50 kilo bomb, enabling the 109 to be used in a *jajdgbomber* (fighter-bomber) role. The Me 109E was now ready to fight the Battle of Britain and challenge the RAF for aerial superiority. It was a circumstance that Professor Willy Messerschmitt could never have imagined when he drew the first pencil lines on his Augsburg drawing board back in 1934.

The day fighters of both sides, however, currently stood-by, awaiting developments.

By night, though, the Germans maintained a degree of pressure, lone raiders prowling over Britain, dropping bombs and causing a general nuisance. On the night of 18/19 June 1940, the greatest attack to date on mainland Britain was launched, with over seventy intruders attacking a wide range of targets.

That moonlit night, the *Luftwaffe* was particularly active over East Anglia, with many 'red' air raid warnings sounding. Oil installations were bombed at Canvey Island, the breached pipeline blazing for hours, and civilians were killed in Cambridge and Southend. At this time, Britain's nocturnal defences were totally inadequate, there being no dedicated night-fighting aircraft, and Airborne Interception radar had yet to appear. Consequently, day fighters, including the Spitfire, which was not a good night-flying aircraft, were pressed into service to patrol after dark, supplementing the twin-engine Bristol Blenheim equipped squadrons.

As a daylight bomber, the Blenheim had proved vulnerable to fighter attack, and the Mk IF version lacked the performance to be an effective day fighter, so instead the latter type provided the backbone of Fighter Command's nocturnal defence force during this early war period. The night in question would see both Spitfires and Blenheims in action over eastern England.

At Rochford, Flight Lieutenant Malan was wide awake and becoming increasingly concerned as the crump of exploding bombs could be heard from a direction of Southend – uncomfortably close to his wife and new-born son in Westcliffe. It was too much for the 'Tiger' to bear: Sailor requested permission to scramble. An anonymous eyewitness described the scene on that clear, moonlit, night:

> Without waiting to dress, Sailor's rigger and fitter, who had already turned in, pushed their feet into gum boots, slung their rifles over their shoulders, put on their tin hats, and reported for duty in their striped pyjamas. Then they rushed out to the dispersal post. While the mechanics worked swiftly to start up the Spitfire, Sailor methodically buckled on the harness of the parachute. By the time he had got his gear on, the engine had started, so he climbed into the cockpit and strapped himself in before opening up the throttle to warm the engine up a bit. Meanwhile, he looked up and tried to pick out a target ahead and saw a He 111 at 6,000ft being held by searchlights. It was making a straight run directly across him. A second glance at the approaching bomber made him decide that the engine was quite capable of warming itself up. Leaping out of the cockpit with his parachute on, he made a dive for a little trench close at hand. The last time he saw the trench it was only about eighteen inches deep, but unbeknown to him the men had continued to dig until it was 5ft deep. He dived in just as the bomber appeared slap overhead, and landed on his face at the bottom.

Immediately the raider had passed overhead, Sailor jumped out of the trench, back into his Spitfire, and hastened off in pursuit; his personal combat report describes events:

> I climbed towards E/A which was making for the coast and held in searchlight beams at 8,000ft. I positioned myself astern and opened fire at 200 yards, closing to fifty yards with one burst. Observed bullets entering E/A and had my windscreen covered in oil. Broke off to the left and immediately below as E/A spiralled out of beam.

This attack – incredibly delivered from as close as fifty yards *at night* – occurred between '0020 hrs to 0030 hrs (approximately)', 'off Foulness'. According to local records this He 111, of *Stab*/KG4 *General Wever*, crashed into the Bishop of Chelmsford's garden in Springfield Road, Chelmsford, at 00.30 hrs; the crew of four baled out and were captured. This was a historic occasion: it was the Spitfire's first nocturnal 'kill'.

At the same time, Flying Officer John Petre of Duxford-based 19 Squadron got yet another KG 4 machine – but return fire from the rear-gunner ignited his Spitfire, which literally blew up in his face; Petre survived, but was badly burned.

Flying Officer Frank Brinsden, of 19 Squadron: 'His Spitfire literally blew up in his face and he suffered terribly disfiguring burns, which, I am happy to say, have become less obvious with the passage of time.'

Flying Officer James Coward:

> I was not there, but a story did the rounds that after Petre had shot down the *Heinkel*, a Scottish soldier recently returned from Boulogne, where the Germans shot all Scottish prisoners [this is untrue, although elements of the *Waffen*-SS did murder large numbers of British prisoners in two well-documented massacres on the road to Dunkirk], saw the pilot descending in the searchlight beam and was waiting for him with bayonet fixed. Apparently the very arrogant German, who spoke excellent English, said 'There is no point you taking me prisoner, the *Führer* will be over here in a week and you will all be prisoners.' To which the Scot is said to have replied 'Who's takin' prisoners?!'
>
> Prodding with his bayonet, he escorted the German to the Guard Room. As I heard it quite a party developed in the ante-room to celebrate Petre's success, when a young officer who was a keen follower of the First World War 'aces' said 'I believe that in the First World War officers captured were brought into the Mess for a drink before being taken off for interrogation.' So, the Duty Officer was asked to fetch the German over for a drink. Apparently, on entering the ante-room he was astonished at the apparent jollity, and as a hush spread through the room at his appearance he said 'It is quite useless to put on this charade for my benefit, but you must realise that the war is as good as over.
>
> When I flew over I could see London in flames.' To which an officer who had just driven back from London said 'Well, I was having a drink in the RAF Club just over an hour ago and it all looked quite normal to me' – whereupon the German lost all his arrogance and burst into tears! Someone said 'This is too depressing for words, for God's sake take him away.'

There was doubtless little truth in Coward's third-hand story, but Pilot Officer Peter Howard-Williams, also of 19, remembered things more accurately:

> On the night of 18 June 1940, I was flying Spitfire R6623 on a local night recce, when I was recalled, and experienced pilots were

scrambled. Petre then shot down the *Heinkel*. One was shut into the cells of the Duxford Guard Room as he proved rather fierce and belligerent. Another German, *Oberleutnant* von Arnim, was brought to the Mess, spoke good English and was well entertained. He was the navigator and captain on the aircraft – which seemed odd to us in those days. I remember giving him a pair of RAF wings. He said that his father was commanding German forces in North Africa.

After a pleasant evening during which there was no hostility as I remember it, I think he was given a room for the night in the Mess. I do remember that there was a stink the next day, as the intelligence people, who were due to question him, didn't think he should have been so well treated. I don't remember Von Arnim saying anything other than the fact that Germany would win the war simply because Hitler said so. There were certainly no tears, and we all had a few beers and enjoyed it all.

Flying Officer Frank Brinsden:

The captain of the He 111 'Johnnie' Petre shot down was at first detained in our Mess and Ladies Room. Eileen Lane [a pre-war racing driving champion, socialite and wife of 19 Squadron's 'A' Flight commander, Flight Lieutenant Brian Lane DFC] called at the Mess to see Brian, who was absent, and shown unwittingly to the Ladies Room by the Duty Officer. On her entry, the German officer rose to his feet and greeted Eileen as an old acquaintance – they had known each other on the motor racing circuits of Europe!

This *Heinkel* was also attacked by Blenheim pilot Squadron Leader 'Spike' O'Brien of Collyweston's 23 Squadron, whose aircraft went into a spin upon breaking away – unable to regain control, O'Brien ordered 'abandon ship', but was the only crew-member to survive a safe parachute descent: Pilot Officer Cuthbert King-Clark baled out but was killed when his body hit the starboard propeller, and Corporal David Little was trapped in the aircraft and killed in the resulting crash.

German bombers still prowled over England, a second falling to the guns of 74 Squadron's Flight Lieutenant Malan at 01.15 hrs:

Climbed to 12,000ft towards another E/A held by searchlights on northerly course. Opened fire at 250 yards, taking good care not to overshoot this time. Gave five two-second bursts and observed bullets entering all over E/A with slight deflection as he was turning to port. E/A emitted heavy smoke and I saw one parachute open very close. E/A went down in spiral dive. Searchlights and I following him right down until he crashed in flames near Chelmsford. As

> I approached target in each case I flashed succession of dots on downward recognition light before moving into attack. I did not notice AA gunfire after I had done this. When following second E/A down I switched on navigation lights for a short time to help establish identity. Gave letter of period only once when returning at 3,000ft from Chelmsford when one searchlight searched for me.

This was incredible – and the switching on of navigation lights, thereby illuminating the Spitfire and making it a target for German gunners, 'to help establish identity', is completely consistent with the careful professional fighter pilot the record proves he was – as opposed to accusations levelled at him over 'Barking Creek'.

The second He 111 destroyed by Sailor belonged to 4/KG4 and was attacked between Wickford to Chelmsford at 12,000ft; the Cork Light Vessel, anchored off Felixstowe reported seeing the enemy bomber crash into the sea at 01.15 hrs, killing all aboard, including the *Staffelkapitän, Oberleutnant* H. Prochnow.

To destroy one enemy aircraft in one night was a feat enough in itself – but two was a huge achievement. Meanwhile, Sailor's wife Lynda and their newly born son, Jonathan, slept soundly, blissfully unaware of the drama unfolding above their heads.

At 01.35 hrs, 19 Squadron's Flying Officer Eric Ball was scrambled from Duxford to:

> investigate a raid over Newmarket. He found the enemy aircraft illuminated by searchlights and recognised it to be a He 111. Over Colchester he attacked from dead astern, closing from 200–50 yards. He broke away and repeated his attack, by which time the enemy aircraft was enveloped in clouds of smoke and losing height. Immediately afterwards the searchlights lost the enemy aircraft and pilot returned to base. The enemy aircraft crashed at Margate, all the crew being killed.

In his subsequent report, Flying Officer Ball made clear 'that without the excellent work put in by searchlights no interception would have been effected'. This was a *Heinkel* of 6/KG4, which fell into the sea off Margate; contrary to the squadron diarist's assessment, only one of the crew was killed, the rest captured.

Over the Norfolk coast, Sergeant Alan Croxton Close of 23 Squadron, flying Blenheim L8687 YP-S, had stalked a He 111 – but was shot down in flames by an alert German gunner. While the 23-year-old pilot from Sale, Cheshire, was killed in the resulting crash, his gunner, LAC Laurence Karasek, safely baled out.

This combat, which vividly lit up the night sky, had not gone unnoticed by Flight Lieutenant Duke-Woolley, also of 23 Squadron, who reported that at 00.50 hrs:

> While flying at 6,000ft three miles north-east of Kings Lynn, I observed aircraft subsequently identified as a He 111 held in searchlights at 8,000ft. Time 0045 hrs. Observed ball of fire which

I took to be a Blenheim in flames break away from behind tail of enemy aircraft (E/A). Climbed to engage E/A and attacked from below tail after searchlights were no longer holding. Range 50 yards. E/A returned fire and appeared to throttle back suddenly. Own speed 130 – 140 mph. Estimated E/A slowed to 110 mph. Delivered five attacks. Air gunner (AC Derek Bell) fired several short bursts at varying ranges. After last front gun attack, Air Gunner reported port engine of E/A on fire. Returned to base and landed, starboard engine unserviceable. Several bullet holes in wings and fuselage of own aircraft including hit in starboard wing and fuselage by cannon.

The enemy raider, a He 111-H4 (fuselage code 5J + DM) of II/KG 4's staff flight, crash-landed in shallow water just offshore at Blakeney Point in Norfolk, a vast expense of flat beach, perfect for a forced-landing. The crew, the *Gruppenkommander*, Major Dietrich Freiherr von Massenbach, *Oberleutnant* Ulrich Jordan, *Oberfeldwebel* Max Leimer and *Feldwebel* Karl Amberger, swam and waded ashore, covered by auxiliary coastguard men from their nearby station. Sensibly, the Germans surrendered and were taken into custody, confirming having shot down Close's Blenheim before being despatched by Duke-Woolley and Bell.

It was a costly night for KG 4, which lost five He 111s over England. Astonishingly, Von Massenbach's Heinkel remained where it crashed off Blakeney Point until 1969, when it was removed on the orders of Trinity House, the charity dedicated to safeguarding shipping and seafarers. (In such shallow water, so close to shore it is difficult to understand how the wrecked German bomber was in any shape or form a navigation hazard. The year of its removal also saw, ironically, release of Guy Hamilton's technicolour and star-studded epic *Battle of Britain* – which really launched the warbird preservation and aviation archaeology movements. If only the *Heinkel* had survived a few more months, it might have been saved, preserved, perhaps, at an appropriate museum. Today, Blakeney Point is owned by the National Trust, which in 2017 reported wreckage from the He 111 being exposed after a storm).

Nothing remains to remind us today of that dramatic incident over eighty years ago, but Blakeney Point is certainly an atmospheric place where the imagination can easily visualise that wrecked bomber rotting in the surf.

After news of the night's action spread on the morning of Wednesday 19 June 1940, Pilot Officer Scott-Malden, still converting to Spitfires at Aston Down, wrote in his diary 'Orderly Officer. Talked to the AA posts, who look forward to some work at last. The "Battle of Britain" starts with an air raid on the East Coast.' This is interesting because it confirms that the night's attack on Britain was so significantly heavy, that it suggested the aerial campaign for which Britain was braced had begun.

The Home Intelligence daily report also documents the reaction to the night's events:

> The air raids and warnings last night have on the whole been taken very calmly: 'not as bad as we expected'. At the same time, areas where bombs fell before sirens sounded are very critical and this reinforces a widespread demand for making ARP a compulsory rather than a voluntary service. The raiding in Wales has strengthened the popular belief that evacuation is not synonymous with safety and the value of 'scatter' as a sensible air-raid precaution needs emphasis. One Region is very critical of the newspaper methods of presenting air-raid news. It is too alarmist and emphasises the number of casualties, rather than their minute numerical proportion. Two Regions report demands by the public for full details of the night's air raids in the 7 o'clock news 'as a reward for hours of discomfort in the shelters'.

The air-raid warning system, managed by Fighter Command in conjunction with the civil defence organisations and police, was a matter of controversy, however. Four levels of warning existed:

Yellow	'Preliminary Caution'. A confidential warning of impending attack provided civil defence organisations, the police, government officials, and large factories.
White	'Cancel Caution', cancelling the Yellow warning, if necessary.
Red	'Action Warning', following a 'Yellow' message, activating air-raid sirens, giving public warning of an impending attack, sending people hurrying to take shelter.
Green	'Raiders Passed', when sirens sounded the 'All Clear', indicating the threat had passed.

On occasion, the warning was adequate, other times not. The government faced a dilemma, torn between its duty to protect the public and not wanting to see production disrupted any more than necessary. The night attacks from this night of 19 June 1940 onwards saw night workers spending up to three hours in shelters, and daytime workers deprived of sleep.

There was, of course, the infamous 'Black Out' after dark, in which no light was permitted to shine forth, thereby potentially assisting the visual navigation of enemy aircraft. And therein lay another dilemma. Factories were permitted some external lighting, which was extinguished in the event of a Red warning. If there were no such alarms, the lights remained on, thereby potentially assisting the enemy. The Government wished to reduce the number of Red warnings owing to the negative impact upon production, but the Home Secretary, Sir John Anderson, declared that factory workers should work on after a Red warning, only sheltering if and when bombs actually exploded.

Originally, the policy had been 'Safety First'. Now it was clearly 'Production First'. The dangers faced, therefore, by those engaged in war production is something often hidden from history, but something which, as our narrative evolves, we will explore.

On 22 June 1940, France formally surrendered. Delivering a very clear message to the French, Hitler was personally present when the armistice was signed – in the very railway carriage at Compiègne that the Germans had surrendered to Marshal Foch on 11 November 1918. General Kietel, OKW Chief of Staff, read a statement on Hitler's behalf to the French delegation:

> Thus did 11 November 1918 inaugurate, in this railway carriage, the sufferings of the German people. Everything that could be inflicted on a race, by way of dishonour, humiliation and moral and material suffering, had its beginnings here. Perjury and breach of promise was heap[ed] upon a race whose only weakness, after more than four years of heroic resistance, was to lend credence to the pledges of the democratic leaders …
>
> France has collapsed after resisting heroically and being beaten in an uninterrupted series of bloody battles. That is why Germany has no intention of giving the armistice terms and negotiations a flavour that would humiliate a gallant adversary.

General Weygand concluded that Germany's terms were 'harsh but not dishonouring'.

After the armistice was signed, German engineers dismantled the historic railway carriage, forever erasing Germany's shame of 11 November 1918. Hitler danced a celebratory jig – then went sightseeing in Paris before returning to Berlin. The German people gave their victorious *Führer* an astonishing triumphal welcome: crowds numbering hundreds of thousands awaited his return, and the flower strewn route from the Anhalter-Bahnhof station to the Reich Chancellery resounded with their cheers. Keitel declared Hitler 'The greatest warlord of all time', and, incited by relentless propaganda and inspired by unprecedented victories, Germany looked forward with enthusiasm to Britain's defeat. Hitler's propaganda minister, Dr Josef Goebbels, predicted 'terrible' consequences for the British, should Germany's terms not be met.

Churchill immediately launched a scathing attack on the French government, telling the House that 'His Majesty's Government have heard with grief and amazement that the terms dictated by the Germans have been accepted by the French government at Bordeaux.'

King George VI felt relieved, as His Majesty explained to his mother: 'Personally I feel happier now that we have no allies to be polite to and to pamper.'

It was now that Air Chief Marshal Dowding's foresight and determination not to squander away precious fighters in France on a battle already lost was given clear justification; his view was simply: 'Thank God we are now alone.'

Again, the Home Intelligence daily report is of interest:

> There has been little change in morale during this period of waiting. People have got over the French collapse and are quite calm ... There is a clear realisation of the danger of invasion and from some Regions come reports that the public think preparations for it have improved ... Air raids were taken philosophically, although, particularly in the South-Western Region, they gave rise to uncontrolled rumours. There is criticism of the midnight news reporting the beginning of a raid: it promoted nervous apprehension. Observers report that one of the main reactions in raided districts is weariness through broken sleep with consequent depression ... Besides waiting for Hitler's terms, people are still waiting for a strong lead.

Flying Officer Frank Brinsden:

> At squadron level I don't think we were fully aware of what was going on. We were just keen to have a crack at the Germans, and the prevalent attitude was that we couldn't wait for them to come. Given that the Belgians and French had proved of little use during the defence of their homelands, we were glad to be on our own. We were absolutely confident that we were better than the enemy and wanted an opportunity to bloody Hitler's nose.

The mood in Fighter Command, nonetheless, was optimistic and enthusiastic. Flight Sergeant George Unwin: 'We never considered being beaten. It was just not possible in our eyes.'

After France surrendered, German forces became an army of occupation in north-west France, while Marshal Phillipe Pétain established a collaborationist regime in Vichy. In London, however, the French General Charles de Gaulle, a member of the French cabinet during the Fall of France, established a French government in exile – rejecting both the armistice and Pétain's Vichy government.

On 18 June 1940, when all appeared hopeless, de Gaulle appealed via the BBC for free French servicemen to join him and continue the fight. Among those who heard, and then answered this clarion call to arms, was one French pilot, René Mouchotte. Born to a wealthy family on 21 August 1914, Mouchotte joined the French Air Force in 1935, completing his statutory military service, becoming a reservist and resuming civilian life in January 1939. Recalled at the outbreak of war, he served as a flying instructor and then converted to twin-engine aircraft at Oran, Algeria. After the armistice, as described in his diaries, first published in 1946, together with fellow airman Henri Lafont, the pair flew to England and joined the RAF. As trained pilots, they were welcome reinforcements.

The hapless Poles, however, again on the losing side, were disappointed with the speed with which France had collapsed, and felt somewhat let down. Now, the Poles in France made their way to join their comrades in Britain. Polish records describe how, on occasions, force had to be used against the French to facilitate this evacuation. Ships were requisitioned at pistol point and sailed to Gibraltar.

Those pilots with French machines flew across the Channel to England, and those with boats crossed sea. Indeed, no possible means of reaching Britain, to continue the fight, was overlooked. Great initiative was shown by many Polish officers, among them Lieutenant Stanislaw Wandzilak, who led over forty Polish Air Force mechanics to the French coast, seizing transport by force and ultimately escaping the chaos of France's defeat by sea. In England, Wandzilak would be praised for his 'coolness and courage'. In Britain, Blackpool became the central collecting depot for Polish personnel, who began the long and often frustrating process of learning a new language, as well as RAF procedures and learning to fly, service and operate Fighter Command's modern fighter types. Together with Free French, Belgians, Dutch and Czechoslovaks, the more numerous Poles were vital reinforcements.

By now, the effect of casualties was being felt on a personal level. Assistant Section Officer Felicity Hanbury:

> My first husband was a 30-year-old fighter pilot killed long before the Battle of Britain, in a flying accident on Gloster Gladiators while serving with 615 Squadron on 1 October 1939, less than a month after the war had broken out. So when I became a 24-year-old WAAF officer I had already been widowed. It was quite a shock coming in at the beginning of everything. I had personally experienced what might also happen to other people which, I suppose, wasn't a bad thing when I was responsible for 250 airwomen at Biggin Hill: operations room plotters, drivers, cooks, people in the armoury, stores, everything. One of my code and cipher officers married a pilot on the base who was shot down and she didn't know whether he would reappear; he did, thank goodness.
>
> The girls of the WAAF came from all walks of life. Some were well educated; others were not. There were so many wanting to join that you could sort them out as suitable for this or that. We had no difficulty recruiting but did have absorbing all the new recruits at such short notice.

On 9 June 1940, an engineering officer from Hornchurch had contacted de Havilland, inquiring as to whether a governor could be fitted to the existing variable pitch propeller, converting the airscrew from two-pitch to constant-speed. Four days later, de Havilland's engineers spent thirty-six hours fitting a Spitfire with such a device, known as the Constant-Speed Unit (CSU), this aircraft being delivered to 65 Squadron at Hornchurch on 15 June. This modified aircraft was found to be able to take off in 225 yards, reach 20,000ft in 7.42 minutes, had a maximum ceiling of 39,000ft – the variable pitch propeller's statistics being 320 yards, 11.8 minutes, and 32,000ft respectively.

The CSU-fitted Spitfires was also more manoeuvrable – and equal in performance to new Spitfires fitted with the Rotol CS propeller. With the benefits being clear, when France surrendered on 22 June the Air Ministry instructed de Havilland to fit, in the field, CSUs and thus convert all Spitfires, Hurricanes and Defiants from the less efficient variable pitch to constant-speed propellers; the work started two days later. So impressed, in fact, was 609 'West Riding' Squadron with the improvement, that its ORB recorded: 'The Spitfire is now an aeroplane.' It was a significant performance improvement – just in time.

At this time, the Air Ministry was concurrently trying to resolve the issue of day-fighter armament, which was a reaction to two things: anticipation of the Germans fitting armour plate to protect their bombers' engines, and secondly the proven destructive power of the 109's Oerlikon. Interestingly, although the Hurricane's wing was thicker – and arguably therefore stronger – trials around achieving a cannon-armed fighter featured almost entirely around the Spitfire. This can only be because the Air Ministry were already looking ahead and recognised that the Spitfire had much potential for development, whereas the Hurricane did not.

Moreover, the cannon – weighing ninety-six pounds each, increased weight-loading. The Spitfire's superior margin in performance was more able to absorb this than the Hurricane, which already lagged behind both the Spitfire and, more importantly, the Me 109. Confusion, however, existed over the best armament configuration and combination. Initially it was thought that just two cannons, one in each wing and without any machine-guns, would suffice.

On 27 June 1940, the first cannon-armed Spitfire, R6761, was delivered to 19 Squadron at Fowlmere. Soon the squadron was entirely equipped with the cannon-armed Spitfire Mk IB. Only one comparable Hurricane existed. This was also fitted with two Hispano-Suiza cannon, but unlike the Spitfire, the wings of which accommodated the cannon internally, the Hurricanes were fitted in two under-wing exterior pods.

During the Battle of Britain, this machine saw action, flown by Flight Lieutenant Dick Smith of 151 Squadron, who later described the aircraft as 'a heavy old cow'. Indeed, in battle, Smith was 'frustrated by the poor performance' of this aircraft. Hawker also produced a four-cannon armed one-off, but although this too was delivered to 151 Squadron it saw no combat (ultimately, however, the Hurricane Mk IIC would be armed with four cannons, but, because of impaired performance, this was employed not as an interceptor day-fighter but as a successful ground-attack and night intruder aircraft).

Flying Officer Frank Brinsden remembered that he and his fellow pilots of 19 Squadron were 'chuffed' to learn that they were to be the first cannon-equipped Spitfire squadron. The CO, Squadron Leader Philip Pinkham, lectured his pilots on 1 July 1940 regarding the advantages and disadvantages of their new weapon. The disadvantages he listed as:

1. Stoppages too frequent. Stoppages of one cannon makes it very difficult to keep a steady sight with the other.
2. Fire period restricted to six seconds, making defence against other fighter aircraft very difficult.
3. Lack of 'spread'.

The advantages, Pinkham explained were:

1. Terrific destructive power.
2. High muzzle velocity decreasing amount of deflection necessary in deflection shooting.
3. Increased range and accuracy.

Pinkham also began exploring new tactical formations so as to maximise his cannon-armed Spitfires' potential. On 4 July 1940, the Squadron flew to practice his new ideas. Instead of flying in the usual 'vics', 'A' Flight's sections dived in echelon from 2,000ft above and to the side of three target aircraft from dead astern. They closed rapidly and gained steady sighting at high speed before breaking away downwards and to one side. The new formation was then posted up at dispersal in diagrammatic form.

This was forward thinking indeed. This new formation relied upon two sections of two flying in line astern and was highly manoeuvrable – similar, in fact, to the *Schwarm*. The only difference and continued drawback being that the Spitfires remained too close together. Still, this was very much a step in the right direction and away from the suicidal vics of three, as stipulated by Fighter Command. What was not, ironically, was the cannon's unreliability.

Flying Officer Frank Brinsden:

> Our initial pleasure at receiving the Mk Ibs soon turned to disappointment when they did not function well in practice. I personally got into several scraps when both jammed after firing only a few rounds. Distortion somewhere, under 'G' forces, was suspected and I proved this on several practice sorties over the Wash when both cannons jammed when 'G' forces similar to those applied in combat built up.

WE NEVER CONSIDERED BEING BEATEN

Armourer Fred Roberts remembered that:

> We took a lot of stick from the pilots over these stoppages. For a while they wanted to blame the armourers and then, when a full magazine of ammunition was expended, the pilots complained that they only had six seconds of firing time against the eighteen seconds of the Browning machine-guns. We had little help and no encouragement from the armament staff at Duxford ... Even the 'experts' who came from RAF Northolt to help could only listen and learn from us!
>
> Most of the trouble stemmed from the cannons being mounted on their sides, the empty shell cases therefore being ejected sideways from the breech and deflected back into it. The nose of the shell dropping slightly and striking the breech end of the barrel, buckling the shell case at the neck caused another kind of stoppage.
>
> We fitted various kinds of deflector plates. We altered the angle of the plates, fitted rubber pads to dampen the force of the spent shell case, but none of these experiments worked. We also had magazine feed trouble, caused by it lying on its side while mounted on the cannon. To counter this we tried varying the tension applied to the magazine spring but that was unsuccessful.

So important was this matter that Dowding himself was involved. In a letter to the Air Minister, Sir Archibald Sinclair, he nailed the problem: 'These guns were designed to operate on their bellies but have been mounted on their sides. This has led to technical difficulties.' It was crucial that these 'technical difficulties' were resolved, but for the present 19 Squadron's frustrations would continue.

Squadron Leader Edward Alford remembered that at Kenley:

> To add a little more to the firepower of the installations on the roof of my station Armoury, I converted a Vickers machine-gun into a serviceable weapon, by fitting a new firing pin to it in place of the truncated one which gave no protrusion, and having tested it on the twenty-five yards range, placed it in as advantageous position as possible on the roof of the Armourers' shop, where it became the 'Belle of the Ball' among the Armourers each time we mustered for action on receipt of an Air Raid Warning.
>
> So enthusiastic did the Armourers become, that these guns received daily, the care and attention a keen gardener would give to his prize flower bed and possession of the post with the Vickers gun covetously regarded by all, and it was because of this efficient maintenance, that when the time did arrive for them to be used in earnest that they all functioned perfectly which, in due course, caused the destruction of one Do 17 before the crew had time to drop their bombs.

Towards the end of June 1940, we received to our great joy, eight 20mm Hispano cannons for ground defence, four of which were installed on the 'drome at Kenley and the others were sent to Croydon. Having sited them we badgered 'Works and Buildings' to complete the bases for the mountings and erect low protecting walls round them to give the gun crews a little protection from the elements as well as from other missiles which might be directed against them. These walls were built to a height of about three ft six inches, which allowed the guns to be brought to a horizontal position should they have had to be used against airborne troops or gliders landing on the drome.

Sandbag stops were built to arrest the rotary traverse of the guns in the horizontal position to ensure that in the excitement of an action, gunners would not be able to fire on each other, but at the same time would have a maximum traverse of 360° when sighting at aircraft. Gunners were trained at an Armament Training Camp in the use of these weapons, but to ensure that their training could be continued we persuaded the driver of an excavator working near a dispersal point, to dig out part of a natural bank in the hillside, and this we converted to a little test range as it was conveniently near one of our cannon gun posts.

From this one gun post the gunners both at Kenley and Croydon were all able to fire a few rounds necessary to keep them conversant with the handling of it and just how it would behave when installed on that particular type of mounting. As it was not possible to indulge in as much actual firing as we would have liked nor to test each gun on its own mounting due to lack of range facilities and ammunition of this type, the syllabus of training was supplemented by constant practice with camera guns, to teach deflection and range judging, which were coupled with lectures on aircraft recognition, by the Intelligence Officer.

While the station concentrated on defence, provision of equipment and ammunition for itself and the resident squadrons, the squadrons patrolled and practiced and the armament ground crews practiced re-arming and re-fuelling at which they became very proficient and a flight of Aircraft could be re-armed in approximately nine minutes.

To attain this time, an established procedure had to be followed and this having been well learned, the armourers made themselves small tools to assist them in awkward points, to save precious seconds. Speed was an essential point but it was not allowed to sacrifice correct stripping and assembly of gun panels, and ammunition tanks just to try and beat the record.

Some difficulties were experienced with Aircraft recognition signals since they were changed from time to time during the day. Where, in the days of peace, Verey pistols had been used, it could not be expected of a fighter pilot to 'Poke his arm through the hood and fire', so an automatic system was installed.

As very often happens when a modification is made to aircraft and new equipment fitted, it is found that a special modified airman is really needed to reach it, and this was almost the case with the Plessey Signal Device. This was placed in the rear of the pilot's seat in the bottom of the fuselage and to effect a change-over of the cartridges when an aircraft was at 'Readiness' used to make all concerned 'Hot under the collar'. Another snag with this device was that should it be fired from a low height, the star from the recognition cartridge did not have time to function before striking the ground, much to the discomfort of the pilot, who knew of the 'Itching fingers on triggers and Firing Controls' of ground crews whenever an Aircraft was seen. To overcome this the Station Engineer Officer undertook to reverse the device to fire upwards through the top of the fuselage. Due thought had to be given to fire risks, but a blast tube fitted to guard against this functioned very well, and in this new position the signal device was more accessible.

Our redoubtable 'Works and Buildings' Department kept a constant watch on the condition of our camouflage and to see someone on the drome or surrounding buildings spraying 'Weed Killer' as we called it, was no uncommon sight. In the early hours of one morning, before the day was really 'aired' a Blenheim forced-landed on our drome, believing it to be a partially ploughed field (report unconfirmed) and the pilot was unfortunate enough to run a wheel over a concealed gun post, which tipped the aircraft over on its nose. This was the cynosure of all eyes when the morning mists cleared away and the 'maintenance boys' soon got busy. It was discovered that the 'Pills' he carried on patrol, were still in positions so the Armament party had to be brought in. All the 'Safety Pins and Collars' could not be found and a temporary arrangement was made to remove the bombs to a safe place.

This presented a problem, for to house 250lb. bombs on a fighter drome one could not please everybody, but a convenient spot, as far as possible from Aircraft dispersals, petrol installations and main road was selected and sandbag traverses were built round the bombs, which were placed as far apart individually as space would permit. Having no Fuze keys or tools available a signal was sent to the station to which the machine belonged requesting them to 'Call and

Collect' as soon as possible, which was the following day, much to everyone's relief.

The advent of glorious June was not so 'Glorious' as we would have liked, with Italy declaring war against Great Britain, which was quickly followed by the grave news from Dunkirk. There were cryptic remarks about 'Eyties' and 'Flying Barrel Organs', but the seriousness of the position was well illustrated when we met old friends who returned from France with only the varied uniform they stood up in, and aircraft returned with bullet holes and shell holes in main planes and fuselages. Sorties were flown from dawn to dusk and due to enemy action at some of our advanced aerodromes near the coast, aircraft had to operate from the parent Station. About this time the special Mk VII B ammunition was issued and when signals were received that we could call at Woolwich Arsenal to collect our share, every effort was made to be 'First in the queue' at Woolwich the following morning.

This ammunition with incendiary rounds was very popular with our pilots, who would, had they been allowed, have filled their ammunition tanks with each type. A very definite method of arming the guns was detailed by Headquarters Fighter Command, however, and many impassioned requests had to be refused. Despite the strenuous and many commitments the squadrons had to meet daily, it was still very necessary to keep an efficient maintenance system working, and gun history sheets with records of rounds fired and number of stoppages or breakages of each gun were compiled while the midnight oil burned low.

Although this did seem irksome at times, extremely useful information was obtained which was used to form a basis for replacement of gun parts before they reached breaking point, thus avoiding, as far as possible, stoppages due to mechanical failures. The supply of spares for Browning guns was not sufficient to enable anyone to keep any 'stored away' and when Wing Commander Healey, the Command Armament Officer visited the station, he was beleaguered with requests for spares. The greatest of these requests were for Transporters and Springs, which he produced at times from the ticket pocket in his uniform like 'Maskelin Devant' would produce 'White Rabbits' from a top hat, and so doing relieved many a 'situation'.

The general bombing of some of our advanced aerodromes gave some information as to the type of bombs used and the method used for fusing them and this information was passed to stations to enable them to prepare to deal with unexploded bombs should the occasion arise. To deal with these I gathered together the necessary equipment, namely, Reels of D.3. wire, Red flags, a dynamo exploder and the explosives required to complete a demolition as detailed in A.P1244. As it might be inadvisable to demolish a bomb 'in situ', a reel of wire rope was added to the list of equipment and defusing devices, which were received as a general issue to all stations especially for use with German fuses.

Detailed instructions were received from Fighter Command as to the method to be employed in handling unexploded enemy bombs, and careful note was made of these and the armament staff were instructed accordingly. When it became known that anti-handling devices were included in German Bombs, some type of equipment was needed to enable them to be dealt with, while the armament staff had a reasonable chance of safety. To effect this, two types of 'Grab Tongs' were designed and station workshops made them up, and with their use it would have been possible, to drag an unexploded bomb along the ground from a safe distance, should it have fallen in a place which seriously jeopardised the operational efficiency of the station. Fortunately we did not have occasion to use these, but it was a comforting thought to know that the equipment was ready.

To keep a second string to their bow, pilots introduced their own patent sights which they used should a failure occur to the bulb of their reflector sight during flight and it was decided by one squadron to mark the front panel of the bullet proof screen with a small centre spot similar to that of the reflector sight, and this was found to be most useful when the normal sight failed or was hit by enemy fire.

Bomber Command also faced a busy time. When Hitler attacked the West on 10 May 1940, the Bomber Command contribution to the AASF was ten squadrons – two equipped with the twin-engine Blenheim, the rest with the Fairey Battle. When this single Merlin-engine-powered and all-metal monoplane, with retractable undercarriage and a three-man crew, entered service in 1937, it appeared modern and was well-received – little wonder, considering the Battle replaced the Hart and Hind biplanes of yore. With a maximum speed of only 240 mph, however, it was soon apparent that the Battle was too slow, the same engine powering the Spitfire and Hurricane having to propel much more weight through the air. The Battle's two machine-guns, one fixed and forward-firing, the other rearwards and operated by a rear-gunner, were inadequate for defence – not least against Me 109s armed with a pair of 20mm Oerlikons.

This inadequacy was tragically confirmed, in fact, during the first few weeks of war, when on one occasion Me 109s destroyed two out of three Battles flying reconnaissance sorties, and four out of five on another. This did not bode well for the task ahead: the AASF and Bomber Command was to work with the Allied armies to stop a German invasion. When that happened, on the first day, thirteen of thirty-two Battles were shot down by AA fire while attacking the Maastricht bridges at low-level. Then, eight Battles attacked the advancing enemy in Luxembourg – seven were shot down while the eighth was shot-up and crashed back at base.

It was a tragic story, but one underpinned by great courage: two Battle aircrew, Flying Officer Donald Garland and his observer, Sergeant Tom Gray, received posthumous Victoria Crosses – the first awarded to the RAF during the Second World War. Within a few days, however, the AASF had been reduced to less than 25 per cent of its original strength, and the Battle was withdrawn from daylight operations.

Excepting the pair of Blenheim squadrons sent to France, Bomber Command's heavier bombers remained at home. On the night of 15/16 May 1940, ninety-six Wellingtons, Whitleys and Hampdens attacked German industrial targets – signalling the start of the Allied strategic bombing campaign against Germany. While the intention, striking at German oil facilities, was necessary, the deteriorating situation in France saw the AASF, BEF and French government clamouring for Bomber Command to concentrate on targets behind the battlefield and thereby directly supporting the ground situation.

Consequently, on 17 May 1940, heavies were ordered to attack the Meuse bridges, while others continued attacking oil targets in Germany. In spite of this dual responsibility, spreading resources, Bomber Command's overall work before and during *Dynamo* definitely delayed the enemy – and every hour counted. At the campaign's start, Bomber Command losses over France were over 20 per cent – dropping to 2 per cent during the evacuation. Why?

Firstly the German fighters also suffered losses as the battle progressed, and secondly, the further Germany advanced, the less concentrated its AA defences became. The most significant reason is the third factor: strong fighter support, which was forthcoming in daylight during *Dynamo*. Heligoland Bight had indicated early on the folly of sending unescorted bombers by day, and the massive reduction in Bomber Command's losses clearly evidenced the immeasurable benefit of fighter escorts. Slowly, the necessary tactics using modern aircraft were becoming apparent.

On 10 June 1940, Mussolini's fascist Italy entered the war on the Axis side; the following night, Bomber Command attacked the Fiat aircraft factory at Turin. And so the war went on. Navigation, the weather, and limited accuracy when bombing Germany night posed difficulties, however. Although bombing after dark was safer for crews, this circumstance, not having been previously considered, had not been planned for in terms of navigational aids and other supporting technology.

What these raids achieved was unknown at the time, and to a degree still is, but at least losses were comparatively light, and once France had fallen, the German oil industry once more became Bomber Command's primary target – but on 20 June 1940 the Air Staff made clear to Bomber Command that its primary objective must from now on be targets 'which will have the most immediate effect in reducing the scale of air attack on this country': aircraft factories in Germany, and airfields in the now occupied lands. Other specified targets included oil, communications, and even forests and crops. Significantly, the Command was to be ready at short notice to attack 'an enemy invading force at the points of departure, and subsequently at sea or at the points of landing in this country'.

So it was that on 30 June 1940, thirty Blenheims bombed German airfields at Rouen and Amiens; the next day saw forty-seven Blenheims attacking Schiphol airfield in the Netherlands and Rouen again. Over the next six weeks, formations of six to twenty Blenheims of 2 Group frequently attacked enemy airfields. The problem, however, was that the *Luftwaffe* now had some 400 airfields available, so Bomber Command found itself under-resourced to make a significant impact against the *Luftwaffe's* bases.

More and heavier bombers were needed, and were in due course provided – but the priority right now, at eleventh hour, was fighters for Dowding.

Chapter 13

'The Beaver'

On the evening of 14 May 1940, the wireless announced in homes all over Britain the last major appointments of Churchill's new administration. The most significant of these was arguably Lord Beaverbrook – the media tycoon and a veritable force of nature – who became Minister of Aircraft Production. There could have been no better choice.

With characteristic almost superhuman drive and energy, 'The Beaver' immediately set about organising his new Ministry for Aircraft Production (MAP). The MP for Uxbridge, Colonel John Llewellin (1st Baron Llewellin) became Beaverbrook's Parliamentary Secretary, while Sir Charles Craven, the Chairman of Vickers-Armstrong assumed responsibility for production, and Air-Marshal Sir Wilfred Freeman, from the Air Ministry, was placed in charge of development.

Perhaps uniquely, the new Ministry was initially based at the Minister's home, Stornoway House, overlooking London's Green Park; the typists were based upstairs, with Beaverbrook and his staff downstairs. Work began at 08.30 hrs each day, or before, with Beaverbrook dictating notes before meetings with Air-Marshals, civil servants and representatives from the aircraft industry from 09.30 hrs onwards. Every night, Beaverbrook personally received telephone reports on the day's output of aircraft from the aircraft factories, maintenance units and engine manufacturers. His final instructions were given at 02.00 hrs daily – and six hours later the cycle resumed. At 61, many marvelled at Beaverbrook's energy, which was an example to all.

The framework of MAP was the Air Ministry's production departments, but these were based at Harrogate in Yorkshire, 200 miles from London. This was no good. Beaverbrook needed his staff to be at hand for personal interview, and so MAP became London-based, at Millbrook. Beaverbrook was himself a civilian pilot and had owned several recreational aircraft, so had first-hand experience of aviation matters. More importantly, his son, Max, was a pilot in the elite 601 Squadron of the AAF, flying Blenheims, so there was a vested family interest in assuring sufficient modern machines for the RAF.

While 'The Beaver' could inspire and imbue all he came into contact with a sense of utmost industry and urgency, he relied upon the industrialist Sir Charles Craven for his knowledge of factories. In fact, he chose his team carefully, drawing upon the huge experience of other industrialists, including Arthur Matthews, who was placed in charge of steel alloy production. Everyone gave their dynamic leader only their best, and being appointed to work at MAP became coveted.

Apart from the obvious need to increase aircraft production, Beaverbrook was also faced with a shortage of materials and components for his factories, inadequate repair facilities for aircraft damaged on operations and engines, and an acute deficiency in instrumentation. All of these things the Minister energetically immersed himself in resolving. But inevitably, there were frustrations; like Dowding, Beaverbrook believed so passionately and deeply in his essential mission that he had no intention of compromising anything – especially Spitfire production.

At that time, the Vickers Supermarine Aviation Works at Woolston, near Southampton, was the main base for Spitfire production. The busy factory was located on the Itchen's east bank, immediately north of the floating bridge, which ferried passengers across the estuary that divided Southampton in two. A few hundred yards to the north of this was the company's so-called 'Itchen Works'. Both factories fronted the Itchen, and there was a 15ft high railway embankment across the road behind the Itchen Works. Beyond the railway, to the east, was the open land of Peartree Green, and built-up area of Woolston. Completed Spitfire major sub-assemblies were transported by road to the company's hangars at Eastleigh airport for final assembly and test flying, so to a degree production was necessarily dispersed.

The first of many bombs fell on Southampton's Millbrook area on the night of 20 June 1940, causing casualties; the city centre was hit on 13 and 14 August and six Sotonians lost their lives, an early confirmation of the city's vulnerability to air attack now that the Germans were just sixty miles due south, at Cherbourg. In any case, it could be assumed that Supermarine would become a prime target for the *Luftwaffe*, and Supermarine was too small a factory to cope efficiently with producing the numbers of Spitfires now required.

Another important factor influencing the numbers of aircraft available to the RAF was that since Italy had entered the war, Britain, unlike Germany at that time, was having to fight on two fronts – and with limited resources. This meant sending aircraft, men and materiel overseas, to the Middle East, to meet the Italians in North Africa – 161 fighters by October 1940, seventy-two of them Hurricanes – but no precious Spitfires. Britain looked to America for aeroplanes, with disappointing results, and the Soviets were also unhelpful. So it was that Britain was almost entirely reliant upon the fighters it could produce at home.

On 3 June 1936, the Air Ministry ordered 310 Spitfires at a cost of £4,500 each (excluding engine, guns, instruments and radios). It was expected that the first production aircraft would be delivered in October 1937, but it soon became apparent that Supermarine – a small company of 500 employees – lacked the capacity to fulfil this large order. By the time those Spitfires were ready, the individual cost had risen to £6,033. In 1937, a further order was placed for another 200 Spitfires. Jeffrey Quill wrote that the cause of problems in mass producing the Spitfire,

> lay in the years of neglect of the aircraft industry by successive governments up to 1936. At the last possible moment they initiated the re-armament programme and expected an industry starved of orders since 1919 suddenly to increase production capacity by four or five times, and change over to building far more complex types of aircraft, all within a space of just two or three years. Of course there were going to be enormous problems and with the best will in the world mistakes were going to be made. It was all very well for the Air Ministry to say to Supermarine 'What you can't do yourselves you must sub-contract'. But where were the sub-contractors to be found with the necessary experience, on the fringes of an industry which hitherto had hardly sufficient orders to keep itself alive.

These observations put into perspective the old accusations that the Spitfire, being technically advanced, required the workforce to learn new production techniques and hence the delay in delivery to the RAF. Supermarine's workforce possessed the necessary skills – it was the size of the factory that was an issue. True, a Spitfire did take two-and-a-half times the man hours than the Hurricane took to produce, so clearly a larger production facility was required.

Before the war, the Nuffield organisation, including Morris Motors, a big automotive manufacturer, had been tasked with building a huge 'shadow' factory at Castle Bromwich, near Birmingham, producing Spitfires. The idea was that the West Midlands were less vulnerable to air attack than the South Coast, being so far inland, and such a factory would alleviate the pressure on Supermarine and through applying the mass production methods of the automotive industry would both assume main responsibility for Spitfire production and substantially boost the numbers thereof.

The required progress had not been made by 1940, so Beaverbrook, acting independently just three days after being appointed Minister, transferred management of the factory from Lord Nuffield to the MAP, and specifically Vickers-Armstrong. Furthermore, Beaverbrook shared Dowding's views regarding the crucial security of the base, and agreed that at this time it was fighters the RAF needed, not bombers. Consequently, Beaverbrook immediately cancelled all Castle Bromwich Aircraft Factory (CBAF) orders for bombers, replacing that with a requirement for Spitfires alone – and the first Spitfires to roll off the Birmingham production line in July 1940 were the improved Mk IIs. CBAF would go on to produce the majority of the 22,000 Spitfires ultimately built, and events during the summer of 1940, as we will see, proved the wisdom of the shadow factory concept and dispersing Spitfire production. The failure of Nuffield to get the huge CBAF into gear much earlier was the main reason, given Supermarine's comparatively small-scale operation, that by the summer of 1940 there were two-thirds more Hurricanes (built at factories including Brooklands and Hucclecote) than Spitfires. The Hurricane, therefore, would bear the brunt of the fighting and was essential to make up the numbers – but it was the Spitfire, with its high-altitude ability and overall superior performance, that was really in demand.

The MAP certainly had a challenge on its hands. After the Fall of France, Dowding possessed just 768 fighters, of which only 520 were operational. In June 1940, 308 Hurricanes were produced against ninety Spitfires. Between 1 June and 1 November 1940, a total 1,367 Hurricanes had come from the factories, and 724 Spitfires. Hurricane losses would amount to 753 (61.7 per cent), Spitfires 467 (38.3 per cent) – a clear indication of why it was so vitally important to accelerate progress at CBAF. The upshot was that thanks to Beaverbrook and MAP, in the battle ahead aircraft production always remained abreast of losses, assuring Dowding of a constant supply of fighters. This was no mean achievement and contributed enormously to Fighter Command's ability to defy the *Luftwaffe*.

It is noteworthy that whatever the myth, the opposing air forces were surprisingly evenly matched by summer 1940. On 10 August 1940, Germany possessed 1,011 single-engine fighters, 805 of these being operational, and would soon concentrate the majority of these in the Pas-de-Calais for the assault on London. By the day that attack came, 7 September 1940, the number of serviceable Me 109s had decreased, owing to attrition, to 533, and only 275 by 1 October 1940. The two sides began their opposition with roughly equal numbers of single-engine fighters – but that Fighter Command's strength exceeded that of the enemy by the end of the Battle of Britain was to the enduring credit of the MAP and British aircraft industry.

The problem for Fighter Command, however, was that with the whole of Britain within range of enemy aircraft, operational fighter squadrons had to be spread around the country and not simply concentrated in southern England. Although entirely necessary, and the wisdom of this strategy would soon become apparent, this significantly reduced the resources available to Air Vice-Marshal Park in the all-important 11 Group covering London and the South-East. This is why Park, having to carefully preserve limited resources while inflicting maximum damage upon the enemy, largely chose to fight the Battle of Britain using small, flexible, formations, rather than commit his forces to action en masse.

This, in due course, would give rise to the impression of Fighter Command defending Britain against overwhelming odds. Squadrons in northern England, however, were of no immediate assistance to outnumbered RAF pilots fighting over south-east England; their small formations were soon to intercept great armadas of German aircraft. If the story of 'The Few' is a myth, this is why – but this series of books will evidence and argue that for Fighter Command's pilots over the battle zone, being outnumbered was no myth.

Thanks to the energy and drive of his friend Beaverbrook, Dowding had no need to worry over the supply of replacement fighters. Indeed, in his post-war Despatch on the Battle of Britain, Dowding described Beaverbrook's appointment 'as magical, and thereafter the supply situation improved to such a degree that the heavy aircraft wastage which was later incurred in the "Battle of Britain" ceased to be the primary danger, its place being taken by the difficulty of producing trained fighter pilots in adequate numbers.' And therein lay another vexing issue.

At the outbreak of the Second World War, Fighter Command was the only Command to oppose Air Ministry plans for establishing special units to convert newly qualified pilots to the type of aircraft they would fly operationally, prior to joining squadrons. Dowding considered that allocating operational aircraft for such conversion training away from squadrons was a waste of aircraft when such instruction could be given by the squadrons themselves – as indeed it had always been to date. Ironically, though, at the time, Fighter Command was the only Command to possess such a unit: 11 Group Pool had been formed at Andover on 16 January 1939, equipped with four Demon biplane fighters with which to train eight pilots at a time on two-month courses. The Air Ministry considered three pools would actually be required to back the thirty-six squadrons of Fighter Command at that time, but shortages of aircraft, personnel and aerodromes delayed this expansion process. By March 1939, 11 Group Pool had moved to St Athan in South Wales, and re-established itself with more modern aircraft – namely eleven Battles and twenty-two Hurricanes.

In September 1939, however, the unit was seriously below establishment while focusing upon the advanced service flying training of volunteer reservists. Shortly after the outbreak of war, the unit's Battles were replaced with Harvard trainers, and soon 11 Group Pool was only five Hurricanes short of its authorised establishment. The course length was halved to four weeks, and syllabus hours reduced from forty-five to thirty hours per pupil. Producing twenty-four pilots every four weeks, it was hoped that the Pool would provide 300 pilots trained to operational standard per year.

Still Fighter Command HQ remained sceptical regarding the value of Pools for training at the expense of front-line strength. Dowding, however, continued to vigorously contest the need, making it clear at conferences on 15 and 21 September 1939 that in his opinion, new pilots from Flying Training School should be trained in squadrons, 11 Group Pool at St Athan being used only for reinforcements to France. The Commander-in-Chief went further, saying that the need for a 12 Group Pool based at Aston Down in Gloucestershire was unnecessary. The Air Ministry parried with the argument that the lack of Group Pools would mean a lack of casualty replacements when the fighting became intense, and if necessary, Group Pool aircraft could be taken for operational use. Fighter Command therefore agreed, albeit reluctantly, to this compromise and opened 12 Group Pool on a limited basis, on the understanding that it did not absorb any Spitfires or Hurricanes. Training was still to be ongoing in squadrons, and the constant need for it was impressed upon Group Commanders.

No.12 Group Pool became operational at Aston Down on 25 September 1939, equipped with six Harvards, three Blenheims and eleven Gladiators. The schedule was to train some 230 pilots per year. Both pools were initially handicapped, though, by a shortage of cine-camera guns, reflector gunsights, lack of proper armouries, and no ground-to-air radio-telephony facilities. Nonetheless, when the general adequacy of Group Pools was compared with FTS output in October, it was found to be satisfactory. The planned Group Pool capacity at full establishment almost equalled that of the FTSs, with a projected figure of 1,100 fighter pilots per year. In reality, the Group Pools were far below establishment and therefore capable of dealing with less than half of those proposed numbers. Due to lack of aircraft, the Pools were able to do little Blenheim training and no Spitfire training at all. To remedy the former deficiency, a few pupils were given conversion courses at Hendon during December 1939.

In January 1940, Fighter Command eventually agreed in principle that an adequate operational training system for fighter squadrons should be established. Both 11 and 12 Group Pools were renamed Operational Training Units the following March, and became Nos. 6 and 5 respectively. The OTUs remained under the command of their respective Fighter Command Group areas (but in June 1940 were placed under the direct control of 10 Group). By 1 April 1940, the fighter training organisation had expanded and three OTUs were planned with a total strength of forty-eight Hurricanes, thirty-four Spitfires, twenty Blenheims, four Defiants, two Gladiators and twenty-four Harvards or Battles.

These decisions were still not altogether welcomed by Dowding, who disagreed that the recent spate of flying accidents, which prompted the Air Ministry's action, was due to inadequate training, and still saw OTUs as an unaffordable luxury. Dowding particularly objected to a third OTU being formed before all front-line squadron requirements were met. His arguments were once again to no avail as the Air Ministry decided to go ahead, regardless. At that time, the total strength of operational aircraft held by OTUs was twenty, as opposed to the authorised 132. Their combined pilot output was barely enough to back the Hurricane squadrons in France serving there with the AASF, and also fulfil the requirement to supply ninety Blenheim pilots to Fighter Command. In France the fighter squadrons criticised the standard of training provided by OTUs, because the replacement pilots being received direct from St Athan and Aston Down had just ten hours flying experience on Hurricanes or Spitfires, and no high altitude, oxygen or fighter attack experience.

In May 1940, the urgent need for replacement, operational, fighter pilots suddenly became acutely apparent when the Hurricane squadrons in France began suffering heavy losses. At that time, 5 and 6 OTUs were achieving a maximum output of eighty pilots per month, against a monthly requirement of 200 for casualty replacement alone. Hitler's attack on the West that month brought the realities of modern warfare into sharp focus, emphasising the urgent need to step-up operational training.

On 1 June 1940, Fighter Command's establishment of pilots was 1,482 (1,200 of which were operational), rising to 1,558 (1,422 operational) by 31 August 1940 (in spite of the number of casualties), thanks to the output of training units. Indeed, by 2 November, the figure had risen to 1,727; partly through reducing the length of operational conversion courses, new pilots typically passed out with just ten hours flying time on the Spitfire and Hurricane during the Battle's crucial period. These figures, however, do not just relate to Spitfire and Hurricane pilots – and in truth they were what really mattered, as Fighter Command's pilots were also spread around Defiant, Blenheim and even a Gladiator-equipped squadron.

Furthermore, as previously mentioned, Dowding's strength was dispersed around Britain, so far from all of these pilots were based in southern England. Interestingly, on 1 June 1940, the German strength of operational Me 109 pilots was 906, the majority of whom were available to fight over Britain, given that Germany was not yet fighting on two fronts. By 1 November 1940, that figure had dropped to 673, whereas Dowding's operational strength of pilots for all his Command's aircraft types had risen to 1,796. Clearly, as with aircraft, thanks to Beaverbrook, Fighter Command would not face a shortage of pilots – but what these new men lacked was combat experience, and that had to be accrued the hard way.

Across the Channel, though, there was indecision.

Chapter 14

'Unleash a Storm of Wrath and Steel Upon the British!'

When writing his memoirs, *Feldmarschall* Albert Kesselring, who had been given command of *Luftflotte* 2 in January 1940, was reminded of an old proverb: 'Lash your helm faster after victory.'

Kesselring highlighted that Hitler 'defied ... this golden rule' after the Fall of France: 'Even if he did believe in the possibility of diplomatic negotiations, to we soldiers it was incomprehensible that the first steps to demobilise the army were being taken before the end of the war was palpably in sight.'

The reduction in Germany's army by a fifth, to 120 divisions, ordered by Keitel on 14 June 1940, was not, however, a preparation for peace. The ongoing war with Britain placed the emphasis on air and sea warfare, so the large army that had rampaged across Western Europe was not required. This meant that the army's older age groups could be released, some of those men returning to factories and thereby alleviating the pressure on German industry, and in any case enough combat troops remained in France to invade southern England, should that prove necessary.

After meeting with the *Führer*, Mussolini's Foreign Minister and son-in-law, Count Galeazzo Ciano, was in no doubt of Hitler's avowed intent, which was to 'continue the struggle and unleash a storm of wrath and steel upon the British!' Goebbels, though, considered that 'Despite everything,' Hitler 'still had a very positive attitude towards England ... He is still not ready for the final blow.'

Hitler was under no illusions that a seaborne invasion of Britain would be difficult, not least given the *Kriegsmarine*'s comparative weakness, and was unconvinced that air power alone could force a decisive decision. Germany was at the zenith of its power, however, and so more than ever, for all Kesselring's misgivings, Hitler genuinely hoped that Britain would come to terms. This aspiration was fuelled by news from Baron von Weizsäcker, State Secretary of the German Foreign Office, on 19 and 22 June 1940 that the Swedish Ambassador to Berlin, with whom he had spoken, believed some influential circles in London favoured negotiation. This emboldened Hitler, who told Brauschitsch on 23 June that Britain was 'coming down a peg', this actually being recorded in the OKW Operational Staff minutes of that day's conference between the two warlords. On 2 July, the *Wehrmacht* was advised that Hitler was in favour of invading Britain, providing certain conditions could be satisfied.

Talk of invasion had been ongoing since Grand Admiral Raeder conferred with Hitler on 21 May 1940. Six days later, Rear-Admiral Fricke, the *Kriegsmarine* operations chief, presented his staff with a memorandum he had prepared, *Studie England*: preliminary planning for a seaborne landing on the south and south-east English coast – not the East Coast, as originally mooted. By now, the *Kriegsmarine* had the experience of the recent invasion of Norway to draw upon, in which surprise had played a major part in that combined operations' success.

Invading Britain, however, was a huge undertaking in comparison. It required time-consuming preparations which were impossible to conceal from the ever-watchful enemy, and considering Britain's state of alertness, coupled with the sheer size of such an invasion fleet, surprise would be impossible. Then, of course, there was the RN, the RAF, and much heavier AA and other defences. Little wonder doubt and indecision held sway.

Fricke offered two potential landing plans: sailing from ports between Texel and Cherbourg to land between Portland and Yarmouth, or departing from the Scheldt to Hanstholm in Denmark to disgorge troops between the Thames estuary and Newcastle. The first was preferred, representing a shorter sea-crossing with less opportunity for the RN to counter-attack or disruption from changeable weather conditions. Mine clearance of the sea lanes involved would also be easier, as would the sowing of protective minefields. Communications would be simpler and air cover more easily provided.

These advantages were offset against the fact that the second proposal's departure points were in, or close to, Germany, therefore providing greater concealment and protection and better port facilities. An invasion fleet assembled there would also be less vulnerable to air attack and the proposed landing areas were less well defended than Britain's South Coast. Those favourable factors, though, were overridden by the operational requirements of the sea-crossing involved. On one thing Fricke was crystal clear: the RAF must not be allowed to interfere with the assembly of the invasion fleet, the crossing or landings. Furthermore, the RN was to be kept at bay via minefields, and the bridgehead's resupply also needed aerial protection. Good weather was also prerequisite.

So great an undertaking was the proposed invasion that long preparations were anticipated, as shipping had to be made ready, provisioned and crewed, the invasion force supplied and assembled, and the substantial minefields laid. Fricke also documented that the *Kriegsmarine* was so small that only the progress of the war would indicate whether 'special opportunities for effective action' would be presented, because the German naval 'inferiority in relation to the British and French navies will scarcely allow fleet operations'. The key, Fricke said, was therefore to rapidly land personnel on the English coast, a task, over such a short distance, the *Kriegsmarine* could achieve if supplemented by 'auxiliary vessels (steamers, fishing-steamers).

On 31 May 1940, Admiral Schuster, the *Kommandierender Admiral Francreich* (Naval Commander-in-Chief in France) and Captain Degenhardt, the Chief of Sea

'UNLEASH A STORM OF WRATH AND STEEL UPON THE BRITISH!'

Transportation (Special Duties), were ordered to survey shipping in the West. On 4 June, given that the *Kriegsmarine* was now concerned with vessels capable of a Channel-crossing in every port, river and canal of the newly occupied lands, this undertaking became the responsibility of the OKM Merchant Shipping Division. Details of all such transports were to be recorded. Meanwhile, the OKM began seriously investigating the potential problems connected with an invasion. The Naval Ordnance Office was instructed to research how best the Dover Strait could be sealed off by heavy artillery. Fricke then received a detailed report from naval intelligence of England's shoreline from the Wash to the Isle of Wight, and between Skegness and Flamborough Head, specifically identifying potentially suitable landing locations along with details of known defences, including the proximity of airfields. This is clear evidence that the *Kriegsmarine* was seriously analysing the possibilities and difficulties connected with a seaborne invasion of Britain.

At a conference with Hitler on 20 June 1940, Raeder first mentioned the possibility of a seaborne invasion of Britain to Hitler – but the *Führer* showed little interest, doubtless preoccupied with the imminent armistice with France and considering what less dangerous options for terminating the war with Britain may arise from that. Hitler, flushed with success and whose priority remained expansion eastward, was starting to believe that Germany could successfully wage war on two fronts, even though Britain remained undefeated.

The need for a decision, however, was increasingly pressing. Halder noted on 22 June 1940 that 'the near future will show whether Britain will do the reasonable thing in the light of our victories, or will try to carry on the war alone. In the latter case, the war will involve Britain's destruction, and many last a long time.' Two days later, the OKH issued orders covering regrouping the Army after the French campaign, which included 'preparations against England', and Halder considered it 'not impossible that we shall be compelled to land in England'. Indeed, there was some enthusiasm for this prospect among certain army factions, the Army Group 'B' War Diary of 28 June critically noted that current orders placed insufficient emphasis on concentrating troops on the Channel coast ready to attack southern England. Clearly, then, as late as the end of June and beginning of July 1940, there was no clear plan or decision forthcoming.

Although no record of the discussion survives, on 18 June 1940, Hitler met Mussolini and talked of an air and seaborne assault on Britain. Ciano noted in his diary, however, that by 30 June, Hitler had not responded to the Duce's offer of Italian aircraft and troops to join the proposed battle against Britain. Hitler, Ciano wrote, was 'going through one of his periods of isolation, which, with him, precede the making of great decisions ... it seems that the German offensive will come only from the air, in grand style, and will take place between 10 and 15 of July.'

The following day, however, Ciano saw Hitler who was 'considering many alternatives', so far as Britain was concerned, and had 'doubts'. The *Führer* was at *Tannenberg*, his battle headquarters in the Black Forest, and was carefully studying Jodl's report of 22 June, on 'Continuation of the War against England'. Three strategies were recommended therein: firstly an alliance of countries with a vested interest in waging war against the wider British Empire, and, secondly, a direct air assault which, 'Allied with propaganda and periodic terror attacks, announced as reprisals ... will finally break the will of the people to resist, and thereby force the Government to capitulate.' Finally, Jodl recommended a seaborne invasion, but not as the main assault, only to occupy and 'finish off' Britain after the country had been militarily defeated by the *Luftwaffe* and *Kriegsmarine*. Göring, however, did not blindly support the proposal for a seaborne invasion. Rightly he recognised that 'the planned operation can only be considered under conditions of absolute air superiority'.

A landing under fire was unnecessary because, like Hitler and Jodl, he believed that the war against Britain had 'already taken on a victorious course' – and for that Göring claimed a disproportionate amount of credit for his *Luftwaffe*. In campaigns to date, however, the Germans had fought much weaker enemies, especially when the Allied air forces failed to perform cohesively on the continent, although the *Luftwaffe*'s role in closely supporting the army was a model to be emulated. What this hid from plain sight was any *Luftwaffe* deficiencies, prompting Göring to exaggerate the air force's capabilities and contribution to victory.

Indeed, in July 1940, Hitler rewarded Göring for having 'created the preconditions for victory', by making him *Reichsmarschall* – and therefore his deputy. The truth, however, was that while the *Luftwaffe* was well-equipped to closely support the army in rapid campaigns against weaker foes, it was ill-equipped and unprepared to embark upon a strategic bombing campaign against England – with its advanced System of Air Defence and modern fighters. To Göring, believing the war already won, none of this mattered; he was sublimely confident: 'My *Luftwaffe* is invincible ... And so now we turn to England. How long will this one last – two or three weeks?'

On the Channel coast, the *Luftwaffe* was reorganised in preparation for the impending air assault on Britain, and divided into two *Luftflotten* – 2, commanded by *Generalfeldmarschall* Albert Kesselring, and 3 by the imposing-looking *Generalfeldmarschall* Hugo Sperrle. The former's headquarters were at Brussels, his *Luftflotte* 2 responsible for north-eastern France and the Low Countries. The latter, whose luxurious tastes matched those of the *Reichsmarschall* himself, was based at the fabulous Palais du Luxembourg, *Luftflotte* 3 embracing north-western France. A line was drawn on the map of the British Isles, north from Southampton, with *Luftlotte* 2 being responsible for targets east of that line, and 3 to the west. From Norway, *Generaloberst* Hans-Jurgen Stumpff's *Luftflotte* 5 was positioned to strike targets in north-east England and Scotland. Between them, *Luftflotten* 2 and 3 possessed 2,600 aircraft, including 1,200 twin-engine bombers, 280 *Stukas*, 220 twin-engine Me 110s and 760 Me 109s.

This represented the bulk of the *Luftwaffe*'s strength, *Luftflotte* 5 having just 190 twin-engine bombers, fighters and reconnaissance aircraft. The *Luftflotten* commanders took their orders directly from Göring. Each specialised element within

'UNLEASH A STORM OF WRATH AND STEEL UPON THE BRITISH!'

each fleet was controlled by a *Fliegerkorps* HQ. The new post of *Jagdfliegerführer* (or *Jafü* – fighter leader) centralised fighter control under the command of one officer answerable to the *Luftflotte* chief, although the bomber *Fliegerkorps* HQ, responsible for many more men and machines, inevitably had a greater say in policy. Consequently, the *Jafü* became little more than a liaison officer, informing the fighter pilots what their bomber counterparts expected of them.

At operational level, each *Luftflotte* was organised into groups – *Geschwader* – *Jagd* (fighters), *Zerstörer* (destroyers, twin-engine Me 110 heavy fighters) and *Kampfgeschwadern* (bomber groups), while aerial reconnaissance was provided by *Küstenaufklarungs* (coastal reconnaissance) units. Each *Geschwader* comprised around 100 aircraft, commanded by the *Geschwaderkommodore*, an officer usually of *Oberstleutnant* (lieutenant-colonel) rank, who flew at the head of his *Geschwaderstab* (Group Staff Flight), which could be up to *Staffel* (squadron) strength. *Stabsoffizier* (staff officers) included the adjutant, technical, operations and communications officers. Each *Geschwader* was sub-divided into three *Gruppen*, designated I-III, each commanded by a *Gruppenkommandeur*, usually a major. Every *Gruppe* also had its own *Stab* and was sub-divided into three *Staffeln* (squadrons) each, numbered 1–12 and commanded by the *Staffelkapitän*, an *Oberleutnant* or *Hauptmann*. Thus 6/KG55 was the sixth *Staffel* of *Kampfgeschwader* 55, and specifically the third *Staffel* in the II *Gruppe*. Each *Gruppe*, therefore, compared to a 'wing' of three RAF squadrons, while a *Geschwader* corresponded to a Bomber Command Group.

The three twin-engine bomber types available to the *Luftwaffe* were the He 111, Do 17 (and 215 variant) and Ju 88. The He 111's maximum bombload was 4,400 lbs, the Do 17's 2,205lbs, and the Ju 88's, 3,300lbs, while the Me 110 fighter-bomber could carry four 551lb bombs externally, beneath the fuselage, and the Ju 87 *Stuka* dive-bomber was armed with either a single 1,102lb bomb, or one 551-pounder and four 110lb bombs. Such payloads, however, were insufficient to wage a strategic bombing campaign – by comparison, the later four-engine British Avro Lancaster carried 22,000lbs of bombs – five times more than the He 111.

The Germans did have at their disposal, however, various types of bomb to drop on Britain. The principal High Explosive (HE) bomb came in three types: the *Sprengbombe-Cylindrisch* (SC), a thin-cased general-purpose bomb; the *Sprengbombe-Dickwandig* (SD), a thickly encased semi-armour-piercing fragmentation bomb, and the *Panzerbombe-Cylindrisch* (PC), an armour-piercing bomb. Collectively known as *Minenbomben*, these bombs had a high ratio for blast effect, contained 55 per cent explosive, and were used primarily for general demolition. In fact, eight of the ten bombs dropped on Britain were SC, weighing between 50 and 2,000kg. These were of a three-piece steel construction with a thick nose welded to a thin-walled cylindrical body. Horizontal stability was provided by a sheet-steel or alloy tail unit. When carried in internal fuselage bomb bays, depending upon the aircraft type the bombs were stored either vertically or horizontally, or when carried externally, beneath the fuselage or wings, held by suspension brackets or bands.

Often a *Kopfring*, a triangular steel ring, was fitted around the nose, preventing deep penetration of the ground and thus achieving maximum blast effect. *Trumpets of Jericho* were sometimes fitted to SC50 and 250 tail units, consisting of carboard tubes, shaped like organ pipes, through which, as the bomb descended, caused a blood-curdling banshee howl. Then there was the *Flammenbombe* (often referred to in British Civil Defence reports as 'oil bombs'), an incendiary containing an oil mixture consisting of 70 per cent petroleum and 30 per cent TNT, and a HE bursting charge. These came in two sizes, 250 and 500kg and were used to start large fires – far more dangerous than the tiny 1kg *Brandbombe* incendiary, which would fall on Britain by the thousand.

To aim their destructive cargoes, each bomber was fitted with the Goerz bombsight for level bombing, or better still the Lofte 7c tachometric sight. The target was sighted through a gyro-stabilised telescope, powered by an electric motor. As the bombardier held the telescope on target, information on the aircraft's flight path was automatically fed into an onboard sighting computer, previously programmed with details of the bombs carried and altitude from which they would be dropped. The computer gave course corrections displayed to the pilot. As the target was approached, the sighting telescope moved to coincide with the angle dictated by the computer and an electrical circuit released the bombs automatically. A run of some forty seconds was needed for a standard level flight attack using this sight, but low-level attacks required the bombs to be dropped manually.

We have previously examined RAF air-to-air and air-to-ground communications, the limitations of which may have contributed to the 'Barking Creek' tragedy, but aerial communications were a real problem for the *Luftwaffe* in 1940. For example, German fighter pilots could speak with each other in the air, but not to either the ground or any bombers. For that reason, the Germans developed a colour-coding system peculiar to each *Staffel*, greatly assisting in the identification of friendly aircraft. For instance, white wingtips, cowling and rudder indicated the first *Staffel* in each *Gruppe*, red the second, yellow the third, while the *Geschwaderstab* and *Gruppenstab* used blue and green respectively. Each aircraft's fuselage bore the national black cross, and in the case of bombers and twin-engine fighters the letter and number to the left indicating the unit, and those to the right particular *Staffel* and individual aircraft. The latter was either painted in or outlined in the colour of the *Staffel* concerned.

The *Jagdwaffe* – the fighter force – was also built up around the same *Geschwader*, *Gruppe* and *Staffel* system. The *Geschwaderkommodore* flew with his *Stabschwarm* (staff-flight), again comprising his technical specialists, and similarly the each *Gruppenkommandeur* had a *Gruppenstabschwarm*. Each *Staffel* comprised three sections of four, each known as a *Schwarm*, which broke in combat into two fighting pairs, each called a *Rotte* and comprising leader and wingman. Individual aircraft within each *Staffel* was marked from 1 upwards, painted in the Staffel colour to the left of the fuselage national cross (if looking at the left-hand side of the aircraft). The marking to the right confirmed the aircraft's

Gruppe: I = no marking, II = a horizontal or vertical bar, and III = a wavy line. The *Geschwaderstab* and *Gruppenstabschwarm* used a system of chevron, horizontal and vertical bars, and circles to identify each technical officer. Each unit's badge also often adorned its aircraft, for example, 1/JG2's Me 109s wore a white Bonzo dog motif, while 3/JG2 preferred a blue pennant bearing a yellow dagger and word '*Horrido*' – being the German fighter pilot's traditional celebratory shout upon recording an aerial victory.

Fighter Command had no substantial Air Sea Rescue (ASR) facility at this time, relying upon just eighteen high-speed launches to search for and rescue downed airmen around Britain's coast, although frequently RAF aircrews owed their rescue to chance encounters with passing friendly vessels. The *Luftwaffe*, however, had the benefit of its *Seenotflugkommando,* ASR units equipped with He 59 floatplanes able to rescue downed airmen from the sea.

Both the German life jacket favoured by fighter pilots, the *Schwimmveste* (either inflated by a pressurised gas bottle or orally), and the kapok-filled bomber crew version were superior to the bulky RAF 'Mae West'. *Luftwaffe* aircrew also had brightly coloured skull-caps to clip over their flying helmets, carried flare pistols and florescent dye to colour the water around them; their aircraft also carried dinghies, which RAF fighters did not at this time. The Channel was, however, also dotted with so-called 'Lobster Pots', RAF rescue buoys containing four bunks with bedding and other essential items a downed airman might need.

In one absolutely crucial area, however, the *Luftwaffe* was significantly lacking: accurate air intelligence, which is to say, up-to-date information about the enemy air force's strength, deployment and plans, with which to shape and inform strategy. *Luftwaffe* Intelligence was one of at least four *Wehrmacht* intelligence services, and the fifth-ranking department within the OKL; additionally, there was a General of Reconnaissance, an aerial photography branch, and the Air Signal Communications Chief, Wolfgang Martin, with his Cipher Office. Within the *Luftwaffe*, however, the intelligence role did not enjoy high prestige, the most promising officers being assigned elsewhere. The long-standing *Luftwaffe* Intelligence chief, *Oberst* Josef 'Beppo' Schmid, also worked as Göring's Ministerial Officer, so was not even a dedicated intelligence specialist. Indeed, Schmid had a demonstrable habit of embellishing reports to his chief and Hitler: to please his masters he told them what they wanted to hear, not always the actual facts – especially about enemy strength and losses.

For example, on 31 March 1939, Schmid reported that the Western powers' aircraft production was 'inadequate to catch up with the major advance in the expansion of the air forces achieved by Germany in the next one to two years'. In 1939, Germany produced 8,295 aircraft, 10,826 in 1940, and 11,776 the following year. Correspondingly, Britain's factories saw 7,940 in 1939, rising to 15,049 in 1940, and 20,094 in 1941.

In January 1940, Schmid estimated that the air forces of Britain and France were 'definitely inferior to the *Luftwaffe* in terms of numbers and equipment', and opined that no decisive improvement could be 'immediately' expected in 1940. Schmid also maintained that the RAF fighters would have little chance against the heavily armed Me 110 twin-engine heavy fighter, which, he said, had 'better dogfight performance'. Again, this was a flawed assessment, based upon the performance of German fighters against unescorted RAF bombers during the Battle of the Heligoland Bight. In the event, the Me 110 was found significantly lacking when facing Spitfires and Hurricanes, but because of Schmid, their production increased at a cost to the superior Me 109. The German success in Scandinavia and in the West gave Hitler and the OKW a false impression of the *Luftwaffe*'s actual capability, this optimism and over-confidence being shared by the OKW, including *Generalmajor* Hans Jeschonnek, the OKL Chief of Staff. Schmid and Jeschonnek believed that once an aerial assault was launched against Britain, the RAF would be destroyed in two to four weeks. The inadequate intelligence and inaccurate analysis would also soon manifest itself in poor target selection and ever-changing battle plans.

On 30 June 1940, Göring issued 'General Directions for the Operation of the *Luftwaffe* against England': 'Acting in concert, the *Luftflotten* are to operate all-out. Their formations, once lined up, are to be launched against defined groups of targets'. According to the *Luftwaffe War Diaries*:

> The primary target was the RAF, its ground organisation and the industry which fed it. On the other hand, Admiral Raeder demanded that the RN, supply convoys and the harbours at which they docked, should also be attacked from the air. Göring was confident that the *Luftwaffe* could fulfil both tasks simultaneously.

The *Luftwaffe* General Staff overrode Raeder, however:

> Until such time as the enemy's air force had been destroyed, the ruling principle of *Luftwaffe* commanders shall be to assault his formations at every available opportunity by day and night, in the air and on the ground – without regard to other commitments.

Still, though, at the end of June 1940, *Luftwaffe* air attacks on Britain remained nothing more than scattered nocturnal night raids and minelaying sorties. Indeed, Home Intelligence reported that 'Air raids were taken calmly. "A bore rather than a terror".'

In Britain, however, there was only one fully equipped division, and that was Canadian. Lord Avon, the War Minister, visited south-east England, which was, he knew, the likely landing grounds for a German invasion, should that come, and afterwards sent Churchill a report, explaining that 'the troops were very well trained ... but there is no anti-tank weapon of any kind ... and no tanks ... and that was the state of it, the cupboard was bare'.

'UNLEASH A STORM OF WRATH AND STEEL UPON THE BRITISH!'

Having already erred by allowing the BEF to escape at Dunkirk, Hitler's indecision at this crucial time would ultimately contribute immeasurably to Germany losing the war – and, perhaps surprisingly, it was not Churchill but the former Prime Minister, Neville Chamberlain, that champion of appeasement, who broadcast a clear warning to Hitler:

> We will fight him in the air and on the sea, we will fight him on the beaches ... we will fight him on every road, in every village and in every house, until he or we are utterly destroyed.

Chapter 15

'Events are Much Livelier'

In Britain, the lull following Dunkirk only served, according to the Home Intelligence report of 1 July 1940, to 'increase the feeling of bewilderment and suspense'. On that day, the Ministry of Information announced to the public that the Channel Islands had been occupied – the war was coming increasingly closer to home.

Pilot Officer Peter Parrott, 145 Squadron:

> We then started a period of comparative ease, my logbook showing flights training replacement pilots. In the past three weeks, we had become a close-knit flight. We now had our camp-kits at Dispersal, and, in the fine weather, enjoyed sleeping in the open air. The squadron worked at readiness roster of twenty-four hours. Readiness was at five, fifteen and thirty minutes. The latter period allowed us time to return to the Mess for a bath, change of clothing, and, if lucky, a meal – which were otherwise brought to Dispersal in hay boxes. We were now up to twenty pilots in the squadron, so could take it in turns to have a day off. We were then transferred to the Tangmere satellite at Westhampnett. Again the flights were dispersed, well apart, with just one Nissen hut each. Again we used our camp-kits. The Mess was a marquee, where we met for meals, which at first were brought over from Tangmere, again in hay boxes. We knew that the big air battle was yet to come and that this would doubtless be accompanied by an attempt by the Germans to invade.

At 06.12 hrs that first morning of July 1940, Flight Lieutenant Ted Graham had led a section of 72 Squadron Spitfires up from Acklington to intercept a 'bandit' eight miles east of Sunderland. Graham identified the enemy aircraft as 'a twin-engine biplane with floats, coloured white and with a large Red Cross on upper surface of upper plane'. This was a He 59 of *Seenotflugkommando* 3, engaged on a mercy mission and searching for a missing German bomber crew. Nonetheless, Graham made the conscious decision to attack, sharing the victory with the two other pilots in his section. The floatplane alighted on the sea, the crew of four, one of whom was badly wounded, took to their dinghy until picked up by HMS *Black Swan*. Suffice it to say, consciously attacking an ambulance aircraft was a direct contravention of the Geneva Convention.

At 10.20 hrs, a German reconnaissance Do 215 was intercepted by a pair of 616 Squadron Spitfire pilots ten miles South of their Leconfield base, but there was nothing as yet to suggest that the pattern of German air activity over Britain was likely to be any different to previous days. The next action of the day would be fought over shipping in the Channel – a new development.

After the Fall of France, the English Channel was deserted – all except for black dust-encrusted colliers of the so-called 'Coal Scuttle Brigade'. To industrial Britain, coal was essential, fuelling power stations, furnaces and railways. According to some estimates, the weekly requirement was for a staggering 40,000 tons. Being rich in coalfields, Britain did not have to import coal, but the miners' yield in Wales and the north-east still had to be transported to London and the South Coast port of Southampton. The only practical means was by sea, to which there was no alternative. From the north-east, the colliers travelled south down the east coast, to Southend, the Thames Estuary and London's docks. East convoys would assemble at Glasgow, making their way south down the west coast, meeting ships from South Wales, chugging across the Bristol Channel, around Land's End, and east to Southampton.

Although there was limited U-boat activity in the comparatively shallow Channel, mainly later on, the greatest threat was, of course, from the air and shelling by German batteries around Calais. E-Boats, fast surface raiders armed with torpedoes, were another threat, and minefields a further danger. Naturally, convoys were afforded protection by the RN, usually in the shape of two destroyers and half-a-dozen armed trawlers. There was, inevitably, a lack of preparedness, however. No major training exercise in convoy cooperation and protection had been held before the war; the small number of convoy passage exercises were inclined more towards the RN practising operation of its primitive submarine detecting radar. There were no specialist aircraft available and nor, as yet, was air integrated into any formal convoy management plan.

At lunchtime on 1 July 1940, one such coal convoy, codenamed *Jumbo*, was steaming towards Plymouth when dive-bombed by *Stukas* from III/StG 51, which had recently moved to operate from newly captured airfields around Cherbourg. Fortunately no ships were sunk, and sections of 213 Squadron's Hurricanes, although having arrived after the Germans' departure, successively kept guard overhead thereafter. This daylight attack on shipping, however, represented a change in German tactics, which continued that afternoon.

Owing to concerns around children being concentrated together, school holidays in Britain began on 18 June 1940, and continued until 1 October. Nonetheless, that first day of July saw the children of Bank Row, a working-class street in Pulteneytown, beside Wick harbour, playing happily in the street – when at 16.20 hrs two bombs exploded, shattering both tranquillity and lives.

Corporal James Clark was serving with the 5th Seaforth Highlanders in Caithness – but his family lived at 4 Bank Row:

> When the bombs were dropped I was sitting on top of the Portland Arms Hotel in Lybster, rigging up a radio aerial. I heard the bombs drop from there, thirteen miles away. We all it felt it or heard it and when I came down a dispatch rider came into the mess and told me that Wick was bombed. I asked where and he said 'Oh! A wee road leading up to the harbour and a shop called Smiths had been bombed, and all the people there killed, and the people next door were killed. I said 'What?!' It was a shock.
>
> My Sergeant-major said 'Get on your bike!' (I had an army motor bike). I went down to Wick and when I got to my house the police would not let me near it because they said there was a delayed action bomb there which might go off. I was not brave, but the thought of my wife and child being there was unbearable. I pushed him aside, went up the hill to the house and climbed in. There were no stairs.
>
> I was fortunate that my wife was out shopping with our son, Hamish, who was three or four years old. Had they been in the house, they would have been killed too – but, luckily, they were in Bridge Street, taking my mother-in-law home. Our house was destroyed, only a few pots and pans and some chairs were saved from it.

Eight children were killed in Bank Row and seven adults. The German aircraft concerned had attacked from low-level, probably aiming for the adjacent harbour. There was no air raid warning. The town was devastated.

That afternoon, for the first time, sixteen bombs were dropped on various targets, including oil storage tanks at Hull, which were set ablaze. These raids were by lone aircraft, however, and fell well short of delivering a 'knockout blow'.

At 17.45 hrs, a section of three Spitfires from Leconfield's 616 Squadron shot down a He 111 of 4/KG4, which had attacked Hull, off Spurn Head. In the South, a section of 64 Squadron Spitfires and one of 145 Squadron Hurricanes intercepted a German reconnaissance bomber, destroying it over the Channel, forty-five miles off Beachy Head. At 19.50 hrs, a 602 Squadron Spitfire pilot damaged a Ju 88 near Dunbar, after which the curtain fell on this first day of daylight fighting. Although the German air attacks on this day represented a significant change of tack, aligned with Göring's recent orders, there was still no invasion plan or order.

The following day, 2 July 1940, it was reported that:

> People are still waiting, most with 'grim determination', others with increasing nervous tension, some with restless criticism. There is an increase in rumour, and yesterday there were many reports of parachute landings and invading troops. Today, there is much talk of

the imminence of invasion, often supported by references to 'official' statements that the invasion is only a matter of hours away. In spite of this atmosphere ... people are not depressed. Many people say they think our defence preparations are inadequate but at the same time say 'we shall beat them off', 'We'll teach them a lesson', 'Let them come' ... Air raids are taken calmly and morale is high in districts where there have been continuous warnings, e.g. Bristol. There is little evidence that air raids are affecting morale adversely.

Hitler, at his *Tannenberg* HQ, discussed with Goebbels the content of a speech the *Führer* would deliver to the Reichstag in four days' time – the essence of which was a final peace offer to Britain. There was little confidence in the Nazi camp, however, that Churchill would even consider coming to terms, and so Hitler, approved Jodl's invasion plan on 2 July 1940. On this day the *Wehrmacht* were informed that landing operations would be considered if certain pre-requisites were met, the priority among which was aerial superiority. It is arguable, therefore, that the Battle of Britain began that day, because German air operations were now directly linked to achieving aerial superiority as the prelude to a seaborne invasion. Indeed, as Air Chief Marshal Dowding wrote in his Despatch: 'It is difficult to fix the exact date on which the "Battle of Britain" can be said to have begun.' – a matter we will explore further as our narrative progresses.

Perhaps ironically, 2 July 1940 did not see a huge daylight effort. That morning, a section of 611 Squadron Spitfires destroyed a lone Do 215 engaged in reconnaissance of the east coast, one of a large number of such machines available to the enemy. Flying alone, however, these spy planes lacked fighter escort and the mutual fire support provided by a bomber formation. For those reasons Fighter Command took a heavy toll of these reconnaissance aircraft, which undoubtedly reduced the accurate information available to *Luftwaffe* Intelligence.

At 17.36 hrs three 7/KG4 Ju 88s attacked the Vickers-Armstrong plant at Elswick, near Newcastle. One of the raiders was hit by AA fire and wrecked in a forced-landing on the Frisians, and bombs fell in Newcastle and Jarrow, killing thirteen people and injuring over a hundred more. Despite the raid having occurred during daylight, the factory was not hit, further evidencing the often-haphazard nature of bombing at this time. A Newcastle barrage balloon was ignited by a Do 17, the bomber being claimed destroyed by AA gunners, this possibly being a *Stab*/KG2 machine which was damaged and crashed on landing back at base.

That afternoon, *Stukas* again sallied forth from Cherbourg to attack Convoy OA177G, twenty-one miles off Start Point. The largest ship in the convoy, the 10,058 tonne SS *Aeneas*, received the most attention, and was fatally hit by two bombs: one through the portside, the other smashing through the after cross-bunker trunkway and blowing out the starboard side. The latter exploded deep within the ship, killing virtually all engineers and stokers. In total, nineteen sailors lost their lives – ten of whom were from Hong Kong (indeed, as we will explore in due course, many of the merchant seamen killed during these Channel battles in 1940 were Chinese and Indian, which remains a comparatively little-known fact). The SS *Aeneas* was abandoned and finally went to the bottom in 55 metres of water two days later.

On 3 July 1940, radar indicated fifty hostile plots approaching Britain throughout the day, 25 per cent of which were reconnaissance aircraft. At 08.40 hrs, Green Section of 616 Squadron, comprising Flying Officer George Moberley, Pilot Officer Hugh 'Cocky' Dundas and Flight Sergeant Fred Burnard, attacked a I/KG3 Do 17 at 4,500ft off Spurn Point. The Spitfires attacked in turn, shooting down the bomber which crashed into the sea near a convoy, then drove off and damaged another raider equally, no doubt intent upon bombing the ships below. Group Captain Sir Hugh Dundas, as he became, later wrote of his elation after that combat:

> Back at Leconfield I experienced for the first time the exhilaration of landing and taxiing in after a successful engagement with the enemy. Those who waited on the ground could always tell when a Spitfire's machine-guns had been fired. Normally the eight-gun ports on the leading edge of each wing were covered by little patches of red-doped canvas. But when the guns were fired these patches were shot away, leaving the ports open, and the plane made a distinctive whistling noise in the glide.
>
> This clear signal that you had been in action could be made more pronounced by a bit of side-slipping, which, though sternly discouraged by the authorities, was hard to resist on such occasions. And so, when they recognised this signal of action, the ground crews, who identified themselves enthusiastically with the pilots whose planes they serviced, would run out in high excitement to hear the news.
>
> They regarded a victory for their plane as a victory for themselves – and justly so, for our reliance on their skills was absolute. I felt twelve-ft tall after that combat, which in retrospect does not seem anything to be particularly proud of. At least I had broken my duck. I could only claim one-third of an enemy aircraft destroyed and one-half of another damaged – but that was better than nothing at all.

At 14.05 hrs, Green Section of 603 'City of Edinburgh' Squadron, which had not participated in the Dunkirk fighting and was dispersed to Dyce, Montrose and Turnhouse in Scotland, shot down a raider of the Stavanger-based 8/KG30 six miles South of Dyce. Shortly after 16.00 hrs, 603 Squadron's CO, Squadron Leader 'Uncle' George Denholm was leading Red Section:

> Patrolling stepped down with Red Section North of Fraserburgh. The Section got dispersed and I was coming South towards and behind

one of the other Spitfires when I saw an aircraft two-three miles to my south-east. He commenced a shallow dive and I climbed up to get the sun behind me. I then did a diving quarter attack from starboard and gave a burst of about three seconds, during which I received several hits and broke off the engagement as my glycol radiator was damaged.

An aircraft engine's coolant system is all-important, because otherwise the powerplant will overheat and stop, possibly catching fire. The glycol header tank, however, was just protected by the thin sheet aluminium engine cowling, and the under-wing radiator was likewise covered in a single sheet. The Spitfire was, therefore, vulnerable to this kind of damage, which was especially dangerous when fighting over the sea. Indeed, all it might take to bring down a Spitfire was a well-aimed or lucky shot with a single rifle-calibre bullet holing a coolant pipe, and the fighter was only going one place: down. Denholm's decision to break off his attack on what he identified as a 'Do 17' was the only sensible course of action. 603's CO considered the effect of his attack on the bomber 'doubtful'.

Sergeant Ivor Arbor was also in action with Squadron Leader Denholm, and reported the engagement having occurred at 16.10 hrs, 10,000ft forty miles East of Peterhead:

> I was Viken [603 Squadron's radio callsign] Red 3, stepped down from the rest of the Section. I first sighted the Enemy Aircraft (E/A) about 2,000ft below, crossing ahead from starboard to port. I went down to investigate and when doing so saw one member of my Section carrying out an astern attack, whereupon I manoeuvred into position for an astern attack, after my other Section member broke away. I closed in to 250 yards and fired three two second bursts. The E/A carried out evasive action by making slight turns both to the left and right.
>
> After breaking away I positioned myself for a Number Two Attack and fired four bursts of two or three seconds each. On completing this attack I found myself very close and immediately astern of the E/A, so I fired the rest of my ammunition and saw sparks appearing from him. Some black smoke also came from the engines and blackened my windscreen. The E/A was now going down in a shallow dive while I positioned myself abreast and about half a mile to starboard.
>
> From this position made a feint beam attack, following this I made two more similar attacks, going very close to the E/A each time. After the last one I turned around and found the E/A had disappeared. I saw a patch of white foam on the sea and could see the silhouette of the machine beneath the surface, the tail fin was just showing and I saw two orange rimmed rubber boats but no personnel. I then fixed the position and headed off home.

While Squadron Leader Denholm had identified the enemy bomber as a 'Do 17', Sergeant Arbor described it as a 'He 111'. The Do 17, however, had a distinctive twin-fin, and Arbor's report refers to a single fin protruding from the sea. Neither were right: it was actually a Ju 88, although no mention of what type was engaged is mentioned in the combat report of Pilot Officer Dudley Stewart Clarke, Red 2. Nonetheless, the bomber was clearly destroyed, the victory being shared equally by the three Spitfire pilots. What they had shot down, in fact, was another 8/KG30 Ju 88, the four crewmen of which remain missing. This is, however, a perfect example of aircraft misidentification of aircraft targets, which was common.

8/KG30 would lose another Ju 88 and its crew to 603 Squadron that day, when at 19.10 hrs, Red Section destroyed a third bomber two miles south-east of Inverbervie. It had been a costly day for the Norway-based unit.

Although the majority of fighting on this day occurred over the south coast and south-east during the afternoon, Flight Lieutenant John Kennedy of 238 Squadron damaged a Ju 88 near Middle Wallop in Hampshire, his Hurricane also being hit in the process, and 56 Squadron's Flight Lieutenant John Coghlan and Flying Officer Richard Brooker claimed a Do 215 'probable' West of Felixstowe.

At 13.10 hrs, a section of 145 Squadron Hurricanes claimed a He 111 'probable' off St Catherine's Point on the Isle of Wight. Two hours later a flight of 54 Squadron Spitfires similarly claimed a Do 215 'probable' off Deal, following an attack on the coastal airfield at Manston. Flight Lieutenant John Ellis, an experienced fighter pilot and leader with a number of aerial victories to his credit already, reported on events occurring at 16.10 hrs:

> I was leading Blue Section of 610 Squadron, with Red Section in line astern, on a patrol between Margate and Dungeness. Both sections had been patrolling for five minutes when we were ordered to intercept one bandit over Hawkinge, below cloud. I saw the bandit, a Do 17, approaching from the North at right angles to our course. I wheeled the Flight around in line astern and gave orders for a No 1 Attack.
>
> I attacked first and opened fire over the coast near Folkestone at 400 yards. After a burst of roughly five seconds, the top rear gunner baled out but I still received constant machine-gun (MG) fire from the bottom gunner. I continued firing until my ammunition was exhausted and noticed, before breaking away, large pieces of cowling, presumably engine cowling, flying off and a small amount of black smoke from the starboard engine. A fire had also started in the top rear gunner's cockpit but I noticed the flames were extinguished just as I broke away.
>
> I turned to follow the aircraft and to watch the remainder of the Flight attack, but soon smelt burning oil and noticed that the oil pressure was zero and the temperature 100°, so immediately set

course for Hawkinge. I switched off over the coast and forced-landed on Hawkinge, where I discovered I had been hit in the oil cooler and in two other places.

Again, this report indicates the vulnerability of another vital component, in this case the oil tank, again simply encowled within the sheet aluminium nose and unprotected by steel armour plate. The Do 17 concerned was accredited as damaged and shared between the six Spitfire pilots involved.

Off Beachy Head at 16.30 hrs, a section of Tangmere-based 43 Squadron Hurricanes damaged another Do 17, then, at 17.00 hrs, nine 32 Squadron Hurricanes intercepted 'Raid 34', a Kenley raider, a Do 17, 8,000ft over Tonbridge.

Pilot Officer Peter Gardner:

> Visibility was very good but interrupted by cloud. I was No 2 of Blue Section and saw the E/A flying West. I broke away from the formation hoping my leader would follow me, but he did not. I chased him among the clouds, firing intermittently. He finally emerged from the cloud bank and when I saw him he was pursued by two other Hurricanes.
>
> I joined in and we all attacked several times. He finally crashed in Paddock Wood. The gunner having been killed in my first burst, the gun was taken up by another member of the crew, who fired throughout the action. Sergeant Bayley, who was firing after me, finally put the last burst into it. No outstanding damage was seen, the engines were not stopped, being protected by armour plating, only being slowed down by having the propellers riddled.
>
> Two of the crew were killed and two taken prisoner. The prisoners gave me some interesting information which is enclosed in another form. I opened fire at 200 yards, closing to fifty.
>
> I would like to suggest that a beam attack is more effective than the astern, as in this instance looking at the aircraft afterwards, the beam attack avoids the armour plating.

Pertinent points indeed from Pilot Officer Gardner, who with other pilots visited the crash-site of 8/KG77 – and also noteworthy is the close-range he engaged from. It was becoming increasingly clear that in spite of pre-war concerns regarding fast, modern, fighter combat, the basic principles of the First World War, including height, sun, surprise and getting in close, ensuring accuracy, still held good.

The final daylight action once more involved a Spitfire pilot of 610 Squadron, namely Pilot Officer Peter Litchfield, at 17.55 hrs:

> I was Green 2 of a Section led by Flying Officer Warner, patrolling a convoy off Folkestone in fine weather. We were returning after

being sent to Hawkinge, to the East end of the convoy and were in the process of changing formation when AA fire from the ships was observed and an aircraft, identified as a Do 215, was seen heading for the French coast.

We gave chase, going into line astern and I joined in, in the nearmost position. We were still well out of range, and diving fast, when the enemy crossed the French coast at Cap Gris Nez and dived into low thin 9/10ths cloud at about 300ft. Heavy AA fire was encountered as we approached and crossed the coast, and the leader appeared to lose sight of the enemy through cloud, and he then led me at high speed as low as possible over the fields.

After about two minutes of this I observed fire from the rear gunner and I gave him a three second burst at 350 yards. He ceased firing and upon getting closer, I gave another burst of three seconds and the aircraft rocked from side to side. As I fired for the last time, the enemy appeared to stand on his tail, and I broke to avoid collision and went over the top of him, as there was no room below.

I did not see him again, although I looked both above and below the cloud. The AA opened up again as I re-crossed the coast, but no damage was done and I re-joined Green Section over the convoy.

The two Spitfire pilots, however, were over dangerous ground, and were lucky not to have been intercepted by Me 109s – so far absent from the renewed daylight battle to date. The attack was made near Marquise, and the enemy aircraft, actually a Do 17 of 4/KG77, is believed to have crashed near Vraucourt; there were no survivors.

On this day, the Germans did lose an Me 109; not to a Hurricane or Spitfire as might be expected, but to a Lockheed Hudson reconnaissance bomber of Coastal Command's 206 Squadron. The Hudson in question was flown by Pilot Officer Burne and navigated by Pilot Officer Rustom, while LACs Deighton and Holywell manned the guns and radio respectively. Burne's aircraft was engaged on a 'dawn recce towards Dutch coast' (ORB) and (the combat report tells us that) 'after bombing a large factory' the:

> Hudson was at 7,000ft, climbing for 10/10ths cloud about 12,000ft, having recently pulled out of a dive from 11,000ft to 7,000ft in a bombing attack. Rear gunner (LAC Deighton) sighted a Me 109 below the Hudson, astern and to starboard about 1,000 yards away. Enemy aircraft was camouflaged a dark colour.
>
> The Hudson continued climbing in order to reach cloud cover and took no avoiding action other than occasional gentle turns or banks to enable air gunner to detect possible E/A behind rudder blind spots. The Messerschmitt climbed up from starboard to port and

turned onto the same course as the Hudson at about 800 yards range. E/A then throttled back until he was climbing at the same speed as the Hudson, and kept station for about half a minute, slightly above the Hudson and in line with turret and port rudder.

Rear-gunner fired a short burst at about 800 yards to check on working of guns and simultaneously the E/A opened his throttle and started to make an attack, diving slightly and apparently attempting to get underneath the Hudson and come up to starboard.

The Hudson rear-gunner opened fire as the E/A was passing astern at about 250 yards range; the first few rounds dropped astern but almost at once the burst caught up with the E/A and registered on its tail and was then concentrated on its fuselage as the Me 109 banked steeply to port. In all, the gunner fired 600 rounds, almost all at ranges between 200 – 300 yards. At no time was the E/A closer than 200 yards.

Pieces flew off the E/A's tail and then flames came out of the fuselage, presumably from fuel tank aft of cockpit, and then E/A went over into a roll and spun down in flames ... AA fire opened up soon after the fighter had been shot down, but evasive action taken at 10,000ft was completely successful.

The Me 109 pilot, of 2/JG54, based at Schiphol, baled out, his aircraft crashing at Assendelft in the Netherlands. It was good shooting.

On the same day, Count Ciano spoke with William Phillips, the American Ambassador to Italy, who confirmed that 'For the moment', the United States did not 'intend to enter the conflict. We are arming on a very large scale, and are helping the British in every way. However, some new fact might decide our intervention, such as a bombardment of London with many victims among the civilian population.'

Ciano noted in his diary that 'This is why Hitler is careful and thinks twice before launching the final adventure' – and on this day there was a very clear indication that Britain was highly unlikely to consider any peace offer made by: the RN attacked the French fleet at its Mers-el-Kébir base, near Oran on the northern Algerian coast.

Under the terms of the recent Armistice, the defeated French – now neutral – were to retain control of their fleet, but Churchill's concern was that being off North Africa, there was a possibility that the ships could be seized by the Italians in Libya and thereby join and benefit the Axis arsenal. This would represent a significant increase in strength for the enemy, sufficient to disrupt Britain's supply lines and engage the RN across the Empire's seas. The War Cabinet, ill-trusting the French following the armistice (about which Churchill remained incensed), consequently gave Operation *Catapault* the go-ahead. The RN bombardment of the French base caused the deaths of 1,297 Frenchmen. One French battleship was sunk and five other ships damaged. Subsequently, the French navy blockaded in Alexandria agreed to disarm and remain in port until hostilities ended.

To Churchill, it had been 'the most hateful decision ... in which I have ever been concerned'. Deep resentment festered over the attack in France and relations with Britain became further strained. Meanwhile Dr Goebbels maximised the propaganda opportunity, but most importantly the Axis were deprived of this bonus resource – which could have bolstered the *Kriegsmarine* for an invasion of Britain. The prospect of a German invasion was very much on Churchill's mind that day, given that he told the War Cabinet such an event may be 'imminent'. The Prime Minister also explained that while he understood why the CAS, Air Chief Marshal Sir Cyril Newall, had ordered Bomber Command to focus on targets connected with the German aircraft industry, so urgent was the hour now that priority needed switching to attacking the enemy's harbours and shipping.

Certainly, on 4 July 1940, things were happening across the Channel. *Oberst* Johannes Fink, *Kommodore* of the Do 17 equipped KG2 *Holzhammer*, based at Cambrai-Épinoy, was appointed *Kanalkampfführer* (Channel Battle Leader) – a clear indication that a determined air effort was in the offing and focused on the Channel. It was not so much the shipping and ports involved that were the *Luftwaffe*'s primary objective, though – these targets were more a means to an end, to draw Fighter Command to battle for destruction over the sea. The Germans would dictate the time and place of battle, and have the height advantage. It was impossible for Fighter Command to mount standing patrols from dawn to dusk, there were insufficient resources to do so, and, even with radar, warning of such attacks was short. The enemy's intention, therefore, was to overwhelm any small formations of fighters patrolling over convoys, then annihilate reinforcing RAF squadrons, which would be met by German fighters sweeping in strength. The adoption of this strategy represented progress, but *Generalfeldmarschall* Kesselring, whose *Luftlotte* 2 would bear the brunt of this fighting, considered that 'The preliminaries to Operation *Seelöwe*, which was to have as its objective the invasion of England, reveal the planlessness of our conduct of the war.'

According to Kesselring, the German army was 'reluctant to tackle an operation against Britain', 'the navy flatly opposed to it', while *Luftwaffe* generals, however, 'were more positively minded'.

Several units, in addition to his own KG2, were put at Fink's disposal at this initial stage: from *Luftflotte* 2 came IV (*Stuka*) *Lehrgeschwader* 1 (LG, Demonstration Unit), commanded by *Hauptmann* Bernd von Brauchitsch, based at Saint-Inglevert, and *Hauptmann* Hannes Trautloft's Me 109s of III/JG51, formed that day at St Omer and under the overall command of the *Geschwaderkommodore*, *Oberst* Theo Osterkamp – a thirty-two victory First World War ace who, now aged 48, had already added two more to the list in this war. *Luftflotte* 3 contributed the *Stukas* of StG1, commanded by *Oberstleutnant* Walter Hagen, the gruppen of which were variously based at Angers, and Caen and Théville in Normandy. It would be the latter unit which scored first blood.

'EVENTS ARE MUCH LIVELIER'

Situated in *Luftflotte* 3's geographic area of responsibility was the HM Naval Base (HMNB) at Portland, in Dorset. The Isle of Portland juts out four miles into the English Channel, creating a huge natural anchorage extending across Weymouth Bay. Equidistant between the two major RN bases at Portsmouth to the east and Devonport to the west, HMNB Portland was originally intended as a fuelling station, over time becoming home to the Channel, Home and Reserve Fleets, while the land-based HMS *Osprey* became a submarine depot. The creation of a floating dry dock in 1914 also saw Portland used for ship repairs and refitting, and the harbour was also used for torpedo testing. An RN hospital was also established and Portland became a centre for research into anti-submarine warfare.

This, then, was clearly an important target – and so was HMS *Foylebank*, which had arrived in Portland harbour on 9 June 1940, anchoring off Castletown's south-east breakwater. Originally launched in 1930 as MV *Foylebank*, this 5,500 tonne grain-carrying merchant vessel was requisitioned by the RN in 1939 and converted into an auxiliary anti-aircraft ship, armed with 0.5-inch machine-guns, two quad 2-pounder 'pom-poms' and four twin 4-inch gun turrets. On 3 July 1940, HMS *Foylebank* was spotted by a German reconnaissance aircraft, which was fired upon but not hit by the ship. It was an ominous occurrence, and the ship was placed on overnight alert.

At 08.00 hrs on the morning of 4 July 1940, German records confirm that twenty-six *Stukas* of III/StG1 took off from their French bases. The enemy formation rounded Portland Bill at 08.30 hrs, following the eastern side of the Isle of Portland – bound for Castletown and HMS *Foylebank*. Above the dive-bombers, their Me 110 fighter escorts provided a protective umbrella – but there would be no reaction from Fighter Command. Why is unclear. That no RAF fighters were scrambled led to both an unfolding tragedy and story of selfless valour.

Ernest Pettiford was aboard HMS *Foylebank*:

> The first bomb hit within seconds. The ship was soon a blazing inferno. People were screaming and shouting and swearing. We had no anti-flash gear and I caught the full blast. I tried to get my gas mask on but that was blown away. I had burns on my face, hands, legs, everywhere. I knew I had to get off the ship, which was completely ablaze.

The *Stukas* accurately bombed their target, the thick black billowing smoke was visible for miles around. One dive-bomber was shot down by the stricken ship, crashing into the sea off Portland Bill, but HMS *Foylebank* was mercilessly battered. During eight terrifying minutes, the ship was bombed, immediately listing to port.

At the time, Brian Wilkins was a 6-year-old pupil at Weymouth's Holy Trinity School:

> We were going to school with my friend Billy Monger, and we just got to Rodwell railway bridge, when there was an explosion

in Portland Harbour. We immediately climbed up on the wall to the bridge, watched the *Stukas* bombing the *Foylebank*. There was one gun on the ship which kept on firing.

The starboard pom-pom crew had opened fire immediately, but seconds later four of the men were killed by an exploding bomb. The three remaining pom-pom crew were all wounded, two of them having also been hit previously. One of those men was 23-year-old Leading Seaman Jack Foreman Mantle – who would posthumously receive the Victoria Cross for his 'signal act of valour' that day:

> Leading Seaman Jack Mantle was in charge of the Starboard pom-pom when FOYLEBANK was attacked by enemy aircraft on the 4th of July, 1940. Early in the action his left leg was shattered by a bomb, but he stood fast at his gun and went on firing with hand-gear only; for the ship's electric power had failed. Almost at once he was wounded again in many places. Between his bursts of fire he had time to reflect on the grievous injuries of which he was soon to die; but his great courage bore him up till the end of the fight, when he fell by the gun he had so valiantly served.

Ernest Pettiford:

> A couple of rescue ships came alongside but I couldn't make it down the gangway. I got on the swinging boom but I couldn't hold on because my hands were badly burned and I crashed down on to the bottom of the rescue boat.

The 'rescue boat' was the Naval Harbourmaster's launch, the coxswain of which was one Edward Sidney Palmer and crewed by A.V. Bailey, S.R. Felmingham, J. Saunders and J. Pierce. Palmer later remembered that fateful day:

> Well things were beginning to happen, fast motor boats coming and going. Naval ships moving at all hours of the night. Ships being sunk out in the Channel, warnings of enemy planes and so on. At the Eastern End of the Harbour, in line with the southern entrance, they had moored a large anti-aircraft guard ship ... HMS *Foylebank*. She used to fly a yellow flag when enemy planes were reported, and a red flag when planes were approaching Portland.
>
> Well, on 4 July 1940, I was proceeding down the inside harbour at about 0830 in the morning, a lovely day, a normal day. I noticed the guard ship was flying the yellow flag, but did not take much notice, for she had been flying that on a number of days lately – when out of the sun they came, enemy dive bombers.

Diving straight down onto the guard ship, machine-gunning and bombing. All hell let loose ... they appeared to have caught us napping. I immediately told my crew that we were going in to pick up the hands and ratings who were jumping and being blown into the water alongside of her. There was a barge with work people alongside of *Foylebank*, but a bomb dropped alongside the barge turned it upside down.

We got in alongside and started to pick up the survivors. Dive-bombers kept coming, machine-gunning and bombing, lifting the launch almost out of the water. Well, we loaded the hands aboard until we could carry no more and made for the nearest jetty. Some of the poor fellows were in a sad mess. We landed as quickly as we could and went back for more.

By this time the enemy dive-bombers had done what they had come to do, the *Foylebank* was on fire and sinking.

Of the 279-man crew on HMS *Foylebank*, 176 died; the ship eventually sank the following day. If not for the bravery of Coxwain Palmer and his crew, the death toll would undoubtedly have been higher; Palmer later received the British Empire Medal for his actions that day.

From the German perspective, this first real action in the *Kanalkampf* was a resounding success, the intelligence report to 5 *Fliegerkorps* recording 'six direct hits' on an 'elderly warship' – HMS *Foylebank* – causing 'severe fires'. AA fire, the report continued, 'of all calibres' was experienced, 'especially from hit warship' – which is perhaps the *Foylebank*'s epitaph. One direct hit was reported on a 'freighter of 10,000 tons', and three more, causing fires, on another half the size. 'Strikes in the immediate vicinity' of several other merchantmen were also documented. Three merchantmen and a harbour tug, in fact, in addition to HMS *Foylebank*, were also sunk. Emboldened, it would be a busy day for the crews of StG1.

On the return flight from Portland, III/StG1 reported a convoy in mid-Channel, North of Cherbourg, steaming east to west. The next target to receive the *Stukas*' unwelcome attention was the fourteen merchantmen of Convoy OA178 – which was attacked at 13.00 hrs by StG1 off Portland. The Germans sank four ships and damaged others.

Yet again, no RAF fighters were patrolling overhead, and nor were any scrambled. This was clearly unacceptable and the RN rightly demanded answers – but there appears no explanation as to why fighters from the Tangmere or Middle Wallop sectors did not intervene. At this time, all of the South coast and south-west was the responsibility of 11 Group, although fortunately the new 10 Group, commanded by Air Vice-Marshal Sir Quintin Brand, responsible for the south-west and with headquarters at Box in Wiltshire, had been formed on 1 June 1940 and would be activated on 13 July 1940 – after which the Germans would far from have it all their own way.

The next action was off the Kentish coast. At midday, one flight of 54 Squadron Spitfires left their base at Rochford to operate from the forward aerodrome at Manston. At 12.30 hrs, a section of the squadron's Spitfires scrambled to investigate an unidentified radar plot off Manston – but was,

> attacked by Me 109s coming very suddenly from the cover of cloud, disappearing immediately after the attack. One machine (Pilot Officer Kemp) was badly damaged (although the pilot managed to land at Manston). Flying Officer McMullen's machine also received a short burst of machine-gun bullets but he was able to continue the patrol and himself attack either a Dornier or a Me 110, firing a short burst at 200 yards. Our pilots were uninjured. [ORB]

The Me 109s were from 2(*Jagd*)/LG1 which had executed a classic ambush from on high. Because the Me 109's engine was fuel-injected and its petrol feed therefore unaffected by gravity, the high-speed hit and run diving attack was a classic tactic which played to the German fighter's technical strengths. First World War-like protracted dogfights between individual fighters were comparatively rare, the enemy pilots much preferring to pounce from on high, attacking in one fleeting pass before diving away, as in this case – the manoeuvre famously described by Sergeant David Cox, a Spitfire pilot on 19 Squadron, as the 'dirty dart'.

The next raid was on a convoy off the Kentish coast at 14.00 hrs, by eighteen II/KG2 Do 17s, escorted by thirty III/JG51 Me 109s. This time, 11 Group responded, scrambling Squadron Leader John Joslin's 79 Squadron Hurricanes from Hawkinge:

> At 1408 hrs, the Squadron [eight aircraft] ... Took off to investigate a raid. As soon as Squadron left ground, AA fire was noticed and bombs were observed dropping, off Deal, on a convoy. Squadron climbed to 6,000ft and intercepted a formation of twelve Do 215 with escort of Me 109s, flying in four sections of three. Rearmost section of Do 215s was attacked.
>
> Squadron Leader Joslin fired all his rounds into a Do 215 but with no effect and landed at 1425 hrs. Sergeant Whitby attacked a Do 215 with no apparent effect. Flight Sergeant Brown attacked a Do 215 but was himself attacked by an Me 109: he evaded three, shot at two, and attacked an Me 109 that was on the tail of Pilot Officer T.C. Parker.
>
> Enemy aircraft were encountered over the Channel. Pilot Officer D. Stones DFC had a dogfight with Me 109. He had a large hole in mainplane caused by cannon of Do 215 [these were actually Do 17s, which had no cannon]. No conclusive casualties were inflicted on the enemy. Flying Officer Mitchell, Pilot Officer Clift and Pilot Officer

Millington landed having fired no rounds. Sergeant Cartwright DFM was missing after the action, and was presumed to have crashed into the sea off St Margaret's Bay, as a report was received from the army that an aircraft was seen to go into the sea during the period of action. [ORB]

Two of the German bombers were damaged in the action, in fact, both returning to France with two wounded crewmen aboard.

On 18 June 1940, 92 Squadron's Spitfires had arrived at Pembrey, in South Wales. From there, the squadron assisted with the defence of Bristol and Swansea, by day and night, and the posting was not without action. Of 92 Squadron, Flight Lieutenant Brian Kingcome later wrote that the squadron,

> always had the special ingredient which sets certain groups apart from the rest – a small, indefinable, quality in the alchemy that gives an edge, a uniqueness. This quality can never be duplicated or planned for, but somehow comes into being and is aptly called 'spirit'. It always begins at the top, and 92's exceptional spirit undoubtedly had its origins in the outstanding personalities of the original squadron and flight commanders. It then continued to flourish in the fertile soil of the rich mix of characters who made up this exceptional fighting unit: determined, committed young men, intent of squeezing the last drop of living from whatever life might be left to them at the same time as they refused to take themselves or their existences too seriously.

Recently arrived on 92 Squadron was a certain replacement pilot, 18-year-old Pilot Officer Geoffrey 'Boy' Wellum, who joined Kingcome's flight. Upon arrival at Pembrey, Wellum had yet to fly a Spitfire at night, so rapidly found himself practising dusk landings prior to his first nocturnal flight on 20 June 1940. 'Terrifying', he described the experience as many years later, 'just a black void. I didn't do very well, it must be said. It was disorientating. I ballsed up the landing, thought I was going to kill myself, collided with a Chance light and broke my Spitfire.'

Fortunately the pilot survived – but was grounded by Squadron Leader Sanders for 'an indefinite period'. Understandably, Flight Lieutenant Kingcome was not best pleased, and incurring his displeasure alone was enough to mortify Wellum, but at least his flight commander talked through the incident and offered sound advice. Ten days later, Geoffrey once more experienced the unparalleled thrill of Spitfire flight – and had no further trouble landing at night.

Pilot Officer Geoffrey Wellum:

> The Spitfire was not a great night flying aircraft, due to the narrow-track undercarriage, poor forward visibility when taxiing, caused by

the long nose, and the glare from six exhaust ports negatively affected night vision. This aircraft was not, though, designed for night flying, do not forget, but as a short-range daylight interceptor. The lack of aircraft specifically designed for night-fighting, however, meant that Spitfires and Hurricanes had to be used in this role.

At 15.15 hrs on 4 July 1940, three 92 Squadron pilots, Pilot Officers Harry Edwards and Sam Saunders, and Sergeant Ron Fokes, intercepted a 4/KG54 He 111 which had attacked the Bristol Aeroplane Company at Filton, damaging the Rodney Works' roof.

Pilot Officer Harry Edwards:

Yellow Section of 92 Squadron was ordered to patrol Filton at Angels 10. When in position I called up Filton [Sector Operations Room] and told them. Shortly afterwards Yellow 2 [Sergeant Fokes] called my attention to AA fire about five miles away and at about 12–13,000ft. I told Yellow 2 to take the lead, and we went for the spot, but before arriving there I tallyhoed what I thought to be a Do 17 overhead and travelling in our opposite direction. We climbed up and turned around but we (Yellow 1 and 2) were too late as he entered cloud with Yellow 3 [Pilot Officer Saunders] on his tail.

I again assumed the lead and ordered Yellow 2 to go below this thin 500ft cloud layer, while I stayed above. We had apparently lost him, so I recalled Yellow 2. I asked Filton Yellow 3s position which they gave me. Returning towards Filton above the cloud layer, I espied a He 111, traveling about 180 mph on a course about 120°.

Yellow 2 had seen him by this time and tried to head him off. I managed to get a 1½ second burst (250–300 yards) from the port quarter before he disappeared in cloud. Yellow 2 went on the starboard and I on the port, where we saw him enter. Yellow 2 called to me as he came out and did a starboard beam while I a port quarter (2–3 secs at 250–300 yards) almost simultaneously. We then noticed thin blue smoke from his port motor and he steadily lost height. The only evasive tactics adopted were at first, when he entered cloud.

When attacking, I noticed that both rear gunners were firing tracers. We continued to attack simultaneously, doing beams and quarters. The port motor at one time appeared normal and didn't smoke. By this time he was about 300ft. I then did a head-on attack (3 secs) while Yellow 3 did a starboard beam. At the moment I broke away he crashed into trees and burst into flames. My motor was very hot and oil and glycol temperatures above normal so I decided to land, thinking I had been hit in the radiator or oil tanks.

'EVENTS ARE MUCH LIVELIER'

> The temperature, I discovered afterwards, was due to the closed radiator near the ground and continually at 2,850 revs or more. I had engaged the E/A at 13,000ft and had closed the radiator as my temperature was low. As I was near the crashed He 111, I took charge and posted an army guard, rescued the maps and documents, dragged two men out of the burning plane and awaited the arrival of the Intelligence Officer from Filton, who took over.

The He 111 crashed at Longmoor Farm, Gillingham in Dorset. Three of the crew, including the pilot, were killed in the crash; only the air gunner, *Unteroffizier* Hermann Krack survived.

The final daylight action on this day was fought at 18.50 hrs off Dungeness, between 32 Squadron's Hurricanes and Me 109s of 2(J)/LG2.

Pilot Officer Rupert Smythe, 32 Squadron:

> I was flying No 3 of Yellow Section in the direction of Manston. Just off Deal six Me 109s appeared out of the clouds and attacked us. I saw one attacking Pilot Officer Grice so attacked it myself. I fired two short bursts and saw glycol starting to stream from the engine. The E/A turned on its side and dived towards the sea. As I was then being attacked by another E/A I could not follow it down.
>
> After a few turns the second E/A broke off the attack and dived to sea level in an attempt to escape. I caught him up about eight miles off the coast and after four bursts he crashed into the sea, the tail breaking away. There was no sign of the pilot reappearing, although I circled for several minutes.
>
> Pilot Officer Grice reported that army troops watching through binoculars near where he forced-landed saw the first Me 109 crash into the sea.
>
> As has happened several times before, the last section was attacked by 109s coming out of the cloud. It would appear that if fighter pilots are to devote their whole attention to looking out for bombers, they must have an escort of Defiants to guard their tail, if there are any enemy fighters in the vicinity.

Only one Me 109 failed to return, however. Pilot Officer 'Grubby' Grice forced-landed at Manston, and similarly Pilot Officer Keith Gillman landed his shot-up Hurricane at Hawkinge.

The events of 4 July 1940, with Fighter Command failing to defend Portland and Convoy OA178, led to the Admiralty closing the Channel to sea traffic, only permitting the colliers of the essential 'Coal Scuttle Brigade'. Dowding, however, reckoned that forty fighter squadrons were required to protect shipping from Land's End to the Humber. He could not afford so many, and his priority were the aircraft factories crucial to resupplying his Command. On 5 July, Churchill was sufficiently concerned to request assurance from the Naval Staff 'that the situation is in hand and that the Air is contributing effectively'. Unsurprisingly, the Admiralty's response was that the matter was far from 'in hand'.

The RAF fighters, however, consistent with Dowding's policy of carefully shepherding and preserving his limited resources, were still not committed to battle *en masse* over the Channel – indeed, they never were, no matter what inducement the enemy prioritised. It was simply a question of resources matching priorities, no matter how much the Prime Minister demanded 'Action this day'.

Thursday, 4 July 1940 was also significant because Air Marshal Charles Portal, Commander-in-Chief of Bomber Command, was formally directed to prioritise attacks on German shipping. The German naval base at Kiel, where capital ships *Scharnhorst* and *Deutschland* rode at anchor, was to become a primary target, along with such ports as Hamburg, Bremen, Wilhelmshaven, Brunsbüttel and Rotterdam. By this time, Spitfires of the Photographic Development Unit (PDU, renamed Photographic Reconnaissance Unit (PRU) on 8 July 1940), supporting Coastal Command, were returning with news of motorised German transportation barges and troopships beginning to assemble at Dutch and Belgian ports.

The reason was obvious: an improvised invasion fleet was being assembled. No.2 Group's Blenheims were tasked with smashing the enemy barges on the waterways of Occupied Europe. This required bombing accuracy, and so these attacks were to be made in daylight and only in suitable weather conditions, in which these unescorted bombers could rely upon cloud cover for protection in much the same way as German reconnaissance bombers and nuisance raiders operated over Britain by day.

In such conditions, 2 Group was to field up to forty-eight aircraft daily, attacking either individually or in small formations. Sensibly, the strategy was to widely spread these raids geographically, thus dispersing the defending German fighter forces. Bomber Command's wider responsibilities continued, with mine-laying and the continued offensive against the enemy aircraft industry and oil, and, to a lesser extent, German communications. That day, twenty 2 Group Blenheims bombed railway marshalling yards in Germany and enemy airfields in Belgium and the Netherlands, in addition to shipping off the Dutch coast; one Blenheim was lost. At night, Wellingtons and Whitleys bombed targets in Germany, while some Hampdens attacked Kiel while others laid mines.

Coastal Command also contributed, through minelaying and coastal patrols. The First World War had already indicated how deadly the submarine could be, and now the enemy's coastline included all the ports from Germany to France's Atlantic coast, the U-Boats and surface raiders were well-placed to blockade Britain, and meeting this threat was Coastal Command's responsibility – albeit with obsolete aircraft at this time. On this day, 4 July 1940, for example, 206 Squadron, operating Lockheed Hudsons out of Bircham Newton in Norfolk, sent two aircraft to search for a missing 44 Squadron Hampden: both were intercepted off the Frisians and shot down by Me 109s of 3/JG51; all eight RAF aircrew involved remain missing. No.236 Squadron's Blenheim fighters, based at Middle Wallop, however, were transferred from Fighter Command to strengthen Coastal Command, and on this day moved to Thorney Island, near Tangmere on the south coast. From there, with a detachment also operating from St Eval in Cornwall, the squadron was to patrol convoys and provide protection for reconnaissance aircraft spying on the French coastal ports, among other things: it would be a busy time ahead for Coastal Command too.

The political polemic *Guilty Men* was published on 5 July 1940. It had been written during the Dunkirk evacuation by Beaverbrook scribes Frank Owen, Michael Howard and Michael Foot, and in which Chamberlain, Baldwin and certain of their ministers were squarely accused of having failed to rearm Britain, imperilling its national security, and thereby betraying the country. The pamphlet was a huge seller, giving fresh impetus to the campaign to remove those responsible for appeasement from office. While Britain had certainly been slow to rearm, and was now paying the price, Munich had bought time – without which, the situation, especially in the air, would have been infinitely worse. Churchill, however, refused these demands and steadfastly kept Chamberlain in his War Cabinet (until, terminally ill, Chamberlain resigned in October 1940; he died on 9 November 1940).

Against the backdrop of *Guilty Men*, the 65 Squadron ORB noted that 5 July 1940 was 'a bit livelier' compared to the squadron's post-Dunkirk experience to date. At 05.35 hrs, Flying Officer Proudman led off five 'B' Flight Spitfires, including Sergeant Patrick Hayes and the new Pilot Officer Brisbane, to patrol Dover. Having been given several vectors by the Controller, Proudman, Blue One, sighted a He 111 and led his Section in line astern to execute a textbook No 1 Attack. At 200 yards, Blue One opened fire before breaking away, and was succeeded in turn, by Blue Two, Sergeant Kilner, and Blue Three, Pilot Officer Hart. Flying Officer Proudman then made a further attack, the enemy bomber turned towards land and lost height, before alighting in the sea and sinking immediately. Only two of this 8/KG1 bomber survived.

According to 611 Squadron based at Digby, the day was 'Cool, with a good deal of cloud'. Nonetheless, while the weather prevented the *Luftwaffe* repeating the previous day's effort, the lone nuisance raiders and reconnaissance bombers were active over Britain once again. The squadron's ORB describes the day's events, typical at this time for a 12 Group fighter squadron patrolling the East Coast:

> Blue Section was ordered off at 1240 hrs to patrol Skegness, to await an 'X' Raid reported at 22,000ft over the North Norfolk coast, going northwards. Identified as a friendly Spitfire, Blue Section was recalled as soon as they reached the patrol line.
>
> At 1640 hrs, Red Section was ordered to patrol Spurn Head at 14,000ft, to investigate two bandits coming in. When over the Outer

Dowsing these raids disappeared. Red 1 (Flying Officer Watkins) and 3 (Sergeant Burt) went down to sea level but saw nothing, Red 2 (Pilot Officer Brown) patrolling at 12,000ft.

The Section was then ordered to investigate another bandit at 12,000ft in their vicinity – Red 3 saw enemy aircraft 6,000ft above and Red 1 and 3 gave chase, but the enemy disappeared into cloud before our aircraft were in range. Red 3 continued patrol below cloud, Red 2 was over Spurn Head when aircraft bombed the Humber, and Red 1 patrolled East of cloud bank.

Later, enemy aircraft emerged from cloud above Red 1 and to the North – Red 1 gave chase and the enemy, a Ju 88, dived at high speed for another bank of cloud, travelling East. Red 1 got to 400 yards range and fired 800 rounds at enemy while I was disappearing into cloud – no results were seen as aircraft was immediately lost in cloud. Red 1 patrolled East of this cloud bank for some time until lack of petrol compelled him to return. Red 2 and Red 3 returned independently. A heavy thunder shower at 1750 hrs made flying extremely difficult but after this the weather cleared up again.

Pilot Officer Peter 'Sneezy' Brown:

At take-off, most pilots would face the aircraft's tail and pass water, most of which went over the tail-wheel. A full or half-full bladder for an hour and a half at 30,000ft was something to avoid. By the time the pilots had finished, the fitters had started the engines and we were ready for take-off. The unusual facet of this story is not that it happened quite regularly, but that towards the end of 1940 a formal letter was sent out by Fighter Command's engineering department giving strict instructions that urinating on the tail-wheel must cease forthwith as it was causing corrosion damage. The letter was treated with great hilarity!

On the evening of 5 July 1940, Spitfires of Kenley's 64 Squadron were also in action, as Sub-Lieutenant Frank Dawson-Paul reported that:

At 1955 hrs as Blue 3, I was ordered with Blue Section to carry out a reconnaissance of the aerodromes at Rouen and Abbeville. We crossed the coast at 11,000ft and at 10,000ft above Rouen observed three Me 109s preparing to attack from astern.

I turned to port and positioned myself for attack. I fired one burst from below at a 109 and broke away. Then I managed to position myself on the tail of another 109. I fired two bursts, both of which hit him. He then did an aileron turn in which I followed him and I fired another burst from about 200 yards, which also hit him. As my height was only 3,500ft then, I broke off the fight and last saw the 109 going down in a steep spiral as if out of control.

Both Blue 1 and 2 (Pilot Officer D.K. Milne) took part in this dogfight and I last observed Blue 2 ... on the tail of a 109. As far as I could see, there was nothing on is tail. I saw neither aircraft after the combat and made my way home.

The action, however, was not yet over for Dawson-Paul:

On returning from my reconnaissance of Rouen and Abbeville via Le Touquet, I flew at 20ft above the sea – made landfall at Lympne and was just turning towards Hawkinge at a height of 200ft when I observed tracers going past me. Looking in my mirror I saw a Me 109 on my tail. Owing to my low altitude I could do but little, so went into a very steep turn to starboard. The 109 followed, firing the whole time. After completing four turns his fire ceased and on looking back there was no sign of him, so I proceeded to Hawkinge and landed. Damage to aircraft are hole in port and starboard wings, one hole in starboard flap and one hole in oil cooler. From various reports from the military, the Me 109 is believed to have spun in, but this is not yet confirmed.

No Me 109 crashed, however, so it could have been Milne's Spitfire, P9449, that had been seen crashing by eyewitnesses on the ground. Although official sources state that Milne crashed near Rouen, given that he remains missing it is more likely that he went into the sea, and could have been the victim of either *Leutnant* Erich Hohagen or *Oberfeldwebel* Johann Illner, both of 4/JG51 and both of whom claimed Spitfires destroyed.

Sub-Lieutenant Dawson-Paul was a pilot seconded to Fighter Command from the FAA. After the AASF's heavy losses in France, the Air Ministry reached an agreement with the Admiralty for the loan of FAA pilots. Originally, Churchill had envisioned the FAA supplying fifty pilots – the enthusiastic answer to the call for volunteers, however, saw sixty-eight FAA pilots reinforcing Fighter Command, although ten were recalled. Eighteen of the remaining volunteers would be killed during the forthcoming Battle of Britain, and Dawson-Paul would become the first of the FAA Few to become an ace.

Pilot Officer Johnnie Johnson, 616 Squadron:

If attacked, the thing to do was go into the tightest turn possible, to out-turn your opponent and thereby turn the tables. If you couldn't out-turn him, the problem was you couldn't just keep on turning and turning all day. At some stage a pilot had to decide to break off – and that could be the end of it. Fortunately, our Spitfires could usually out-turn the Me 109E the Germans were using in 1940.

That night, sixty Bomber Command Blenheims, Hampdens, Wellingtons and Whitleys also took advantage of the prevalent cloud cover, attacking airfields in the Netherlands and ports in Germany. One bomber attacked the liners *Europa* and *Bremen* in Hamburg, both of which were being fitted out for use in Operation *Seelöwe*, but no hits were scored. This, though, was the start of Bomber Command's 'Battle of the Barges'. It was dangerous work; given the importance of the ports, the Germans had bolstered defences with 6,700 light and 2,600 heavy flak guns.

Pilot Officer Andrew Jackson, 149 Squadron, Mildenhall:

> Despite these formidable defences, the RAF Bombers pressed home their attacks, inflicting heavy damage on the Invasion Fleet and ancillary equipment. With my own crew, we bombed the shipping tied up in the ports of Calais, Dunkirk, Ostend and Antwerp, suffering ack-ack damage, severe enough for two of our aircraft to be grounded for repair. One Wellington had two large holes ripped out of its fuselage. There were other hazards in a crowded airspace. On a return flight from bombing Ostend docks, an aircraft outward bound passed directly overhead with about fifty ft to spare – a very close call!

On 5 July 1940, with the recent failure of Fighter Command to defend Portland in mind, Squadron Leader John Scatliff Dewar DSO, DFC led his 87 Squadron Hurricanes from Church Fenton in Yorkshire to Exeter in Devon, there to provide aerial protection to the Western Approaches and in particular the ports of Plymouth and Bristol.

'Johnny' Dewar was born in Lahore, India, where his father was a Civil Servant, on 10 August 1907. Later, he was educated at King's School, Canterbury, where he became a sergeant in the OTC, and then entered Cranwell as a flight cadet in 1927. Tours as an army and naval cooperation pilot followed – the latter partially at sea, at home and abroad, with the FAA. On 10 July 1937, Johnny Dewar married Kay Bowyer, the daughter of Southampton Alderman Percy Vincent, the couple having met ice-skating in Southampton a year previously. Soon afterwards, the couple moved to Martlesham Heath, where Johnny was posted to test armament with the A&AEE at Martlesham Heath – contributing to the development of both the Spitfire and Hurricane prototypes. On 1 February 1938, Dewar was promoted to squadron leader and became Senior Operations Officer (SOO) at RAF Thorney Island in West Sussex – where Kay Dewar became a code and cipher clerk.

On 10 November 1939, by which time Squadron Leader Dewar was among the RAF's most experienced pilots, he was posted to 11 Group for reassignment to a fighter squadron: three weeks later, he took command of 87 Squadron, which was flying Hurricanes in France. During this 'Phoney War' period, 87 Squadron received various important visitors, including both His Majesty the King, and the British Prime Minister, Neville Chamberlain. When the German attack on the

'EVENTS ARE MUCH LIVELIER'

West began on 10 May 1940, 87 Squadron was, needless to say, heavily engaged. Two weeks later, its airfields overrun, the unit was evacuated back to England. On 31 May, *The London Gazette* announced that Squadron Leader Dewar was among the first officers to be awarded the 'double' of the DFC and DSO for his services in France. The citations respectively read:

> This officer has shot down five enemy aircraft and led many patrols with courage and skill.
>
> Before intensive operations started, this officer injured his right shoulder in a severe flying accident. Despite this, he flew regularly and led his squadron with skill and dash, more than sixty enemy aircraft being destroyed by them. He remained in command of the squadron throughout the operations, in spite of the injured shoulder, trained his new pilots well and continued throughout to be a very efficient commander, inculcating an excellent spirit in his squadron.

Upon returning home, of his shoulder injury Johnny simply told his wife, 'Oh, don't worry about that.' The fact is, Johnny Dewar was clearly both an exceptional fighter pilot and leader – and COs with both abilities were in short supply at the time.

No.87 Squadron had been but briefly withdrawn to Church Fenton for rest and refit. During that time, on 5 June 1940, Squadron Leader Dewar and Pilot Officer Dennis 'Hurricane' David, also of 87 Squadron, were called to an investiture at Buckingham Palace to receive their decorations gazetted for their courageous service during the Battle of France. The pair flew down to London, stayed overnight, and lunched with David's mother. He later wrote:

> She fell under his spell, as did everyone who knew him. Altogether it was a much-needed break from the stress we had been under. We returned to Church Fenton refreshed and in good spirits. We did our best with the fresh pilots to get them as much flying practice as we could before the air battles which we knew lay before us, because we were aware that although our boys had more than enough courage and dedication, they were as yet no match for the experienced German pilots.

On 5 July 1940, Squadron Leader Dewar led 87 Squadron down to Exeter. As the squadron's ORB commented:

> By this time the capitulation of France had completely altered the whole strategic situation of this war, and the South West of England suddenly found itself vulnerable to attack, instead of being a safe assignment. There was therefore considerable speculation as to when the *Blitzkrieg* would be launched against England.

Exeter was, in fact, a civilian airport procured by the RAF and in the process of changing over to a war and service footing. 213 Squadron had arrived a fortnight previously, 'and naturally had occupied the best parts of the station. The officers were billeted at the Rougemont Hotel in Exeter, and the men at Farringdon House, not far from the aerodrome.' Recognising the significance of the phase of air operations 87 Squadron was about to be engaged in, the charismatic and popular Squadron Leader Dewar addressed his pilots:

> No one is going to stop the Huns invading this country in the next month or so – except us. When we have cleared the bastards out of the skies over the Channel and the south coast, they won't be able to invade by sea – so we are going to stop them. There's nobody else and we are in a proud position and the luckiest people at this time. This is what we are here for, so now let's get on with it!

And get on with it, 87 Squadron soon would.

According to 65 Squadron, 6 July 1940 was 'back to normal' and another quiet day generally – providing Fighter Command an opportunity to strengthen certain sectors, given that by now squadrons' losses during the Fall of France and Dunkirk fighting had been made good. 609 'West Riding' Squadron's Spitfires, moved from Northolt to the Middle Wallop Sector, as Pilot Officer David Crook recalled:

> Our stay at Northolt was now almost up because on Thursday morning, 4 July 1940, the enemy bombed Portland. There was no fighter opposition from us, and so orders came through later in the morning that 609 were to move to Warmwell aerodrome as reinforcements.
>
> We were very pleased about this – not many people like Northolt – and while there, it was always possible that one would get another of those accursed French patrols! So, we thought that we were well out of it.
>
> The squadron accordingly moved down on the Thursday afternoon ... We were the only squadron in that Sector at the time, and so did not get any time off, and got up at 0330 hrs and went to bed again about 2330 hrs, altogether a pretty long day.
>
> We had a number of alarms and went out into Weymouth Bay as hard as we could, hoping to see some enemy, but I think most of these scares were quite without foundation and after a day or so, I concluded that I might spend months at this game and never see any action. How little I knew!
>
> On the Sunday we moved up to Middle Wallop (unlovely name) – a new aerodrome between Salisbury and Andover. This is a very good strategic base for the defence both of Southampton,

and Portland, and it was to be our home for some time to come. We continued, however, to use Warmwell as an advanced base and we flew down at dawn every day and returned to Wallop at dusk.

The first RAF fighter squadron to see action on 6 July 1940 was 74 Squadron, based at Hornchurch – and specifically Blue Section, which scrambled at 05.05 hrs to investigate an 'X' Raid. Blue 1, Flight Lieutenant William Measures, reported on this 'Interception Patrol over the coast, near Dover, at 7,000ft':

> When flying in a SE direction approximately seven miles West of Dover, I sighted a He 111 flying NE about a quarter of a mile to my right. I immediately turned onto his tail and fired a short burst at approximately 300 yards range. E/A returned fire from top gun, with no effect. I then closed range rapidly, as E/A was entering cloud, and flew through cloud formating on enemy in line astern.
>
> After some seconds we passed out into clear air, and I fell back to 200 yards and delivered several bursts. I noticed de Wilde ammunition [tracer] hitting his fuselage and engine and saw one burst demolish the top rear gun turret. No return fire was being given by now, and E/A was giving out white smoke from both engines, and a stream of oil from port engine, which partially obscured my windscreen. E/A then descended to 100ft, making gentle turns to right and left, and making eastwards across the Channel.
>
> I followed at 3,000ft, having no ammunition left. Eventually the port engine slowed down but E/A carried on, on the starboard engine, and eventually landed on the beach of the French coast, NE of St Ingelvert. I then returned alone to base, Blue 2 (Pilot Officer D.H.T. Dowding) and Blue 3 (Sergeant C.D.E. Skinner) having been separated from me at the beginning of the action.
>
> My own aircraft was not hit. AA fire over Dover was quite good, and assisted us very much in locating the E/A. I learned later that Blue 2 and 3 chased a second E/A.

The He 111 was claimed as 'confirmed' destroyed.

Blue 2, Pilot Officer Derek Hugh Tremenheere Dowding – son of the Commander-in-Chief – reported as follows, having also been guided to the enemy by bursting AA fire:

> On approaching AA fire I sighted first one and then another He 111, which on sighting us flew into cloud, pursued by Blue Section. I lost Blue 1 in this cloud but after two seconds caught a glimpse

of a He 111 ahead, through a clearer patch. Then he vanished, and I thought I had lost him.

After a few more seconds flying, still in clouds, I saw something fall just in front of my spinner, and saw the He 111 fifty yards ahead and above, unloading his bombs as fast as possible. I pulled up the nose and gave him 10 second burst at very close range. I could see my ammunition, especially the de Wilde incendiary, hitting the aircraft all the time.

Eventually the starboard engine blew up in a big black cloud of smoke, several large pieces fell away and the wheels came down. The aircraft then fell away sharply to the right, into cloud, and I lost him, being unable to turn quickly enough. I then returned to base and landed. I observed black cross and lettering on fuselage as E/A fell away. Camouflage appeared to be normal.

This He 111 was claimed as a 'probable'. Blue 3, Sergeant Skinner, appears to have made no combat claim; all three 'Tiger' Squadron pilots involved were experienced operators, having already experienced combat and made claims over Dunkirk.

Later that day, Red Section of 603 Squadron, based at Turnhouse, successfully intercepted a high-flying German reconnaissance machine, as Pilot Officer George 'Sheep' Gilroy reported on the combat, which took place between 12.38 and 13.06 hrs:

While climbing at 17,000ft on vector of 180° from Peterhead I observed a short vapour trail through broken cloud (20,000ft). Height of E/A estimated 23,000ft. E/A was flying on same course, about five to eight miles south-west of our position. After sighting E/A I did not alter course but continued climbing through the broken layer of cloud to about 23,000ft, north-east of E/A. After flying over Aberdeen, E/A turned onto 090° and started to climb.

Being north-east I was able to cut the corner and putting my Section into line astern began very slowly to come up on E/A. We climbed to about 27,000ft without coming into range. Suddenly, E/A went into a long steep dive to broken cloud at about 3,000ft. I had about 400 Indicated Air Speed (ASI). My rev-counter began to flicker and stopped. I throttled back a little and veered South a little. We were coming into range faster in the dive and I wanted to come in and attack out of the sun.

Red 3 (Sergeant J.K. Caistor) in a new aircraft delivered an attack and broke away to port. I came in on E/A's starboard quarter and E/A levelled out among thin, broken, cloud. I came into the astern position and E/A turned steeply to port. I was obliged to cease fire, being unable to allow enough deflection, but resumed fire when E/A straightened out. E/A took advantage of cloud but after several bursts the port engine took fire. I broke away and watched the E/A go down in sea, within a mile.

The kill was shared equally between the three Spitfire pilots of Red Section, which also included Pilot Officer Dudley Stewart-Clarke flying the Red 2 position. The pilots described their target as a 'Do 215', but it was actually an Me 110 of *Aufklärungsgruppe Oberbefehlshaber der Luftwaffe* (*Aufl*.ObdL, the reconnaissance unit of the *Luftwaffe* Commander-in-Chief), which crashed into the North Sea 100 miles east-north-east of Aberdeen; all three enemy crewmen aboard were killed.

While Red Section celebrated, a certain Pilot Officer Richard Hillary, and Pilot Officers Colin Pinckney and Peter Pease, reported for duty with 603 Squadron direct from 5 OTU at Aston Down, and were promptly sent off to join the squadron's 'B' Flight at Montrose. In his classic memoir *The Last Enemy*, Hillary wrote:

> Montrose was primarily an FTS where future pilots crowded the air in Miles Masters. As the only possible enemy raids must come from Norway, half a squadron was considered sufficient for its protection.
>
> At our Dispersal Point at the north-west corner of the aerodrome there were wooden huts. One of these was the Flight Commander's office; another was reserved for the RT (Radio Telephone) equipment and technicians; the third, divided into two, was for the pilots and ground crew respectively ... From the ceiling [in the third hut] hung several models of German aircraft, on the back wall by the stove were pasted seductive creatures by Petty [the artist George Petty, an American pin-up artist], and on a table in the middle of the room a gramophone was playing, propped up at a drunken angle on a pile of old books and magazines.
>
> In a corner there was another table on which were a couple of telephones operated by a corporal. Two beds standing against the longer walls, and several old chairs, completed the furniture.

It was a scene repeated at every airfield across Britain.

Further South, enemy air activity over Britain was slight, although twenty-five bombs destroyed civilian dwellings in Shotton and Plymouth, and at Guillemont Barracks, Aldershot, a lone He 111 caused damage, leaving eleven dead and fifty-nine injured in its destructive wake.

No.2 Group's Blenheims were busy this day, nineteen aircraft being despatched to attack enemy airfields and barges. Owing to the weather, only six aircraft bombed. Three Blenheims of West Raynham's 18 Squadron 'took off to attack and reconnoitre aerodromes in N France and Belgium. Two aircraft dropped no bombs and the third failed to return to base.' The missing aircraft had been shot down near Rotterdam by 2/JG54 Me 109s, the three-man crew all being captured.

Coastal Command's 254 Squadron also lost two Blenheims, which were providing aerial cover to RN vessels off Norway; one was shot down by a Me 110, the other by a 109. Both crews ditched and rescued by RN destroyers, but the pilot of one had been killed; a crewman of the other aircraft later died of his injuries.

That night, Bomber Command sent forty-three aircraft into the night sky to sow mines and bomb German ports and airfields in Holland. No.37 Squadron lost a Wellington destroyed and its crew killed, and a 102 Squadron Whitley crew was brought down and captured.

A day of thundery showers over southern England, 7 July began with RAF fighters destroying several German reconnaissance bombers over the Channel. Yellow Section of 145 Squadron, led by Squadron Leader John Peel, was up from Tangmere at 05.00 hrs:

> On this patrol a Do 17 was sighted five miles away, travelling northwest at about 20,000ft. Leaving Flying Officer Rowley with the convoy, he and Pilot Officer Wakeham gave chase and eventually shot the Dornier down into the sea, at a point 20 miles SSW of The Needles.

The four-man crew of this Do 17, of 2(F)/121, were all killed.

No.54 Squadron's Spitfires were operating from the forward base at Manston:

> [09.30 hrs]. A second and most disastrous day at Manston. 'B' Flight lost three machines, two being complete write-offs. Green Section were attacked by a number of He 112s, while themselves attacking a He 111. Pilot Officers Campbell and Coleman were both shot down, but managed to make forced-landings near Deal. The pilots suffered from minor injuries but the machines were completely wrecked. Flying Officer McMullen, the leader, was also damaged but managed to land at Manston. The He 111 disappeared unscathed. The fundamental lesson of 'looking everywhere in the sky at once' has been learnt at a very high price. [ORB]

The Spitfires had not, however, been ambushed by 'He 112s', which was a prototype single-engine fighter never to see operational service, but which appears frequently in RAF fighter pilots' combat reports from the period. 54 Squadron had, in fact, been bounced by the Me 109s of 7/JG51.

At 09.47 hrs, a Do 17 of 3(F)/121 was intercepted off Brighton by Yellow Section of Tangmere's 43 Squadron; Pilot Officers Brunner and Cruttenden, and Sergeant Buck equally shared the enemy aircraft as 'damaged'. Then, at 10.26 hrs, Tangmere's so-called 'Millionaire's Mob' – namely the auxiliary 601 Squadron, also struck against 2(F)123, at 10.25 hrs. Squadron Leader Max Aitken DFC – son of Lord Beaverbrook – was leading and reported that:

> Flight ordered to patrol base and later vectored out to sea. Enemy aircraft seen flying south-west. No 1 Attack delivered. Boxes of wine were thrown out at me as I attacked and enemy went into steep dive.

> I broke away after my attack and the rest of the Flight continued the attack and shot E/A down into sea.

Whether the 'boxes of wine' being thrown was true or tongue in cheek, given the auxiliaries known irreverence towards service discipline, is unclear, but the kill was shared between Aitken and Flying Officer William Clyde DFC; the German crew all perished.

Further west, at 17.10 hrs Pilot Officer Ken Dewhurst of 234 Squadron, based at St Eval in Cornwall, damaged a Ju 88 over Plymouth, on one of the fourteen interception patrols flown by the squadron that day. The main action of the day, however, was yet to come.

The enemy reconnaissance aircraft were closely watching a convoy steaming east, making for the Thames Estuary. Naturally, the Germans aimed to attack where the ships were most vulnerable: the Dover Strait. By early evening, the convoy was off Folkestone, hoping to negotiate the Strait, under ever watchful German eyes, after dark.

Above, 11 Group fielded a constant protective umbrella of at least nine fighters, flying 215 sorties between noon and 20.00 hrs. The enemy had other ideas, however.

At 19.30 hrs, forty-five Do 17s of I and II/KG2 took off from their bases around Arras, heading for the convoy. In response, 64 Squadron was scrambled from Kenley, and at 20.15 hrs, Flight Lieutenant 'Sammy' Saunders led off 65 Squadron's 'B' Flight from Hornchurch – Pilot Officer Hart and Sergeant Franklin joining him in Blue Section, while Flying Officer Proudman, Pilot Officer Brisbane and Sergeant Hayes made up Green Section. Before the Spitfires arrived, however, bombs fell on the convoy, one ship being sunk and three others damaged. By the time 65 Squadron appeared over the Strait, Me 109s were sweeping over Kent and Sussex to counter such a threat to the bombers.

The scenario already had disaster for the defending fighters written all over it.

Flight Lieutenant Saunders:

> I was leading Blue Section ... Green Section was in line astern of me. We were patrolling between Folkestone and Dungeness at approximately 10,000ft. Green One reported to me that he had seen some aircraft and I told him to lead his Section in their direction and I would follow. Green One turned fairly steeply and dived through some clouds. I followed and after coming out of clouds could not locate Green Section as there was another cloud layer below.
>
> I was then told by Blue Two that there were aircraft were diving on us from behind, I turned sharply and saw five Me 109s who immediately opened fire. Blue Section then broke formation and I found myself behind and above an Me 109, he half-rolled and dived steeply for the sea.
>
> I followed and in the dive was attacked by another Me 109 and was forced to break away slightly. I then saw the first Me 109 flying

towards France, just on top of the water. I chased him and when within range (3–400 yards) gave three long bursts. After the third burst he hit the sea and was skidding on top of the water, throwing up a lot of spray. At that moment I was again attacked by a second Me 109 and had to break-away in a steep turn and discovered that I had practically no ammunition left.

By now I was ¾ of the way across the Channel so I headed back to England. The second Me 109 followed and started to attack from above and behind, and opened fire well out of range. I did two steep turns and again headed for England and was not followed again.

Flight Sergeant Franklin:

At 2020 hrs ... I was Blue Two and sighted five Me 109s attacking us from the rear. I informed Blue One and the Section broke up and manoeuvred to attack enemy aircraft. I pursued one enemy aircraft nearly to Calais, fired a short burst and enemy aircraft crashed into sea.

Returning to the English coast I sighted several Me 109s protecting bombers. They were roughly in two vics of three and four respectively. I climbed above and attacked several times four to five aircraft. One machine was hit in the engine and pulled away towards France through clouds. I followed, firing at intervals and finally saw machine make a forced descent in sea about ten miles from the English coast. The enemy aircraft sank.

Returning towards land, I saw what I thought to be another 'Me 109' and attacked it but recognised it to be a Hurricane. I looked for markings and saw none. I examined aircraft closely and the only markings visible were a red 'dope' centre (not identification red) and a dark blue outer circle on wings. No marking on fuselage visible. I was doubtful and returned to base without firing.

The CO of 79 Squadron, Squadron Leader John Joslin, a Canadian, however, had been shot down by a Spitfire, baling out of his Hurricane at 20,000ft. His Section, comprising Pilot Officers Don 'Dimsy' Stones DFC and Tom Parker, had been attacked from above and behind, Stones and Parker turning into their attackers whom they recognised as Spitfires. Certain sources suggest that this was 65 Squadron's 'B' Flight, but the circumstances do not, in fact match: Saunders and Franklin: clearly state that they were attacked first by the enemy aircraft they engaged, not the other way around, as the 79 Squadron pilots describe. Whatever happened, Squadron Leader Joslin was killed, as a result of his parachute failing to open.

As the battle over the convoy continued, the pilots of 65 Squadron's Blue Section returned safely to Hornchurch between 21.00 and 21.15 hrs.

Of Green Section, however, nothing was ever heard again. Flying Officer Proudman, Pilot Officer Brisbane and Sergeant Hayes simply disappeared, the Squadron diarist scribing their simple epitaph: 'It is tough luck losing three of our boys like this but such is war.'

But what had happened to Green Section?

On 19 July 1940, Squadron Leader Cooke, CO of 65 Squadron, reported on the action to the Station Commander at Hornchurch, concluding that on Blue Section's 'return they kept a look-out for them. R/T also failed to elicit any reply. Green Section were therefore not seen since the beginning of the engagement and no news is available in spite of considerable enquiries.' All three pilots were posted 'Missing'. Three days later, Station Commander reported to the Air Ministry that after Flying Officer Proudman had been ordered by Flight Lieutenant Saunders to lead the way for the close engagement of the raiders:

> In the ensuing fight no contact was made with Green Section ... It appears probably that the Section was surprised in or below clouds and engaged by superior numbers of the enemy. Flying Officer Proudman had considerable experience and was a very excellent fighter pilot. The loss of this officer and the other two pilots with him is deeply regretted.

On 2 January 1941, the Air Ministry, in anticipation of officially presuming the death of the three pilots, wrote to their next-of-kin, enquiring as to whether they had received any news. Mr Hayes, who had regularly communicated with the Red Cross in case information was received that his son Patrick was a prisoner, replied in the negative. Death officially presumed for legal purposes was one thing, though – the emotional lack of closure for families of the missing quite another.

In fact, as late as 23 October 1945, after the war in Europe was over, Flying Officer George Proudman's uncle, the Reverend A.J. Proudman of St Mary's, Evesham, Worcestershire, wrote to the Air Ministry requesting an investigation into his nephew's disappearance. The response, dated 17 November 1945, confirmed that the operational conditions involved coupled with the 'complete absence of news, can only point to the conclusion that the aircraft came down in the sea and that your nephew lost his life'.

German records are incomplete, but we can ascertain that the following *jagdfliegern* claimed Spitfires destroyed over the Channel that evening:

Leutnant Hermann Segatz	5/JG51	SW Dover
Leutnant Hermann Striebel	5/JG51	South of Hastings
Leutnant Herbert Huppertz	6/JG51	NW Dungeness
Oberfeldwebel Fritz Beek	6/JG51	East of Dungeness
Unteroffizier Eduard Hemmerling	6/JG51	NW Folkestone

It is highly likely that certain of these enemy pilots from what was, in fact, the only German fighter group in the Pas-de-Calais at this time, surprised and shot down Green Section, the pilots of which crashed into the Channel. All three are remembered on the Air Forces' Memorial on Cooper's Hill, Runnymede in Surrey, dedicated to more than 20,000 airmen and women of the Commonwealth air forces lost on operations flying from bases in the United Kingdom and North and Western Europe, and who have no known grave.

On 7 July 1940, two more 2 Group Blenheims fell to Me 109s while on sorties to attack the now usual airfields and barges. Coastal Command attacked enemy shipping off Terschelling, Obrestad and Karmoy, and Skuas of 801 Squadron FAA attacked oil installations at Bergen, although no damage was caused. That night, Bomber Command sent fifty-four aircraft to various targets, and sowed more mines, losing a 61 Squadron Hampden to flak.

Yet again, the fighting began on 8 July 1940 with the interception of a German reconnaissance bomber, this one up from Villacoublay to photograph the airfield and aircraft factories at Filton, Bristol. Spitfires of 92 Squadron caught it at 09.20 hrs.

Flight Lieutenant Robert Stanford Tuck:

> Blue Section was ordered to patrol Filton at 20,000ft from Hullavington. After patrolling Filton for approximately fifteen minutes at a given height, received order to vector 220°. After having been on this vector for three minutes, I sighted six miles on my port beam and 10,000ft below one twin-engine aircraft heading north-west, i.e. towards Bristol. On turning and diving towards aircraft it put down its nose and dived very steeply towards the nearest cloud, which was straight ahead on its course.
>
> We intercepted it in range approximately three to four miles before it went into cloud, by which time we had identified it as a Do 17. We all delivered one attack before it disappeared into the cloud. I estimated E/A speed at 370 mph. I followed him straight into this cloud and overtook him.
>
> In the cloud I was very close on his tail. It was then imminent that I should collide with it, so I broke away. I pulled directly upwards and came out on top of the cloud. I then went straight ahead on the course I estimated the bomber to be taking and saw it come out the other side of the cloud below and slightly behind me. I turned down towards him and delivered a quarter attack ahead of the beam at close range.
>
> By this time smoke was pouring from its starboard engine and oil was strewn across the top of the starboard wing and right down the starboard fuselage. After this attack it did a gentle right-hand turn into the next cloud. I went straight ahead above the cloud and waited

for him to come out the other side. He came out where I estimated
he would and I was in an ideal position to carry out a head-on attack,
which I did.

I opened fire at about 800 yards range and held my fire to the last
minute, when I broke away directly over him and quickly turned.
He then did a right-hand turn into another cloud and I lost sight of
him and was unable to make contact again. The place at which I lost
contact I estimate to be seven miles NNE of Filton.

The bomber was claimed as destroyed and jointly accredited to all three pilots of Blue Section, the others being Pilot Officer Bob Holland and Sergeant 'Titch' Havercroft. The Do 17, however, was only damaged, and made it home.

A little later, at 11.00 hrs, Blue Section of 74 Squadron, comprising Flight Lieutenant Measures, Pilot Officer Dowding and Sergeant Skinner, was scrambled from Manston to patrol base at 'Angels 5':

One He 111 was sighted. Flight Lieutenant Measures attacked first,
inflicting serious damage. Pilot Officer Dowding arrived and carried
on the attack, silencing the rear-gunner. Sergeant Skinner closed the
combat and observed enemy aircraft dive into the sea, in flames.

This combat reportedly occurred immediately South of Manston, over Pegwell Bay.

Certain accounts state that this He 111, apparently of *Stab*/KG1, was also attacked by a sole Hurricane of Squadron Leader Peter Townsend's 85 Squadron, based at Martlesham Heath in Essex. This was flown by one of the very early, exceptional, aces, namely the 27-year-old Yorkshireman, Sergeant Geoffrey 'Sammy' Allard – a Halton apprentice who was able to become a fighter pilot as the result of the 1936 Expansion Plan and who had already done very well during the Fall of France. Allard's combat, however, took place earlier, at 10.23 hrs and much further North, at 8,000ft ten miles south-east of Felixstowe; Allard reported that:

I took-off from Martlesham at 1008 hrs to patrol aerodrome West of
clouds. At 1015 hrs ordered back to vector 200°. After two minutes
I approached doubtful aircraft heading East. In closing the attack
the rear-gunner of E/A opened fire. I positioned myself to attack and
dropped from 8,000 to 7,000ft. I delivered a line astern attack and
gave two bursts of three seconds, following the E/A down through
cloud to 3,000ft. At this height I met the E/A in a diving position.
As I came through the clouds a few seconds later, I noticed a line
of oil on the surface of the water but there was no sign of the E/A.
I returned to Martlesham at 1047 hrs.

Clearly, then, Allard was back on the ground when 74 Squadron's Blue Section engaged their He 111. Allard was credited with this He 111 destroyed, which, according to the 85 Squadron ORB, 'went into a steep dive and crashed into the sea six miles south-east of Felixstowe', i.e. conclusive. This brought the number of enemy aircraft shot down by Flight Sergeant Allard and confirmed to eleven.' This He 111, though, appears to have been confirmed on the basis of little evidence – who, for example, actually saw it crash? Not Allard himself. Even so, it could not have been the same aircraft intercepted by 74 Squadron.

According to German records, a He 111 of *Stab*/KG1 ditched off Boulogne, the crew of which were drowned – but as so often happens, this only further confuses the issue, given that 74 Squadron's pilots clearly saw their victim crash into Pegwell Bay, and Allard believed, having seen nothing more than oil on the water, that his had gone in off Felixstowe – neither of which locations, of course, are anywhere near Boulogne. Could it be, then, that the oil witnessed by Allard was nothing whatsoever to do with a crashed aircraft, and 'his' He 111, therefore, went on to ditch off Boulogne?

Next blood, nonetheless, went to Catterick's 41 Squadron, as reported by Flight Lieutenant Tony Lovell, the action occurring at 11.32 hrs:

> I was leading Blue Section ... at 1130 hrs I sighted a Ju 88 seven miles NE of Scarborough at 18,000ft. When I was certain of the black crosses on the fuselage, I ordered No 1 Attack. I carried out this attack from slightly below but found slipstream very upsetting, so attacked from slightly above. After my second burst he dropped all his bombs at once. He was firing cannon from the top rear turret. After my fourth burst I saw large fragments come from the fuselage and tail, and the cannon stopped. He then did a stall turn and started gliding towards land. Having finished all my ammunition I broke away to the right. I saw three Hurricanes carry out one quarter attack each without any further ill effect on the bomber. I followed the bomber down and did a quick dive past him to get the lettering on the fuselage, all I could see was a large yellow 'A', on the cockpit side of the black crosses.

The Hurricanes were those of 249 Squadron's Green Section, based at Church Fenton. The three Hurricane pilots, Flying Officer D.G. Parnell, Pilot Officer H.J.S. Beazley and Sergeant A.D.W. Main, shared the kill with the two Spitfire pilots of 41 Squadron's Blue Section, namely Flight Lieutenant Lovel and Sergeant W.J. Allison. There was certainly no mistaking the outcome: this 9/KG4 Ju 88A-1, 5J+AT, which had been intercepted on its return flight from Sunderland, crashed in flames at Hornsea, Yorkshire, at 11.42 hrs. Killed aboard the aircraft was the *Staffelkapitän, Hauptmann* K. Rohloff, although the other three members of the crew baled out and were captured.

'EVENTS ARE MUCH LIVELIER'

After the morning reconnaissance incursions, the afternoon saw an attack on a convoy off Dover. At 13.45 hrs, Pilot Officer William Warner led Blue Section of 610 Squadron up from Biggin Hill. Flying alongside him were Pilot Officer Arthur Raven and Sergeant Peter Else:

> Attacked nine Do 215s, ten miles out to sea. No 2 silenced the rear gunner of one of the enemy aircraft. No 3 saw a Spitfire on fire in the sea, six miles off Dover. This was probably No 2 of Section, Pilot Officer Raven, who failed to return. The pilot was seen to leave the aircraft and swim.

Sadly, Pilot Officer Arthur Lionel Boultbee Raven was never seen again.

At 14.56 hrs, Red and Green Sections of 610 Squadron were scrambled to assist the convoy, which was now five miles South of Hythe. Red 2, Pilot Officer Joe Pegge reporting that the Spitfires,

> contacted enemy bombers, Do 215s, about seven, which were attacking a convoy off Dungeness. Red Section at 5,000ft prepared to attack three enemy bombers in vic formation. They broke up and we split up. I attacked three Do 215s in succession. The first two I gave two two second bursts and the last one a three second burst. The last one had smoke coming from the starboard engine from a previous attack. When it entered a cloud I broke away and saw three Me 109s after a Spitfire, slightly above me. One of the Me 109s went into a cloud and I went after the second 109. From a range of about 100–150 yards I gave it a three second burst and it dived towards the sea with black smoke coming from it. When I last saw it, it was over the vertical. I was then attacked from behind so climbed to the right into a cloud.

The Me 109 was credited as destroyed, having been confirmed by Sergeant Norman Ramsay, also of 610 Squadron. All 610 Squadron aircraft had returned safely to base at 16.39 hrs.

At 15.00 hrs Yellow Section of 32 Squadron scrambled from Hawkinge and hastened towards the convoy, West of Dungeness. The three Hurricane pilots, Pilot Officers Grice, Gillman and Smythe climbed rapidly to 3,000ft before Gillman was forced to go home owing to oil trouble. Smythe and Grice pressed on, attacking 'three He 112s' (ORB, *sic*), which were actually Me 109s of II/JG51. At 15.50 hrs, Grice claimed a German fighter destroyed, but unconfirmed, but Smythe was shot-up, a bullet furrowing his leather flying helmet. Lucky to survive the experience, the Hurricane pilot landed his damaged machine back at Hawkinge.

At 15.15 hrs, nine Hurricanes of 79 Squadron scrambled from Biggin Hill 'to patrol Dover area, several enemy aircraft in the vicinity'. There were indeed: Me 109s on a *Freiehunt* (fighter sweep), which bounced the hapless Hurricanes:

> Pilot Officer J. Wood and Flying Officer E.W. Mitchell were missing after the patrol. Pilot Officer Wood was shot down in flames over the Channel; he baled out and was picked up by a Naval patrol boat but had died of burns. Flying Officer Mitchell crashed at Temple Ewell, in flames, the aircraft burnt for an hour or more after crashing and it was not possible to identify the body. Identification was made by checking the gun numbers.

Next on the scene were nine Spitfires of 65 Squadron, scrambled, from Hornchurch, at 15.29 hrs and vectored towards the convoy: 'Several enemy aircraft were observed in pairs and threes, and the Squadron broke up into sections line astern' (ORB).

Flight Sergeant William Franklin:

> We saw several enemy aircraft, which had already been engaged as they were in no formation. I saw a bomb burst near Dover and proceeded to investigate. While circling around I noticed below me an Me 109 stalking Blue 1. I attacked, and after a three second burst beginning with deflection and ending dead astern, I saw the flaps out and one leg of undercarriage come down. Then there was an explosion behind the cockpit and bursting into flames. The E/A crashed into the sea about eight miles off Dover.

Squadron Leader Henry Sawyer, attached to 65 Squadron as supernumerary, to gain current operational experience before succeeding Squadron Leader Desmond Cooke in command, was attacked by a *schwarm* of Me 109s, one of which he hit before making good his escape. Squadron Leader Cooke, however, led his Section into cloud but upon emerging, the CO 'was nowhere to be seen; attempts were made to contact him over the R/T but he was never seen or heard of again'. No.65 Squadron's popular CO had been shot down by *Oberleutnant* Josef Fözö of 4/JG51; the 33-year-old's name is also included on the Runnymede Memorial. As the 65 Squadron diarist noted: 'Another nice effort by Flight Sergeant Franklin but it is certainly shaky losing the CO in this way.'

At 16.00 hrs, Sergeant E.A. 'Boy' Mould (Red 1) and Pilot Officer Peter Stevenson (Red 2) of 74 Squadron were patrolling Manston at 6,000ft when, as Red 2 reported:

> Four Me 109s were sighted at 5,000ft, approaching from the South, in line astern. Two enemy aircraft broke away and flew towards the

> East. I gave chase, followed Red Leader. Red Leader gave the E/A a short 30° deflection burst. The enemy aircraft then did a vertical stall down to the right, and as it dived down I flew onto its tail as I saw Red Leader was unable to do so.
>
> I followed the E/A down to ground level from 5,000ft to 50ft. I fired at it on the way down. I noticed the enemy aircraft firing his guns ion the dive and also when we flew along a road. I gave several long bursts and hit both the radiators in the first burst. The E/A flew very low over Folkestone, then turned inland. In my longest burst of eight seconds I punctured his oil tank underneath the fuselage. The E/A was enveloped with black oil smoke. I followed the E/A for five minutes, low flying the whole time at full speed.
>
> I broke away when I saw a machine flying behind me. When I had broken away I saw it was a Hurricane.

After his first attack, Mould had blacked out. Coming to, he saw a 109 at low-level, which he pursued. This was the same aircraft he had first fired at, also being attacked by Red 2. After the breath-taking low-level and high-speed chase, the German pilot, *Leutnant* Johann Böhm of 4/JG51 forced-landed on Bladbean Hill, Elham. Sergeant Mould orbited overhead until satisfied that the German had been made a prisoner of war.

Much further to the west, Blue Section of St Eval's 234 Squadron's 'B' Flight (Flight Lieutenant Pat Hughes, Flying Officer Keith Lawrence and Sergeant George Bailey) scored the unit's first confirmed kill at 18.15 hrs; the three Spitfire pilots collectively reported that:

> Blue Section was on convoy patrol, with Blue 1 patrolling above a cloud layer with Blue 2 and 3 guarding the convoy under 7/10ths cloud at 1,000ft. E/A first seen by Blue 2 diving steeply on an easterly course at 4,000ft and he turned immediately towards convoy to intercept it. Blue 3 sighted E/A at this time. E/A on sighting our fighters climbed steeply through cloud layer where Blue 1 sighted it.
>
> Blue 2 carried out an attack from dead-astern, opening fire at 300 yards and closing to fifty yards, firing all his ammunition and breaking away to port. Blue 1 attacked the E/A which climbed into cloud. Blue 1 followed and fired all his ammunition, using slight deflection as E/A was turning to port slightly, in the cloud.
>
> On emerging from the cloud, Blue 1 broke away to port and downwards. Blue 3 immediately attacked from dead astern. The E/A gradually lost height in a slow left-hand turn, attempted to climb but eventually landed on the water. It floated for about twenty minutes and then sank, leaving three men on the surface. The estimated speed of the E/A during the attacks was about 200 mph. The rear top gunner

continued to fire until the aircraft settled on the water, when a small amount of flames were seen issuing from it.

No slipstream effect was encountered and the evasive tactics carried out were climbing and diving and slight turns to either side. There appeared to be two guns firing on top of the fuselage and one underneath, both firing tracer bullets, which left the muzzle with a green flash. Camouflage was dark green on top, light blue underneath, with usual national markings.

The number of rounds fired was:

Blue 1. F/Lt Hughes. 2,492, one cross-feed.
Blue 2. P/O Lawrence. 2,395, one cross-feed.
Blue 3. Sgt Bailey. 1,320, no stoppages.

The sighting used by all three pilots was a range of 150 yards ... the apparent cause of destruction was engine failure as the E/A appeared under control until hitting the water. It is thought that considering the number of rounds fired at such short-range, this aircraft was heavily armoured.

The three pilots of 234 Squadron equally shared destruction of this LG1 Ju 88, the crew of which were not rescued from the sea. Interestingly, it is worthy of note that Flight Lieutenant Hughes was an Australian, Pilot Officer Lawrence a New Zealander, and Sergeant Bailey British – indicating the increasingly multi-national force the RAF had become.

That evening, returning to the action over Kent, Me 109s remained active over Dover into the evening. At 19.30 hrs, three sections of 54 Squadron's Spitfires took-off from Rochford, and clashed with I/LG2 between Deal and Dover. Flight Lieutenant Basil 'Wonky' Way was leading the patrol, which had been ordered to Dover at just 3,000ft; needless to say, the Me 109s were much higher:

I was informed by R/T that there were three Me 109s at 12,000ft in the vicinity. I was at 5,000ft and proceeded to climb. I saw two aircraft behind Green Section, which was above and in front of my Section. I warned Green Section that they might be enemy aircraft and former turned towards the cloud. I continued to climb and the unidentified aircraft began to execute climbing spiral turns. I got right behind them (identifying them as Me 109s – black crosses and general appearances).

They were in a 'vic' formation and I attacked the rear one, giving it a three second burst at 200 yards. I do not think E/A could have seen me until the moment of my attack. Glycol began to pour from its port radiator, together with a certain amount of black smoke.

I left this E/A and turned to attack the second one (I did not continue pursuit of the first as the second would probably have got on my tail).

The second E/A dived straight down and I managed to get a long burst in at 250 yards. E/A continued diving, skirting the edge of the cloud (9,000ft) over the coast; it came below the cloud, went up into the fringe of it again, came below and at about 5,000ft the pilot baled out. I judged his position to be about five miles inland NW of Deal. The parachute opened. There was no enemy rear fire.

The last Me 109 Way attacked crashed near Sandwich in Kent, the pilot, *Leutnant* Albert Striberny of 3/LG2, being captured. Way was credited with one Me 109 destroyed five miles north-west of Deal, shared with Pilot Officer Garton, and the other confirmed destroyed at Sandwich.

The final combat of the day, at 19.35 hrs, represented another success for 602 Squadron. Flight Lieutenant Sandy Johnstone was leading Green Section on patrol at 20,000ft and 'saw a He 111 going East and gave chase, caught up in thick cumulus but overshot E/A. Pilot Officer Paul Webb contacted and set port engine afire, last seen diving through cloud' (ORB).

The He 111 was claimed by Webb as 'damaged' – but was actually destroyed. This reconnaissance bomber, of 1(F)/120, crashed into the North Sea, killing the crew, the remains of all three of which later washed up on the enemy coastline.

That day, fifty-one 2 Group Blenheims were sent to attack various targets in the Netherlands, Belgium and France, although only twenty-four of these aircraft found and bombed their objectives owing to cloud cover. Three of these, in fact, made a low-level strafing and bombing attack on II/KG3's base at Laon, just as the Do 17s of 4/KG3 were taking off, two being damaged. By night, sixty-four Bomber Command 'heavies' attacked ports in northern Germany and airfields in the Netherlands, and laid more mines; one Whitley was lost. Again, though, German bombers were active over Britain, bombing starting on various targets at 00.47 hrs, continuing until 05.00 hrs – eight people were killed and forty-three injured.

On Tuesday 9 July 1940, Home Intelligence reported that:

> Morale continues to be high: there are indications that invasion is ceasing to be the terrifying and novel idea that it once was. In coastal areas evidences of preparation make the subject dominant in public and private conversation and there is keen anxiety below a calm surface.
>
> In other slightly less vulnerable areas military confidence has been transmitted to the civilian population and, as one observer remarked, 'everyone is so keyed up, I can't think what will happen if Hitler doesn't come after all'. There is still a good deal of questioning about the Government's evacuation plans, although people are

satisfied on certain points, and many people have now completed their private plans for 'crash' evacuation. On the whole there is more talk of invasion than of air raids, which everywhere have been taken calmly. There is considerable increase of public confidence in siren policy.

The threat of invasion brings strongly to the front popular demand for aggressive leadership.

While the air battles continued, the Home Front had found a means of hitting back: the 'Spitfire Fund'. In June 1940, a Jamaican newspaper, the *Gleaner*, cabled the MAP inquiring how much a bomber cost to build. Lord Beaverbrook decided upon the round figure of £20,000 – this sum soon being raised by *Gleaner* readers and a cheque donated accordingly. A week later *The Straits Times* of Singapore cabled £250,000 and the Gold Coast £100,000. According to Gordon Beckles, 'The affair assumed the proportion of an Empire round game played by people with a lot of money to spend. The people of England, groaning under heavy taxation, read the announcements with envious interest.'

Beaverbrook's letters of thanks to donors were prominently published in the press. Donations were not always large; children emptied their money-boxes, the elderly sent in their meagre pensions – all were acknowledged with thanks by Beaverbrook. By the beginning of July 1940, the newspapers were full of notices from Beaverbrook acknowledging donations.

A Canadian mining millionaire, Sir Harry Oakes, then inquired how much a Spitfire cost: £5,000 was the figure set. A Wolverhampton alderman, Mr Morris Christopher, gave a cheque for £50 to the Editor of the *Express and Star* newspaper, suggesting that the Black Country town should raise £5,000 for a Spitfire. The paper opened a 'Spitfire Fund' and rapidly achieved £6,000 – this clearly being, as Beckles wrote, 'an obvious challenge to the civic pride and patriotism of other cities'. By doing nothing other than embark upon a correspondence campaign, Beaverbrook had started what remains a significant lesson in the art of propaganda.

On 3 July 1940, the *Worcester Evening News and Times* reported its decision to present a 'Fighter Plane' to the government. In what was a leading front-page article, reference was made to an appeal published that day in the *Daily Express*, calling upon 'Worcester and Wallasey, Gloucester and Greenock, Wigan and Wimbledon', and all other towns with a population exceeding 50,000, to 'buy a "home-town" aeroplane to fight for Britain. An aeroplane built with your money, named after your town.'

The editor of the *Worcester Evening News and Times*, Mr Ivor Griffiths, subsequently cabled the *Daily Express* as follows: 'Have read your appeal to buy a home-town aeroplane. Worcester responds and determines to buy a fighter plane carrying the City's name and coat-of-arms. We are cooperating with the Mayor of the City in raising necessary cash to transmit to Lord Beaverbrook.' The article went on to appeal to 'firms and individuals' to send their donations to either the Mayor or the newspaper. A 'rapid telephonic enquiry among local leading firms and citizens' assured the editor that 'enthusiastic support would be given to this effort'.

Two days later, the front page trumpeted that the appeal had raised £2,400 on the first day alone, and that the decision to 'present a fighter plane' had been 'hailed with enthusiasm by people in the City'. From the outset tactics were clear: the names of donors were to be published alongside the amount of their gift. For example, Mr C.W.D. Perrins, 'one of the four surviving Freemen of the City', immediately gave £500, and the Worcester Royal Porcelain Company Ltd sent in £50. An anonymous donation of £500 was also reported, together with £250 from Kay and Company Ltd and various other large figures from prominent local firms. Interestingly, though, the front-page article that day proclaimed that 'What pleased us greatly was the way small subscriptions came pouring in and we appeal that they should continue, so as to make the gift a fully representative one.' The same day's back page published a letter from the Mayor of Wimbledon, acknowledging that Worcester was Wimbledon's 'competitor' but suggesting that the two exchanged fund-raising ideas. A full list of donations, ranging from £500 to pence was also published, numbering around 100 in total.

The technique of reporting established during the first three days of Worcester's appeal continued. On 6 July 1940, the front page not only provided details of major contributions by firms but highlighted that an 'Old Age Pensioner' had sent in 10 shillings, and a widow had donated her late husband's 'English lever watch'. The back page reported how the appeal's 'representatives' had 'called on club secretaries and hoteliers, inviting their cooperation'. 'Collecting Cards' were also distributed, the article reported, the intention being to raise £5,000 in ten days – that being 'half the time taken by Wolverhampton'. Subsequent editions over the next few days were of an identical format, the back page of 8 July mentioning 'the schoolboy who said "It'll be grand to think that I paid for part of the plane"', concluding that 'That's the spirit of the whole thing.' This patriotic fervour developed into a great effort which gave the public an indirect means of hitting back at Hitler's bombers. And on 9 July 1940, those bombers came back.

First light saw Britain shrouded in cloud and rain, the poor flying weather, restricting operations that morning, although the enemy's reconnaissance bombers continued prowling overhead. At 05.55 hrs, Hurricane pilots Flight Lieutenant Noel Hall, Pilot Officer Charles Frizzell and Sergeant Ron Forward were scrambled to intercept an 'X' Raid. Having climbed away from Northolt to the south-west, a Do 17 was sighted at 06.20 hrs over Newbury, as Sergeant Forward reported:

> Do 17 seen flying on a course approximately 240 when Blue 3 was at same height, 22,000ft, on course of 210. Markings clearly seen on fuselage, indistinguishable markings on tail fins, fuselage black cross, white edges. Normal enemy camouflage. Quarter attack from starboard and astern, very slightly above, range 400 yards, burst

of four seconds. E/A banked and dived to port in almost vertical dive. Deflection shot made when E/A in turn, twelve second burst 200–300 yards. One further short burst when E/A in dive. No effect noticed at any time. Hurricane on full throttle, could not hold the E/A in dive and E/A disappeared in cloud. All; ammunition expended. No return fire noticed. Cloud conditions too bad to attempt to return to base. Landed at Ford.

Although it was concluded that 'no confirmation that the E/A was hit', Forward's shooting could have been more effective than even he thought: although identified as a 'Do 17' this 'E/A' is believed to have been a Do 17 of 4/KG3 – which crashed in near Antwerp after being intercepted and damaged on its return flight from the Midlands.

The first clash between opposing fighters occurred between the Hurricanes of 43 Squadron, up from Tangmere, and Me 110s of *Luftflotte* 3's Alençon-based V(Z) LG1, as Squadron Leader George Lott reported:

Leading Red Section I was detailed to intercept six E/A near Selsey Bill at 1140 hrs and was later directed to St Catherine's Point. Flying above 10/10ths cloud in this direction I observed a total of twelve aircraft which came up through the clouds about eight to ten miles ahead in four sections of three and heading SSW. Giving a 'Tally Ho!' I gave chase at 6½lbs boost, climbing slightly.

When about twenty miles South of the Isle of Wight, the two leading formations, believed to be Ju 87s, dived down through clouds and the rear two sections of Me 110s went into line astern and turned about. They spread out and attacked head-on, and I turned into No 2 of the enemy who opened fire at about 800 yards. His fire did not appear to be well-aimed and I held my own fire until about 300 yards range. After a ½ second burst I received some hits in my aircraft and a piece of glass or Perspex entered my right eye.

Being uncertain of the extent of the injuries I had received, I called the other members of my formation by R/T and said that I had been hit and was leaving the fight. I dived for cloud and managed to remain in it long enough to set a northerly course and informed base that I had been hit and was doubtful if I could reach base. I climbed above the cloud and throttled well back as glycol was escaping from the engine and the temperature gauge had gone on strike.

I saw land through a gap in the cloud and thought I recognised Southampton Water. I asked base for a homing bearing. This I received and asked to be informed when I was over base. On being told I was three miles North of base I turned South and descended through cloud to about 800ft, just under the cloud-base and saw

Arundel. Set course for Tangmere but glycol fumes were increasing and engine was failing, so released my harness and prepared to abandon aircraft. The engine finally stopped about four miles short of base and as the windscreen was obscured and I had the use of only one eye, I decided to take to parachute.

I removed the side panel and abandoned ship at what must have been about 700ft and landed successfully, though with rather a bump, on my back in the middle of the road. A doctor on the spot took me into camp.

Squadron Leader Lott's wounds were such that he lost an eye. He was replaced as CO by Squadron Leader J.V.C. 'Tubby' Badger. Two of the Me 110s were claimed destroyed by the Hurricane pilots, which was accurate: one of the German fighters was missing and another crash-landed back at base minus the rear-gunner, who had baled out over the sea.

During the afternoon a cold front moved eastwards with South Wales, enjoying better weather earlier than southeast England, being targeted by nuisance raiders. A lone German bomber passed over Grangetown before turning to attack Cardiff Docks – one of the world's biggest coal ports. In this raid, the British steamer SS *San Felippe*, laden with timber, received a direct hit from a bomb in the hold – killing seven seamen, who were the city's first fatal casualties of the war.

Tim O'Brien, a burly docker, became hero of the hour when he braved the smoke-filled and damaged hold to drag an injured man out to safety, although the casualty, 61-year-old Jeremiah Savage, died of his wounds. Twice more O'Brien entered the inferno and emerged with injured men; his bravery was later recognised by the award of an industrial medal.

LAC P.D. Baxter was an airframe fitter at RAF Penrhos, also in South Wales, and recalled that afternoon:

> We were in a hut ... when an almighty bang rent the air. One of the hut walls parted company with the building. We had been thrown to the floor and thought that the boiler had exploded. Picking ourselves up and rushing outside, we saw a Dornier overhead with its machine-guns rattling away. We dived for cover. Practically the whole camp was running around by now, and it took some minutes for the panic to die down.
>
> It transpired that the Officers' Mess had suffered the worst of this attack and two officers had been killed [Flying Officer Brian Page and Pilot Officer Geoffrey Goldsmith-Jones, the latter a Canadian]. One wing of three blocks had been completely shattered by several bombs and room contents spread over a wide area. Two other bombs, which had fallen on different parts of the camp, had not exploded – could these have been delayed action types? One had hit

> the face of the Maintenance Hangar a glancing blow and travelled a considerable distance before coming to rest outside Station HQ (SHQ). It's trajectory was visible as skid-marks on the camp roads. Both bombs were safely defused and later mounted either side of the main entrance to SHQ as a grim reminder that Penrhos had entered the war.
>
> Considerable damage was caused by machine-gun bullets, including several lorries damaged by fire and two Henley aircraft destroyed. After this raid by a single aircraft we were dreading a repeat performance and ordered to sleep in air raid shelters.

Although such raids were not going to deal a telling blow on the British economy or defences, clearly, they were both disruptive and destructive.

As the weather cleared to the east, convoys once more came under fire – and the day would see the heaviest aerial fighting over the Channel so far.

At 12.45 hrs, the Dover Chain Home RDF Station reported heavy enemy activity behind the Pas-de-Calais. There was constant air traffic in the area, as German aircraft travelled to and fro for varying purposes, but this build-up was greater than anything seen previously. In anticipation of the weather clearing, but there still being sufficient cloud cover remaining to enable the Germans to approach unseen and attack the convoy currently in the Thames Estuary, Air Vice-Marshal Park brought six 11 Group squadrons to 'Available'. Various squadrons patrolled over the convoy and coast without incident. Then, at 14.20 hrs, Biggin Hill's 610 Squadron caught a Do 215 snooping over the Channel; Squadron Leader Andrew Smith:

> While leading 'A' Flight of 610 Squadron after a patrol from Dungeness to Dover and Cap Gris Nez we were directed to Hawkinge; when flying at 14,000ft a Do 215 was sighted above and to port, just below cloud.
>
> No 1 Attack was delivered at 16,000ft for about eight seconds. Smoke observed coming from starboard motor. No return fire from bomber on break-away. Second attack delivered at 2,000ft off Cap Gris Nez for three or four seconds, when E/A was flying right-wing low with starboard wing enveloped in black smoke and losing height rapidly. When breaking away saw some black objects pass my aircraft.
>
> Yellow 3 (Sergeant CA Parsons) did a final attack while E/A was diving for the ground over land, but after breaking away could not see him any more.

This aircraft was accredited as destroyed, shared between Smith and Parsons. It was, in fact, a Do 17 of StSt/KG76 which actually crash-landed back at base.

'EVENTS ARE MUCH LIVELIER'

At 15.05 hrs, Red and Yellow Sections of 79 Squadron took-off from Hawkinge; the first of the Hurricane pilots to engage was Pilot Officer William Millington, at 15.36 hrs:

> I was flying Red 2 of 'A' Flight and carrying out interception in company with Yellow Section at about 15,000ft over mid-Channel, SE of Dover. E/A were sighted some 7–8,000ft overhead, heading for Dover, making full use of moderate cloud. We lost Yellow Section and Red 3 among cloud as we were climbing to intercept E/A. Red 1 and I orbited, maintaining height at approximately 20,000ft. A dogfight developed between Hurricanes and Me 109s and Red 1 and I joined in at full-speed.
>
> After milling about for a short time I climbed up behind two Me 109s who ventured from the base of thick cloud at about 19,000ft, in formation. I carried out an astern attack on the rear E/A, opening fire at 300 yards and holding my burst for about three seconds. Pieces flew from E/A and my tracer converged on his cockpit. E/A with thick black smoke pouring from it headed for the sea, diving steeply and crashed a few miles from the French coast. In the meantime the other E/A had gone down in a diving turn and another Hurricane, which eventually proved to be Yellow 1, and myself, chased him towards the French coast with black smoke pouring from it and appeared to be losing height rapidly.
>
> As I was due to change over onto reserve tank I broke away some miles from the French coast and returned to base. Hurricane with Rotol airscrew and at full throttle with emergency boost control pulled appeared to be rapidly overtaking the Me 109.

Pilot Officer 'Dimsy' Stones of 79 Squadron reported his combat as having occurred at 15.40 hrs, also East of Dover:

> I was leading 'A' Flight as Yellow 1 in that Section and ordered to patrol base at 15,000ft, subsequently reduced to 10,000ft. I was then vectored on 135° and told to orbit in mid-Channel. I then observed eight enemy aircraft above us, heading for Dover. I called up my Section and told them I was climbing to intercept E/A. They turned slightly to the West and a dogfight ensued. Two Me 109s did a stern attack on me as soon as my Section broke up and it was not until after about ten minutes milling around that I was able to single one out. I got on his tail and he dived towards the French coast and just before crossing the coast decided to break away. I observed some MTBs, presumably enemy, patrolling the French coast East of Calais, about two miles out, heading East. No AA fire was experienced from these

craft. Returned to base at '0'ft and landed at 1604 hrs. R/T was very good. Intercepted R/T message from enemy leader in which word 'Angels' was used.

Millington's Me 109 was confirmed as destroyed, but not Stones's. Midshipman Maurice Birrell, on loan from the FAA, claimed a 109 damaged in the skirmish. Later that day, 79 Squadron received orders to withdraw to Turnhouse the following morning, having served in the front line of Britain's air defence since March 1937.

The Spitfires of 65 Squadron had been at readiness throughout the day on 9 July 1940, and would soon meet a large enemy raid:

At 1535 hrs, three sections were ordered from Manston to intercept raiders off the North Foreland. One aircraft failed to start and another returned to base almost immediately with engine trouble. The remaining seven aircraft climbed to 10,000ft and almost at once sighted about seventy E/A heading for the Thames Estuary. The E/A were in vics of five, seven and nine, stepped up from 8,000 to 14,000ft, three vics abreast in line astern. There was a layer of bombers well protected above and at the sides by Me 109s and Me 110s.

Flight Lieutenant Saunders, who was leading, climbed to 18,000ft and finding himself slightly above five Me 109s, dived down onto one of them and opened fire with full deflection at 400 yards. He then came into position dead astern and fired a short burst, causing the E/A to pull up steeply and do a half-roll. Flight Lieutenant Sanders then gave a final burst at 100 yards when the enemy aircraft fell away and something appeared to break off the tail. Blue 2, Flying Officer Grant, attacked an E/A from above and behind, firing a three second burst when white smoke was observed pouring from the enemy.

The E/A dived away but Blue 2 was unable to follow as there were at least two other E/A on his tail., and was therefore only able to claim a probable. Red 1, Flying Officer Walker, on sighting a number of E/A over Margate ordered his Section into line astern and manoeuvred himself behind a section of E/A. He dived down onto a Me 110, firing a short burst from astern and below, opening at 200 yards, the E/A attempting evasive tactics, went into a turning dive with smoke and flames pouring from the fuselage. A few seconds later, while evading attacks of two other Me 109s, he saw the enemy aircraft which he had first attacked falling towards the sea, just above cloud at 3,000ft.

While all this was happening, Red 2, Flight Sergeant Phillips, had also joined in the attack, firing short bursts at several aircraft in turn. Red 2 finally fired a five second burst at a Me 109 and saw it go into a vertical dive about five miles NE of Ramsgate, he followed and fired two further bursts and saw the E/A fall out of control. An Me 109 was subsequently found to have crashed near where the combat took place. From this operation all our aircraft returned safely ... Quite a good day's work all-round, and no casualties, events are much livelier. [ORB]

As ever, the Me 109s engaged were those of II/JG51, but only *Leutnant* Hermann Striebel of 5/JG51 was lost.

The Hurricanes of 151 Squadron's 'A' Flight were up from North Weald and being led by the Station Commander himself, that indomitable Irishman, Wing Commander Victor Beamish. Pilot Officer Jack Hamar:

At 1430 hrs, 'A' Flight of 151 Squadron was ordered to patrol a large convoy about five miles off the coast, just north of the Thames Estuary. I was flying as Red 2 in the formation. At 1540 hrs a large number of E/A in several waves were sighted flying NW at about 10,000ft. It was impossible to attack the first wave, consisting of He 111 bombers, because of the large number of escorting fighters, which were very near us.

Red 1, therefore, ordered line astern and attacked the nearest formation of fighters, which consisted of twelve Me 110s. No 1 Fighter Attack was used, and after Red 1 had broken away and attacked the rear Me 110, I closed to 150 yards and gave it a five second burst. I saw my bullets tearing into the fuselage and wings of the E/A, which staggered badly. I then had to break away quickly as the air seemed full of enemy aircraft.

I then saw bombs exploding near the convoy which I approached at full throttle. I chased a section of three E/As away from northern end of the convoy but failed to get into a position to open fire. I then continued to patrol the convoy for about fifteen minutes as the air had by this time cleared of E/A. No ships in the convoy had been hit, so I returned to base as my fuel was running low.

Red 1 was Wing Commander Beamish:

On receipt of a warning by R/T we saw what I estimate at sixty German aircraft, consisting of about twenty-one bombers escorted by about forty fighters, Me 110s and Me 109s. We immediately attacked the squadron of Me 110s, who got into a circle, line astern, to attack us. I got long bursts into a Me 110 and saw my shots going into it, but owing to the number of E/A I could not wait to see results. We formed into line astern and made a number of attacks. Immediately,

I returned to the convoy as I had little ammunition left. A few bombs were dropped but hit nothing, and no enemy bombers came near me while remaining over the convoy until my fuel was practically exhausted.

This was the biggest raid so far; 151 Squadron ORB:

> It is estimated that almost 100 E/A were engaged, their objective being one of our convoys. During the fight Flying Officer Milne shot down a Me 109 and Midshipman Wightman did the same, in each case seeing the enemy fall into the sea. Another enemy fighter – Me 110 – was seen to go down, but as Wing Commander Beamish, Flying Officer Forster and Pilot Officer Hamar each attacked and badly damaged one of these, it is impossible to say which of them is to be credited with it. Flight Lieutenant Ironside was wounded in the face when his cockpit cover was hit by a bullet and he is now in St Margaret's Hospital, Epping. Midshipman Wightman was shot down himself after accounting for his Me 109 and after baling out he was picked up by a trawler and taken to Sheerness. Later in the evening he reported back here.

This was a bold thrust by the enemy. The circle Wing Commander Beamish described the Me 110s was known as the *Abwehrkreis*, a defensive circle, later termed the more aggressive *Angriffskreis*, or 'attack circle'. The Me 110s concerned were those of Major Johann Schalk's III/ZG26, based at Barley in *Luftflotte* 2, this being the unit's first bomber escort mission over *Der Kanal*, losing one aircraft of 8/ZG26 in the combat arising.

Shipping was not the only target this day. That afternoon two He 111s of I/KG53 bombed Norwich with devastating results. Twenty-seven civilians were killed – the first of 350 killed by bombing in Norwich throughout the war – the youngest of whom was 16-year-old Fred Wright, a labourer at Boulton-Paul's Riverside Works; the oldest was Kate Lovett, a 60-year-old housewife.

Bombs also cascaded down upon Salhouse Road, the Barnard Works, Carrow Hill Works and Thorpe railway station. There was no air raid warning, accounting for the high death toll. 17 Squadron, at Debden in Essex, shot down a He 111 at 16.55 hrs, approximately fifty miles out to sea off Orfordness, but this was not a Norwich raider; Pilot Officer Geoffrey Bennett (Red 3):

> While on patrol with Red Section a He 111 was sighted at 1655 hrs by Red 2 (Sergeant Griffiths) at 6,000ft. We were at 8,000ft and we immediately turned towards it. The E/A, which was proceeding due West, immediately turned and jettisoned its bombs and made off East, at sea level. After a chase of approximately fifteen minutes

'EVENTS ARE MUCH LIVELIER'

> Red 1 (Pilot Officer Manger) opened fire, followed by Red 2 and then myself in a No 1 Attack. Desultory fire was observed from the E/A but no hits were sustained. The top rear gun alone was brought to bear on us. When I opened fire the E/A was already throwing out clouds of smoke and slowing down. My shots went into its starboard engine. The weather was good with high cloud about 6/10ths, and we attacked out of sun.

The three pilots shared destruction of the He 111, a machine of 3/KG3, the crew of which were killed. At the time, Debden was in 12 Group (later being absorbed by 11), the Group Commander, Air Vice-Marshal Leigh-Mallory sending 17 Squadron a congratulatory signal: 'Well done 17 Red'.

There was also action late that afternoon off the Scottish coast for Red Section of 602 Squadron. At 17.50 hrs, Flight Lieutenant Dunlop Urie, up from Drem in East Lothian, shot down a Ju 88 ten miles east of Fifeness, and Flying Officer Donald Jack damaged another. But it was southern England that was already facing the brunt of the *Luftwaffe*'s assault – and the day's fighting was far from over.

At this time, owing to the fighting over the sea, various 11 Group fighter squadrons were going forward at first light to operate from coastal airfields, such as Manston and Hawkinge. No.54 Squadron, for example, was based at the Hornchurch sector station and went forward to patrol from Manston and Rochford (Southend), thereby increasing range while decreasing interception times.

Flight Lieutenant Al Deere, of 54 Squadron's 'B' Flight, recalled that:

> For the time being, the Squadron continued to operate in flight or section strength, one section always being in position over a convoy when it was within the Hornchurch area of responsibility while the other section was at stand-by or readiness on the ground as a reinforcement, the actual state depending on the weather conditions prevailing at the time. If an important convoy was in the area the patrol was usually increased to a flight and the remaining aircraft on the ground brought to stand-by.

On Deere's fourth patrol of 9 July 1940, he 'ran into trouble while leading my flight to investigate what was reported as unidentified activity five miles east of deal'. The 'trouble' was in the form of another red-cross-emblazoned He 59 rescue seaplane, searching for the missing *Leutnant* Striebel of 5/JG51, who had earlier fallen victim to 65 Squadron's Spitfires.

Deere, Red 1, espied the He 59, which had a civilian registration (D-ASUO), and was in a quandary as to how to proceed; Pilot Officer Johnny Allen, Yellow 1, then reported nine Me 109s above and behind the seaplane, escorting it. That made up Deere's mind: the seaplane was enemy and therefore fair game. Ordering Yellow Section to deal with the He 59, Deere led Red Section to attack the 109s –

which, alerted, split into two formations, one climbing steeply and turning tightly to the right, the other similarly left. According to Deere:

> The Hun leader had timed his break perfectly and he had certainly put us at a disadvantage by splitting his force. There was only one thing to do: break formation and have a go, each pilot for himself ... we were outnumbered ... and more likely to confuse the Hun in this way, thus diverting attention from Jonny who had just ordered his Section to attack the seaplane.

What followed was straight out of the *Boy's Own* paper, as Deere wrote:

> Fastening to the tail of a yellow-nosed Me 109 I fought to bring my guns to bear as the range rapidly decreased, and when the wingspan of the enemy aircraft fitted snugly into the range scale bars of my reflector sight, I pressed the firing button. There was an immediate response from my eight Brownings which, to the accompaniment of slight buffeting from my aircraft, spat a stream of lethal lead target-wards.
>
> 'Got you,' I muttered to myself as the small dancing yellow flames of exploding De Wilde bullets spattered along the Me 109's fuselage. My exultation was short-lived: before I could fire another burst two Me 109s wheeled in behind me. I broke hard into the attack, pulling my Spitfire into a climbing, spiralling turn as I did so, a manoeuvre I had discovered in previous combats with 109s to be particularly effective. And it was no less effective now: the 109s literally fell out of the sky as they stalled in an attempt to follow me.
>
> I soon found another target. About 300 yards directly ahead of me and at the same level, a 109 was just completing a turn before re-entering the fray. He saw me almost immediately and rolled out of his turn towards me so that a head-on attack became inevitable. Using both hands on the control column to steady the aircraft and thus keep my aim steady, I peered through the reflector sight at the rapidly closing enemy aircraft. We opened fire together and immediately a hail of lead thudded into my Spitfire. One moment the 109 was a clearly defined shape, its wingspan nicely enclosed within the circle of my reflector sight, and the next it was on top of me, a terrifying blur which blotted out the sky ahead. Then we hit.
>
> The force of the impact pitched me violently forward on to my cockpit harness, the straps of which bit viciously into my shoulders. At the same moment, the control column was snatched abruptly from my gripping fingers by a momentary but powerful, reversal of elevator load. In a flash it was over. There was clear sky ahead of me and I was still alive'.

'EVENTS ARE MUCH LIVELIER'

Alive Deere was, having collided with *Oberfeldwebel* Johann Illner (4/JG51), who was also miraculously unhurt – but the Spitfire pilot was still far from safe:

> Smoke and flame were pouring from the engine which began to vibrate, slowly at first but with increasing momentum causing the now regained control column to jump back and forth in my hand. Hastily I closed the throttle and reached forward to flick off the ignition switches but before I could do so the engine seized and the airscrew stopped abruptly. I saw with amazement that the blades had been bent almost double with the impact of the collision; the 109 must have been just that fraction above me as we hit.
>
> With smoke now pouring into the cockpit I reached blindly forward for the hood release toggle and tugged at it violently. There was no welcoming and expected rush of air indicating that the hood had been jettisoned. Repeatedly I pulled at the toggle but there was no response. In desperation I turned to the normal release catch and exerting my full strength endeavoured to slide back the hood. It refused to budge; I was trapped. There was only one thing to do: try to keep the aircraft under control and head for the nearby coast. The speed had by now dropped off considerably, and with full backward pressure on the stick I was just able to keep a reasonable gliding attitude. If only I could be lucky enough to hit in open country where there was a small chance I might get away with it.
>
> Frantically I peered through the smoke and flame enveloping the engine, seeking with streaming eyes for what lay ahead. There could be no question of turning. I had no idea what damage had been done to the fuselage and tail of my aircraft, although the mainplane appeared undamaged, and I daren't risk even a small turn at low level, even if I could have seen to turn.
>
> Through a miasmatic cloud of flame and smoke the ground suddenly appeared ahead of me. The next moment a post flashed by my wingtip and then the aircraft struck the ground and ricocheted into the air again, finally returning to earth with a jarring impact, and once again I was jerked forward onto my harness. Fortunately the straps held fast and continued to do so as the aircraft ploughed its way through a succession of splintering posts before finally coming to a halt on the edge of a cornfield. Half blinded by smoke and frantic with fear I tore at my harness release pin. And then with my bare hands wielding the strength of desperation, I battered at the Perspex hood which entombed me. With a splintering crash it finally cracked open, thus enabling me to scramble from the cockpit to the safety of the surrounding field.

The Kiwi Flight Lieutenant, already an ace decorated with the DFC, was lucky, although as he later recalled: 'my hands were cut and bleeding; my eyebrows were singed; both knees were badly bruised; and blood trickled into my mouth from a slightly cut lip. But I was alive!' This lucky escape would be one of many for Al Deere, who, appropriately entitled his wartime memoir *Nine Lives*.

In the action with 4/JG51, which had taken place over the sea, three miles South of Deal, Deere was credited with a 109 confirmed destroyed and one unconfirmed, the same for Sergeant N.A. Lawrence. Apart from damage to Illner's machine during the collision with Deere, the enemy reported no losses, however – although two 54 Squadron pilots were killed in action: Pilot Officers Jack Garton and Tony Evershed; of the latter, who remains missing, Deere later remembered that, 'He was one of the brightest new boys. I had high hopes of him turning into a good section leader.'

Red Section had kept the 109s totally occupied, however, enabling Pilot Officer Allen and Yellow Section to force the He 59 to land on the Goodwin Sands at 19.30 hrs. The enemy ambulance aircraft was later towed ashore by the Walmer lifeboat and the crew captured. Intelligence gleaned from prisoners of war was, of course, essential, and British Intelligence was even provided an unlimited budget to listen-in on German prisoners' conversations through hidden microphones. *Luftwaffe* aircrew were first accommodated at Trent Park, a country house near Cockfosters in London, known as the 'Cockfosters Cage'.

The information arising gave a vital insight into various matters, including the enemy's mindset, psyche and morale, in addition to details of aircraft performance and opinions on the leadership and course of the war. The AAII(g) intelligence department evaluated shot-down German aircraft, that information also being fed into the system and overall picture. Indeed, the Air Intelligence (AI) branch of the Air Ministry was much more successful than the Germans in providing accurate and up-to-date appreciations of the *Luftwaffe* Order of Battle throughout the war.

This success was owed in no small part, we now know, to the 'boffins' working behind the scenes on top secret decoding at the now famous Bletchley Park. The encoded signals traffic of the *Luftwaffe* ENIGMA cipher machine was cracked, providing the British accurate information from 22 May 1940 onwards. This meant AI had up to the minute details of *Luftwaffe* strength, disposition and deployment, aircraft serviceability, losses, wastage and reserves available in all theatres, daily reports on operations and much else besides. This essential information, known as ULTRA, accurately informed AI, meaning that British strategy could be realistically planned. ULTRA had less impact on a daily tactical level, but was arguably informing this indirectly through the strategic planning.

Returning to the events of 9 July 1940, the final raid of daylight hours zeroed in on Portland again, which was attacked at 19.00 hrs by twenty-seven Ju 87s, escorted

'EVENTS ARE MUCH LIVELIER'

by Me 109s of 1/JG2 and Me 110s from 13/LG1. By this time, 609 Squadron had moved to Middle Wallop and was now operating out of Warmwell, just inland of Weymouth, on a daily basis; when the attack came in, Green Section was already on patrol, comprising Flying Officer Peter Drummond-Hay, with Pilot Officers David Crook and Michael Appleby.

Pilot Officer David Crook:

> At about 6.30 p.m. we were ordered to patrol Weymouth, and so Drummond, Michael and I took off. Drummond leading.
>
> We circled Weymouth for about three quarters of an hour, and saw nothing at all. Drummond was getting very fed up with this apparently unnecessary flying, and we circled round Warmwell and ask permission to land. We were told, however, to continue our patrol and turned out again over Weymouth at about 7,000ft. A moment later, looking out towards the left, I saw an aircraft dive into a layer of cloud about two miles away and then reappear. I immediately called up Drummond on the R/T, and told him and he swung us into line astern, and turned left towards the enemy.
>
> We had been told to expect two or three enemy aircraft, and a moment later I saw one or two more appear and recognised them as *Junkers* 87 dive bombers. I immediately turned on my reflector sights, put my gun button onto 'Fire', and settled down to enjoy a little slaughter of a few Ju 87s, as they are rather helpless machines.
>
> I was flying last on the line, and we were now travelling at very high speed, and rapidly approaching the enemy, when I happened to look round behind and above, and to my intense surprise and dismay, saw at least nine *Messerschmitt* 110s about 2,000ft above us. They were just starting to dive on us when I saw them, and as they were diving, they were overtaking us very rapidly.
>
> This completely altered the situation. We were now hopelessly outnumbered, and in a very dangerous position and altogether I began to see that if we were not jolly quick, we should all be dead in a few seconds.
>
> I immediately called up Drummond and Michael and shouted desperately 'Look out behind, *Messerschmitt's* behind', all the time looking over my shoulder at the leading enemy fighter, who was now almost in a range.
>
> But though I kept shouting, both Drummond and Michael continued straight on at the bombers ahead, and they were now almost in a range and about to open fire.
>
> I've never felt so desperate or so helpless in my life, as when in spite of my warnings, these two flew steadily on, apparently quite

oblivious of the fact that they were going to be struck down from the rear in a few seconds.

At that moment, the leading *Messerschmitt* opened fire at me, and I saw his shells and tracer bullets going past me. I immediately did a very violent turn to the left and dived through a layer of cloud just below.

I emerged from the cloud going at very high speed – probably over 400 mph – and saw a Ju 87 just ahead of me. I opened fire (my first real shot of the war!) and he seemed to fly right through my tracer bullets, but when I turned around to follow him, he had disappeared.

I then climbed up into the cloud again and fired without result at an Me 110 above me. He turned away immediately and I lost him.

At that moment I saw dimly a machine moving in the cloud on my left and flying parallel to me.

I stalked him through the cloud and when he emerged into a patch of clear sky, I saw that it was a Ju 87. I was in an ideal position to attack, and opened fire and put the remainder of my ammunition – about 2,000 rounds – into him at very close range.

Pieces flew off the fuselage and cockpit covering, a thin stream of smoke appeared from the engine and a moment later he burst into flames and dived down vertically. Somewhat fascinated by the sight, I followed him down and saw him hit the sea with a great burst of white foam. He disappeared immediately, and apart from the patch of foam there was no sign that anything had happened. The crew made no attempt to get out and there is no doubt that they were killed by my first burst of fire.

Crook had shot down none other than the *Gruppenkommander* of I/StG77, *Hauptmann* Friedrich-Karl Freiherr von Dawigk and his gunner, *Feldwebel* Karl Götz, neither of whom were ever seen again. After the combat, Crook reflected:

I had often wondered what my feelings would be when killing somebody like this, and especially when seeing them go down in flames. I was rather surprised to reflect afterwards that my only feeling had been one of considerable elation – and a sort of bewildered surprise because it had all been so easy.

I turned back for the coast – we were about ten miles out to sea by this time – and started to call up Drummond and Michael on the R/T. But there was no response, and as far as Drummond was concerned, I was already calling to the void.

Crook was right; Flying Officer Drummond-Hay had been shot down, by either Me 109 pilots *Oberleutnant* Anton Mader or *Unteroffizier* Willi Reins, the 31-year-old Spitfire pilot crashing into the Channel, never to be seen again.

Crook continues:

> Moments later I saw another Spitfire flying home on a very erratic course, obviously keeping a very good look behind. I joined up with it and recognised Michael and together we bolted for the English Coast like a couple of startled rabbits.
>
> Everybody was very pleased when we got back and full of congratulations, as it was the first machine the squadron had definitely shot down since Dunkirk.
>
> Michael had left his R/T in the 'Transmit' position instead of 'Receive' and so had not heard my warning shouts at the beginning of the action.
>
> Fortunately for him, however, he turned it over just in time and heard me say *'Messerschmitt'*. He whipped round and found himself being attacked by three Me 110s. He had very great difficulty in escaping, got into a spin, recovered, and then spun the other way! – and came home having fired almost all his rounds at various Me 110s and Ju 87s, though without being able to see any results.
>
> He last saw Drummond about a mile away, being attacked by several enemy fighters, but could not go to his aid owing to his own troubles.
>
> As soon as our machines were refuelled and re-armed, six of us flew out into the bay to look for Drummond.
>
> But there was no sign of him at all, and his body was never recovered.
>
> I think there is no doubt that he also had left his R/T on 'Transmit' and so did not hear my warnings, or else perhaps he was thinking that there were only a very few enemy, as we had been told, and therefore the possibility of attack from the rear simply did not occur to him. There had been so many false alarms that he was rather in the frame of mind – 'nothing can ever happen at Weymouth'.
>
> We took off just before dusk to return to Wallop. Gordon [Pilot Officer Gordon Mitchell, who would be killed in action on 11 July 1940, see Volume II of this series] could not come as he had damaged his machine earlier in the day and I left him standing outside the tent, looking rather disconsolate because he had not been able to take part in the action with Michael and me. It was the last time I ever saw him.

No.609 had been raised as an auxiliary squadron, its personnel hailing from Yorkshire's West Riding. Such squadrons had a strong sense of family, almost;

before joining up these men were frequently already friends, or knew each other, or were even related. While such close bonds generated a strong *esprit de corps*, the downside was that casualties affected morale worse than in regular units. Crook also commented on this in his memoir, *Spitfire Pilot*:

> I went up to my room at Wallop. Everything was just the same as Drummond and I had left it only eighteen hours before – his towel was still in the window where he had thrown it during a hurried dressing. But he was dead now. I simply could not get used to such sudden and unexpected death, and there flashed across my mind the arrangements we had made to go up to Town together on the following day. It all seemed so ironical, so tragic, so futile.
>
> I felt that I could not see sleep in that room again, and so I took my things and went into Gordon's bed next door and slept there.
>
> But I could not get out of my head the thought of Drummond, with whom we had been talking and laughing that day, now lying in the cockpit of his wrecked Spitfire at the bottom of the English Channel.

Although 13/LG1's Me 110 pilots claimed two Spitfires destroyed, only Drummond's was lost. In addition to Crook's *Stuka*, the enemy also lost an Me 110, the crew of which came down in the sea and were captured. Three 609 Squadron Spitfires alone, however, were understandably unable to prevent the Ju 87s successfully attacking Convoy CW2, the *Talvadis* being sunk three miles of Prawle Point, and other freighters were damaged between Weymouth Bay or off Portland.

On this day, 2 Group's Blenheims were busy, with twenty-six Blenheims undertaking 'various' tasks – but the day went badly for the Lossiemouth-based 21 and 57 Squadrons, as the former' ORB notes: 'Attack on Stavanger Sola airfield ordered. Six aircraft took off at 10.00 hrs together with six aircraft of 57 Squadron. Target successfully located and heavily bombed.'

The problem was, the Blenheims had poked a hornets' nest:

> Heavy AA fire was encountered and all except three aircraft were attacked by Me 110s and 109s. Four of our aircraft were shot down off the coast, also two of 57 Squadron. Aircraft piloted by Wing Commander Bennett, with Sergeant Summers as Observer and Sergeant Burt as Wireless Operator/Air Gunner, was heavily attacked by fighters but reached cloud cover successfully.
>
> W/T message (1145 hrs) was received stating that through fighter attack the aircraft was damaged and might be forced to come down in the sea. Trace of this aircraft's course was maintained by Kinloss until 1231 hrs, after which nothing further was heard. Sweeps of

area were arranged between Coastal Command and ourselves, but no trace of aircraft or crew could be found....

The one aircraft of 21 Squadron to return, piloted by Pilot Officer Rodger, sustained numerous holes in the wings and fuselage and also had both undercarriage tyres burst. Sergeant Spillard, Observer, was slightly wounded on the leg by an incendiary bullet. The rear-gunner of this aircraft, Sergeant James, successfully accounted for an Me 109, which was seen to crash in flames into the sea. [21 Squadron ORB]

James had shot down and killed *Unteroffizier* Gerhard Weber of 5/JG77, but it was a poor exchange for the loss of six Blenheims and all crews killed.

Coastal Command's Shetland-based 201 Squadron lost a Short Sunderland flying boat engaged on a North Sea patrol, neither the aircraft, shot down by a 3/ZG76 Me 110, nor its crew of ten were seen again. Noteworthy is that fact that the victorious German pilot was one *Oberleutnant* Gordon Gollob – whose first victory had been recorded during the Battle of the Heligoland Bight, followed-up by this Sunderland and a 233 Squadron Hudson, shared with *Oberfeldwebel* Herbert Schob, later the same day. Later, Gollob, an Austrian, would fly Me 109s over England with II/JG3, and score heavily over the Soviet Union, ending the war with 150 victories.

That night, Bomber Command despatched fifty-five Hampdens and Wellingtons to attack various targets and continue minelaying operations, but bad weather dictated nineteen Wellingtons being recalled; in contrast to daylight hours, there were no RAF bombers lost on operations that night and nor did the enemy cause any substantial damage after dark.

Clearly then, there had been increasingly bitter fighting over the Channel since 2 July 1940, often against large enemy formations. But was this the Battle of Britain? If not, why not? And if not, should it have been?

Chapter 16

'I Have Therefore, Somewhat Arbitrarily Chosen the Events of 10 July as the Opening of the Battle'

Although we will explore the details later in this overall narrative, it is important at this stage to appreciate that what became the Battle of Britain was considered to be Germany's first signal reversal of the Second World War. Without intending any disrespect whatsoever to the RN, the fear of which was clearly a primary factor in influencing the *Kriegsmarine*'s view of a proposed seaborne invasion, this outcome was essentially decided through an unprecedented aerial campaign. As we have seen, although the aircrew of Fighter Command were directly involved with the air fighting over Britain's seas and shores, both Bomber and Coastal Command also contributed.

Nonetheless, when it was agreed to honour RAF airmen who had taken part in the Battle of Britain through a special award, rightly or wrongly this was specifically a consideration for Fighter Command aircrew. On 8 May 1945, the war in Europe ended with the total defeat of Germany, and on 24 May 1945 the Air Ministry announced that there would be a special clasp to the 1939–45 Star indicating that the recipient had been fighter aircrew during Britain's darkest days. The start and finish dates of the Battle, however, had to be decided, in addition to which of Fighter Command's aircrew would be eligible. These were not easy questions to answer.

On 23 July 1945, the Air Ministry further announced the issue of the clasp and appended rosette, to be worn on the medal ribbon, to 'aircrew personnel who flew in fighter aircraft engaged in the Battle of Britain between 10 July 1940 and 31 October 1940'. Over time further qualification criteria emerged, which will be discussed in future volumes; what is significant to this account is the start-date of 10 July 1940.

On 11 September 1946, Air Chief Marshal Dowding's Despatch on the Battle of Britain was published in *The London Gazette*. In this important document, Dowding clearly felt the start-date unclear and ambiguous himself, commenting that:

> The Battle may be said to have started when the Germans had disposed of the French resistance in the summer of 1940, and turned

their attention to this country. The essence of their strategy was to so weaken our fighter defences that their air arm should be able to give adequate support to an attempted invasion of the British Isles.

It is difficult to fix the exact date on which the 'Battle of Britain' can be said to have begun. Operations of various kinds merged into each other almost insensibly, and there are grounds for choosing 8 August, on which was made the first attack in force against land objectives in this country, as the beginning of the Battle.

On the other hand, the heavy attacks made against our Channel convoys probably constituted, in fact, the beginning of the German offensive; because the weight and scale of the attack indicates that the primary object was rather to bring our fighters to battle than destroy the hulls and cargoes of the small ships engaged in coastal trade. While we were fighting in Belgium and France, we suffered the disadvantage that even the temporary stoppage of an engine involved the loss of pilot and aircraft, whereas, in similar circumstances, the German pilot might be fighting again the same day, and his aircraft be airborne again in a matter of hours.

In fighting over England these considerations were reversed, and the moral and material disadvantages of fighting over enemy country may well have determined the Germans to open a phase of fighting in which the advantages were more evenly balanced. I have therefore, somewhat arbitrarily chosen the events of 10 July as the opening of the Battle. Although many attacks had previously been made on convoys, and even land objectives such as Portland, 10 July saw the employment by the Germans of the first really big formation (seventy aircraft) intended primarily to bring our fighter defence to battle on a large scale.

Dowding continued by briefly outlining the issues he faced in preserving a force of sufficient size to adequately defend Britain, concluding that 'the Battle of Britain began for me in the autumn of 1939' – which was an undeniable fact.

Significantly, Dowding acknowledged that the enemy's ultimate objective was invasion. That being so, surely the enemy's invasion plans appended to *Luftwaffe* air operations dictated when the Battle of Britain began? We know that on 2 July 1940, the OKW informed the *Wehrmacht* that the invasion of England was to proceed, providing certain conditions were obtained, essentially control of the air. Arguably, then, that is the day that the Battle of Britain began, because from then on, until the proposed invasion was eventually postponed, there was a plan and stated intention to land in southern England – notwithstanding Hitler's delusional hopes that Britain would accept peace terms.

Some have argued that the Dunkirk air fighting was the start of what became the Battle of Britain – but that was clearly not the case given that those air battles were not connected to any invasion plan. Indeed, at that time, this book clearly evidences the simple fact that Hitler's policy in the ongoing war against Britain was blockade, not invasion. Dowding mentions 8 August 1940 as a potential start-date, when the Germans began stepping up attacks on land targets, but clearly, as far as the enemy was concerned, military preparations, in the air, on land and at sea, had begun the previous month, so, again, we return to the OKW directive on 2 July 1940.

Certainly Air Commodore Al Deere, the celebrated fighter ace from New Zealand, writing in 1959, was convinced that the start-date was 2 July 1940. Indeed, a line in his 54 Squadron's ORB, dated 10 July 1940, is telling: 'As a result of the first phase of the Battle of Britain, the Squadron could only muster eight aircraft and thirteen pilots.'

That 'first phase', as far as 54 Squadron was concerned, was the period 2–9 July 1940. And yet, officially, the Battle of Britain did not actually commence until the following day.

Why, though, does it matter, all these years later, when the Battle of Britain really began?

An obvious answer is that history deserves an accurate account and interpretation, but more so is the memory of those aircrew who were killed or maimed between 2 and 9 July 1940 inclusive. While this book has sought to demonstrate and pay due acknowledgement to the aircrew of other Commands involved, and the RN, as we have seen the official focus when recognising combatants was solely Fighter Command. That being so, it is the fighters that are also considered here, with regard to whether those involved in the fighting between 2 and 9 July 1940 should also have been awarded the Battle of Britain Clasp?

Think, for a second, of those like 54 Squadron's Yellow 2, shot down by an Me 109 on 9 July 1940 and who was heard over the radio screaming for help, to no avail, and was killed upon crashing into the sea; or poor Squadron Leader George Lott of 43 Squadron, who survived the trauma of being shot down on the same day but lost an eye – which kept him out of action throughout the Battle of Britain's official dates. Those men's names will not be found among those of The Few, to the chagrin and disappointment, very often, of their loved ones. Indeed, some families remain resentful even today that there was no recognition forthcoming – but there is no doubt whatsoever that those aircrew also gave their lives serving in Fighter Command and in the defence of this country – and deserve to be remembered for it. That they did not receive the same recognition as Fighter Command aircrew who flew operationally between 10 July and 31 October 1940 can only be considered a sad omission and injustice.

In the forthcoming Volume IV we will visit Churchill's famous speech of 20 August 1940, in which he paid tribute to 'The Few', and examine whether the Prime Minister was talking exclusively about Fighter Command or the RAF collectively. What is important here and now, however, is the impression of RAF fighter pilots fighting against overwhelming numbers – which we have already seen in these early skirmishes. In truth, the MAP kept the aircraft coming, and

Training Command provided sufficient replacement pilots, albeit lacking in combat experience, and the opposing air forces were in many ways equally matched. The origins of this perception of a fight against overwhelming odds are found in this book, however, and are all about how Fighter Command was deployed and the tactics used.

As we have seen, Britain was divided into groups, and being unsure as to whether the Germans would attack northern England in strength, flying from bases in Norway, and given that the whole of Britain was with range of German bombers, Fighter Command's resources had to be spread throughout the land – not concentrated in southern England, which after the Fall of France became the main battle area.

The lack of British experience and understanding of modern, fast-moving, fighter tactics before the war, and the limitations of aerial communication in which pilots could talk to their own squadron and ground controller, but not pilots from other squadrons or different sector ground controllers, dictated that the flight of six, or section of three, was seen as the preferred formation size, rather than even a whole squadron flying together. Although at Dunkirk Air Vice-Marshal Park's squadrons eventually travelled across the Channel in multiple squadron convoys, once over the French coast they fought independently (although with friendly fighters consequently in the immediate vicinity, help was close at hand).

It is important, though, to understand that these convoy formations were not cohesive fighting units, and had no bearing, in fact, on subsequent tactics or arguments regarding formation size during the Battle of Britain. After Dunkirk, small Fighter Command formations continued responding to enemy attacks, until, as we will see, 12 Group's controversial 'Big Wing' first sallied forth on 7 September 1940 – much more of which later. For now, we are focused upon the small formations in use at this early time.

In this book, providing the background to, and an account of, the first week of fighting – before the official start-date – we have repeatedly seen how flights and just sections of three were frequently used, both for patrols and interceptions. At first, after Dunkirk, the enemy's daylight air activity largely comprised countless reconnaissance sorties by lone, unescorted, bombers, a number of which fell victim to defending fighters, depriving the Germans of important intelligence. As the battle wore on over the Channel and South coast, however, larger enemy formations came into play, outnumbering the single section and flight – but small formations remained essential for flexibility and the preservation of limited resources.

On paper, therefore, the two air forces may well have been evenly matched, but statistics in this case miss the essential point: Fighter Command aircrew meeting the *Luftwaffe* from 2 July 1940 onwards were invariably outnumbered, not because of an overall lack of aircraft or pilots, but because of the tactics it was necessary for Air Vice-Marshal Park to use. In that sense, and in practical terms, the RAF fighters *were* fighting against overwhelming odds – and it was little comfort to Al Deere and outnumbered comrades to know, when facing a horde of German bombers and fighters over the Channel in early July 1940, that statistically it was an even fight, and that the Germans feared the RN. So we can see already, in this book, the start of how the Battle of Britain would be fought and why it was – and is – still seen as a fight against the odds. And as far as Fighter Command's aircrew were concerned fighting over southern England and the Channel, more often than not it was.

The skill and courage of Fighter Command's aircrew can never be doubted, and it is right that, even while recognising and paying tribute to essential contributions by other Commands, the focus of any narrative concerning the dramatic events of summer and autumn 1940 primarily focuses on the RAF's fighter battle – which, although not statistically, most often – in the air, where it mattered – really was against all odds.

Moving on, in this book we have explored many threads which collectively, over a long period of time, represent what was a gathering storm, how Britain's defences were organised to meet this threat, and the events leading up to Hitler agreeing to a seaborne invasion of England, and the first, tentative but often fierce, aerial thrusts involved. The fighting on 10 July 1940, the official start-date, it is true, saw even heavier fighting, with a great air battle involving over 100 aircraft, so Volume II will graphically relate the breaking storm between 10 July and 12 August 1940 – the *Kanalkampf* (Channel Battle) proper – the officially recognised first phase of battle.

To be continued …

Appendix

RAF Fighter Command Operational Aircraft and Aircrew Casualties
2–9 July 1940

4 July 1940		
79 Squadron, Hawkinge	Hurricane Mk I, N2619	Sgt H. Cartwright DFM shot down and killed in combat with Me 109s over St Margaret's Bay.
5 July 1940		
64 Squadron, Kenley	Spitfire Mk IA, P9507	PO D.K. Milne shot down and killed by Me 109 on reconnaissance sortie over France.
7 July 1940		
54 Squadron, Manston	Spitfire Mk IA, R6711	PO A.R. McL Campbell, shot down by Me 109 and wounded off Deal.
	Spitfire Mk IA, P9390	PO E.J. Coleman, as above.
65 Squadron, Hornchurch	Spitfire Mk IA, R6615	FO G.V. Proudman. Shot down by Me 109s off Dover; missing.
	Spitfire Mk IA, R6609	PO N.J. Brisbane, as above.
	Spitfire Mk IA, N3129	Sgt P.S. Hayes, as above.
79 Squadron, Hawkinge	Hurricane Mk I, P2756	Sqn Ldr J.D.C. Joslin shot down in flames on patrol over Dover, allegedly by Spitfires.

8 July 1940		
65 Squadron, Hornchurch	Spitfire Mk IA, K9907	Sqn Ldr D. Cooke, shot down off Dover by Me 109 and killed.
79 Squadron, Hawkinge	Hurricane Mk I, N2384	PO J.E.R. Wood, shot down by Me 109 off Dover, baled out by died of wounds.
	Hurricane Mk I, P3461	FO E Mitchell, as above, over Kent.
610 Squadron, Biggin Hill	Spitfire Mk IA, R6806	PO A.L.B. Raven, shot down in combat with German bombers off Dover, baled out but never found.
9 July 1940		
43 Squadron, Tangmere	Hurricane Mk I, P3464	Sqn Ldr G.C. Lott DSO DFC, shot down by Me 110, crashed landed, wounded, near Fontwell; lost an eye, consequently.
	Hurricane Mk I, L1824	PO J. Cruttenden, shot down and safely baled out after combat with German bombers off Beachy Head.
54 Squadron, Manston	Spitfire Mk IA, N3183	Flt Lt A.C. Deere, collided with Me 109 in combat over Channel, crash-landed, wounded, near Manston.
	Spitfire Mk IA, R6705	PO J.W. Garton, shot down and killed in combat with Me 109s off Manston.
	Spitfire Mk IA, L1093	PO SJA Evershed, as above.

151 Squadron, North Weald	Hurricane Mk I, P3806	Mid O.M. Wightman, shot down over Thames Estuary and rescued by trawler.
	Hurricane Mk I, P3309	Flt Lt H.H.A. Ironside, shot-up and wounded over Thames Estuary but returned to base safely.
609 Squadron, Warmwell	Spitfire Mk IA, R6637	FO P. Drummond-Hay, shot down by Me 109 over Portland, missing.

The foregoing casualties represent eight pilots killed or missing, seven wounded and two more who later died of their wounds.

Bibliography

The National Archives

The National Archives is the main repository for primary source documents; the following documents were consulted during the course of research for this book.

Operations Record Books:

AIR27/235	17 Squadron
AIR27/243	18 Squadron
AIR27/252	19 Squadron
AIR27/263	21 Squadron
AIR27/287	23 Squadron
AIR27/360	32 Squadron
AIR27/424	41 Squadron
AIR27/441	43 Squadron
AIR27/460	46 Squadron
AIR27/511	54 Squadron
AIR27/528	56 Squadron
AIR27/537	57 Squadron
AIR27/589	64 Squadron
AIR27/592	65 Squadron
AIR27/601	66 Squadron
AIR27/624	72 Squadron
AIR27/640	74 Squadron
AIR27/664	79 Squadron
AIR27/703	85 Squadron
AIR27/743	92 Squadron
AIR27/984	145 Squadron
AIR27/1018	151 Squadron
AIR27/1177	201 Squadron
AIR27/1222	206 Squadron
AIR27/1315	213 Squadron
AIR27/1371	222 Squadron
AIR27/1439	234 Squadron

AIR27/1445	236 Squadron
AIR27/1453	238 Squadron
AIR27/1498	249 Squadron
AIR27/1526	257 Squadron
AIR27/1547	263 Squadron
AIR27/1553	264 Squadron
AIR27/2068	601 Squadron
AIR27/2074	602 Squadron
AIR27/2079	603 Squadron
AIR27/2093	607 Squadron
AIR27/2102	609 Squadron
AIR27/2106	610 Squadron
AIR27/2109	611 Squadron
AIR27/2123	615 Squadron
AIR27/2126	616 Squadron

Combat Reports:

AIR50/9	17 Squadron
AIR50/10	19 Squadron
AIR50/11	23 Squadron
AIR50/16	32 Squadron
AIR50/18	41 Squadron
AIR50/19	43 Squadron
AIR50/20	46 Squadron
AIR50/21	54 Squadron
AIR50/22	56 Squadron
AIR50/24	64 Squadron
AIR50/25	65 Squadron
AIR50/26	66 Squadron
AIR50/30	72 Squadron
AIR50/32	74 Squadron
AIR50/33	79 Squadron
AIR50/36	85 Squadron
AIR50/40	92 Squadron
AIR50/62	145 Squadron
AIR50/63	151 Squadron
AIR50/83	213 Squadron
AIR50/51	222 Squadron
AIR50/89	234 Squadron
AIR50/91	238 Squadron
AIR50/96	249 Squadron
AIR50/100	257 Squadron
AIR50/103	263 Squadron

AIR50/104	264 Squadron
AIR50/165	601 Squadron
AIR50/166	602 Squadron
AIR50/167	603 Squadron
AIR50/170	607 Squadron
AIR50/171	609 Squadron
AIR50/172	610 Squadron
AIR50/173	611 Squadron
AIR50/175	615 Squadron
AIR50/176	616 Squadron

Casualty Packs:

AIR81/2347	Sergeant H. Cartwright
AIR81/1003	Pilot Officer D.K. Milne
AIR81/1033	Pilot Officer A.R. McL Campbell
AIR81/1034	Pilot Officer E.J. Coleman
AIR81/1038	Flying Officer G.V. Proudman
AIR81/1039	Pilot Officer N.J. Brisbane
AIR81/1059	Sergeant P.S. Hayes
AIR81/1036	Squadron Leader J.D.C. Joslin
AIR81/1042	Squadron Leader D. Cooke
AIR81/1043	Flying Officer E. Mitchell
AIR81/1046	Pilot Officer A.L.B. Raven
AIR81/1058	Squadron Leader C.G. Lott
AIR81/1055	Pilot Officer J.W. Garton
AIR81/1064	Pilot Officer S.J.A. Evershed
AIR81/1056	Flight Lieutenant H.H.A. Ironside
AIR81/1061	Flying Officer P. Drummond-Hay
AIR81/1059	Pilot Officer G.D. Goldsmith-Jones & Flying Officer B.P.H. Page

Miscellaneous Documents:

AIR4/21	Flying Log Book, Flight Lieutenant D.M. Crook DFC
AIR4/58	Flying Log Book, Squadron Leader B.J.E. Lane DFC
AIR9/136	Air Ministry, memorandum concerning invasion precautions, October 1939
AIR9/447	Air Ministry, Director of Plans, 'Employment of Air Striking Force', 8 July 1940
AIR14/41	Air Historical Branch Narrative, Battle of France
AIR16/300	Report on German Fighter Tactics
AIR16/301	Report on German Bomber Tactics
AIR16/960	Fighter Command Victory Claims & Casualties
AIR16/365	Fighter Command, Operational Strength of Squadrons and Order of Battle

AIR16/142	Trials of Cannon-Armed Spitfires
AIR18/636	Handling Trials of Prototype Spitfire K5054
AIR22/293	Cabinet Statistical Branch, Statistics on Aircraft Production, Imports and Exports, Schedule D, Exports of Fighters
AIR22/262	Daily Returns of Casualties to RAF Aircraft, 25 June – 29 September 1940
AIR22/296	Cabinet Statistical Branch, Personnel, Casualties, Strength, Establishment of the RAF
AIR35/121	Report by Squadron Leader P. Halahan on Comparative Trials of Hurricane v Me 109, 7 May 1940
AVIA6/2394	Me 109: Handling and Manoeuvrability Tests, September 1940
AVIA18/636	Report on Turning Circles of Me 109, Spitfire and Hurricane, 9 June 1940
AVIA18/763	Me 109 Fighter: Brief Handling Trials, A&AEE, 10 June 1940

German Documents

OKW Directives for Invasion of the UK, Operation *Seelöwe*, Summer and Autumn 1940, Bundesarchiv

Luftflotte 2 War Diary, available via Digital History Archive (see website detailed below)

German fighter combat claims can be found in the OKL records of the *Chef für Ausz. und Dizsiplin Luftwaffe-Personalamt LP(A)V* (available via various online sources)

German loss records can be found in the *Oberfehlsaber der Luftwaffe Genst. Gen. Qu/6 Abteilung/40.g. Kdos.I.C*, records, preserved by the Imperial War Museum.

Unpublished Sources

Correspondence, papers and interviews, Dilip Sarkar Archive
Papers: Air Vice-Marshal J.E. Johnson
Memoir, Air Commodore J.B. Coward
Original manuscript of *Spitfire Pilot*, Flight Lieutenant D.M.C. Crook

Published Sources

Addison, P., and Crang, J.A. (Eds), *The Burning Blue: A New History of the Battle of Britain*, Pimlico, London, 2000
_____, *Listening to Britain: Home Intelligence Reports on Britain's Finest Hour – May to September 1940*, Vintage Books, London, 2011

'AHE', 'Cranwell and its Traditions', *Journal of the Royal Air Force College*, 1930

Allen, Wg Cdr H.R., *Fighter Squadron: A Memoir 1940–42*, Granada, London, 1982

Anon, *The Second World War, RAF 1939–45, Flying Training: Volume One, Policy & Planning*, HMSO, London, 1941

Anon, *The Battle of Britain: August–October 1940*, Ministry of Information on behalf of the Air Ministry, London, 1941

Anon, *The Battle of Britain*, Air Ministry Pamphlet 156, Issued by the Department of the Air Member for Training, August 1943

Anon, *The Rise & Fall of the German Air Force 1939–45*, Air Ministry Pamphlet 248, Public Record Office, London, 2001

Ashworth, C., *RAF Coastal Command: 1936-1969*, PAL, Sparkford, 1992

Bader, Group Captain Sir D.R.S., *Fight for the Sky: The Story of the Spitfire and Hurricane*, Sidgwick & Jackson, London, 1973

Balfour, H., *Wings Over Westminster*, Hutchinson & Co Ltd, London, 1973

Beckles, G., *Birth of a Spitfire*, first edition, Collins, London, 1941

Bekker, C., *The Luftwaffe War Diaries*, Corgi Books, London, 1972

_____, *Hitler's Naval War*, Corgi, London, 1976

Benoist-Méchin, J., *60 Days That Shook the West*, Jonathan Cape Ltd, London, 1963

Bialer, U., *The Shadow of the Bomber: The Fear of Air Attack and British Politics 1932-39*, Royal Historical Society, London, 1980

Bishop, E., *The Battle of Britain*, George Allen & Unwin Ltd, London, 1960

Bolitho, H., *A Penguin in the Eyrie: An RAF Diary 1939 to 1945*, Hutchinson, London, 1955

Boot, H., and Sturtivant, R., *Gifts of War: Spitfires and Other Presentation Aircraft in Two World Wars*, first edition, Air-Britain Historians Ltd., Tonbridge, 2005

Bouverie, T., *Appeasing Hitler: Chamberlain, Churchill and the Road to War*, Vintage, London, 2019

Bowyer, M.J.F., *2 Group RAF: A Complete History, 1936–1945*, Faber & Faber, London, 1974

Branson, N., & Heinemann, M., Britain in the 1930s, Weidenfeld & Nicolson, London, 1971

Calder, A., *The People's War: Britain 1939–45*, Pimlico, London, 2008

_____, *The Myth of The Blitz*, Pimlico, London, 2008

Caldwell, D., *The JG26 War Diary: Volume One, 1939–42*, Grub Street, London, 1996

Cannandine, D. (ed), *The Speeches of Winston Churchill*, Penguin, London, 1990

Churchill, W.S., *The Second World War, Vol II, Their Finest Hour*, Cassell & Co, London, 1949

Clapson, M., *Britain in the Twentieth Century*, Routledge, Abingdon, 2009

Collier, B., *The Defence of the United Kingdom*, HMSO, London, 1957

Cornwell, P., *The Battle of France, Then & Now: Six Nations Locked in Aerial Combat September 1939 – June 1940*, Battle of Britain Prints International Ltd, Old Harlow, 2007

BIBLIOGRAPHY

Cox, S., & Probert, H., (eds), *The Battle Re-Thought: A Symposium on the Battle of Britain*, Airlife, Shrewsbury, 1991

Cox, S., 'RAF & Luftwaffe Intelligence Compared' in Handel, MI (ed), *Intelligence & Military Operations*, Frank Cass, Abingdon, 1990

Cull, B., *First of The Few: 5 June – 9 July 1940*, Fonthill Media Ltd, Stroud, 2013

Dean, Sir Maurice, *The Royal Air Force in Two World Wars*, Cassell, London, 1979

Deere, Air Cdre A.C., *Nine Lives*, Hodder Paperback Ltd, London, 1959

Deighton, L., *Fighter: The True Story of the Battle of Britain*, Triad/Panther Books, St Albans, 1979

Deist, W., *The* Wehrmacht *and German Rearmament*, The MacMillan Press Ltd, Basingstoke, 1986

Dimbleby, J., *The Battle of the Atlantic: How the Allies Won the War*, Penguin, London, 2015

Donnelly, M., *Britain in the Second World War*, Routledge, London, 1999

Dowding, A.C.M., *Lord HCT, Despatch: The Battle of Britain*, London Gazette, London, 1946

Dundas, Grp Capt Sir H.S.L., *Flying Start*, Stanley Paul, London, 1988

'Ellan, Squadron Leader B.J.' (pseudonym for Brian Lane), *Spitfire! The Experiences of a Fighter Pilot*, John Murray, London, 1942

Foreman, J., *RAF Fighter Command Victory Claims of World War Two, Volume One*, Air Research Publications, Red Kite, Walton-on-Thames, 2003

Foxley-Norris, ACM Sir C.F.N, *A Lighter Shade of Blue: The Light-hearted Memoirs of an Air-Marshal*, Ian Allen Ltd, London, 1978

Franks, N., *Air Battle for Dunkirk 26 May – 3 June 1940*, Grub Street, London, 2006

Galland, A,. *The First and the Last: Germany's Fighter Force* in the Second World War, Fontana, London, 1954,

Gilbert, M., *The Second World War: A Complete History*, Weidenfeld & Nicolson, London, 1989

Green, W., *Aircraft of the Battle of Britain*, MacDonald & Co (Publishers) Ltd and Pan Books Ltd, London, 1969

Haig-Brown, A.R., *The OTC in the Great War*, Country Life Publications, London, 1915

Handel, M.I. (ed), *Intelligence and Military Operations*, Frank Cass, Abingdon, 1990

Hastings, M., *All Hell Let Loose: The World at War 1939-1945*, Harper Press, London, 2011

Hillary, R., *The Last Enemy*, MacMillan & Co Ltd, London, 1950

Hough, R., and Richards, D., *The Battle of Britain: The Jubilee History*, Hodder & Stoughton Ltd, London, 1990

James, J., *The Paladins: The Story of the RAF up to the Outbreak of World War II*, Futura Publications, London, 1990

James, T.C.G., *The Battle of Britain*, Frank Cass, London, 1990

Jefford, J., 'Aircrew Status in the 1940s', Royal Air Force Historical Society Journal, No 42, 2008

Johnson, Air Vice-Marshal J.E., *Wing Leader*, Chatto & Windus, London, 1956

Kesselring, Field-Marshal A., *The Memoirs of Field-Marshal Kesselring,* Greenhill Books, London, 1997

Kershaw, I., *Hitler: 1936–1945, Nemesis*, Penguin, London, 2001

Lisiewicz, Squadron Leader M (Ed), *Destiny Can Wait: The Polish Air Force in the Second World War*, William Heinemann Ltd, London, 1949

Lunde, H.O., *Hitler's Pre-emptive War: The Battle for Norway, 1940*, Casemate, Philadelphia and Newbury, 2008

Quill, J.K., *Spitfire*, Arrow Books, London, 1983

Manvell, R., and Fraenkel, H, *Goering*, Greenhill Books, London, 2005

Mason, F.K., *Battle Over Britain*, Aston Publications, Bourne End, 1990

McKee, A., *The Coal-Scuttle Brigade*, Souvenir Press Ltd, London, 1957

Middlebrook, M., and Everitt, C., *The Bomber Command War Diaries: An Operational Reference Book 1939-1945*, Midland Counties Publications, Hinckley, 1996

Mitchell, Dr G., *RJ Mitchell. World Famous Aircraft Designer: From Schooldays to Spitfire*, Nelson & Saunders, Olney, 1986

Morgan, E., & Shacklady, E., *Spitfire: The History*, Key Publishing, Stamford, 1987

Mowatt, C.L., *Britain Between the Wars*, Methuen & Co Ltd, London, 1976

Muggeridge, M. (Ed), *Ciano's Diary 1939-1943*, William Heinemann Ltd, London, 1947

Orange, V., *Park: The biography of Air Chief Marshal Sir Keith Park*, Grub Street, London, 2001

Orange, V., *Dowding of Fighter Command: Victor of the Battle of Britain*, Grubb Street, London, 2008

Orwell, G., *The Lion and the Unicorn: Socialism and the English Genius*, Penguin, London, 1982

Overy, R., *The Air War 1939-1945*, first edition, Europa Publications Ltd, London, 1980

―――――――, *The Battle of Britain*, Penguin, London, 2004

―――――――, *Goering: The Iron Man*, Bloomsbury Revelations, London, 2021

Penny, J., *Bristol at War*, Derby Books Publishing Company Ltd, Derby, 2010

Pope, R., *War & Society in Britain 1899-1948*, Longman, Harlow, 1991

Pugh, M., *We Danced All Night: A Social History of Britain Between the Wars*, Bodley Head, London, 2008

Price, A., *Spitfire at War*, Ian Allan, Shepperton, 1974

―――――――, *The Hardest Day*, MacDonald & Janes, London, 1979

―――――――, *The Spitfire Story*, second edition, Arms & Armour Press, London, 1995

Priestley, J.B., *English Journey*, Mandarin, London, 1994

BIBLIOGRAPHY

_____, *Postscripts*, Heinemann, London, 1940

Ramsay, W. (Ed), *The Battle of Britain: Then & Now, Mk V Edition*, Battle of Britain Prints International Ltd, London, 1986

_____, *The Blitz Then & Now, Volume 1*, Battle of Britain Prints International Ltd, London, 1989

_____, *The Blitz Then & Now, Volume 2*, Battle of Britain Prints International Ltd, London, 1990

Richards, D., *RAF Bomber Command in the Second World War: The Hardest Victory*, Penguin, London, 2001

Roberts, F.V., *Duxford to Karachi: An RAF Armourer's War*, Victory Books, Worcester, 2006

Sarkar, D., *Douglas Bader*, Amberley Publishing, Stroud, 2013

_____, *The Final Few*, Amberley Publishing, Stroud, 2015

_____, *How the Spitfire Won the Battle of Britain*, Amberley, Stroud, 2010

_____, *Spitfire Squadron: The Full Story of a Unique Battle of Britain Fighter Squadron*, Pen & Sword Ltd, Barnsley, 2019

_____, *Letters From The Few: Unique Memories From the Battle of Britain*, Pen & Sword Ltd, Barnsley, 2020

_____, *Battle of Britain 1940: The Finest Hour's Human Cost*, Pen & Sword Ltd, Barnsley, 2020

_____, *Sailor Malan: Freedom Fighter*, Pen & Sword Ltd, Barnsley, 2021

Schenk, P., *Operation Sealion: The Invasion of England*, Greenhill Books, Barnsley, 2019

Simpson, G., *A History of the Battle of Britain Fighter Association: Commemorating The Few*, Pen & Sword, Barnsley, 2015

Smith, M., The RAF. In Addison, J, & Crang, JA (Eds), *The Burning Blue: A New History of the Battle of Britain*, Pimlico, London, 2000

Stevenson, J., *British Society 1914–45*, Penguin, London, 1994

Townsend, Group Captain P., *Duel of Eagles: The Classic Account of the Battle of Britain*, Weidenfeld & Nicolson, London, 1990

Trevor-Roper, H.R. (ed), *Hitler's War Directives 1939–45*, Pan Books, London, 1966

Vasco, J.J., and Cornwell, PD, Zerstörer: *The* Messerschmitt *110 and its Units in 1940*, JAC Publications, Norwich, 1995

Williams, C., *The Battle of the Atlantic*, BBC Worldwide Ltd, London, 2002

Wheatley, R., *Operation Sealion*, Oxford University Press, Oxford, 1958

Wood, A.C., & Sutton, A, *Military Aviation of the First World War*, Fonthill Media Ltd, Stroud, 2016

Wood, D., and Dempster, D., *The Narrow Margin: The Battle of Britain*, Arrow Ltd, London, 1969

Wright, R., *Dowding and the Battle of Britain*, Corgi, London, 1970

Ziegler, F.H., *The Story of 609 Squadron: Under the White Rose*, MacDonald, London, 1971

Websites

The National Archives:	www.nationalarchives.gov.uk
Commonwealth War Graves Commission:	www.cwgc.org
Battle of Britain Memorial Trust:	www.battleofbritainmemorial.org
Battle of Britain: The People's Project:	www.battleofbritainthepeoplesproject.com
Dilip Sarkar:	www.dilipsarkarauthor.com
Digital History Archive:	www.digitalhistoryarchive.com
Kenley Revival Project:	www.kenleyrevival.org
Battle of Britain London Monument:	www.bbm.org.uk

Films

Although produced for either propaganda purposes or popular culture, the following films can provide an idea of the timeframe this book concerns:

Triumph Des Willens ('Triumph of the Will'), directed by Leni Riefenstahl (Universum Film AG, 1935).
Things to Come, directed by William Cameron Menzies (London Films, 1936).
The Gap, directed by Donald Carter (Gaumont-British Instructional, 1937).
The Warning, edited by RQ McNaughton (British National Films, 1939).
The Lion Has Wings, directed by Michael Powell, Adrian Brunel and Brian Desmond Hurst (London Films 1939).
Target for Tonight, directed by Harry Watt (Crown Film Unit, 1941).
A Yank in the RAF, directed by Henry King (Twentieth Century-Fox, 1941).
Mrs Miniver, directed by William Wyle (Metro-Goldwyn-Mayer, 1942).
The First of the Few, directed by Leslie Howard (British Aviation Pictures, 1942).
The Flemish Farm, directed by Jeffrey Dell (Two Cities Films, 1943).
Reach for the Sky, directed by Lewis Gilbert (The Rank Organisation, 1956).
Dunkirk, directed by Leslie Norman (Metro-Goldwyn-Mayer, 1958).
Battle of Britain, directed by Guy Hamilton (Spitfire Productions, 1969).
Dunkirk, directed by Christopher Nolan (Warner Brothers, 2017).
Darkest Hour, directed by Joe Wright (Perfect World Pictures, 2018).
Munich: The Edge of War, directed by Christian Schwochow, (Netflix, 2022)

Television

The World at War, directed by David Elstein (ITV, 1973).
A Piece of Cake, directed by Ian Toynton (Holmes Associates, 1988).

Other Books By Dilip Sarkar

Spitfire Squadron: No 19 Squadron at War, 1939–41
The Invisible Thread: A Spitfire's Tale
Through Peril to the Stars: RAF Fighter Pilots Who Failed to Return, 1939–45
Angriff Westland: Three Battle of Britain Air Raids Through the Looking Glass
A Few of the Many: Air War 1939-45, A Kaleidoscope of Memories
Bader's Tangmere Spitfires: The Untold Story, 1941
Bader's Duxford Fighters: The Big Wing Controversy
Missing in Action: Resting in Peace?
Guards VC: Blitzkrieg 1940
Battle of Britain: The Photographic Kaleidoscope, Volumes —IV
Fighter Pilot: The Photographic Kaleidoscope
Group Captain Sir Douglas Bader: An Inspiration in Photographs
Johnnie Johnson: Spitfire Top Gun, Part I
Johnnie Johnson: Spitfire Top Gun, Part II
Battle of Britain: Last Look Back
Spitfire! Courage & Sacrifice
Spitfire Voices: Heroes Remember
The Battle of Powick Bridge: Ambush a Fore-thought
Duxford 1940: A Battle of Britain Base at War
The Few: The Battle of Britain in the Words of the Pilots
Spitfire Manual 1940
The Sinking of HMS Royal Oak In the Words of the Survivors (re-print of Hearts of Oak)
The Last of the Few: Eighteen Battle of Britain Pilots Tell Their Extraordinary Stories
Hearts of Oak: The Human Tragedy of HMS Royal Oak
Spitfire Voices: Life as a Spitfire Pilot in the Words of the Veterans
How the Spitfire Won the Battle of Britain
Spitfire Ace of Aces: The True Wartime Story of Johnnie Johnson
Douglas Bader
Fighter Ace: The Extraordinary Life of Douglas Bader, Battle of Britain Hero (re-print of above)

Spitfire: The Photographic Biography
Hurricane Manual 1940
River Pike
The Final Few: The Last Surviving Pilots of the Battle of Britain Tell Their Stories
Arnhem 1944: The Human Tragedy of the Bridge Too Far
Spitfire! The Full Story of a Unique Battle of Britain Fighter Squadron
Battle of Britain 1940: The Finest Hour's Human Cost
Letters from The Few: Unique Memories of the Battle of Britain
Johnnie Johnson's 1942 Diary: The War Diary of the Spitfire Ace of Aces
Johnnie Johnson's Great Adventure: The Spitfire Ace of Ace's Last Look Back
Sailor Malan – Freedom Fighter: The Inspirational Story of a Spitfire Ace
Spitfire Ace of Aces – The Album: The Photographs of Johnnie Johnson
The Real Spitfire Pilot
The Real Hurricane Pilot: Arise to Conquer
Bader's Big Wing Controversy: Duxford 1940
Bader's Spitfire Wing: Tangmere 1941
The Battle of Britain on the Big Screen
Battle of Britain: The Movie (contributor to and publisher of the now late Robert Rudhall's original edition (2000), and editor and substantial contributor to 2022 revised edition)
Spitfire Down
Forgotten Heroes of The Battle of Britain
Faces of The Few
Spitfire Faces
I Had a Row With A German (introduction)
Rene Mouchotte: Free French Spitfire Pilot (with Jan Leeming)
Faces of HMS Royal Oak

Index

Aeroplane and Armament Experimental Establishment, 20, 174
Aircraft,
   Armstrong Whitworth Siskin, 46
   Bolton-Paul Defiant, 32–4, 44–5, 131–2, 139–40, 161–2, 164, 169, 187, 201, 202, 229
   Bristol Beaufighter, 33
   Bristol Blenheim, 31–4, 66, 99, 110, 133, 138, 161, 177–8, 180–2, 191, 193–6, 200, 201–202, 230–1, 239, 244, 251, 268–9
   Bristol Bulldog, 15–16
   De Havilland Tiger Moth, 8, 96–7, 153
   Dornier Do 17, 55, 87, 95, 109, 146, 158, 159–60, 189, 207, 215–20, 222, 226, 228, 240–1, 244–5, 251, 253–4, 256
   Dornier Do 18, 109
   Dornier Do 215, 157, 159, 207, 213, 215, 218, 220, 226, 239, 247, 256
   Eastleigh, 27, 197
   Fairey Battle, 67, 133, 193, 201
   Fairey Fulmar, 33
   Gloster Gauntlet, 8, 17, 21–2, 25, 30–1
   Gloster Gladiator, 33, 36, 66, 109, 118, 123, 124, 186, 200–202
   Gloster Sea Gladiator, 33
   Grumman Martlet, 33
   Hawker Audax, 68
   Hawker Demon, 15, 21–2, 200
   Hawker Fury, 15–16, 20, 24
   Hawker Hart, 16, 20, 68, 72, 96–7, 193
   Hawker Hartebeeste, 96
   Hawker Hurricane, 21–3, 24, 25, 26, 27, 28, 31 *et seq*
   Heinkel He 59, 209, 212, 261, 264
   Heinkel He 111, 55, 87, 89, 109, 123, 128, 131, 141, 147, 152, 163, 178, 180–2, 207, 214, 218, 228–9, 231, 237–40, 245–6, 251, 259–61
   Heinkel He 115, 109
   Junkers Ju 88, 55, 87, 92, 109, 123, 131, 137, 139, 141–2, 148, 159, 164, 207, 214, 215, 218, 232, 241, 246, 250, 261
   Junkers Ju 87, 87, 122, 124, 131, 133, 135, 138–9, 145, 153–6, 164, 206–207, 213, 225, 254, 264–8
   Messerschmitt Me 109, 33, 35–6, 44, 87–93, 100, 110–11, 129, 131, 137, 139–40, 143–7, 151–2, 154–8, 161–5, 170, 174–7, 187, 193, 199, 202, 206, 209–10, 220–2, 226, 229,

231–3, 239–42, 244, 247–51, 257–65, 268–9, 272
Messerschmitt Me 110, 33, 92, 111, 137, 143, 146–7, 159, 161–4, 175–6, 182, 206–207, 210, 223, 226, 239, 254–5, 258–60, 265–9
Miles Magister, 68, 71–2
Miles Master, 31, 71–2, 143, 239
North American Harvard, 67, 200–201
Northolt, 21–4, 46, 189, 236, 253
Short Sunderland, 264
Supermarine Spitfire, 12, 16–17, 26–30 et seq
Westland Whirlwind, 33

Airfields, Depots and RAF Stations in the United Kingdom,
Aston Down, 68, 171, 182, 200–201, 239
Bentley Priory, 40, 45, 47, 52, 58, 66, 123
Biggin Hill, 71–2, 129, 150, 161, 186, 247–8, 256
Blackpool, 186
Brooklands, 20–1, 37, 199
Catterick, 66, 246
Church Fenton, 31, 234–5, 246
Coltishall, 75
Croydon, 68, 117, 190
Debden, 62–4, 260–1
Digby, 62–4, 231
Duxford, 8, 28, 30, 46, 62–4, 66, 74, 99, 105, 128, 140, 149, 154, 162, 179–81, 189
Dyce, 216
Eastleigh, 27, 197
Exeter, 234–6
Farnborough, 1, 27, 174
Gravesend, 71, 165
Halton, 75, 245
Hamble, 8
Hanworth, 68
Hastings, 97

Hatston, 33
Hawkinge, 36, 46, 108, 150, 218–20, 226, 229, 233, 247, 256–7, 261
Heathrow, 68
Hendon, 5, 24, 46, 102, 136, 156, 201
Heston, 34–5, 68
Hornchurch, 71–2, 100–101, 103, 136–7, 142–3, 149–50, 153–5, 162, 186–7, 237, 241–3, 248, 261
Horsham St. Faith, 131
Kenley, 108, 189–90, 219, 232, 241
Kirton-in-Lindsey, 56, 161
Leconfield, 213–14, 216
Lympne, 150, 233
Manston, 135, 138, 150, 153, 155, 162, 218, 226, 229, 240, 245, 248, 258, 261
Martlesham Heath, 20, 139, 161, 234, 245
Middle Wallop, 68–9, 71, 218, 225, 231, 236, 265
Montrose, 216, 239
North Weald, 44, 100–101, 167, 259
Pembrey, 227
Penrhos, 255–6
Rochford, 142, 146, 157, 178, 226, 250, 261
South Cerney, 68
St. Athan, 67, 200–201
St. Eval, 231, 241, 249
Stanmore, 40, 42
Staverton, 96
Sutton Bridge, 66
Tangmere, 24, 46, 136–8, 153, 212, 219, 225, 231, 240, 254, 255
Thorney Island, 231, 234
Turnhouse, 23, 216, 238, 258
Upavon, 38
Uxbridge, 8, 36, 46, 68–9

INDEX

Warmwell, 236–7, 265
West Raynham, 64, 239
Air Ministry, 7, 10, 13–18, 20–1, 26–8, 32, 36, 38–9, 44–7, 55–6, 59–60, 65–7, 83–4, 93, 106, 108, 123, 134, 136, 153, 187, 196–8, 200–201, 233, 243, 264, 270
   Pamphlet No. 248, 93
Air Raid Precautions, 53, 183
Aldridge, Pilot Officer, 71
Alford, Squadron Leader Edward George GM, 36, 99, 108, 117, 189
Allen, Wing Commander Herbert Raymond, 74, 143, 261, 264
Anderson, Sir John, 183
Arbor, Sergeant Ivor, 217–18
Aitken, Squadron Leader Max, 240–1
Auxiliary Fire Service, 53, 117

Bader, Group Captain Sir Douglas, 161–3
Baldwin, Stanley, 6–7, 19, 83, 169, 231
Ball, Flying Officer Eric, 31, 181
Balfour, Harold 1st Baron, 34–5
Barrage Balloons, 52, 215
Barking Creek, 94–112, 161, 181, 208
Battle of Britain, xii–xiii, 19, 33, 36, 39, 41, 45–8, 58, 75, 87, 91, 103, 109, 144, 150, 169–71, 174, 177, 186–7, 199–200, 215, 269–73
   Dowding's Despatch, 125, 199, 215, 270
   Kanalkampf, 222, 225, 274
Battle of Britain Clasp, 270, 272
Battle of Britain (film, 1969), 67, 182
Battle of Britain Memorial Trust, xii
   National Memorial to The Few, xii, xiii
Battle of Britain (Official Pamphlet, 1943), 47–52
Battle of France, 67–8, 167, 171, 174, 235
   Fall of France, 166, 174, 185, 199, 203, 213, 236, 245

Battle of the Barges, 234
Battle of the Heligoland Bight, 111, 210, 269
Battle of the River Plate, 120
Beachy Head, 214, 219
Beamish, Wing Commander Victor, 259–60
Beaverbrook, Max Aitken, 1st Baron, 196–9, 202, 231, 240, 252
Bennett, Pilot Officer Geoffrey, 260–1
Birmingham, 61, 66, 96, 198
Blakeney Pont, 182
Bolitho, Hector, 99, 105, 106
Boris, Leutnant Karl, 131
Bouchier, Air Vice Marshal Sir Cecil, 143
Brand, Air Vice-Marshal Quintin, 225
Brighton, 175, 240
British Army,
   Royal Engineers, 1, 54, 129
   Bomb Disposal Units, 54
British Broadcasting Corporation, 69–70, 105–106, 185
British Expeditionary Force, 98, 123, 127, 132, 134–5, 140, 145–6, 149, 165–8, 170, 194, 211
Brinsden, Flying Officer Frank, 179–80, 185, 188
Broadhurst, Air Chief Marshal Sir Harry, 109
Brothers, Air Commodore Peter Malam, 25, 129, 145
Brown, Pilot Officer Peter, 151
Bulman, P.W.S., 20, 25
Bushell, Squadron Leader Roger, 161–2
Byrne, Flying Officer Paddy, 102–103, 161

Calshot, 14
Canvey Island, 166, 177
Camm, Sir Sydney, 16, 19–21, 24, 26–7, 31
Castle Bromwich Aircraft Factory, 198

Chamberlain, Neville, 26, 34–5, 95, 97, 120–1, 123, 127–8, 171, 211, 231, 234
Chelmsford, 178, 180–1
Cheltenham, 96
Churchill, Winston, xii, 7, 19, 24, 34–5, 115, 120, 128–9, 134–5, 145, 149, 167–71, 184, 196, 210, 215, 221–2, 230–1, 233, 272
Clark, Corporal James, 214
Clouston, Flight Lieutenant, 31
Coventry, 66
Coward, Flying Officer James Baird, 7–8, 179
Cozens, Squadron Leader Henry, 30
Cranwell, RAF College, 3–4, 9, 36, 234
Craven, Sir Charles, 196
Crook, Pilot Officer David, 236, 265–8

Dawson-Paul, Sub Lieutenant Frank, 232–3
Dean, Sir Morris, 5–7
Deere, Air Commodore Alan Christopher, 142–4, 148, 158, 261–4, 272–3
Derby, 14, 61, 64, 66
Dewar, Squadron Leader John Scatliff, 234–6
Denholm, Squadron Leader George, 216–18
Dixon, Captain Bertram, 1
Dixon, Pilot Officer Peter, 136
Donaldson, Air Commodore Edward, 101, 135, 138, 149, 164, 167
Donaldson, Squadron Leader Jack, 123, 125
Dowding, Air Chief Marshal Sir Hugh, xii, 15–16, 19, 37–47, 52, 55–67, 90, 91, 98–9, 123, 125, 133–5, 139–40, 146, 150, 161–2, 168, 170, 172, 174, 185, 189, 195, 197–202, 215, 229–30, 237, 245, 270–2
Dowding's Despatch, 125, 199, 215, 270

Dowding System, 37–55
Dowding, Pilot Officer Derek, 146, 160
Dover, 48, 83, 140, 142, 150, 163, 231, 236–7, 241, 243, 247–8, 250, 256–7
Drobinski, Squadron Leader Boleslaw, 108
Dundas, Group Captain Sir Hugh, 216
Dunkirk, 135, 140–2, 146–7, 149–53, 156–60, 162–4, 166–71, 173–4, 179, 192, 234, 238
Duke-Woolley, Flight Lieutenant Raymond, 181–2
Dungeness, 218, 229, 241, 243, 247, 256
Dunkirk Evacuation, *see Dynamo*, Operation
Dynamo, Operation, 145, 150–73, 174, 194, 211, 212, 216, 231, 236, 267, 271, 273

Eastbourne, 175
Edwards, Pilot Officer Harry, 228–9
Edge, Flight Lieutenant Gerry, 139
Ellis, Flight Lieutenant John, 218
Enigma, 264

Fall Gelb, Operation, 126–49
Fall of France, 166, 174, 185, 199, 203, 213, 236, 245
Fink, Oberst Johannes, 222
Folkstone, 218–19, 241, 243, 249
Forbes, Admiral Sir Charles, 113, 122
Forbes, Lieutenant The Master of, 95
Forward, Sergeant Ron, 253–4
Foxley-Norris, Air Chief Marshal Sir Christopher, 132
Franklin, Pilot Officer William, 242, 248
Freeborn, Pilot Officer John, 102–103, 140–2, 147, 151, 158, 161

Galland, General Adolf, 88
Gayner, Flying Officer Richard, 144

INDEX

Gillan, Squadron Leader John, 21, 23–4
Gilroy, Pilot Officer George, 238
Goebbels, Richsleiter Joseph, 184, 203, 215, 222
Göring, Reichsmarschall Hermann, 77–84, 106, 117, 126, 167, 171, 206, 209–10, 214
Gort, General The Viscount, 98, 127, 140, 145–6, 149–50, 166
Gossage, Air Marshal Leslie, 40, 56–8, 66, 101
Graham, Flight Lieutenant Ted, 212
Grant, Flying Officer Stan, 159, 258
Gray, Pilot Officer Colin, 151
Gray, Sergeant Tom, 194
Green, Sergeant William James, 9, 68
Greig, Flight Lieutenant D'Arcy, 14
Grice, Wing Commander Douglas, 25, 229, 247

Hamar, Pilot Officer Jack, 135, 137–8, 148, 164, 167, 259–60
Hanbury, Assistant Section Officer Felicity, 186
Harlow, 64
Harvey-Kelly, Lieutenant, 1
Hastings, 243
Hawker Aircraft Limited, 20
  Hurricane prototype K5083, 20, 25
Hayes, Sergeant Patrick, 158–9, 231, 241, 243
Henshaw, Alex, 12
Hillary, Pilot Officer Richard, 239
Hispano-Suiza, 19, 187
Hitler, Adolf, 5, 11, 19, 26, 33–6, 47, 66, 76–85, 88, 94, 104, 110, 115, 118–21, 125–8, 137, 145–6, 156, 167, 171, 174, 180, 184–5, 193, 201, 203–206, 209–11, 215, 221, 251, 253, 271–2, 274
  Mein Kampf, 80–1
Hogan, Air Vice-Marshal H.A.V., 4

Hogan, Squadron Leader, 68, 71
Home Guard, 53, 116–17
Hulton-Harrop, Pilot Officer John, 102
Hulton-Harrop, Pilot Officer Montague, 101
Hunter, Squadron Leader, 131, 161–2, 164
Hove, 173
Howard-Williams, Pilot Officer Peter, 179

Inskip, Sir Thomas, 43
Irwin, Sergeant Charles Albert, 155

Jackson, Pilot Officer Andrew, 234
Jersey, 68, 138
Jeschonnek, Generalmajor Hans, 85, 210
Johnson, Air Vice-Marshal James Edgar, 9, 11, 89, 233
Johnson, Sergeant Reg, 56
Joslin, Squadron Leader John, 226, 242

Kay, Pilot Officer H.S., 131
Kell, Herman, xii
Kesselring, Feldmarschall Albert, 84–5, 203, 206, 222
Kingcome, Flight Lieutenant Brian, 137, 227
King George VI, 184, 234
King-Clark, Pilot Officer Cuthbert, 180
Kinkead, Flight Lieutenant S.M., 14
Knowles, Squadron Leader, 101

Lane, Flight Lieutenant Brian, 106, 126, 154–5, 180
Larkhill, 1
Lawson, Wing Commander G.M., 59
Leathart, Air Commodore James Anthony, 143
Leigh-Mallory, Air Chief Marshal Sir Trafford, 40–1, 58, 61–7, 132, 139–40, 164, 261
Litchfield, Pilot Officer Peter, 219

Local Defence Volunteers, *see* Home Guard
London, 40, 51, 56, 62–4, 66, 69, 99–101, 104–105, 116–17, 161, 169, 173–4, 179, 185, 196, 199, 203, 213, 221, 235, 264
Lott, Squadron Leader George, 254–5
Lovell, Flight Lieutenant Tony, 246
Lucking, Group Captain D.F., 101–102
Ludlow-Hewitt, Air Chief Marshal Sir Edgar, 44, 58
Luftwaffe, 5, 19, 34, 47, 81 *et seq*
Lyne, Pilot Officer Michael, 149, 153–5

Malan, Group Captain Adolf Gysbert, 100–103, 140–3, 147–8, 150, 157, 159–60, 178, 180
Mantle, Leading Seaman Foreman, 224
Margate, 173, 181, 218, 258
McClean, Sir Robert, 17–18
Measures, Flying Officer William, 142, 160, 237, 245
Mermagen, Squadron Leader Herbert, 56, 161–3
Milch, Erhard, 82–3
Millington, Pilot Officer William, 227, 257–8
Ministry of Aircraft Production, 196–9, 206, 252, 272
Mitchell, Flying Officer, 226
Mitchell, Flying Officer E.W., 248
Mitchell, Gordon, 15, 17, 27, 30, 267
Mitchell, Reginald Joseph, 13–17, 19–20, 26–9, 31, 99
Mölders, Werner, 88
Morris, Bob, 75
Mouchotte, Commandant René, 185
Mould, Pilot Officer P.W., 109, 248
Mould, Sergeant Tony, 142, 147, 248–9
Munich Crisis, 24, 34, 36, 47

Nash, Guardsman Percy, 95
National Fire Service, 53

Newall, Air Chief Marshal Cyril, 1st Baron Newall, 38, 40, 134, 222

Observer Corps, 39–40, 42, 48, 49, 50, 52–3, 100
Orlebar, Squadron Leader A.H., 14

Palmer, Edward Sydney, 224–5
Park, Air Chief Marshal Sir Keith, 12, 45–7, 55–6, 58–9, 66–7, 144, 150, 156, 161, 164–5, 168–70, 199, 256, 273
Parrott, Pilot Officer Peter, 128, 136, 138, 152, 160, 167, 212
Peel, Squadron Leader John, 240
Pegge, Pilot Office Joe, 247
Petri, Flying Officer John, 155, 179, 180
Pettiford, Earnest, 224
Pile, General Sir Frederick, 51–2
Pinkerton, Flight Lieutenant George, 109
Pinkham, Squadron Leader Philip, 188
Price, Alfred, 17

Quill, Jefferey, 27–8, 150, 198

Radar, 39–42, 47, 52, 58, 70–1, 101, 103, 153, 160, 216, 222, 226, 256
 Airborne Interception radar, 177
 Chain Home, 41, 256
 Chain Home Low, 41
Raeder, Admiral Eric, 119–20, 204–205, 210
RDF, *see* Radar
Reynolds, Quentin, 140, 147
Rolls-Royce, 14, 17–18, 20, 27, 32, 64, 66
 Kestrel engine, 87, 97
 Merlin engine, 17, 20, 27, 32, 44, 90
Roberts, Aircraftman 1st Class Fred, 149, 189
Royal Aircraft Establishment, 27

INDEX

Royal Air Force,
  Advanced Air Striking Force, 98, 108, 110, 133, 135, 193–4, 201, 233
  Air Defence of Great Britain, 15, 39, 46
  Auxiliary Air Force, 9–11, 68, 71, 97, 128, 161, 196
  Bomber Command, xii, 44, 58, 98, 110–11, 122, 124, 193–5, 207, 222, 230, 234, 244, 251, 269
  Groups,
    2 Group, 195, 230, 239, 244, 251, 268
  Coastal Command, xii, 33, 122, 230, 231, 244, 269–70
  Elementary Flying Training School, 8, 68
  Expansion Programme, 5, 11, 33, 35, 39, 47, 126, 128, 200, 245
  Fighter Command, xii, 26, 32–4, *et seq*
  Groups,
    10 Group, 41, 201, 225
    11 Group, 36, 40, 47, 49, 56, 58, 63, 66–7, 101, 140, 144, 149–50, 153, 161, 165, 199–201, 225–6, 234, 241, 256, 261
    12 Group, 40–1, 56, 58–9, 63, 65–6, 131, 139–40, 153, 161, 200–201, 231, 261, 273
    13 Group, 41, 65
  22 (Army Co-operation) Group, 40
  RAF Volunteer Reserve, 11, 75, 96–7
  squadrons,
    No.1 Squadron, 109, 174
    2 Squadron, 44
    5 Squadron, 41
    8 Squadron, 41
    13 (Army Co-operation) Squadron, 132

15 Squadron, 41
16 Squadron, 38, 91
17 Squadron, 260–1
18 Squadron, 239
19 Squadron, 5, 8, 28, 30, 34, 55, 65–6, 73, 99, 106, 128, 140, 149, 153–6, 161, 179–81, 187–9, 226
21 Squadron, 268–9
23 Squadron, 180–1
32 Squadron, 25, 71, 73, 129, 145, 219, 229, 247
37 Squadron, 240
41 Squadron, 162, 246
43 Squadron, 24, 44, 219, 240, 254, 272
44 Squadron, 230
46 Squadron, 65, 109, 123–5
48 Squadron, 45
54 Squadron, 101, 140, 142–4, 151, 158, 162, 218, 226, 240, 250, 261, 264, 272
56 Squadron, 100, 101, 218
57 Squadron, 268
61 Squadron, 244
64 Squadron, 31, 165, 214, 232, 241
65 Squadron, 101, 131, 136–7, 139, 158–9, 162, 187, 231, 236, 241–3, 248, 258, 261
66 Squadron, 74–5, 99, 131, 139
72 Squadron, 212
74 Squadron, 100–101, 103, 140, 142–4, 147, 151, 157–60, 180, 237, 245–6, 248
79 Squadron, 226, 242, 248, 257–8
84 Squadron, 44
85 Squadron, 245–6
87 Squadron, 234–6
92 Squadron, 143–4, 161–2, 227–8, 244

111 Squadron, 21, 46, 55, 109
141 Squadron, 66
144 Squadron, 111
145 Squadron, 136, 138, 152, 160, 167, 212, 214, 218, 240
149 Squadron, 234
151 Squadron, 100–101, 135, 137–8, 148, 164, 167–8, 187, 259–60
201 Squadron, 269
206 Squadron, 220, 230
213 Squadron, 64, 213, 236
222 Squadron, 56, 65, 161–3
229 Squadron, 65
233 Squadron, 121, 269
234 Squadron, 241, 249–50
236 Squadron, 231
238 Squadron, 218
247 Squadron, 33
249 Squadron, 246
254 Squadron, 239
263 Squadron, 33, 123–5
264 Squadron, 66, 131–2, 139, 161–2, 164
266 Squadron, 66, 105
501 (County of Gloucester) Squadron, 9–10, 68
601 (County of London) Squadron, 161, 196, 240
602 (City of Glasgow) Squadron, 66, 109, 214, 251, 261
603 (City of Edinburgh) Squadron, 66, 109, 216–18, 238
605 (County of Warwick) Squadron, 139
607 (County of Durham) Squadron, 66, 109, 128, 136, 167
609 (West Riding) Squadron, 187, 236, 265, 267–8

610 (County of Chester) Squadron, 66, 218–19, 247, 256
611 (West Lancashire) Squadron, 66, 151, 215, 231
615 (County of Surrey) Squadron, 144, 186
616 (South Yorkshire) Squadron, 65, 75, 213–14, 216, 233
University Air Squadrons, 9
Oxford, 46
Royal Flying Corps, 1–3, 38, 41, 44–5, 103
Royal Naval Air Service, 1
Royal Navy,
Fleet Air Arm, 33, 124, 233–4, 258
801 Naval Air Squadron, 244
804 Naval Air Squadron, 33
808 Naval Air Squadron, 33
Foylebank, HMS, 223–5
H.M.N.B. Portland, 223–5, 229, 234, 236–7, 264, 268, 271

Salmond, Air Marshal Sir John, 38, 46
Satchell, Squadron Leader Jack, 136
Saunders, Squadron Leader Gerald, 241–2
Schmid, Oberst Josef 'Beppo', 209–10
Sealion, Operation, 203–206, 222, 234
Scott-Malden, Pilot Officer David, 171, 182
Sheerness, 166, 260
Sholto Douglas, Marshal of the Royal Air Force William, 1st Baron Douglas of Kirtleside, 43–4, 46
Smith, Able Seaman Arthur, 113
Smith, Flight Lieutenant Dick, 187
Smith, Jo, 27, 29
Smith, Squadron Leader Andrew, 256
Smythe, Pilot Officer Rupert, 229, 247
Southampton, 13–14, 27, 197, 206, 213, 234, 236, 254

INDEX

Spitfire Fund, 252–3
Stainforth, Wing Commander George, 15, 175
Stephen, Pilot Officer H.M., 158
Stephenson, Squadron Leader Geoffrey, 153–4, 156, 158, 161
Stevenson, Pilot Officer P.C.F., 157–8, 248
Stones, Pilot Officer Donald, 257–8
Stumpff, Generaloberst Hans-Jürgen, 82, 85, 89, 206
Summers, Captain Joseph 'Mutt', 27–8
Summers, John, 96
Sunderland, 212, 246
Supermarine, 12–14, 17–19, 26–9, 87, 96, 150, 197–8
  Funding of the Spitfire, 17–18

Taylor, A.J.P., 5
Townsend, Group Captain Peter, 24, 245
Treacy, Flight Lieutenant W.P., 103, 143, 146–7, 160
Trenchard, Marshal of the Royal Air Force, Hugh Montague, 3–7, 38, 44–6, 76, 111, 128
Tuck, Wing Commander Robert Roland Stanford, 161–2, 244

Udet, Generaloberst Ernst, 83
ULTRA, 264
Unwin, Wing Commander George Cecil, 30, 128, 156, 185

Vickers-Armstrong, 17–18, 196, 198, 215

Waghorn, Flight Lieutenant H.R.D., 14
Wainwright, Pilot Officer Michael, 31, 165
Walker, Flight Lieutenant William, 75, 258
Wandzilak, Lieutenant Stanislaw, 186
Way, Flight Lieutenant Basil, 250–1
Welford, Flying Officer, 137
Wellum, Squadron Leader Geoffrey, 32, 227–8
Welsh, Air Marshal Sir William, 66–7
Weserübung, Operation, 112–25
White, Squadron Leader Laurie, 142–3, 147
Wilkinson, Sergeant Ken, 95, 97
Wilkinson, Squadron Leader Rodney, 105
Wolston, 197
Wolverhampton, 66, 252–3
Worrall, Air Vice-Marshal John, 73
Wray, John, 8–9